Surgery for Stroke

Surgery for Stroke

Edited by

R. M. Greenhalgh, MA, MD, MChir, FRCS

Professor of Surgery and Chairman,
Department of Surgery,
Charing Cross & Westminster Medical School
London, England

and

L. H. Hollier, MD, FACS, FACC

Chairman, Department of Surgery,
Ochsner Clinic and Alton Ochsner Medical Foundation
Louisiana, New Orleans, USA

W. B. SAUNDERS COMPANY LTD
London · Philadelphia · Toronto · Sydney · Tokyo

W. B. Saunders 24–28 Oval Road
London NW1 7DX

The Curtis Center
Independence Square West
Philadelphia, PA 19106–3399

55 Horner Avenue
Toronto, Ontario M8Z 4X6, Canada

Harcourt Brace Jovanovich (Australia) Pty Ltd,
30–52 Smidmore St
Marrickville, NSW 2204, Australia

Harcourt Brace Jovanovich Japan Inc.
Ichibancho Central Building, 22–1 Ichibancho
Chiyoda-ku, Tokyo, 102, Japan

British Library Cataloguing in Publication Data
A catalogue record for this book is available from the British Library.

ISBN 0-7020-1759-0

This book is printed on acid-free paper ∞

Editorial and Production Services by Fisher Duncan
10 Barley Mow Passage, London W4 4PH

Typeset by Dobbie Typesetting Limited, Tavistock, Devon
and printed and bound in Great Britain by The University Press, Cambridge

Contents

TIMING OF CAROTID SURGERY

TECHNIQUES OF CAROTID SURGERY

INTRAOPERATIVE MONITORING

List of Contributors

B. A. J. ANGELSEN, PhD
Department of Biomedical Engineering
Trondheim University Clinic
7006 Trondheim
Norway

C. ARGENTINO, MD
Department of Neurological Sciences
University of Rome "La Sapienza"
00161 Rome
Italy

C. ANTONINI, MD
Department of Neurological Sciences
University of Rome "La Sapienza"
00161 Rome
Italy

H. J. M. BARNETT, MD
Principal Investigator, NASCET
The John P. Robarts Research Institute
100 Perth Drive, PO Box 5015,
London, Ontario N6A 5K8, Canada

N. BARRETT, MD FRCS
Consultant Radiologist
Regional Vascular Service
Department of Surgery
Charing Cross & Westminster Medical
  School
Charing Cross Hospital
Fulham Palace Road
London W6 8RF, UK

A. A. B. BARROS D'SA
Consultant Vascular Surgeon,
Vascular Surgery Unit
Royal Victoria Hospital
Grosvenor Road, Belfast, N. Ireland

S. BASTIANELLO, MD PhD
Department of Neurological Sciences
University of Rome "La Sapienza"
00161 Rome
Italy

J. D. BEARD, FRCS
Royal Hallamshire Hospital
Room 120, Floor 1, Glossop Road
Sheffield S10 2JF, UK

P. R. F. BELL, MB ChB MD FRCS
Department of Surgery
Clinical Sciences Building
Leicester Royal Infirmary
PO Box 65, Leicester LE2 7LX, UK

J. DE BELLEROCHE, MD
Department of Biochemistry
Charing Cross & Westminster Medical
  School
Charing Cross Hospital
Fulham Palace Road, London W6 8RF,
UK

R. BENECKE, MD
Professor of Neurology
Department of Neurology
Heinrich-Heine-Univ., Moorenstrasse 5
D 4000 Dusseldorf, Germany

J. BERENDES
Department of Neurology
Catharina Hospital
Michelangelolaan 2
5632 EJ Eindhoven, The Netherlands

S.-E. BERGENTZ, MD
Professor of Surgery
Lund University
Department of Surgery
Malmö General Hospital
Malmö, Sweden

D. BERGQVIST, MD
Associate Professor
Department of Surgery
Lund University
Malmö General Hospital
S 21401 Malmö, Sweden

G. BISCHOF, MD
University Clinic of Surgery I
University of Vienna
Alser Strasse 4
A 1090 Vienna
Austria

S. D. BLAIR, MS FRCS
Lecturer and Honorary Senior Registrar
Department of Surgery
Charing Cross & Westminster Medical
  School
Charing Cross Hospital
Fulham Palace Road
London W6 8RF, UK

J. BUTH, MD PhD
Department of Surgery
Catharina Hospital
Michelangelolaan 2
5632 EJ Eindhoven, The Netherlands

W. B. CAMPBELL, MS MRCP FRCS
Royal Devon & Exeter Hospital
Wonford, Exeter EX2 5DW, UK

M. COLONNA, MD
Department of Vascular Surgery
University of Rome ''La Sapienza''
00161 Rome
Italy

A. CUCINA, PhD
Department of Clinical Surgery
University of Rome ''La Sapienza''
00161 Rome
Italy

R. CUMING, BSc
Research Associate
Charing Cross & Westminster Medical
  School
Charing Cross Hospital, Fulham
  Palace Road, London W6 8RF, UK

T. DAHL, MD
Department of Surgery
Trondheim University Hospital
Trondheim 7006, Norway

E. H. DILLON, MD
Department of Radiology
University Hospital Utrecht
PO Box 85500
3508 Utrecht
The Netherlands

M. C. DONALDSON, MD
Harvard Medical School
Birgham & Womens Hospital
75 Francis Street, Boston,
Massachusetts 02115, USA

C. DOSSA, MD
Senior Vascular Fellow
Division of Vascular Surgery
Henry Ford Hospital
Detroit, Michigan, USA

P. van EERTEN, MD
Department of Surgery
Catharina Hospital
Michelangelolaan 2
5632 EJ Eindhoven, The Netherlands

B. C. EIKELBOOM, MD PhD
Professor of Vascular Surgery
University Hospital Utrecht
PO Box 85500
3508 Utrecht
The Netherlands

M. ELLIS, BSc
Chief Technician
Department of Surgery
Charing Cross & Westminster Medical
  School
Charing Cross Hospital
Fulham Palace Road
London W6 8RF, UK

C. B. ERNST, MD
Clinical Professor of Surgery
University of Michigan Medical School
Ann Arbor, Michigan
Head, Division of Vascular Surgery
Henry Ford Hospital
Detroit, Michigan, USA

C. FIESCHI, MD
Department of Neurological Sciences
University of Rome "La Sapienza"
00161 Rome
Italy

P. FIORANI, MD
Professor and Head of Vascular
  Surgery
University of Rome "La Sapienza"
00161 Rome
Italy

M. FIORELLI, MD PhD
Department of Neurological Sciences
University of Rome "La Sapienza"
00161 Rome
Italy

C. FORSSELL, MD PhD
Associate Professor
Department of Surgery,
Lund University,
Malmö General Hospital,
S-21401 Malmö, Sweden

P. J. FRANKS, PhD
Lecturer in Epidemiology
Charing Cross & Westminster Medical
  School
Charing Cross Hospital
Fulham Palace Road
London W6 8RF, UK

G. GEROULAKOS, MD FRCS
Vascular Research Fellow
Vascular Section
Academic Surgical Unit
St Mary's Hospital Medical School
St Mary's Hospital
Praed Street, London W2 1NY, UK

P. DE GIER, MD
Department of Surgery
Catharina Hospital
Michelangelolaan 2
5632 EJ Eindhoven
The Netherlands

G. L. GILLING-SMITH, FRCS
Senior Registrar
Department of Vascular Surgery
St Mary's Hospital, Praed Street,
London W2 1NY, UK

E. GODEHARDT, MD
Professor of Statistics and
  Mathematics
Department of Thoracic and
  Cardiovascular Surgery
Heinrich-Heine-Univ., Moorenstrasse 5
D 4000 Dusseldorf, Germany

M. C. GORI, MD
Department of Neurological Sciences
University of Rome ''La Sapienza''
00161 Rome
Italy

R. M. GREENHALGH, MA MD MChir FRCS
Professor of Surgery
Chairman of Department of Surgery
  and Clinical Dean
Charing Cross & Westminster Medical
  School
Charing Cross Hospital
Fulham Palace Road
London W6 8RF, UK

R. HAAVERSTAD, MD
Department of Surgery
Trondheim University Hospital
Trondheim 7006, Norway

H. HILLEN, MD
Department of Internal Medicine
Catharina Hospital
Michelangelolaan 2
5632 EJ Eindhoven, The Netherlands

R. W. HOBSON II, MD
UMDNJ-NJ Medical School
185 S Orange Avenue, G532
Newark, NJ 07103, USA

L. HOLLIER, MD FACS FACC
Chairman, Department of Surgery
Ochsner Clinic and Ochsner
  Foundation Hospital
1514 Jefferson Highway
New Orleans, LA 70121, USA

M. KAIL, MD
University Clinic of Surgery I
University of Vienna
Alser Strasse 4
A 1090 Vienna
Austria

P. KASPRZAK, MD
Nuernberg Medical Centre,
Flustr. 17, D-8500,
Nuernberg, Germany

R. KOLVENBACH, MD
Associate Professor
Department of Vascular Surgery
  and Kidney Transplantation
Heinrich-Heine-Univ., Moorenstrasse 5
D 4000 Dusseldorf, Germany

G. KRETSCHMER, MD
University Clinic of Surgery I
University of Vienna
Alser Strasse 4
A 1090 Vienna
Austria

F. LAMMERS, MD
Department of Neurology
Catharina Hospital
Michelangelolaan 2
5632 EJ Eindhoven, The Netherlands

M. VAN LEEUWEN, MD
Department of Diagnostic Radiology
University Hospital Utrecht,
PO Box 8550
3508 Utrecht, The Netherlands

A. D. LEGATT, MD PhD
Assistant Professor of Surgery
Department of Neurology
Albert Einstein College of Medicine
Montefiore Medical Center,
111 East 210th Street Bronx
New York 10467-2490, USA

C. LEGEIN, MD
Department of Ophthalmology
Catharina Hospital
Michelangelolaan 2
5632 EJ Eindhoven, The Netherlands

B. LINDBLAD, MD PhD
Associate Professor
Department of Surgery
Lund University
Malmö General Hospital
S-21401 Malmö
Sweden

J. A. MANNICK, MD
Harvard Medical School
Birgham & Womens Hospital
75 Francis Street, Boston,
    Massachusetts 02115, USA

S. R. MATHISEN, MD
Department of Surgery
Trondheim University Clinic
7006 Trondheim
Norway

C. McCOLLUM, MD FRCS
Department of Surgery
University Hospital of
    South Manchester
Research & Teaching Building, Nell Lane
West Didbury, Manchester M20 8LR, UK

J. McIVOR, MD
Consultant Radiologist
Regional Vascular Service
Department of Surgery
Charing Cross & Westminster Medical
    School
Charing Cross Hospital
Fulham Palace Road
London W6 8RF, UK

M. MITTLBÖCK, MD
University Clinic of Surgery I
University of Vienna
Alser Strasse 4
A 1090 Vienna
Austria

S. R. MONEY, MD
Fellow in Vascular Surgery
Ochsner Clinic and Ochsner
    Foundation Hospital
1514 Jefferson Highway
New Orleans, LA 70121, USA

H. O. MYHRE, MD
Department of Surgery
Trondheim University Hospital
Trondheim 7006, Norway

A. R. NAYLOR, MD FRCS
Lecturer in Surgery
Leicester Royal Infirmary
PO Box 65
Leicester LE2 7LX, UK

A. N. NICOLAIDES, MS FRCS
Professor of Vascular Surgery
Director Irvine Laboratory
Vascular Section
Academic Surgical Unit
St Mary's Hospital Medical School
Honorary Consultant Vascular
    Surgeon
St Mary's Hospital
Praed Street, London W2 1NY, UK

J. W. NORRIS, MD
Stroke Research Unit, Sunnybrook
    Health Science Centre
University of Toronto
2075 Bayview Avenue
Toronto, Ontario, M4N 3MS, Canada

D. M. NOTT, MD
Senior Lecturer in Surgery
Regional Vascular Service
Department of Surgery
Charing Cross & Westminster Medical
    School
Charing Cross Hospital
Fulham Palace Road
London W6 8RF, UK

G. NOVELLI, MD
Department of Vascular Surgery
University of Rome "La Sapienza"
00161 Rome
Italy

T. F. PANETTA, MD
Assistant Professor of Surgery
Division of Vascular Surgery
Albert Einstein College of Medicine
Montefiore Medical Center
111 East 210th Street Bronx
New York 10467-2490, USA

A. PANNONE, MD
Department of Vascular Surgery
University of Rome "La Sapienza"
00161 Rome
Italy

G. D. PERKIN, MD
Consultant Neurologist
Regional Vascular Service
Department of Surgery
Charing Cross & Westminster Medical
   School
Charing Cross Hospital
Fulham Palace Road
London W6 8RF, UK

P. POLTERAUER, MD
University Clinic of Surgery I
University of Vienna
Alser Strasse 4
A 1090 Vienna
Austria

J. T. POWELL, PhD MD
Reader in Cardiovascular Biology
Charing Cross & Westminster Medical
   School
Charing Cross Hospital
Fulham Palace Road
London W6 8RF, UK

T. PRATSCHNER, MD
University Clinic of Surgery I
University of Vienna
Alser Strasse 4
A 1090 Vienna
Austria

S. PUIG, MD
University Clinic of Surgery I
University of Vienna
Alser Strasse 4
A 1090 Vienna
Austria

D. RAITHEL, MD
Chief of Vascular Surgery
Nuernberg Medical Centre
Flustr. 17, D-8500, Nuernberg
Germany

M. RICCI, MD
Department of Neurological Sciences
University of Rome "La Sapienza"
00161 Rome
Italy

P. M. ROTHWELL, MB ChB MRCP
Research Fellow in Neurology
Department of Clinical Neurosciences
Western General Hospital
Crewe Road,
Edinburgh EH4 2XU, UK

C. V. RUCKLEY, MB ChM FRCSE
Consultant Surgeon
Vascular Research Office
University Department of Clinical
   Surgery
The Royal Infirmary
Edinburgh EH3 9YW, UK

M. I. SACCHETTI, MD
Department of Neurological Sciences
University of Rome "La Sapienza"
00161 Rome
Italy

O. D. SAETHER, MD
Department of Surgery
Trondheim University Clinic
7006 Trondheim
Norway

W. SANDMANN, MD
Professor of Surgery
Chairman, Abt. f. Gefaßchirurgie u.
  Nierentransplantation
Heinrich-Heine-Univ., Moorenstrasse 5
D 4000 Dusseldorf, Germany

E. SBARIGIA, MD
Department of Vascular Surgery
University of Rome "La Sapienza"
00161 Rome
Italy

T. V. SCHROEDER, MD DMSc
Dept of Vascular Surgery, University
  Hospital
Blegdamsvej 9
DK 2100 Copenhagen, Denmark

G. SETTE, MD
Department of Neurological Sciences
University of Rome "La Sapienza"
00161 Rome
Italy

A. D. SHEPARD, MD
Clinical Assistant Professor of Surgery
University of Michigan Medical School
Ann Arbor, Michigan
Senior Staff Surgeon
Division of Vascular Surgery
Henry Ford Hospital
Detroit, Michigan, USA

T. N. SONECHA, MD FRCP DTM&H
Senior Research Fellow
St Mary's Hospital Medical School
St Mary's Hospital
Praed Street, London W2 1NY, UK

F. SPEZIALE, MD
Department of Vascular Surgery
University of Rome "La Sapienza"
00161 Rome
Italy

A. V. STERPETTI, MD
Department of Surgery
Charing Cross & Westminster Medical
  School
Charing Cross Hospital
Fulham Palace Road
London W6 8RF, UK

R. TAKOLANDER, MD
Division for Vascular Surgery
Surgical Clinic, Karolinska Hospital
10401 Stockholm, Sweden

M. TAURINO, MD
Department of Vascular Surgery
University of Rome "La Sapienza"
00161 Rome
Italy

J. E. THOMPSON, MD
Former Chief of Surgery and Vascular
  Surgery
Baylor University Medical Center
Dallas, Texas
Clinical Professor of Surgery
University of Texas Southwestern
  Medical School, Dallas
3900 Miramar Avenue, Dallas
Texas 75205, USA

D. TONI, MD PhD
Department of Neurological Sciences
University of Rome "La Sapienza"
00161 Rome
Italy

J. F. TOOLE, MD
Teagle Professor of Neurology and
  Professor of Public Health Sciences
Bowman Gray School of Medicine of
  Wake Forest University
Medical Center Boulevard,
  Winston-Salem, NC 27157-1074, USA

E. TURKOF, MD
University Clinic of Surgery I
University of Vienna
Alser Strasse 4
A 1090 Vienna
Austria

F. VEITH, MD
Professor of Surgery
Division of Vascular Surgery
Albert Einstein College of Medicine
Montefiore Medical Center
111 East 210th Street Bronx
New York 10467-2490, USA

J. WADE, MD
Consultant Neurologist
Regional Vascular Service
Department of Surgery
Charing Cross & Westminster Medical
  School
Charing Cross Hospital
Fulham Palace Road
London W6 8RF, UK

C. WARLOW, BA MB BChir MD FRCP
Professor of Medical Neurology
Department of Clinical Neurosciences
Western General Hospital, Crewe Road
Edinburgh EH4 2XU, UK

A. D. WHITTEMORE, MD
Harvard Medical School
Birgham & Womens Hospital
75 Francis Street, Boston
Massachusetts 02115, USA

F. WILLEKE, MD
Department of Vascular Surgery and
  Kidney Transplantation
Heinrich-Heine-Univ., Moorenstrasse 5
D 4000 Dusseldorf, Germany

I. M. WILLIAMS, FRCS
Department of Surgery, University
  Hospital of South Manchester
Research & Teaching Building, Nell Lane
West Didbury, Manchester M20 8LR
UK

J. H. N. WOLFE, MS FRCS
Consultant Surgeon
St Mary's Hospital
Praed Street, London W2 1NY, UK

Preface

The title of this volume is very topical. As described by Dr Jesse E Thompson in the opening chapter, carotid surgery has been with us now for over 40 years, long enough for the technique to have become well established. For most operations, clear indications are established in a short time, but the effectiveness of and precise indications for carotid endarterectomy still remain controversial in some respect. Only since the recent publication of the North American and European Symptomatic Carotid Endarterectomy Trials, has some controversy been reduced in this area. Now, at least it is widely accepted that carotid stenosis of greater than 70% in symptomatic patients should be operated upon. There still remain areas of controversy. It is not absolutely certain as yet whether operation is superior to best medical treatment for symptomatic lesions of 30% to 70% but the trials remain in progress and it is important for recruitment to these trials to continue so that an answer will emerge as soon as possible. It becomes clear that for stenoses of less than 30%, operation is not indicated and best medical treatment is preferable.

The place of carotid surgery for the severe asymptomatic lesion is also by no means established. These issues of established techniques, indications and the findings of clinical trials form the central thrust of this book. Other forms of surgery for stroke, such as vertebral artery and intracranial artery surgery are not considered as highlighted items.

There have been many recent advances in the optimal investigations, before, during and after carotid surgery using colour code Doppler imaging, digital subtraction angiography and transcranial Doppler monitoring. It still remains controversial whether it is sensible to dispense with a conventional angiogram before carotid surgery, especially as new imaging modalities are becoming available.

We feel that this book explores the current place of carotid surgery for stroke and covers appropriately aspects of disease causation, investigation of patients thought suitable for the operation, indications, timing, techniques and the effectiveness of the procedure.

R.M.G.
L.H.H.

Dr Jesse E. Thompson

It is with great pleasure that we dedicate this book to Dr Jesse E. Thompson of Dallas, Texas. No one has made a greater contribution to this subject over the years than he. Educated either side of the Atlantic, both at Harvard and as a Rhodes scholar at Oxford, he has maintained his European links and contributed regularly to this series of annual vascular monographs since the first in 1978. It is fitting also that he introduced the editors to each other and we each thank him warmly for his teaching, guidance, example and friendship over the years.
R.M.G.
L.H.H.

THE HISTORY OF CAROTID SURGERY

Carotid Artery Surgery — Historical Review

Jesse E. Thompson

With changing concepts in aetiology and management of ischaemic stroke syndromes during the past forty years has come an increasing interest in surgery of the carotid artery. So much so that carotid endarterectomy has become the most commonly performed operation in peripheral vascular surgery in the USA. My remarks will be limited largely to surgery for cerebrovascular insuffiency.

The word 'carotid' is derived from the Greek, meaning to stupefy or plunge into a deep sleep. Figure 1 shows the 31st metope from the south side of the Parthenon in Athens, now safely ensconced in the British Museum among the Elgin Marbles, and demonstrates that the ancient Greeks were aware of the significance of the carotid artery, with a centaur applying left carotid compression to the neck of a Lapith warrior.

Ambroise Paré in the sixteenth century called these vessels 'the right and left carotides or sleepy arteries'.[1] According to Dandy,[2] Hippocrates and Galen were aware that hemiplegia resulted from a lesion in the opposite side of the brain.

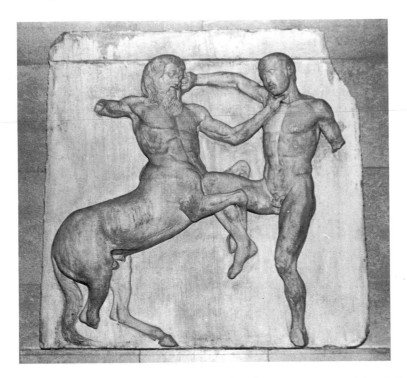

Fig. 1. The 31st metope from the Parthenon, showing a centaur applying left carotid compression to the neck of a Lapith warrior. (Photograph taken by the author in the British Museum. By permission of Churchill Livingstone.)

In the eighteenth century it was observed that the function of the brain might be normal even if one carotid was totally obliterated. Thus, Jean Luis Petit in 1765 described the case of a patient with an aneurysm at the bifurcation of the right carotid which underwent spontaneous cure. At autopsy, seven years later, the carotid and aneurysm sac were observed to be obliterated.[3,4]

The first operations on the carotid artery were quite naturally ligation procedures for injury or haemorrhage. Most likely, Hebenstreit of Germany in 1793 reported the first ligation for injury,[3,5,6] although John Abernethy in England is credited with the first deliberate ligation following control of haemorrhage by compression, of the torn left carotid artery from a goring injury by the horn of a cow. This probably took place in 1798, although the exact date cannot be ascertained. Unfortunately this patient died 30 hours later of cerebral causes and Abernethy abandoned the procedure, reporting his fatal case in 1804.[3,6–8]

The first successful ligation of the carotid artery was performed by David Fleming on 17 October 1803. David Fleming was a young naval surgeon aboard His Majesty's Ship *Tonnant*, the greatest two-decker in the British Navy, carrying 80 guns, and cruising off the Spanish coast during the Napoleonic era. Mark Jackson, a servant, attempted to commit suicide by cutting his throat on 9 October 1803. The knife grazed the outer and muscular coats of the carotid artery but the vessel was intact. Eight days later, on 17 October, the carotid ruptured. Fleming cut down on the artery proximal to the rupture and ligated it. He had not done this before, nor had he heard of Abernethy's case. The patient survived and made an uninterrupted recovery. The case was reported in 1817 by Dr Richard Warren Coley, an assistant surgeon on HMS *Tonnant*. Unquestionably this was the first authentic successful case of ligation of the carotid artery.[9,10]

The first successful ligation of the carotid artery in the USA was carried out by Dr Amos Twitchell, of Keene, New Hampshire, on 18 October 1807, on a soldier sustaining an accidental gunshot wound of the neck in a mock fight. Dr Twitchell, in a life-saving effort to stop haemorrhage, ligated the common carotid and packed the wound. The patient made an uneventful recovery. This operation was performed eight months prior to Cooper's successful operation, to be described below.[3,11]

Sir Astley Cooper in London was the first to ligate the carotid for cervical aneurysm on 1 November 1805. The patient died of sepsis, but on 22 June 1808 Cooper repeated the operation, this time successfully, and the patient lived until 1821.[12]

In 1809, Benjamin Travers first ligated the common carotid for a carotid-cavernous fistula, and in 1885 Victor Horsley ligated the cervical carotid for non-fistulous intracranial aneurysm. By 1868 Pilz had been able to collect 600 reported cases of carotid ligation for haemorrhage or cervical aneurysm with a mortality of 43%.[8]

Until fairly recently the prevailing notion held by most physicians was that strokes were caused by intracranial vascular disease. William Osler in his *Principles and Practice of Medicine* in the 7th edition of 1909, the last edition which he himself wrote, attributed apoplectic stroke largely to cerebral haemorrhage. No mention is made of extracranial occlusive disease, and in the section dealing with cerebral softening where embolism and thrombosis are mentioned, emphasis is upon blockage of intracranial vessels.[13] This is somewhat curious in view of the fact that Gull in 1855,[14] Savory in 1856,[15] Broadbent in 1871,[16] and Penzoldt in 1881[17] had all described occlusive lesions in the extracranial segments of the main arteries supplying the brain, and noted their association with symptoms of cerebral ischaemia. In fact, in 1905 Chiari described the ulcerating plaque, and found that emboli could break away from carotid-sinus-area plaques and cause strokes.[18]

A most significant article was that of J. Ramsay Hunt of New York City in 1914, who called attention to the importance of extracranial occlusions in cerebral vascular disease. He recognized that both partial and complete occlusions of the innominate and carotid arteries could be responsible for cerebral intermittent claudication.[19]

The next significant contribution was the report of Egas Móniz in Portugal, who in 1927 first described the technique of cerebral arteriography.[20] The first report of carotid thrombosis demonstrated by arteriography was that of Sjöqvist in 1936.[21] The following year, 1937, Móniz, Lima, and de Lacerda reported four patients with occlusion of the cervical portion of the internal carotid diagnosed by arteriography.[22] Egas Móniz received a Nobel Prize in 1949, not for cerebral arteriography, but for his work with prefrontal lobotomy. By 1951 Johnson and Walker were able to collect from the literature 101 instances of carotid thrombosis all diagnosed by this technique.[23]

In the same year, 1951, and again in 1954, Dr Miller Fisher working in Montreal, but later in Boston, published two important papers.[24,25] Fisher reemphasized the relationship between, and frequency of, disease of the carotid artery in the neck and cerebrovascular insufficiency. He defined the basic nature of the lesion as atherosclerosis, noted again partial and complete occlusions, and described several syndromes. He observed that with severe stenosis at the carotid bifurcation the distal vessels could be entirely free of disease. He realized the importance of these observations, and stated: 'It is even conceivable that some day vascular surgery will find a way to bypass the occluded portion of the artery during the period of ominous fleeting symptoms. Anastomosis of the external carotid artery or one of its branches with the internal carotid artery above the area of narrowing should be feasible.'

In the same year, 1951, E. J. Wylie had introduced into the USA the procedure of thromboendarterectomy for the removal of atherosclerotic plaques from the aortoiliac segments but it had not been used on the carotid artery.[26]

Fisher's prophecy of surgical reconstruction of the carotid artery in the neck as therapy for occlusive disease was soon fulfilled. The first successful surgical reconstruction of a carotid artery was performed by Carrea et al. in Buenos Aires on 20 October 1951, after reading Fisher's article, and was reported in 1955.[27] In a male patient with a stroke who had stenosis of the left internal carotid in the neck, they performed an anastomosis between the external carotid and the distal internal carotid arteries following partial resection of the stenosed area. The patient made an uneventful recovery and was still alive and well 31 years after the operation.

On 28 January 1953, Strully et al. first attempted thromboendarterectomy of the cervical internal carotid but were unable to obtain retrograde flow. They suggested that endarterectomy should be feasible in such cases when the distal vasculature was patent.[28]

The first successful carotid endarterectomy was performed by Dr Michael DeBakey on 7 August 1953. In a 53-year-old male patient with a frank stroke and total occlusion of the left carotid, thromboendarterectomy was carried out with good retrograde flow from the internal carotid. An arteriogram performed postoperatively on the operating table showed the internal carotid to be patent in both its extracranial and intracranial portions. This patient lived for 19 years without having further strokes and died in 1972 of coronary artery disease.[29]

The operation which gave the greatest impetus to the development of surgery for carotid occlusive disease was that of Eastcott *et al.* performed at St Mary's Hospital in London on 19 May 1954, and reported in November of 1954.[30] In this case, a woman, having suffered 33 transient ischaemic attacks, with stenosis of the left carotid bifurcation, underwent resection of the bifurcation with restoration of blood flow by end-to-end anastomosis between the common carotid and distal internal carotid arteries. Hypothermia was used as a cerebral protective mechanism during carotid clamping. The patient was completely relieved of her symptoms and was alive and well at the age of 86. Figure 2 is a photograph taken during the performance of this operation.

In February 1956, Francis Murphey of Memphis, Tennessee, performed successful carotid endarterectomies for both partial and total occlusions.[31]

On 9 August 1956, the late Champ Lyons accomplished a successful bypass from the right subclavian to the right carotid artery in the neck employing a nylon graft.[32]

The author's first carotid endarterectomy was performed on 16 April 1957.[33] With increasing experience the various procedures just listed were abandoned, with the exception of endarterectomy, which has become the standard operation. Table 1 lists in chronological order the early carotid procedures performed for the treatment of extracranial cerebrovascular disease.

A fascinating aspect of this subject is the study of famous people who have had strokes.

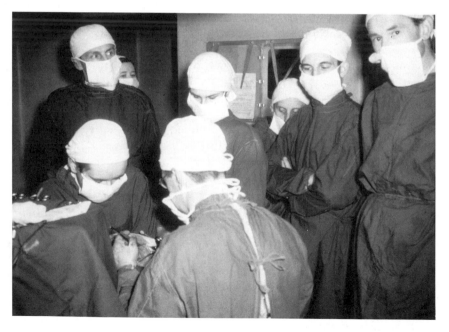

Fig. 2. Photograph taken at St Mary's Hospital, 19 May 1954, of the historic carotid reconstruction operation. Mr Eastcott is seated operating. Professor Rob is standing, on the far right. (Courtesy of Dr George R. Dunlop.)

Table 1. The first carotid reconstructions for cerebrovascular insufficiency, listed in chronological order

Author	Date of operation	Degree of stenosis	Procedure	Restoration of flow
Carrea et al.[27]	20 Oct 1951	Partial	End-to-end anastomosis external carotid to internal carotid	Yes
Strully et al.[28]	28 Jan 1953	Total	Thromboendarterectomy followed by ligation and resection	No
DeBakey[29]	7 Aug 1953	Total	Thromboendarterectomy	Yes
Eastcott et al.[30]	19 May 1954	Partial	End-to-end anastomosis common carotid to internal carotid	Yes
	June 1954	Partial	Thromboendarterectomy	Yes
Denman et al.[34]	14 July 1954	Total	Resection with homograft	Yes
Lin et al.[35]	Dec 1955	Partial	Resection with saphenous vein graft	Yes
Murphey and Miller[31]	6 Feb 1956	Total	Thromboendarterectomy	Yes
	24 Feb 1956	Partial	Thromboendarterectomy	Yes
Cooley et al.[36]	8 Mar 1956	Partial	Endarterectomy	Yes
Lyons and Galbraith[32]	9 Aug 1956	Partial	Subclavian–carotid nylon bypass graft	Yes

Louis Pasteur had a series of transient ischaemic attacks involving largely his speech area, before he finally died in 1895.[37,38]

Several intriguing reports have speculated on the fate of nations as affected by strokes occurring in their leaders. One world-famous figure who suffered from, and eventually died of, cerebrovascular deterioration was Marshal Paul von Hindenburg. Certainly his action in authorizing Hitler to form a cabinet in 1933 was a decision that altered the course of history. Whether or not anyone could have stopped Hitler at this time is subject to speculation, but in his senile and demented state von Hindenburg refused or was unable to involve himself in trouble or controversy. His mental deterioration was such that his Secretary of State had to write down for him word for word the questions put to any caller.[39]

In Russia, V. I. Lenin also suffered from cerebrovascular troubles. He experienced several transient ischaemic episodes; finally he had a complete right hemiplegia and died of his third stroke at the early age of 54. Prior to his illness Lenin had been responsible for elevating Joseph Stalin to several important positions in the government, but in the last years of his life he had grave doubts about Stalin and wanted Leon Trotsky to assume the more important posts. Had Lenin lived to make Trotsky his heir apparent instead of Stalin, who knows what the course of modern history might have been.[37,39]

In the USA no less than ten American presidents have suffered from, or died of, cerebrovascular insufficiency.[37,40,41] A very dramatic example is the case of Woodrow Wilson, who had several strokes which resulted finally in near-total incapacitation. It has been stated by those who have studied the President's illness in detail that Wilson's cerebrovascular disease significantly contributed to the defeat of the United States' support for the League of Nations. Wilson died of a massive stroke on 3 February 1924.[37,39,40]

The illness of Franklin Delano Roosevelt is well known. In 1943 he reportedly had severe symptoms of cerebrovascular insufficiency. How this disease affected the Yalta Agreements of 1945 and the subsequent Cold War is a matter of speculation. His sudden death at the Georgia Warm Springs was said to be due to a massive cerebral haemorrhage, but no autopsy was performed.[37,40,41]

The most recent cerebrovascular episodes in a Chief Executive were experienced by President Dwight Eisenhower. His 'little strokes' were said to be due to intracranial disease. His death came ultimately from complications of heart disease rather than stroke.

By contrast, the late Mayor Richard Daley, of Chicago, after having transient cerebral ischaemia, was subjected to carotid endarterectomy in April of 1974 with complete success and restoration of brain function to normal levels.

In cerebrovascular insufficiency, morbidity at times may be more important than mortality. Thus, the quality of survival is emphasized as a feature of this disease, more so perhaps than in coronary artery disease, and underlines the main role of carotid endarterectomy as one of stroke prevention.[42]

The surgeon's role in the treatment of cerebral ischaemic syndromes by means of carotid endarterectomy has been substantiated by the recent reports of results of two large randomized trials, the North American Symptomatic Carotid Endarterectomy Trial[43] and the MRC European Carotid Surgery Trial,[44] demonstrating the efficacy of surgery in preventing strokes.

ACKNOWLEDGEMENTS

I am indebted to Leslie W. Ottinger MD for providing me with information regarding David Fleming and Amos Twitchell. Portions of the text were taken from J. E. Thompson, History of Carotid Artery Surgery, in *Progress in Stroke Research* Vol. 2, edited by Roger M. Greenhalgh and F. Clifford Rose, 1983, by permission of Churchill Livingstone.

REFERENCES

1. Paré A: The Workes of the famous Chirurgion Ambrose Parey. Translated out of Latine and compared with the French, by Thomas Johnson. From the first English edition, London 1634. New York: Milford House Inc, 1968
2. Dandy WE: Surgery of the Brain. Hagerstown: WF Prior Co Inc, 1945
3. Cutter IS: Ligation of the common carotid — Amos Twitchell. Surg Gynecol Obstet Int Abst Surg 48:1–3, 1929
4. Petit JL: Chirug Mem de l'Acad Roy des Sciences, 1765
5. Hebenstreit EBG: Zusatze zu Benj. Bell's Abhandlung von den Geschwuren und deren Behandlung, 1793
6. Wood JR: Early history of the operation of ligature of the primitive carotid artery. NY J Med July: 1–59, 1857
7. Abernethy J: Surgical observations. *In* Surgical Works, Vol 2, London, pp. 193–209, 1804
8. Hamby WB: Intracranial Aneurysms. Springfield, Ill: Charles C Thomas, 1952
9. Coley RW: Case of rupture of the carotid artery, and wounds of several of its branches, successfully treated by tying the common trunk of the carotid itself. Med Chir J Rev 3 (13):1–4, 1817

10. Keevil JJ: David Fleming and the operation for ligation of the carotid artery. Br J Surg 37:92–95, 1949
11. Twitchell A: Gun-shot wound of the face and neck. Ligature of the carotid artery. N Engl Q J Med Surg 1 (2):188–193, 1842
12. Cooper A: Account of the first successful operation performed on the common carotid artery for aneurysm in the year 1808 with the postmortem examination in the year 1821. Guy's Hosp Rep 1:53–59, 1836
13. Osler W: The Principles and Practice of Medicine 7th edn. New York: D Appleton and Co, 1909
14. Gull WW: Case of occlusion of the innominate and left carotid. Guy's Hosp Rep 1:12, 1855
15. Savory WS: Case of a young woman in whom the main arteries of both upper extremities and of the left side of the neck were throughout completely obliterated. Med Chir Tr Lond 39:205–219, 1856
16. Broadbent WH: Absence of pulsations on both radial arteries, vessels being full of blood. Tr Clin Soc Lond 8:165–168, 1875
17. Penzoldt F: Uber thrombose (autochtone oder embolische) der carotis. Deutsches Arch Klin Med 28:80–93, 1881
18. Chiari H: Uber des verhalten des teilungswinkels der carotis communis bei der endarteriitis chronica deformans. Verhandl Dtsch Path Ges 9:326–330, 1905
19. Hunt JR: The role of the carotid arteries in the causation of vascular lesions of the brain, with remarks on certain special features of the symptomatology. Am J Med Sci 147:704–713, 1914
20. Moniz E: L'encephalographie arterielle son importance dans la localisation des tumeurs cerebrales. Rev Neurol (Paris) 2:72–90, 1927
21. Sjöqvist O: Uber intrakranielle aneurysmen der arteria carotis und deren beziehung zur ophthalmoplegischen migraine. Nervenarzt 9:233–241, 1936
22. Moniz E, Lima A, de Lacerda R: Hemiplegies par thrombose de la carotide interne. Presse Med 45:977–980, 1937
23. Johnson HC, Walker AE: The angiographic diagnosis of spontaneous thrombosis of the internal and common carotid arteries. J Neurosurg 8:631–659, 1951
24. Fisher M: Occlusion of the internal carotid artery. Arch Neurol Psychiat 65:346–377, 1951
25. Fisher M: Occlusion of the carotid arteries. Arch Neurol Psychiat 72:187–204, 1954
26. Wylie EJ, Kerr E, Davies O: Experimental and clinical experiences with use of fascia lata applied as a graft about major arteries after thromboendarterectomy and aneurysmorrhaphy. Surg Gynec Obstet 93:257–272, 1951
27. Carrea R, Molins M, Murphy G: Surgical treatment of spontaneous thrombosis of the internal carotid artery in the neck. Carotid–carotideal anastomosis. Report of a case. Acta Neurol Latinoamer 1:71–78, 1955
28. Strully KJ, Hurwitt ES, Blankenburg HW: Thromboendarterectomy for thrombosis of the internal carotid artery in the neck. J Neurosurg 10:474–482, 1953
29. DeBakey ME: Successful carotid endarterectomy for cerebrovascular insufficiency. J Am Med Assoc 233:1083–1085, 1975
30. Eastcott HHG, Pickering GW, Rob C: Reconstruction of internal carotid artery in a patient with intermittent attacks of hemiplegia. Lancet ii:994–996, 1954
31. Murphey F, Miller JH: Carotid insufficiency—diagnosis and treatment. J Neurosurg 16:1–23, 1959
32. Lyons C, Galbraith JG: Surgical treatment of atherosclerotic occlusion of the internal carotid artery. Ann Surg 146:487–496, 1957
33. Thompson JE, Austin DJ, Patman RD: Carotid endarterectomy for cerebrovascular insufficiency: Long term results in 592 patients followed up to thirteen years. Ann Surg 172:663–679, 1970
34. Denman FR, Ehni G, Duty WS: Insidious thrombotic occlusion of cervical arteries treated by arterial graft, a case report. Surgery 38:569–577, 1955
35. Lin PM, Javid H, Doyle EJ: Partial internal carotid artery occlusion treated by primary resection and vein graft. J Neurosurg 13:650–655, 1956
36. Cooley DA, Al-Naaman YD, Carton CA: Surgical treatment of arteriosclerotic occlusion of common carotid artery. J Neurosurg 13:500–506, 1956

37. Fields WS, Lemak NA: A History of Stroke. New York: Oxford University Press, 211 pp. 1989
38. Fishbein M: Strokes 1. Some literary descriptions. Postgrad Med 37:194–198, 1965
39. Friedlander WJ: About three old men: An inquiry into how cerebral arteriosclerosis has altered world politics. Stroke 3:467–473, 1972
40. Fishbein M: Strokes 2. American Presidents who had strokes. Postgrad Med 37:200–208, 1965
41. Robertson CW: Some observations on Presidential illnesses. Boston Med Quart 8:33–43, 76–86, 1957
42. Thompson JE: Carotid endarterectomy, 1982—the state of the art. Br J Surg 70:371–376, 1983
43. North American Symptomatic Carotid Endarterectomy Trial Collaborators: Beneficial effect of carotid endarterectomy in symptomatic patients with high-grade carotid stenosis. N Engl J Med 325:445–453, 1991
44. European Carotid Surgery Trialists' Collaborative Group: MRC European carotid surgery trial: interim results for symptomatic patients with severe (70–99%) or with mild (0–29%) stenosis. Lancet 337:1235–1243, 1991

PATHOPHYSICAL ASPECTS

Mechanisms of Cerebral Damage Following Cerebral Artery Occlusion

J. de Belleroche

The mechanism through which cerebral ischaemia leads to cell death is poorly understood. Recently, emphasis has focussed on the importance of three key intermediaries in this process—glutamate, intracellular calcium and free radicals. Levels of all three agents have been shown to be elevated in association with the ischaemic insult.

Although glutamate is abundant throughout the body, playing a significant role in protein synthesis and N-metabolism, it is of greatest importance in the central nervous system (CNS) as the predominant excitatory neurotransmitter. Most fast excitatory responses in the CNS are mediated by glutamate; the pyramidal nerve cells of cerebral cortex utilize glutamate in corticospinal, corticocortical and corticostriatal pathways.

Glutamate, calcium and free radicals each have an established physiological action in normal tissue but when tissue is damaged in ischaemia their effects become exaggerated, leading to massive and uncontrolled amplification of their normal actions. The consequences are lethal in the nervous system. For example, in the case of glutamate the normal tissue concentration is high, 5–10 mM, and even following very localized tissue damage, extracellular concentrations of glutamate arising from the damaged cells can increase dramatically. In compromised tissue the normal mechanisms for rapid removal of glutamate such as high affinity uptake, will be defective and glutamate will produce a persistent excitation in surrounding neurones which leads to neuronal death as a consequence of 'overexcitation'. Glutamate neurotoxicity has been demonstrated at the major classes of glutamate receptor subtype, the α-amino-3-hydroxy-5-methyl-4 isoxazole propionic acid (AMPA) and kainate receptors, N-methyl-D-aspartate (NMDA) receptors and quisqualate receptors. AMPA and kainate receptors gate sodium channels whilst NMDA receptors gate channels which transport both sodium and calcium. The quisqualate receptor is a G-protein receptor linked to the generation of inositol trisphosphate.

Emphasis has concentrated on the NMDA receptor in the pathology of ischaemic insults in view of this effect on calcium entry which is also implicated in tissue injury, although much evidence is indirect. However, the involvement of the kainate receptor has been clearly demonstrated in the encephalopathy that results from ingestion of a naturally occurring glutamate analogue, domoic acid, in mussels contaminated with phytoplankton, which produces high concentrations of domoic acid.[1] Domoic acid is selective for the kainate receptor, produces limbic seizures and is neurotoxic for neurones which possess the kainate receptor in particular. The resulting neuronal necrosis in cases that came to autopsy were specifically localized to hippocampus and amygdala in regions corresponding to the distribution of the kainate receptor.

In other conditions where endogenous glutamate is elevated as a result of trauma, seizure activity or stroke, all glutamate receptors in the vicinity are likely to be activated

DE BELLEROCHE

Regions sensitive to damage in experimental seizures (e.g. CA_1 region of hippo-campus) possess a high concentration of NMDA receptors and are protected by treatment with NMDA antagonists. Following tissue damage, secondary effects mediated through kainate and AMPA receptors may increase the level of depolarization, increasing glutamate release and enhancing glutamate action at the NMDA receptor. Normally, elevated concentrations of glutamate at the synapse are very efficiently dealt with through the Na^+-dependent high affinity uptake system, the glutamate transporter, and elevated intracellular levels of calcium can be buffered through binding to calcium binding proteins such as calmodulin and calbindin. However, if the capacity of the calcium binding proteins is exceeded, the buffering capacity is lost and calcium activation of proteinases and calpains occurs which lead to a cytoskeletal disruption and cell death. Amplification of the injury response is further affected by the interaction between glutamate receptor mediated damage and free radical production. Glutamate receptors, NMDA receptor subtype, are linked to the production of arachidonic acid through activation of phospholipase A_2. Arachidonic acid metabolism through the cyclo-oxygenase pathway is associated with free radical generation which in turn can contribute to the level of free radicals in the damaged tissue. Further, free radical generating systems directly damage tissue, leading to enhanced glutamate release and therefore contribute to a self-perpetuating vicious cycle (Fig. 1).

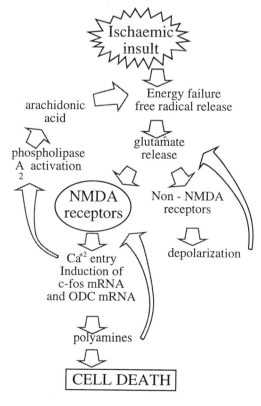

Fig. 1.

Many glutamate pathways in the central nervous system have been shown to demonstrate adaptive responses and are thought to contribute to associative learning paradigms, e.g. long-term potentiation of synaptic potentials. This complex response is associated with rapid effects on gene expression which can be detected within a few hours. Ischaemic and excitotoxic injury also have a profound effect on gene expression, initially causing a rapid induction of immediate early genes (IEGs).[2,3] These genes encode transcription factors which in turn regulate the expression of other genes, known as late genes. We have characterized one such late gene, ornithine decarboxylase, which is induced during ischaemia, trauma and seizure, and is potentially likely to contribute to neuronal cell death.[4,5] Inhibition of the enyzme product with the dimethylfluoro-ornithine (DFMO) is neuroprotective against glutamate mediated neurotoxicity.[6] Overall, the ischaemic insult leads to a massive amplification of a normal physiological response, not only at the level of local toxic agents but further through the amplification of the expression of potentially toxic enzymes. The amplification process is undoubtedly likely to extend the area of tissue damage and hence a knowledge of the precise mechanisms involved will be valuable in targeting treatments to limit the infarct volume following a stroke.

In order to characterize this system in more detail we have investigated the time course of the expression of genes involved in the injury response, IEGs and late genes,[7] their effect on infarct size and the mediators leading to their induction.

MIDDLE CEREBRAL ARTERY OCCLUSION

This model has been used extensively for studying focal ischaemia. In the investigation described here, conditions were used which have been previously characterized for their consistency in yielding ischaemic tissue in the region served by the middle cerebral artery. Unilateral middle cerebral artery occlusion was carried out with bipolar diathermy forceps distal to the lenticular striate branch under pentobarbital anaesthetic. In addition, cannulation of the left femoral artery and vein were carried out for administration of anaesthetic and monitoring of blood gases, glucose and blood pressure. A rectal probe was used for maintenance of body temperature at 37°C. Test neuroprotective drugs were administered 10 min prior to ischaemia. At various times after ischaemia (up to 5 h) animals were sacrificed and tissues taken from five regions ipsilateral to ischaemia and five of the corresponding contralateral regions. The regions dissected were from the frontal cortex overlapping with anterior cerebral artery territory, the core region corresponding to the area served by the middle cerebral artery, and the surrounding 'penumbra' region. The occipital lobe supplied by the posterior cerebral artery territory and the hippocampus were also dissected. Tissue was immediately frozen in liquid nitrogen and stored at −70°C prior to RNA extraction. Extraction was carried out in guanidinium thiocyanate using a polytron ultrasonic homogenizer. RNA was analysed by Northern slot and slot blot analysis using probes specific for and complementary to messenger RNAs of interest.[8] Following hybridization, high stringency washes were used to remove non-specifically hybridized labelled probes and levels of messenger RNAs for the injury response genes were related to levels of mRNA from β-tubulin.

EFFECT OF ISCHAEMIA ON LEVELS OF c-fos mRNA

At 4 h following ipsilateral ischaemia a massive induction of c-fos mRNA was detected in core and penumbra regions of the cerebral cortex ipsilateral to the occlusion, increasing five- to eightfold above the level in the contralateral tissue. A significant increase (threefold) was also seen in occipital cortex. Little induction was seen in the contralateral cortex and in hippocampus from both regions. A significant induction in two other immediate early genes, c-jun and jun-B was also detected with a similar time course. It was noteworthy that the induction extended beyond the immediate area of the middle cerebral artery territory to the occipital lobe, hence indicating the widespread involvement of cortical tissue resulting from a relatively localized area of ischaemia. Pretreatment with MK-801, 3 mg/kg, completely prevented the induction in the core and occipital regions, and reduced induction by 70% in the penumbra region. The marked effect of this agent, which is specific for the NMDA receptor, indicated the substantial involvement of the NMDA receptor in mediating the injury response. This neuroprotective effect of NMDA antagonists obtained in this model of focal ischaemia contrasts with that obtained in global ischaemia where four vessel occlusion is carried out and a reduced level of protection is achieved. Induction of ODC mRNA also occurred within 4 h of the ischaemic insult and was sensitive to treatment with MK-801. This is consistent with large increases in ODC enzyme activity and putrescine that accompany ischaemia.[9]

FUTURE PERSPECTIVES FOR TREATMENT

Studies of experimental ischaemia allow the characterization of the injury response. This response is clearly complex but a number of processes have been identified and their time course determined. These changes occur in the immediate vicinity of the ischaemia but profound effects can be detected in tissue surrounding this core area and these are likely to contribute to the final extent of the infarct area. The results obtained so far indicate that treatment with calcium antagonists can only briefly attenuate early damage due to the initial voltage dependent Ca^{2+} entry. Glutamate antagonists would be extremely effective over the first few hours (4–8 h) after infarct, but their effective use would be limited to the first 24 h. Combination treatment of glutamate antagonists with free radical scavengers (α-tocopherol, allopurinol) would also be indicated since these agents have been shown to be protective in experimental focal ischaemia.[10] It is clearly important to establish whether significant clinical improvement can be achieved with these regimes and hence whether the cost of rapid treatment of stroke patients within 24 h is merited.

REFERENCES

1. Perl TM, Bedard L, Kosatsky T et al.: An outbreak of toxic encephalopathy caused by eating mussels contaminated with domoic acid. N Engl J Med 322: 1175–1780, 1990
2. Wood H, de Belleroche J: Induction of c-fos mRNA in cerebral cortex by excitotoxin stimulation of cortical inputs: involvement of N-methyl-D-aspartate receptors. Brain Res 545: 183–190, 1991

 3. Welsh FA, Moyer DJ, Harris VA: Regional expression of heat shock protein-70 mRNA and c-fos mRNA following focal ischaemia in rat brain. J Cereb Blood Flow Metab 12: 201–212, 1992
 4. Reed LJ, de Belleroche J: Induction of ornithine decarboxylase in cerebral cortex by excitotoxin lesion of nucleus basalis: association with postsynaptic responsiveness and N-methyl-D-aspartate receptor activation. J Neurochem 55: 780–787, 1990
 5. Wood H, de Belleroche J: Induction of ornithine decarboxylase mRNA in cerebral cortex in response to kainate lesion of nucleus basalis: involvement of NMDA receptors. Neurosci Lett 11: 176–182, 1990
 6. Markwell MAK, Berger SP, Paul SM: The polyamine synthesis inhibitor of α-difluoro-methylornithine blocks NMDA-induced neurotoxicity. Eur J Pharmacol 182: 607–609, 1990
 7. de Belleroche J, Aspey BS, Collaço-Moraes Y, Harrison MJ: Focal ischaemia causes an extensive induction of immediate early genes which is sensitive to treatment with MK-801 (In prep.)
 8. de Belleroche J, Bandopadhyay R, King A: Regional distribution of cholecystokinin messenger RNA in rat brain during development: quantitation and correlation with cholecystokinin immunoreactivity. Neuropeptides 15: 201–212, 1990
 9. Paschen W: Polyamine metabolism in reversible cerebral ischemia. Cerebrovasc Brain Metab Rev 4: 59–88, 1992
10. Siesjö BK: Pathophysiology and treatment of focal cerebral ischemia. Part II: Mechanisms of damage and treatment. J Neurosurg 77: 337–354, 1992

Revascularization Pathophysiology After Acute Cerebral Infarction

M. I. Sacchetti, M. Fiorelli, D. Toni, C. Argentino, G. Sette, M. C. Gori, G. Antonini, M. Ricci, S. Bastianello and C. Fieschi

A sufficient amount of clinical information has been collected to enable us to state that pharmacological reperfusion is a well tolerated and non-threatening therapy for acute ischaemic stroke patients. A reperfusion injury (of both metabolic and haemorrhagic nature) has been hypothesized, but the clinical relevance of such a phenomenon has never been studied.

At present, efficacy trials on thrombolysis in acute ischaemic stroke must focus their attention on administering drugs as soon as possible after the onset of stroke to establish the clinical usefulness and safety of thrombolysis and to produce widely applicable clinical strategies. Nothing would justify any delay in treatment even if addressing important pathophysiological questions. However, during the first 48 hours following hospitalization and treatment, selected clinical centres, which are able sequentially to perform computed tomography (CT), single photon emission computed tomography (SPECT) and neurological evaluations without delaying therapy, should collect data in an attempt to answer whether early clinical and instrumental parameters are useful in selecting patients at risk for reperfusion injury.

Only recently it has been understood that thromboembolic occlusion of cerebral intracranial vessels, either isolated or associated with an extracranial lesion, is the main cause of acute ischaemic stroke.[1-3]

When, as a consequence of the acute arterial occlusion, the cerebral blood flow (CBF) starts decreasing from the normal values of about 50 ml/100 g/min, preservation of cellular functions is initially maintained by haemodynamic and metabolic compensatory adjustments.[4]

As soon as mismatching between brain CBF and oxygen metabolic demand occurs, the fall of CBF compromises various cellular functions. At CBF levels of 16–20 ml/100 g/min the ATP synthesis falls and neurons become unable to excite postsynaptic membranes sufficiently. This CBF value has been named the 'threshold for electrical failure'[5] (Fig. 1). In such condition of a neuronal 'idling',[6] called ischaemic penumbra, tissue is functionally silent but still structurally intact, thus potentially salvageable by treatment.[7] A further decrease in CBF, below values of 6–10 ml/100 g/min (the 'energy' failure threshold), leads to an additional decrease of ATP synthesis with subsequent transneuronal ions homeostasis failure, and to irreversal ischaemia[8] (Fig. 2).

It has been postulated that early recanalization, by restoring CBF over the ischaemic threshold, would lead to a burst of aerobic metabolism and to a rapid return of cellular energy, thus preventing (or reducing) the extension of the definite infarcted area. Nonetheless, several experimental studies indicate that reperfusion of ischaemic tissue may be responsible for an aggravation of

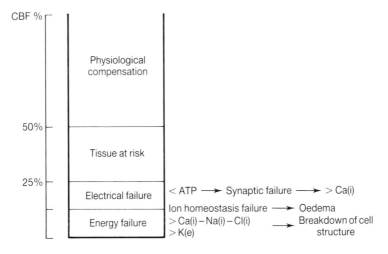

Fig. 1.

ischaemia itself,[9-11] possibly voiding the beneficial effect of early restoration of CBF.

Since early pharmacological revascularization of symptomatic occluded vessels has been suggested as a well tolerated and potentially effective therapy for acute ischaemic stroke, at least 2000 patients have been treated in a non-controlled and non-randomized manner. A recent meta-analysis of those cases has shown an incidence of severe oedema, symptomatic cerebral parenchimol haemorrhage (PH) and haemorrhagic infarction (HI), not unlike those reported for the 'natural history' of stroke.[12]

At present, at least six large, multicentre, controlled clinical trials are underway to test the clinical efficacy of thrombolytic therapy in acute ischaemic stroke (Table 1); the question of whether early reperfusion is followed by a clinically relevant reperfusion injury, however, remains unanswered.

In this paper we summarize the main pathophysiological mechanisms responsible for the maturation of ischaemic brain damage and for the so called reperfusion injury. Furthermore, in an attempt to answer the question of whether early instrumental parameters (CT or SPECT) together with a close neurological evaluation can be used to identify patients at risk for a reperfusion injury, a clinical strategy is proposed.

The maturation of ischaemic brain damage occurs over a time period which varies from a few minutes to several hours, mainly depending on the level of CBF through the collateral blood supply, on the duration of ischaemia and on the selective neuronal vulnerability.[13]

The ischaemic 'cascade' is summarized in Fig. 2.[5,8]

As can be argued from Fig. 2, the morphological expression of necrosis is a process as much dependent on the duration of the ischaemic insult as on its severity. In fact, transgressing the electrical or membrane failure threshold the same pathophysiological events occur more or less instantaneously. It is thus possible for an infarct to develop at a regional CBF (rCBF) that is depressed but above the membrane failure threshold, if the flow is compromised for a sufficiently long interval of time.

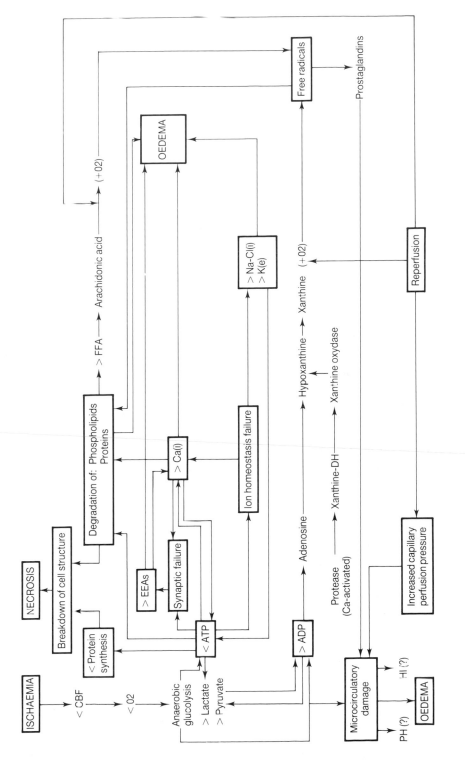

Fig. 2.

Table 1. Ongoing randomized placebo-controlled studies on thrombolysis in acute ischaemic stroke

	Patient no.	Study length (months)	Delay in treatment	Drug	Outcome measures	Follow-up
MAST-Italy (Open Trial)	1500	30	6 h	SK + ASA	Rankin Death rate	6 months
NINDS t-PA Stroke Trial	140 140	27	90 min 90–180 min	rt-PA	NIH Barthel Rankin CT Infarct volume	2–24 h 7–10 days 3 months
MAST (Double blind)	600	24	6 h	SK + ASA	Death rate Orgogozo + Scandinavian Rankin Haemorrhages	6 months
ASK Trial	600	?	6 h	SK	Death rate Rankin	
Yamagouchi	?	?	6 h	rtPA	Recanalization HHS Barthel CT infarct volume Haemorrhages	?
ECASS	600	24	6 h	rtPA	Scandinavian SS NIH Barthel Index Rankin	24 h 7 day 30 day 3 months

Even if very precocious, reperfusion does play a role in the context of a suffering tissue where the ischaemic cascade is present (Fig. 2).

Experimental studies have shown that the reperfusion injury consists of two components: damage due to the re-oxygenation of the ischaemic tissue and the circulatory events consequent to the increased capillary hydrostatic pressure (CHP).[9–10] The main mediators of the so-called 're-oxygenation injury' are free radicals. Their dangerous effect is primarily on the neuronal membrane and organelles (in particular mitochondria) with subsequent excess of pyruvate and aggravation of lactic acidosis.[11] Free radicals may thus represent the "meeting point" between irreversible damage and penumbra salvation.[14]

Since 1950, the haemorrhagic transformation (HI) of a pale lesion has been postulated to be due to the increased CHP in a vascular tree already damaged by ischaemia.[15] This hypothesis has been more recently supported by many authors[16–18] but the negative prognostic role of HI has never been demonstrated. Nonetheless, the pharmacological reperfusion of an already necrotic tissue, by increasing CHP, may induce massive PH and be responsible for early neurological deterioration and poor clinical outcome.

Reperfusion may also increase the amount of water in the context of the ischaemic tissue leading to both vasogenic and cytotoxic oedema. Cytotoxic oedema seems to be related to the overproduction of free radicals which indirectly aggravate the lactic acidosis (Fig. 2).[19] The increasing CHP and the breakdown of the blood–brain barrier, with subsequent leakage of protein-rich fluid into the interstitial space, seem to be responsible for an immediate vasogenic oedema formation.

In conclusion, by inserting the pathophysiological mechanisms responsible for ischaemia itself, reperfusion may obviate the beneficial effect of revascularization.

Although clinical experience has not yet provided any clear evidence of an early reperfusion injury, the hypothetical reperfusion injury, together with the potential haemorrhagic risk related to thrombolysis, call for a careful evaluation of the risk/benefit ratio of this treatment on acute ischaemic stroke patients.

Which strategies might we use to evidentiate a possible reperfusional injury in acute ischaemic stroke patients?

The authors of a study which correlated collateral blood supply at the time of early angiography, infarct extension at computed tomography (CT), clinical outcome and time for recanalization as detected by transcranial doppler (TCD) have indicated that only the combination of good collateral flow and rapid recanalization predicts a benign outcome.[20] The early development of irreversible microcirculatory and cell membrane damage at the time of revascularization in patients with absent or poor collaterals might explain this result. In these cases reperfusion might be harmful.

Angiography is time consuming and not widely applicable in the context of multicentre efficacy trials; furthermore, collateral circulation is variable. Consequently a poor collateral circulation at early angiography does not necessarily mean that the whole territory involved is already irreversibly damaged. In this perspective functional parameters such as those provided by CT scan and/or SPECT images, might be more informative.

Brain CT scan is necessary for a correct diagnosis at entry and to exclude haemorrhages. Furthermore, recently it has been postulated that both the direct and the indirect signs of the ongoing ischaemic lesion evidenced by early CT images, are indicative of the absence of a sufficient collateral blood supply to prevent damage.[21-22]

SPECT studies have been successfully used to evaluate the residual CBF in acute ischaemic stroke patients.[23] Over the last few years it has been demonstrated that SPECT data correlates well with the final CT brain damage, the collateral blood supply at early angiography and the clinical outcome.[24] Furthermore, the CBF levels before treatment can be evaluated, by means of the split-dose method, without inducing any delay in the administration of therapy.[25]

Neurological deterioration after stroke is a common event, with progressing stroke occurring in 14–42% of all strokes. In our experience progressing strokes have a poor outcome in a high percentage of cases.[26] The mechanisms underlying progression of symptoms[27] are likely to be very similar to those suspected for reperfusion injury.[9-11] Therefore, if it is important to monitor the neurological evolution during the first hours after treatment, it is also of primary importance to correlate the early neurological changes with both clinical and instrumental parameters able to suggest more detailed pathogenic information about the nature of the clinical deterioration.

Our proposal is to submit patients to parallel evaluations of clinical neurological course, CT, and SPECT images before treatment and during the first 48 hours of hospitalization, trying to document whether patients who develop a massive oedema, HI or PH associated with stable neurological deterioraton, had at entry early signs predictive of the subsequent clinical worsening.

Therapeutic strategies for acute phase stroke should not only restore the CBF but also antagonize the events responsible for both the maturation of ischaemic damage and the reperfusion injury, trying to minimize the possible deleterious effect of early reperfusion. In this perspective the effectiveness of thrombolysis associated with a drug for brain protection should be tested in a four-arm clinical trial.[28]

REFERENCES

1. Fieschi C, Argentino C, Lenzi GL *et al.*: Clinical and instrumental evaluation of patients with ischemic stroke within the first 6 hours. J Neurol Sci 91: 311–322, 1989
2. Mohr JP, Caplan LR, Melski JW *et al.*: The Harvard Cooperative Stroke Registry: A prospective registry. Neurology 28(8): 754–762, 1978
3. The rt-PA Acute Stroke Study Group: An open safety/efficacy trial of rt-PA in acute thromboembolic stroke: Final Report. Abstracts of the Stroke Council, 16th International Joint Conference on Stroke and Cerebral Circulation, 29, 1991
4. Baron JC, Bousser MG, Rey A *et al.*: Reversal of focal 'misery-perfusion syndrome' by extracranial arterial bypass in hemodynamic cerebral ischemia: A case study with $^{15}O_2$ positron tomography. Stroke 12: 454–459, 1981
5. Siesjo BK: Pathophysiology and treatment of focal cerebral ischemia. Part I: Pathophysiology. J Neurosurg 77: 169–184, 1992
6. Perkins SA, Magargal LE, Augsburger JJ, Sanborn GE: The idling retina: reversible visual loss in central retinal artery obstruction. Ann Ophthalmol 13: 3, 1987
7. Olsen TS: Regional cerebral blood flow after occlusion of middle cerebral artery. Acta Neurol Scand 73: 321–337, 1986
8. Garcia JH, Anderson ML: Physiopathology of cerebral ischemia. CRC Critical Reviews in Neurobiology 4: 303–323, 1989
9. Halsey JH, Conger KA, Garcia JH, Sarvay E: The contribution of reoxygenation to ischemic brain damage. J Cerebr Blood Flow Met 11: 994–1000, 1991
10. Ito U, Ohno K, Nakamura R, Suganuma F, Inaba Y: Brain edema during ischemia and after restoration of blood flow. Measurement of water, sodium, potassium content and plasma protein permeability. Stroke 10: 542–547, 1979
11. Halsey JH, Conger KA, Hudetz AG *et al.*: The role of tissue acidosis in ischaemic tissue injury: the concept of PH integral. Neurol Res 10: 97–104, 1988
12. Wardlow JM, Warlow JP: A meta-analysis of all published data on the use of thrombolytic drugs to treat acute ischemic stroke. 2nd International Symposium on Thrombolytic Therapy in Acute Ischemic Stroke. La Jolla 1–2 May 1992 (Abstract)
13. Siesjo BK: Cerebral circulation and metabolism. J Neurosurg 60: 883–908, 1984
14. Sakamoto A, Ohnishi ST, Ohnishi T, Ogawa R: Relationship between free radical production and lipid peroxidation during ischemia-reperfusion injury in the rat brain. Brain Res 554: 186–192, 1991
15. Fisher M, Adams RD: Observation of brain embolism with special reference to hemorrhagic infarction. J Neuropathol Exp Neurol 10: 92–94, 1951
16. Garcia JH, Lowry SL, Briggs L *et al.*: Brain capillaries expand and rupture in areas of ischemia and reperfusion. *In* Cerebrovascular Diseases, Reivich M, Hurtig H (Ed.). New York: Raven Press, pp 169–179, 1991
17. Ogata J, Yutani C, Imakita M *et al.*: Hemorrhagic infarct of the brain without reopening of the occluded arteries in cardioembolic stroke. Stroke, 20: 876–883, 1989
18. Okada Y, Yamaguchi T, Minematsu K *et al.*: Hemorrhagic transformation in cerebral embolism. Stroke 20: 589–603, 1989
19. Todd NV, Picozzi P, Crockard HA, Ross Russel RW: Duration of ischemia influences the development and resolution of ischemic brain edema. Stroke 17: 466–471, 1986
20. Ringelstein EB, Biniek R, Weiller C *et al.*: Type and extent of hemispheric brain infarctions and clinical outcome in early and delayed middle cerebral artery recanalization. Neurology 42: 289–298, 1992

21. Bozzao L, Bastianello S, Fantozzi M *et al.*: Ipodensità precoce alla TC nell'ictus ischemico in fase acuta. *In*: Neuroradiologia, Pardatscher K (Ed.). Udine: Centauro Ed, pp 467–471, 1989
22. Bozzao L, Fantozzi L, Bastianello S, Bozzao A, Fieschi C: Early collateral blood supply and late parenchimal brain damage in patients with middle cerebral artery occlusion. Stroke 20: 735–740, 1989
23. Lenzi GL, Giubilei F, Perani P *et al.*: Emittion tomographic functional follow-up studies in stroke. Circ Metab Cerveau 5: 7–13, 1988
24. Giubilei F, Lenzi GL, Di Piero V *et al.*: Predictive value of brain perfusion single-photon emission computed tomography in acute ischemic stroke. Stroke 21: 895–900, 1990
25. Pantano P, Di Piero V, Ricci M *et al.*: Motor stimulation response by Ticnicium-99m hexamethylpropylene-amine oxyme split-dose method and single-photon emission tomography. Eur J Nucl Med 1992 (in press)
26. Argentino C, Toni D, Sacchetti ML, Fieschi C: Progressing strokes: Clinical and pathogenetic aspects and therapeutic implications. J Neurol 238: 112, 1991
27. Toni D, De Michele M, Argentino C, Fieschi C: Pathogenetic mechanisms of ischemic stroke progression: a paradygm of treatable strokes? Platelets 1991. Course and treatment of occlusive vascular disease: role of antiplatelet agents, p. 37, 1991
28. Sacchetti ML, Toni D, Argentino C *et al.*: Early fibrinolysis and brain protection: design of a four-arm trial in brain infarction. *In*: Pharmacology of Brain Ischemia, Kriegelstein J, Operpichler H (Eds). Stuttgard: Wissenschaftliche Verlagsgesellschaft, pp 573–577, 1990

Localization and Nature of the Carotid Plaque

Antonio V. Sterpetti and Alessandra Cucina

THE CAROTID PLAQUE

Atherosclerosis has reached epidemic proportions in the Western world. Although the disease is a generalized process, the abdominal aorta, coronary and carotid arteries are the most common targets. Currently 50% of all deaths in developed countries are related to atherosclerotic disease including myocardial infarction and stroke.

Atheroma is the fundamental lesion of this disease. Histologically, the plaque is characterized by an increased number of lipid-laden intimal smooth muscle cells and macrophages, accumulation of connective tissue, including collagen and proteoglycans and lipid deposits. The above-mentioned features occur in varying proportions, leading to different plaque characteristics.

The fibrous carotid plaque is composed of a superficial part made up of collagen and smooth muscle cells, and a deeper part characterized by a mass of lipid-laden smooth muscle cells and macrophages, cholesterol clefts and cellular debris. Inflammatory cells are sometimes present. Smooth muscle cells are the principal cell of the early atherosclerotic lesion and abnormal proliferation of arterial smooth muscle cells is a key event in the formation of the atherosclerotic plaque. Fibrous atherosclerotic plaques can undergo a series of changes leading to the complex plaque. Carotid plaques that are clinically significant, causing flow reduction or embolization are usually complex plaques. Clinically significant carotid plaques are characterized by ulceration, superimposed thrombosis and intraplaque haemorrhage.[1,2] The mechanisms leading to these events are poorly understood.

Haemorrhage results from rupture of the thin-walled intraplaque capillaries. The haemorrhage leads to plaque enlargement and eventually to breakdown of the normal surface with consequent embolization, ulceration and supraimposed thrombosis. Thrombosis occurs most often on ulcerated plaques and may lead to occlusion of the lumen, embolization or, following incorporation in the plaque, to plaque enlargement.[3,4]

CAROTID PLAQUE LOCALIZATION AND HAEMODYNAMIC FEATURES OF THE CAROTID BIFURCATION

Although atherosclerosis is a generalized process, the abdominal aorta and the orifice of its major branches are susceptible to atheroma formation more commonly than the thoracic aorta. The superficial femoral artery and the coronary and carotid vessels are also frequently involved. Other arteries such as the upper limb arteries are usually spared. Even in susceptible arteries, plaque deposition is focal. In the carotid system atherosclerotic plaque localizes mainly to the bifurcation of the common carotid artery and to the internal carotid siphon. The majority of the lesions are at the carotid bifurcation, a lesion readily amenable to endarterectomy. Frequently severe changes at the carotid bifurcation occur with minimal or no changes in the common or distal internal carotid artery.

Thirty years ago Bauer et al.[5] reported that the carotid plaque forms along the outer wall of the carotid sinus. Subsequently these findings were confirmed by autopsy studies.[6] This peculiar and focal localization of the carotid plaque has led to the hypothesis that flow disturbances play an important role in its formation. There is general evidence that fluid dynamics are a determining factor in the development of atherosclerosis. It is often regions of the arterial branching and sharp curvature that have the greatest predilection for the development of atherosclerotic lesions. Why is the carotid bifurcation particularly prone to plaque formation? Firstly it is a branching point and secondly the proximal portion of the internal carotid artery enlarges to form the bulb. The bulb diameter is twice that of the distal internal carotid artery leading to flow abnormalities which might predispose to atherosclerosis.

Lo Gerfo et al.[7,8] (Fig. 1) used plexiglass models of carotid bifurcation with a dye flow visualization technique to analyse flow dynamics. The models were based on angiograms comparable with the human carotid both for dimensions and geometry. Under steady physiological flow conditions, Reynolds number of 500, boundary layer separation was observed in the sinus, on the outer wall (the side opposite the external carotid). Under these conditions a region of very slow moving, stagnating fluid was present along the outer wall of the sinus. Autopsy and angiographic studies[5,6] have shown that the atherosclerotic plaque commonly localizes to the outer wall of the sinus, opposite to the external carotid artery. In a series of experiments Zarins et al.[9,10] and Ku et al.[11,12] have demonstrated areas of flow separation, low shear stress, slow clearance and flow oscillation at the outer wall of the carotid bulb and they have correlated these findings with the development of the early atherosclerotic plaque. Hydrogen bubble flow visualization demonstrated deviation from the laminar

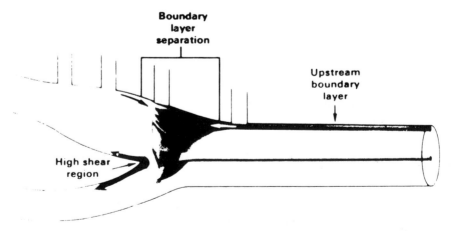

Fig. 1.   Dye flow visualization technique in a plexiglass model human carotid bifurcation shows boundary layer separation at the level of the outer wall of the bulb where the atherosclerotic plaque localizes. From Lo Gerfo et al.[8] with permission.

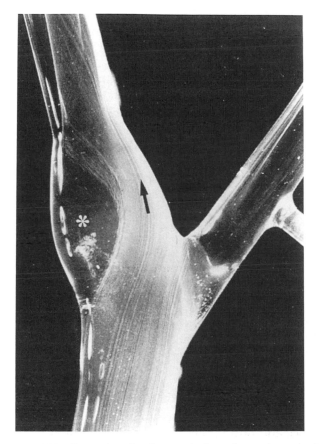

Fig. 2. Hydrogen bubble flow visualization technique in a glass model human carotid bifurcation shows laminar flow in the inner wall of the bulb and area of flow separation in the outer wall where the atherosclerotic plaque localizes. From Zarins et al.[9] with permission.

flow in the carotid bifurcation (Fig. 2). Along the inner wall of the bulb, flow remains laminar with high velocity and high shear stress, whereas in the outer wall there were areas of flow separation, stasis and non-laminar flow. A reversal of axial flow with a complex oscillating shear stress pattern was evident at this level. During systole the region of flow separation disappeared; however, it reemerged during diastole. This flow pattern provides for an increased residence time and decreased clearance at the outer wall of the bulb leading to the possibility of longer interaction between blood cells and vessel wall. Doppler analysis demonstrated high velocity rates in the inner part of the bulb and low velocity in the outer part where early plaque localizes, areas of complex secondary and tertiary flow pattern, but no evidence of turbulence.

In summary, the early atherosclerotic plaque occurs in the outer wall of the carotid sinus where there is low flow velocity, low shear stress, shear stress oscillation and stasis. Plaque formation is minimal in the inner wall of the bulb where shear stress is high, with high velocity laminar flow.

CORRELATION BETWEEN FLOW DYNAMICS AND ATHEROSCLEROSIS FORMATION

How do these abnormal flow dynamics influence plaque formation? Zarins[13] suggests that oscillating shear stress increases endothelial permeability with increased ingress of plasma constituents into the subintima. Endothelial cells align to the direction of flow.[14,15] Alterations in flow direction may lead to reorganization of cytoskeleton and cell junctions with resultant increases in permeability. Alternatively, the area of flow stagnation and low shear stress could have a detrimental effect on the rate of exchange of solutes between arterial wall and lumen. Caro *et al.*[16] have suggested that low wall shear stress influences early plaque formation by affecting the transport of metabolites away from the vessel wall. Also it is possible that platelets may be stimulated to aggregate by the prolonged wall contact. Similarly, flow stagnation could facilitate interaction between lipid particles and the vessel wall. The decreased clearance in areas of flow stasis also could promote interaction between the vessel wall and other cellular elements involved in the formation of atherosclerotic plaque.

However, if the hypothesis that low shear stress, low flow velocity and flow stagnation favour plaque formation was correct, we could not explain why arteries distal to an occlusion, where flow velocity and shear stress are low, usually are spared from atherosclerosis progression. Similarly why does atherosclerosis not form in the venous system, where flow stagnation is common. Thus it is probable that the problem is more complex and other factors including vasomotor tone are involved.

GROWTH FACTORS AND SMOOTH MUSCLE CELLS

Smooth muscle cells are the principal cellular element of the carotid plaque and the abnormal proliferation of smooth muscle cells is a key event in the formation of the atherosclerotic plaque. An important mitogen for cultured smooth muscle cells was originally identified and purified from human platelets; it was called platelet derived growth factor (PDGF).[17,18] PDGF is a 27–31 kilodalton protein which exists as a dimer of two distinct but highly similar polypeptides, termed A chain and B chain.[19,20] PDGF has also been shown to be chemotactic for smooth muscle cells and fibroblasts.[21,22] Because of the specificity of PDGF for connective tissue cells and the release of PDGF from platelets at sites of injury, it has been postulated that PDGF may play a major role in the development of atherosclerotic lesions. However, several findings indicate that abnormal proliferation of smooth muscle cells, which occurs early in atherogenesis, does not require mitogens of platelet origin.[23–25] Arterial smooth muscle cells in culture produce peptide growth factors which may initiate and sustain smooth muscle cells growth in an autocrine manner.

Smooth muscle cells from atherosclerotic plaque can synthesize PDGF-like molecules and the RNA for the oncogene c-sis, which encodes a molecule apparently identical to PDGF, can be identified in human arterial smooth muscle cells.[26,27] Thus the abnormal proliferation of smooth muscle cells which accompanies atherosclerosis can be initiated by a paracrine/autocrine mechanism based on the release of PDGF-like mitogen by the smooth muscle cells themselves.

CORRELATION BETWEEN HAEMODYNAMIC FORCES AND THE GROWTH AND RELEASE OF PDGF BY SMOOTH MUSCLE CELLS

In order to determine whether haemodynamic forces modulate the release of autocrine growth factors from smooth muscle cells we performed a series of experiments to determine the correlation between haemodynamic forces and the proliferation rate and release of mitogens from cultured smooth muscle cells.[28,29]

In these experiments we used smooth muscle cells derived from the aortic media of calves cultured on plastic dishes. Bovine arterial smooth muscle cells (SMC) were subjected to laminar flows of 50 cc/min, 100 cc/min and 150 cc/min in an *in vitro* system. These velocities gave a shear stress of 3, 6, 9 dyne/cm^2 respectively. We determined 1) growth curve and DNA synthesis, 2) flow cytometry pattern, 3) mitogenic activity.

1. Shear stress significantly reduced the growth rate of SMC ($p<0.001$) (Fig. 3). After exposure to shear stress, SMC remained in a quiescent state for at least 24 hours (Fig. 4). Smooth muscle cell proliferation, measured by tritiated thymidine incorporation into DNA, was reduced significantly ($p<0.001$) in SMC subjected to laminar flow (Fig. 5) and decreased SMC proliferation remained evident after flow cessation (Fig. 6).
2. Flow cytometry demonstrated that a lower number of cells were in S phase when SMC were exposed to shear stress and the effect was proportional to the level of shear stress (20% for 0 dyne/cm^2; 11% for 3 dyne/cm^2; 10% for 6 dyne/cm^2; 8% for 9 dyne/cm^2) ($p<0.01$).
3. Conditioned medium from SMC subjected to shear stress stimulated SMC proliferation compared with negative controls and threefold as compared with conditioned medium from SMC not exposed to flow. This effect was proportional to the level of shear stress; SMC subjected to shear stress produced a conditioned medium which was capable of stimulating cellular proliferation in cultures of other cells, including 3T3 cells. In contrast, conditioned medium from SMC not subjected to shear stress did not stimulate cellular proliferation of 3T3 cells. The proliferative effects of the conditioned medium from shear stressed SMCs could be inhibited by preincubation with antibodies to PDGF (Fig. 7).

PDGF-like molecules were detected in the conditioned medium using an antibody based assay.

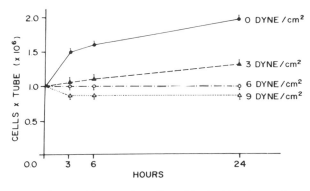

Fig. 3. Growth curves of smooth muscle cells subjected to shear stress. Increasing shear stress reduced significantly the growth rate of the cells.

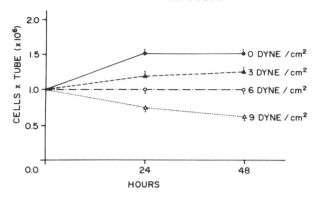

Fig. 4. Growth curves of smooth muscle cells 48 h after flow cessation. After exposure to shear stress, the cells remained in a quiescent state for at least 48 h.

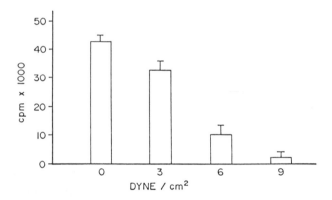

Fig. 5. Tritiated thymidine uptake was reduced in smooth muscle cells subjected to shear stress.

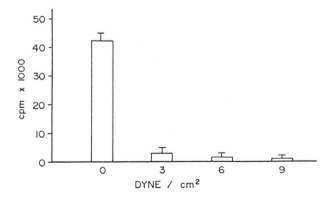

Fig. 6. Tritiated thymidine uptake by smooth muscle cells was significantly reduced after flow cessation.

DISCUSSION

In our *in vitro* model we confirmed that SMC are able to release a PDGF-like mitogen and that increasing shear stress facilitates this phenomenon. Extrapolation of the findings of our *in vitro* study to the clinical setting might explain how disturbance in haemodynamic forces may predispose to early plaque formation. Very low shear stress can facilitate abnormal proliferation of SMC, and high flow shear stress favours release of mitogens.

Thus, flow separation is an important determinant of cellular proliferation with areas of SMC prone to proliferate and areas of SMC releasing increased amounts of mitogens. The latter could influence directly the neighbouring SMC, subjected to low shear stress, by a paracrine mechanism (Fig. 7).

Previous workers have stressed the importance of low shear stress and low flow.[10,11,16] From our investigations it is evident that low shear stress *per se* has only a limited effect. It is the variation of shear stress, as it occurs in areas of flow separation that favours SMC proliferation and plaque formation, by a double effect on cellular growth rate and release of mitogens. The presence of flow separation and the simultaneous occurrence of areas with high and low shear stress may not be an initiator of atherosclerosis, but they are important factors in the localization of the disease in patients at risk.

Extension of the findings of our study to the clinical setting raises the possibility that any type of injury, mechanical or chemical, to the quiescent SMC might disturb the delicate equilibrium which exists in conditions of flow separation and initiate the abnormal proliferation of SMC which characterize early plaque formation. Clinical efforts to control systemic risk factors such as smoking, dyslipidaemia, and high blood pressure are effective in decreasing the morbidity of atherosclerosis. It is possible that control of local factors might reduce the incidence of atherosclerosis. For example anti-PDGF monoclonal antibodies might be used in high risk patients to reduce the

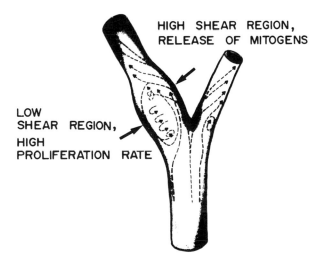

HIGH SHEAR REGION,
RELEASE OF MITOGENS

LOW
SHEAR REGION,
HIGH
PROLIFERATION RATE

Fig. 7. See text (modified from Zarins *et al.*[9]).

effects of PDGF-like mitogens in plaque formation. However, not all of the mitogenic effect of the conditioned medium was attributable to PDGF. Purification, sequencing and cloning of these other mitogens in the future will be needed to give a complete picture of SMC mitogen production in conditions of flow separation. Therefore, other anti-mitogenic factors including antibodies against basic fibroblast derived growth factor might have an important role in preventing plaque formation.

The rationale for controlling local factors for atherosclerosis, may be used after carotid endarterectomy. It is logical to assume that if plaque development and progression is due to the abnormal flow characteristics of the carotid bulb, recurrent stenosis rate will be high if the geometry of the carotid bifurcation is left unchanged after endarterectomy. Primary closure of the endarterectomized carotid leaves the vessel geometry unchanged. Patching with Dacron after endarterectomy might be beneficial in preventing recurrent carotid stenosis merely by altering the anatomy of the carotid bulb which originally caused the haemodynamic conditions responsible for plaque formation and development. Therefore in some situations primary closure after carotid endarterectomy may not be appropriate. The modern vascular surgeon should be aware of the biological phenomena leading to atherosclerosis formation, progression and recurrence, because new developments will be made possible by a closer application of biology knowledge in the clinical setting.

REFERENCES

1. Imparato AM, Riles TS, Gorstein F: The carotid bifurcation plaque: Pathologic findings associated with cerebral ischaemia. Stroke 10: 238–245, 1979
2. Lusby RJ, Ferrell LD, Ehrenfeld WK *et al.*: Carotid plaque haemorrhage. Its role in production of cerebral ischaemia. Arch Surg 117: 1479–1489, 1982
3. Sterpetti AV, Hunter WJ, Schultz RD: Carotid plaque ulceration: its role in cerebral ischaemia. J Cardiovasc Surg 32: 154–158, 1991
4. Moore WS, Hall AD: Importance of emboli from carotid bifurcation in pathogenesis in cerebral ischaemic attacks. Arch Surg 101: 708–716, 1970
5. Bauer RB, Sheehan S, Weehsler N *et al.*: Arteriographic study of sites, incidence and treatment of arteriosclerotic cerebrovascular lesions. Neurology 12: 698–711, 1962
6. Solbert LA, Eggen DA: Localisation and sequence of development and atherosclerotic lesions in the carotid and vertebral arteries. Circulation 43: 711–724, 1971
7. Lo Gerfo FW, Nowak MD, Quist WC *et al.*: Flow studies in a model carotid bifurcation. Arteriosclerosis 1: 235–241, 1981
8. Lo Gerfo FW, Nowak MD, Quist WC. Structural details of boundary layer separation in a model human carotid bifurcation under steady and pulsatile flow conditions. J Vasc Surg 2: 263–269, 1989
9. Zarins CK, Giddens DP, Bharadvaj BK *et al.*: Carotid bifurcation atherosclerosis: Quantitative correlation of plaque localisation with flow velocity profiles and wall shear stress. Circ Res 53: 502–518, 1983
10. Zarins CK: Pathology of carotid artery atherosclerosis. *In* Current Therapy in Vascular Surgery, Vol. 1, Ernst CB, Stanley JC (Eds). p. 1, 1992
11. Ku DN, Giddens DP, Zarins CK *et al.*: Pulsatile flow in a model carotid bifurcation. Atherosclerosis 3: 31–39, 1983
12. Ku DN, Giddens DP, Zarins CK *et al.*: Pulsatile flow and atherosclerosis in the human carotid bifurcation: positive correlation between plaque location and low and oscillating shear stress. Atherosclerosis 5: 293–302, 1985
13. Zarins CK: Hemodynamics in atherogenesis. *In* Vascular Surgery, Moore WS (Ed.). p. 97, 1986

14. Sterpetti AV, Cucina A, Santoro L: Shear stress induces changes in the morphology and cytoskeleton organisation of endothelial cells. Eur J Vasc Surg (in press)
15. Eskin SG, Ives CL, McIntire LV *et al.*: Response of cultural endothelial cells to steady flow. Microvasc Res 28: 87–94, 1984
16. Caro CG, Fitzgerald JM, Schroter RC: Atheroma and arterial wall shear: observation correlation and proposal of shear dependent mass transfer mechanism for atherogenesis. Proc R Soc Lond 177: 109–159, 1977
17. Ross R, Glomset J, Kariya B, Harker L. A platelet-dependent serum factor that stimulates the proliferation of arterial smooth muscle cells *in vitro*. Proc Natl Acad Sci USA 71: 1207–1210, 1974
18. Rosenfeld ME, Bowen-Pope DF, Ross R: Platelet-derived growth factor: morphologic and biochemical studies of binding, internalizing and degradation. J Cell Physiol 121: 263–274, 1984
19. Ross R, Raines EW, Bowen-Pope DF. The biology of platelet derived growth factor. Cell 46: 155–169, 1986
20. Gronwald RGK, Grant FJ, Haldeman BA *et al.*: Cloning and expression of a cDNA coding for the human platelet-derived growth factor receptor: Evidence for more than one receptor class. Proc Natl Acad Sci USA 85: 3435–3439, 1988
21. Heldin CH, Westermark B, Wasteson A: Specific receptors for platelet-derived growth factors on cells derived from connective tissue and glia. Proc Natl Acad Sci USA 78: 3664–3668, 1981
22. Nilsson J, Thyberg J, Heldin CH *et al.*: Surface binding and internalization of platelet-derived growth factor in human fibroblast. Proc Natl Acad Sci USA 80: 5592–5636, 1983
23. Joris I, Zhand T, Nunneri JJ *et al.*: Studies on the pathogenesis of atherosclerosis. I Adhesions and emigration of mononuclear cells in the aorta of hypercholesterolemic rats. Am J Pathol 113: 341–358, 1983
24. Faggiotto A, Ross R, Harker L: Studies of hypercholesterolemia in the nonhuman primate I. Changes that lead to fatty streak formation. Arteriosclerosis 4: 323–340, 1984
25. Reidy MA: A reassessment of endothelial injury and arterial lesion formation. Lab Invest 53: 513–520, 1985
26. Walker LN, Bowen-Pope DF, Reidy MA: Production of platelet derived growth factor-like molecules by cultured arterial smooth muscle cells accompanies proliferation after arterial injury. Proc Natl Acad Sci USA 83: 7311–7315, 1986
27. Barrett TB, Benditt EP. Sis (platelet derived growth factor b chain) gene transcript levels are elevated in human artherosclerotic lesions compared to normal artery. Proc Natl Acad Sci USA 84: 1099–1103, 1987
28. Sterpetti AV, Cucina A, Santoro L *et al.*: Shear stress modulates the proliferation rate protein synthesis and mitogenic activity of arterial smooth muscle cells. Surgery (in press)
29. Sterpetti AV, Morena AR, Cucina A *et al.*: Shear stress stimulates the release of interleukin-1 and interleukin-6 by endothelial cells. Surgery (in press)

Irradiation-Induced Carotid Lesions

Hans O. Myhre, Rune Haaverstad and Torbjørn Dahl

INTRODUCTION

Damage to the carotid arteries following irradiation may be acute or chronic leading to either stenosis, occlusion, disruption or aneurysm formation. While the time interval to rupture is within a few weeks or months, the delayed consequences of irradiation like arterial stenosis may become apparent from a few months to more than 20 years until the onset of symptoms.[1-3] The primary diagnosis varies and most reports refer to patients treated for Hodgkin's disease and lymphoma or carcinoma of the larynx. Carotid obstruction has also been reported in patients suffering from thyroid carcinoma, carcinoma of the parotid gland, breast cancer and sarcoma in the neck and throat. There are also reports of late carotid artery lesions following irradiation for certain benign lesions, including hyperthyroidism, tonsillitis, laryngeal papilloma and pituitary adenoma. The dose of irradiation is not always mentioned in the reports, but most patients have been exposed to more than 50 Gy in the neck region (Table 1).[2-10,12,14-18]

Arterial wall necrosis caused by irradiation together with extensive operative procedures for carcinoma of the oropharyngeal region usually cause dramatic symptoms. These tend to occur when the operation is complicated by tissue necrosis, infection or salivary fistula.[1,3,19-21]

INCIDENCE

The incidence of irradiation-induced carotid artery lesion is largely unknown. Only about 70 cases of symptomatic extracranial carotid artery stenosis have hitherto been

Table 1. Summary from some reports of irradiation-induced carotid stenosis including three or more cases

First author (year)	No. of patients	Irradiation dosage, Gy (median and range)	Interval (years) from irradiation to symptoms (median and range)
Levinson (1973)[4]	3	95.5 (75–116)	32 (24–34)
Bladin (1977)[5]	3	–	19 –
Silverberg (1978)[6]	9	55 (43–120)	7.5 (1.5–30)
McCready (1983)[3]	3	65 (55–75)	17 (7–24)
Bergqvist (1987)[7]	3	50 (50–73)	22 (13–27)
Atkinson (1989)[8]	7	62 (35–70)	12 (4–22)
Call (1990)[9]	3	40 (36–50)	2 (1–3)
Piedbois (1990)[10]	5	55 (47–70)	4 (3–11)
McGuirt (1992)[11]	9	50 (41.5–68)	7 (2–18)

reported, but there are no prospective studies following patients after irradiation therapy. Furthermore, it may take several years until arterial obstruction or symptoms of cerebrovascular insufficiency occur. It is likely that many of these lesions have been reported as ordinary atherosclerotic obstructions since there are several similarities.

In a retrospective study of 910 patients receiving cervical irradiation for malignant disease, 6% had undergone cerebral infarction. This was significantly higher than in a matched control population.[22] Other studies have also indicated that the incidence of significant carotid stenosis following cervical irradiation is much higher than in a sex- and age-matched normal population and compared with control patients with comparable malignant disease, who did not receive irradiation therapy.[11,22,23]

Investigations based on duplex ultrasound technique have been made to estimate the incidence of carotid stenosis following high dose irradiation therapy. In one series 28 irradiated patients with malignant tumours of the head and neck were compared with 556 patients of the same age.[24] The mean follow-up period was more than 7 years and the incidences of carotid artery obstruction were 21% and 9% respectively. In another investigation an incidence of 30% of the irradiated group was reported compared with 6% in control patients.[23] To summarize, there seems to be a five times higher risk of developing moderate to severe carotid stenosis following irradiation therapy than in the normal population.[23]

VASCULAR REACTION TO IRRADIATION

Irradiation-induced damage to blood vessels has been known since 1899 when Gassmann[25] described the histological picture of blood vessel damage in the skin following irradiation. Since then, several animal studies have focused on irradiation-induced stenosis of various major arteries.[26-30] Occlusion of vasa vasorum may be one pathogenetic mechanism for the irradiation-induced changes of the larger vessels.[27,31] The first irradiation damage to major arteries in man was described by Thomas and Forbus in 1959.[32] The connection between irradiation of the neck and carotid artery stenosis has since been reported by several authors.[1,2] Both in animal studies as well as in specimens from operations the morphological changes are similar to atherosclerotic degeneration.[18,31] The intima becomes fibrotic and proliferated and there is destruction of the internal elastic membrane, which may lead to increased lipid accumulation of the vessel wall.[28,30] In cases with rupture, myointimal proliferation as well as extensive adventitial necrosis has been observed.[19]

Animal experiments support the theory that both high cholesterol diet and hypertension potentiate the effect of irradiation on major blood vessels.[28,30,33,34] Furthermore, decreased fibrinolytic activity and synthesis of prostacycline has been measured following irradiation.[35] The critical level of irradiation necessary to induce carotid lesions is not easily defined. Factors such as overlapping between irradiation fields, repeated series of treatment and the combination of surgery and irradiation in the same area are thought to be predisposing.[1] Although controversial, late changes in arteries which have been exposed to irradiation are similar to those found in atherosclerosis, supporting the view that the obstructions are most probably caused by an acceleration of the development of atherosclerosis.

CLINICAL PRESENTATION AND LABORATORY FINDINGS

Most symptoms from irradiation-induced carotid artery stenosis are identical to those observed in ordinary atherosclerotic obstruction. Thus, amaurosis fugax, transient ischaemic attacks and stroke have been described.[2,6,8] Some patients may have noticed an ipsilateral bruit.

The patient will present typical irradiation-induced skin changes such as pigmentation, atrophy, induration and scarring of the area of previous cervical irradiation. An eventual audible bruit tends to be located more proximally than in ordinary carotid stenosis since the obstruction often affects the common carotid artery. For the same reason the carotid pulse of the neck may be decreased. The arterial changes are usually bilateral and the carotid artery on one side may be occluded.[2] In this case there is no palpable pulse on the actual side of the neck.

Most of the reported cases have been studied with arteriography and the location of the process is atypical compared with ordinary atherosclerotic obstructions, which generally develop at the bifurcation area. In contrast, irradiation-induced stenosis usually involves the common carotid artery, often bilaterally (Fig. 1). The arterial obstruction usually affects a more extensive part of the carotid artery and may be multisegmental, depending upon the field and technique of irradiation. The rest of the arterial tree is healthy without signs of occlusive disease.[6,8,16]

The patients usually have few other risk factors for the development of atherosclerosis like smoking, hypertension, hypercholesterolaemia etc. also suggesting irradiation injury as the most important aetiological factor.[6,8] If associated risk factors are present it is believed that they could accelerate the degenerative effect of irradiation, promoting a premature arterial lesion.[2] Thus, the patients are generally 10 years younger than control patients having ordinary atherosclerotic lesions.

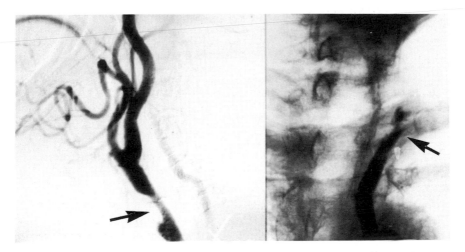

Fig. 1. Irradiation-induced stenosis of the right common carotid artery (→). The left common carotid artery was occluded (←). The patient had received irradiation following operation for thyroid carcinoma 25 years previously. He presented with multiple transient ischaemic attacks and was successfully treated by endarterectomy and patch graft angioplasty.

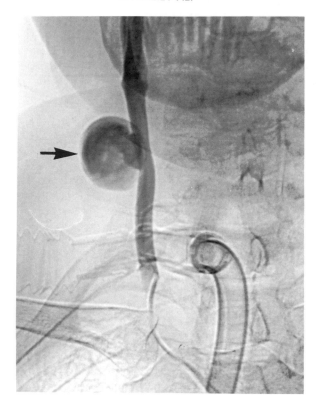

Fig. 2.   Arteriogram showing a false aneurysm (→) of the right common carotid artery. The patient had undergone extensive surgery followed by irradiation therapy (70 Gy) for undifferentiated carcinoma of the right hypopharynx. The operation was complicated with salivary fistula requiring revision surgery. The pseudoaneurysm ruptured and ligation of the carotid artery was performed without neurological sequelae. The patient is doing well 10 months after arterial ligation.

Rupture of the carotid artery will develop dramatic clinical signs of pseudoaneurysm formation (Fig. 2), haematoma with acute respiratory distress or haemorrhage, which is often fatal.[20,21]

TREATMENT AND PREVENTION

Some patients present relative contraindications against carotid surgery because of advanced age, decreased general condition or stroke. Conservative treatment is then indicated. The patients' primary disease must be taken into consideration since many of them have a decreased life expectancy due to their malignancy.[2]

The skin is usually affected by irradiation therapy with scar formation and decreased healing tendency.[5] The dissection can be difficult due to periadventitial fibrosis and less defined tissue planes. The plaques of irradiation-exposed arteries tend to involve more of the arterial wall and may even include the whole circumference of the artery in contrast to non-irradiated arteries.

Surgical treatment usually consists of endarterectomy. Since arterial obstruction is frequently quite extensive, a vertical skin incision is recommended to achieve sufficient exposure. Gentle handling of the skin is necessary to avoid necrosis and to promote healing. Sharp dissection is advised and should be minimized to what is necessary for arterial control. Particular attention should be given not to undermine the subcutaneous tissue. Patch graft angioplasty using autologous material prevents arterial narrowing and makes it possible to take bigger bites in the arterial wall, thereby avoiding tearing and haemorrhage. Prophylactic antibiotics should be given.

In most reports the results of endarterectomy are comparable with those obtained by endarterectomy for non-irradiated atherosclerotic lesions.[2,8] In some patients alternative surgical techniques have to be used. If the lesion is in the proximal part of the common carotid artery, a median sternotomy may become necessary.[13,16] If the lesion involves the whole arterial wall or is extensive, endarterectomy may become risky and an interposition graft or a bypass could be indicated using either autologous saphenous vein or a prosthetic graft.[10,13,16] Extra-anatomic reconstruction has also been used in these lesions as a subclavian-carotid bypass or a 'crossover' bypass from one carotid artery to the other.[6,7] The future role of endovascular surgery in this area is unknown, but balloon angioplasty has been used successfully for subclavian artery stenosis.[1] In the postoperative period proper control of the blood pressure and observation in the intensive care unit the first day is mandatory.

With carotid artery rupture the situation is dramatic and ligation of the artery is usually the only possibility of treatment. The sutures should be reinforced by autologous vein material to avoid tearing of the fragile artery. If the patient does not succumb from immediate haemorrhage, carotid artery ligation can be performed without neurological complications in about 75% of the cases depending upon the adequacy of the collateral circulation.[20,21]

CONCLUSION

Carotid artery stenoses occur several years after irradiation treatment of the neck region. Because of the good prognosis in patients with Hodgkin's lymphoma treated by irradiation therapy, this group of patients is most frequently considered for carotid artery disease. Patients surviving carcinoma of the neck and throat make up the second most important group. The carotid lesion has atypical location and usually involves the common carotid artery within the area exposed to irradiation. The patients are somewhat younger than those with regular atherosclerosis and usually have no concomitant atherosclerosis in other arterial areas. They also have few risk factors of atherosclerosis. Some cases have had a higher dose of irradiation than is usually accepted as safe.

Symptoms from irradiation-induced carotid artery disease are similar to the symptoms in non-irradiated patients and may give rise to severe morbidity or become lethal. It is important to be aware of these consequences despite the relatively few symptomatic cases being admitted to hospital. Screening programmes have shown a high incidence of plaque formation and significant stenosis of the carotid artery following irradiation therapy. It has therefore been recommended to start a follow-up programme with serial duplex ultrasound investigations, at least 5 years following treatment. Although medical prophylaxis with aspirin has been considered following cervical irradiation, at least in patients with additional risk factors of atherosclerotic disease, no firm conclusions regarding such prophylaxis can yet be made. Additional risk factors should in general be minimized. In symptomatic patients with irradiation-induced carotid stenosis, surgical therapy with endarterectomy is advised since the outcome is usually favourable.

REFERENCES

1. Bergentz SE, Bergqvist D (Eds): Iatrogenic Vascular Injuries. Stuttgart: Springer Verlag, pp. 63–76, 1989
2. Murros KE, Toole JF: The effect of radiation on carotid arteries. Arch Neurol 46: 449–455, 1989
3. McCready RA, Hyde GL, Bivins BA, Mattingly SS, Griffin WO: Radiation-induced arterial injuries. Surgery 93: 306–312, 1983
4. Levinson SA, Close MB, Ehrenfeld WK, Stoney RJ: Carotid artery occlusive disease following external cervical irradiation. Arch Surg 107: 395–397, 1973
5. Bladin PF, Royle J: Post-irradiation extracranial cerebrovascular disease. Clin Exp Neurol (Proc Aust Assoc Neurol) 14: 8–14, 1977
6. Silverberg GD, Britt RH, Goffinet RD: Radiation-induced carotid artery disease. Cancer 41: 130–137, 1978
7. Bergqvist D, Jonsson K, Nilsson M, Takolander R: Treatment of arterial lesions after radiation therapy. Surg Gynecol Obstet 165: 116–120, 1987
8. Atkinson JLD, Sundt TM, Dale AJD, Cascino TL, Nichols DA: Radiation-associated atheromatous disease of the cervical carotid artery: Report of seven cases and review of the literature. Neurosurgery 24: 171–178, 1989
9. Call GK, Bray PF, Smoker WRK, Buys SS, Hayes JK: Carotid thrombosis following neck irradiation. Int J Radiat Oncol Biol Phys 18: 635–640, 1990
10. Piedbois P, Becquemin JP, Blanc I, Mazeron JJ *et al.*: Arterial occlusive disease after radiotherapy: a report of fourteen cases. Radiother Oncol 17: 133–140, 1990
11. McGuirt WF, Feehs RS, Bond G, Strickland JL, McKinney WM: Irradiation-induced atherosclerosis: A factor in therapeutic planning. Ann Otol Rhinol Laryngol 101: 222–228, 1992
12. Glick B: Bilateral carotid occlusive disease following irradiation for carcinoma of the vocal cords. Arch Pathol 93: 352–355, 1972
13. Hayward RH: Arteriosclerosis induced by radiation. Surg Clin North Am 52: 359–366, 1972
14. St Louis EL, McLoughlin MJ, Wortzman G. Chronic damage to medium and larger arteries following irradiation. J Can Assoc Radiol 25: 94–104, 1974
15. Kearsley JH: Late cerebrovascular disease after radiation therapy—Report of two cases and a review of the literature. Australas Radiol 27: 11–18, 1983
16. Loftus CM, Biller J, Hart MN, Cornell SH, Hiratzka LF: Management of radiation-induced accelerated carotid atherosclerosis. Arch Neurol 44: 711–714, 1987
17. Jones TR, Frusha JD: Carotid revascularization after cervical irradiation. South Med J 79: 1517–1520, 1986
18. Conomy JP, Kellermeyer RW: Delayed cerebrovascular consequences of therapeutic radiation. Cancer 36: 1702–1708, 1975
19. Fajardo LF, Lee A: Rupture of major vessels after radiation. Cancer 36: 904–913, 1975
20. Razack MS, Sako K: Carotid artery hemorrhage and ligation in head and neck cancer. J Surg Oncol 19: 189–192, 1982

21. Heller KS, Strong EW: Carotid arterial hemorrhage after radical head and neck surgery. Am J Surg 138: 607–610, 1979
22. Elerding SC, Fernandez RN, Grotta JC et al.: Carotid artery disease following external cervical irradiation. Ann Surg 194: 609–615, 1981
23. Moritz MW, Higgins RF, Jacobs JR: Duplex imaging and incidence of carotid radiation injury after high-dose radiotherapy for tumours of the head and neck. Arch Surg 125: 1181–1183, 1990
24. Bootz F, Dienter HC: Bestrahlingsbedingte Schädigung grosser arterien. HNO 35: 24–26, 1987
25. Gassmann A: Zur Histologie der Roentgenulcera. Fortschr Geb Rontgenstr Nuklearmed Erganzungsband 2: 199, 1899
26. Lindsay S, Kohn III, Dakin RL et al.: Aortic arteriosclerosis in the dog after localized aortic X-irradiation. Circ Res 71: 268–273, 1962
27. Fonkalsrud EW, Sanchez M, Zerubavel R, Mahoney A: Serial changes in arterial structure following radiation therapy. Surg Gynecol Obstet 145: 395–400, 1977
28. Lamberts HB, de Boer WGRM: Contributions to the study of immediate and early X-ray reactions with regard to chemoprotection: VII X-ray induced atheromatous lesions in the arterial wall of cholesterolemic rabbits. Int J Radiol Biol 6: 343–350, 1963
29. Sams A: Histological changes in the larger blood vessels of the hind limb of the mouse after X-irradiation. Int J Radiat Biol 9: 165–174, 1965
30. Upadhaya BR, Chakraarti RN, Wahi PL: Post-irradiation vascular injury and accelerated development of experimental atherosclerosis. Indian J Med Res 60: 403–608, 1972
31. Huvos AG, Leaming RH, Moore OS: Clinicopathologic study of the resected carotid artery. Am J Surg 126: 570–574, 1973
32. Thomas E, Forbus WD: Irradiation injury to the aorta and the lung. Arch Pathol 67: 256–263, 1959
33. Gold H: Production of arteriosclerosis in the rat: Effect of X-ray and a high-fat diet. Arch Pathol 71: 268–273, 1961
34. Hopewell JW, Wright EA, Path FC: The nature of latent cerebral irradiation damage and its modification by hypertension. Br J Radiol 43: 161–167, 1970
35. Sinzinger H, Firbas W, Cromwell M: Strahlenvaskulopathie—bedingt durch Änderungen der gefässeigenen Prostacyklinsynthese? Wien Klin Wochenschr 95: 761–765, 1983

The Influence of Smoking and Lipids on Restenosis after Carotid Endarterectomy

Janet T. Powell, Rachel Cuming and Roger M. Greenhalgh

Recurrent stenosis after carotid endarterectomy is common. For most patients the mild restenosis which results from myointimal hyperplasia is part of the normal healing process. More severe restenosis of $\geq 50\%$, occurs in about 20% of patients following carotid endarterectomy.[1-4] Even this more severe restenosis appears to be a benign process of low clinical impact, since symptomatic restenosis develops in <5% of patients.[1-4] Serial duplex scanning has demonstrated that restenosis develops rapidly, appropriate to the healing process, and within 2 years of endarterectomy, restenosis of $\geq 50\%$ develops in 20% of men and 35% of women.[5] Several other reports also have demonstrated an increased incidence of carotid restenosis in women.[6,7] In addition, studies have indicated hypercholesterolaemia as a risk factor for recurrent carotid stenosis.[4,8,9] Subsequently, a clinical trial of aggressive lipid lowering therapy after carotid endarterectomy has been proposed.[10] Since the number of carotid endarterectomies performed appears set to increase following the reporting of the European Carotid Surgery Trial and the North American Symptomatic Carotid Endarterectomy Trial for symptomatic 70–99% carotid stenosis,[11,12] it is timely to consider carefully the evidence concerning aetiological factors associated with carotid stenosis.

CAROTID ENDARTERECTOMIES 1987–1991

In our own centre, 113 patients underwent carotid endarterectomy between 1987 and 1991 for symptomatic disease, with preoperative internal carotid stenosis in the range 60–99%. A Dacron patch was used selectively to ensure that the final diameter of the internal carotid artery was >5 mm. Of these 107 patients (71 men and 36 women) were alive and close enough to Charing Cross Hospital to attend for routine follow-up visits during the first year after endarterectomy. The median age of these patients was 70 (range 41–84) years and 12 (11%) had diabetes mellitus. The indications for surgery were amaurosis fugax (21), transient ischaemic attack (61) and established stroke (25). Forty-six patients were known to have ischaemic heart disease (angina or previous myocardial infarction) and the same number of patients had peripheral arterial disease (ankle/brachial systolic pressure index <0.8).

Colour coded duplex ultrasonography (Acuson 128) was used for pre and post-operative assessment: postoperative assessments were at 3, 6 and 12 months. Fasting blood samples were obtained preoperatively and analysed for cholesterol, triglycerides and apolipoprotein B. Further serum samples were obtained at 3 and 12 months postoperative follow-up for the analysis of serum cotinine. The data were analysed using life tables with significant values being obtained from the log-rank method.

RESTENOSIS AFTER CAROTID ENDARTERECTOMY

Mild recurrent asymptomatic stenosis (26–49%) developed in 47 patients (44%) and more severe restenosis (50–90%) in 18 patients (17%) in the first year following carotid endarterectomy. Among the patients with more severe restenosis, 15 were asymptomatic and three had recurrent transient ischaemic attacks. These three patients were treated with aspirin and none progressed to a completed stroke. One further patient, with no evidence of restenosis, developed recurrent transient ischaemic attacks which also were successfully treated with aspirin. Age, sex, side of operation, patch, hypertension, diabetes, ischaemic heart disease and peripheral arterial disease had no influence on carotid restenosis (Table 1). The data for men and women are shown in Fig. 1.

LIPIDS, SMOKING, BODY MASS INDEX AND RESTENOSIS

There were 42 patients with <25% restenosis, 47 patients with 26–49% restenosis and 18 patients with ≥50% restenosis at one year. The median cholesterol levels were similar in each of the three groups (Table 1). The median triglyceride and apolipoprotein B levels increased with increasing grade of restenosis (Table 1), but these differences did not reach statistical significance. When the patients were separated into two groups above and below median cholesterol levels there was a trend to greater incidence of restenosis ≥50% in the patients with below median cholesterol, but this failed to achieve statistical significance (Fig. 2). Patients with above and below median triglyceride levels had similar incidence of restenosis.

Women undergoing carotid endarterectomy had significantly higher cholesterol and apolipoprotein B levels than their male counterparts (Table 2). For men alone those with recurrent stenosis ≥50% had significantly lower cholesterol levels than those with lesser degrees of restenosis (Table 2). For women the converse was true

Table 1. Patient characteristics

	Restenosis in the first year after carotid endarterectomy		
	0–25% n = 42	*26–49%* n = 47	*≥50%* n = 18
Median age (range)	68.5 (46–84)	70 (41–81)	70 (60–84)
Males (%)	27 (64)	33 (70)	11 (61)
Diabetes (%)	6 (14)	5 (11)	1 (6)
Hypertension (%)	27 (64)	28 (61)	9 (50)
Ischaemic heart disease (%)	18 (44)	18 (40)	9 (50)
Peripheral arterial disease (%)	18 (44)	19 (41)	9 (50)
Cholesterol mmol/l median (range)	6.55 (4.4–13.3)	6.65 (4.4–14.7)	6.1 (5.0–9.7)
Triglyceride mmol/l median (range)	1.49 (0.51–5.98)	1.54 (0.59–9.06)	1.68 (0.64–4.06)
Apolipoprotein B g/l median (range)	0.69 (0.50–1.11)	0.73 (0.49–1.10)	0.75 (0.53–1.02)
Serum cotinine ≥200 nmol/l	12 (29%)	25 (54%)	12 (67%)
Body mass index kg/m^2 (range)	26.1 (17.9–35.0)	26.0 (17.5–42.2)	24.9 (18.5–29.1)

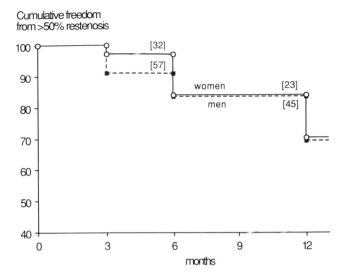

Fig. 1. Carotid restenosis in men (■) and women (○). The number entering each time interval is shown in parenthesis.

and women with recurrent stenosis ≥50% had higher levels of cholesterol and apolipoprotein B than women with lesser degrees of restenosis (Table 2): these differences failed to achieve statistical significance.

Smoking and body mass index were associated with both mild (26–49%) and more severe (≥50%) restenosis. Smokers were defined from having a serum cotinine of ≥200 nmol/l at follow-up visits. Patients with cotinine levels of 100–200 nmol/l could have been light smokers or heavily exposed to passive smoking: such patients were categorized as non-smokers. Restenosis of ≥50% developed in 39% of smokers

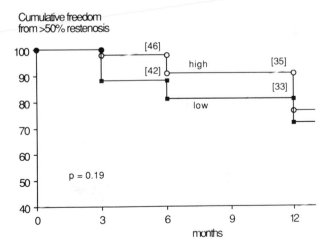

Fig. 2. Carotid restenosis and serum cholesterol: ○: patients with above median cholesterol levels; ■ those with lower levels. The number entering each time interval is shown in parenthesis.

Table 2. Lipids in men and women

| | Cholesterol (mmol/l) *(apolipoprotein B g/l)* | | |
	Total group	*<50% Restenosis*	*≥50% Restenosis*
Men	6.4 (4.4–13.3)	6.5 (4.4–13.3)	5.7 (5.0–6.9)*
n = 71	*0.69 (0.50–1.11)*	*0.69 (0.5–1.11)*	*0.65 (0.53–0.89)*
Women	7.4 (4.4–14.7)**	6.95 (4.4–14.7)	8.1 (5.8–9.7)
n = 36	*0.81 (0.49–1.10)**	*0.80 (0.49–1.10)*	*0.86 (0.69–1.02)*

The data is presented as median (range).
*Significantly different from men with <50% restenosis $p = 0.002$ (Mann–Whitney U test).
**Significantly higher than for the men, $p = 0.006$ (cholesterol), $p = 0.008$ (apolipoprotein B).

compared with only 16% of non-smokers, increased relative risk 2.96 in smokers $p = 0.023$ (Fig. 3). Conversely, increased body mass index at 1-year follow-up was associated with a lower rate of restenosis. Restenosis of ≥50% developed in only 18% of patients with above median body mass index compared with in 35% of the less obese patients (Fig. 4), an increased relative risk of restenosis of 3.03 in the thinner patients, $p = 0.027$.

HOW CAN WE REDUCE RESTENOSIS AFTER CAROTID ENDARTERECTOMY?

Our knowledge concerning restenosis after carotid endarterectomy has increased rapidly with the widespread availability of duplex scanning. In large part the restenosis is a benign healing process and very few patients develop symptomatic restenosis.[1-5] Clearly it would be useful to identify and remedy risk factors associated with the potential for rapid, symptomatic restenosis.

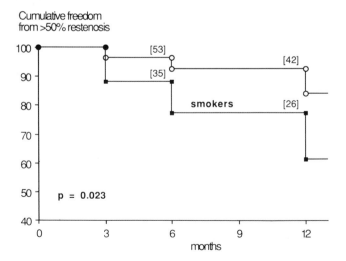

Fig. 3. Smoking and carotid restenosis. Smokers (■) (cotinine ≥200 nmol/l), have a significantly increased risk of restenosis compared with non-smokers (○) (cotinine <200 nmol/l). The number entering each time interval is shown in parenthesis.

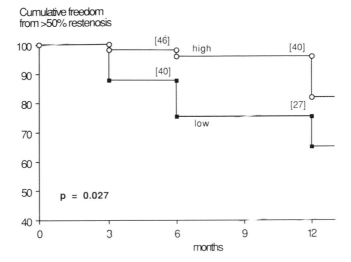

Fig. 4. Carotid restenosis and body mass index. More obese patients (○) (above median body mass index), have a significantly lower risk of restenosis than those with below median body mass index (■). The number entering each time interval is shown in parenthesis

There is little argument that the restenosis results principally from intimal hyperplasia.[13] Simple geometric considerations suggest that intimal hyperplasia in an artery of small diameter will effect greater 'restenosis' than in an artery of larger diameter. This is a topic that requires urgent investigation—do small calibre internal carotid arteries suffer more from restenosis? Should such small calibre arteries be patched? (see chapter: Carotid Endarterectomy with Selected Dacron Patching, p. 157). Is this the explanation for so many reports that restenosis is more common amongst women?[5-7] In our study, where only <5 mm diameter internal carotid arteries were patched, we did not observe that stenosis was significantly more common in women (Fig. 1).

In the Charing Cross series, restensosis was not associated with either female sex or with hyperlipidaemia. Women represented one-third of the patients undergoing carotid endarterectomy. When men and women are considered separately it is evident that women have significantly increased levels of cholesterol and apolipoprotein B compared with the men undergoing carotid endarterectomy (Table 2). When women only are considered there is some indication that increased cholesterol and apolipoprotein B levels could be associated with an increased risk of restenosis, but the numbers are too few for these trends to be significant (Table 2).

Too many authors have investigated aetiological factors associated with carotid restenosis in retrospective case control studies: identifying a few patients undergoing recurrent endarterectomy and comparing them with patients with no significant postoperative restenosis.[4,6-9] Such studies are intrinsically flawed since only survivors can be included and women are overrepresented in the cases (up to 55%). Life table methods should be used for analysis and this has been emphasized recently.[5] Three of these case control studies have reported hypercholesterolaemia as a risk factor for carotid restenosis.[4,8,9] Such studies must not be used as a basis for proposing a clinical trial of aggressive lipid lowering therapy after carotid endarterectomy.[10]

Our results, based on life table analysis, clearly show that hypercholesterolaemia is not a general risk factor for restenosis. Women undergoing carotid endarterectomy have higher cholesterol levels than men. This is not a reason to conclude that hypercholesterolaemia is a risk factor for restenosis.

Although previous studies have indicated that smoking is a risk factor for carotid restenosis this has not been considered seriously. Rapp writes 'In attempting to construct an effective treatment program for patients after carotid endarterectomy, we have concentrated on the lipid levels because tobacco cessation therapy is notoriously unsuccessful, . . .'.[10] Let us face the facts: we now have nicotine patches and more effective anti-smoking counselling but still it remains easier to prescribe lipid lowering drugs. Our study shows that smokers have a threefold increase in the relative risk of developing carotid restenosis in the first year following endarterectomy.

In many patient groups smoking history is unreliable.[14] Nearly all the Charing Cross patients (95/107) admitted to a prolonged smoking history and self-reported current smoking status was not associated with restenosis. Cotinine, a long lived metabolite of nicotine, provides a more specific marker of smoking. Patients with high levels of serum cotinine at postoperative follow-up were those at highest risk of restenosis after carotid endarterectomy (Fig. 3) This confirms an earlier study where it was noted that 95% of patients with recurrent stenosis continued to smoke following endarterectomy.[6]

Weight gain is an established feature of smoking cessation.[15] The mean body mass index of 889 former smokers (men) was 26.4 compared with only 25.1 in 748 continuing smokers.[15] In our study the median body mass index of those with recurrent carotid stenosis was 24.9 compared with 26 in those with lesser degrees of restenosis (Table 1). The association of an improved prognosis for those with above median body mass index may be a consequence of the presence of many former smokers in this group.

Smoking adversely influences restenosis after carotid endarterectomy: the mechanism may relate to the stimulation of intimal hyperplasia in smokers. There is little evidence to suggest the hypercholesterolaemia promotes intimal hyperplasia, neither does hypercholesterolaemia influence carotid restenosis in men. Whilst we may continue to investigate whether hypercholesterolaemia adversely effects restenosis in women, there is no justification in recommending aggressive lipid lowering therapy after carotid endarterectomy.[10] Efforts should be focused on dissuading patients from smoking.

ACKNOWLEDGEMENTS

We thank the Tobacco Products Research Trust for support, P. Worrell and P. Franks for laboratory analyses and data analysis.

REFERENCES

1. Zierler BE, Bandyt DF, Thiele BL, Strandness DE: Carotid artery stenosis following endarterectomy. Arch Surg 117:1408–1415, 1982

2. Colgan MP, Kingston V, Shanik G: Stenosis following carotid endartectomy. Arch Surg 119:1033–1035, 1984
3. DeGroote RD, Lynch TG, Jamil Z, Hobson RW: Carotid restenosis: long-term non-invasive follow-up after carotid endarterectomy. Stroke 18:1031–1036, 1987
4. Salenius J-P, Haapanen A, Harju E, Jokela H, Riekkinen H: Late carotid restenosis: Aetiologic factors for recurrent carotid artery stenosis during long term follow up. Eur J Vasc Surg 3:271–277, 1989
5. Healy DA, Zierler E, Nicholls SC, et al.: Long term follow up and clinical outcome of carotid restenosis. J Vasc Surg 10:662–669, 1989
6. Clagget GP, Rich NM, McDonald PT, et al.: Etiologic factors for recurrent carotid artery stenosis. Surgery 93:313–318, 1983
7. Nicholls SC, Phillips DJ, Bergelin RO, et al.: Carotid endarterectomy: Relationship of outcome to early restenosis. J Vasc Surg 2:375–381, 1985
8. Rapp JH, Qvarfordt P, Krupski WC, Ehrenfeld WK, Stoney RJ: Hypercholesterolaemia and early restenosis after carotid endarterectomy. Surgery 101: 277–282, 1987
9. Colyvas N, Rapp JH, Phillips NR, et al.: Relation of plasma lipid and apoprotein levels to progressive intimal hyperplasia after arterial endartectomy. Circulation 85:1286–1292, 1992
10. Rapp JH: The effect of lipid lowering on the incidence of recurrent carotid stenosis. J Vasc Surg 15:884–885, 1992
11. European Carotid Trial Collaborative Group: MRC European Carotid Surgery Trial: interim results for symptomatic patients with severe (70–99%) or mild 0–29%) carotid stenosis. Lancet 337:1235–1243, 1991
12. Clinical Alert. Benefit of carotid endarterectomy for patients with high grade stenosis of the internal carotid artery. National Institute of Neurological Disorders and Stroke Publication, 1991
13. Claggett CP, Robinowitz M, Youkey JR, et al.: Morphogenesis and clinicopathologic characteristics of recurrent carotid disease. J Vasc Surg 3:10–23, 1986
14. Sillet R, Wilson MB, Malcolm RE, Ball KP: Deception among smokers. Br Med J 65:197–200, 1978
15. Williamson DF, Madans J, Anda RF, et al.: Smoking cessation and severity of weight gain in a national cohort. N Engl J Med 324:739–745, 1991

PREOPERATIVE INVESTIGATION
OF
CAROTID DISEASE

Duplex Scanning: Non-invasive Assessments Before, During and After Carotid Surgery

Rachel Cuming, Stephen D. Blair and Roger M. Greenhalgh

Until early 1988 it was our practice to assess asymptomatic patients following carotid endarterectomy after 3 months. Scans were not performed until the first follow-up occasion. However, 235 patients were reviewed who had been operated upon between 1 January 1980 and 17 February 1988 and on one occasion, a completely unsuspected total occlusion of the operated internal carotid was detected at 3 months. This male patient had been operated upon for transient ischaemic attacks (TIAs). A patch had not been used and a shunt was used during surgery. The patient was completely asymptomatic afterwards but non-invasive assessment including colour duplex scan revealed an asymptomatic occlusion of the internal carotid. This raised the question of the asymptomatic internal carotid occlusion occurring between the operation and the 3-month period. Accordingly, it was determined to adopt a different protocol from then onwards. The wound would be closed with subcuticular prolene and covered with a plastic dressing on the skin. This would enable continuous wave Doppler frequency analysis and colour duplex scanning to be performed at any time in the postoperative period. If the patients had the slightest symptom in the postoperative period, immediate assessment would be performed in the recovery room but otherwise assessment would be delayed until the following day and then again at 3 months.

In addition we experienced a patient who had presented with crescendo TIA and a 99% internal carotid stenosis. The patient was scheduled for next-day surgery and at operation the stenosis had thrombosed and the internal carotid artery was full of a recent thrombus.[1] At operation the clot was removed and an endarterectomy performed and the flow was reestablished. There was no way of knowing if all the clots had been removed and in the postoperative period the patient suffered a fatal stroke. After this most unfortunate experience, it was determined that continuous wave duplex scanning would be performed on the morning of the operation for all patients with lesions of greater severity than 90% stenosis.[1]

PROTOCOL FOR INVESTIGATION AND PATIENT SERIES

From February 1988 until October 1992, 118 patients have been investigated by the new protocol. Of the patients, 80 were male and 38 female, aged 67.3 ± 8.2 years. All patients were encouraged to stop smoking at the first consultation and at the time of surgery, 12 admitted to current smoking (10.0%), 27 (22.9%) were non-smokers and 79 (67.0%) were former smokers. Of the 118 patients 16 (13.4%) were diabetic and 64 (53.8%) were treated for hypertension at some stage. Also, 51 (42.9%) had symptoms of peripheral arterial disease and 41 (35%) had symptomatic coronary artery disease either with previous myocardial infarction or current angina.

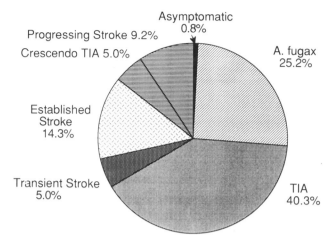

Fig. 1. Presenting symptoms.

Presenting symptoms are demonstrated in Fig. 1. Of the 118 patients, 47 (40.3%) presented with contralateral TIA, and 30 (25.2%) with amaurosis fugax. Together these transient symptoms accounted for 55.5% of the series. Only one patient facing cardiac surgery was operated upon in an asymptomatic state and the remainder in this series were operated upon for transient stroke (5.0%), established stroke (14.3%), crescendo TIA (5.0%) or progressing stroke (9.2%), the Marseille classification being used.[2]

Preoperative non-invasive assessment

At the first consultation, continuous wave frequency (velocity) analysis of the carotid bifurcation was performed (Fig. 2) as well as colour duplex scan of the carotid bifurcation (Fig. 3). A computed tomographic (CT) scan of the brain and arch flush angiogram was performed and then, on the basis of the opinion of a consultant neurologist, surgery was planned.

The operation

For internal carotid or common carotid lesions >90% stenosis, colour duplex scanning was performed on the day of the operation to make certain that the artery was still open before premedication and general anaesthesia were undertaken. A standard carotid endarterectomy was performed. A 5 mm Dacron patch was applied where the dimensions of the carotid artery suggested the appropriateness (see pp. 157–166, Greenhalgh *et al.*, this volume). The Dacron patch was used for 49/118 patients (41.2%). Immediately after closure of the arteriotomy, continuous wave frequency (velocity) analysis was performed at operation by placing a Doppler pencil probe into a sterile polythene sheath containing either acoustic jelly or even simple saline. A little saline was placed around the carotid bifurcation and the sheathed

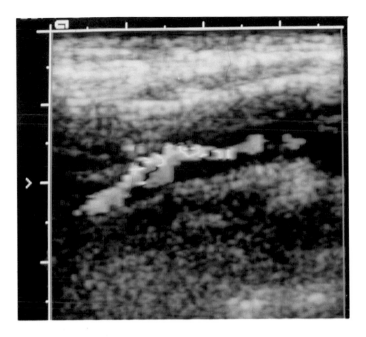

Fig. 3. Colour duplex scan of the internal carotid artery performed at the initial assessment and immediately before on the day of operation for severe (>90%) stenosis (Acuson). This is consistent with a 75% diameter reduction.

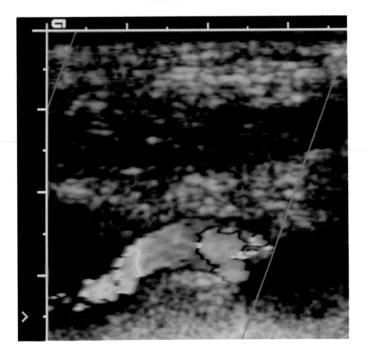

Fig. 6. Colour duplex scan of the internal carotid artery 24 hours after operation. No significant diameter reduction.

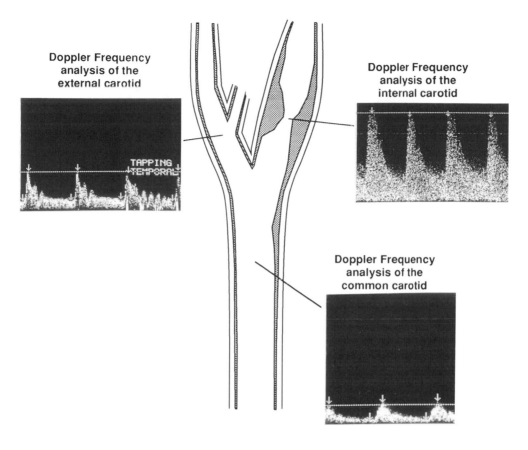

Fig. 2. Continuous wave frequency analysis of carotid bifurcation at the initial assessment before operation. Vasoflow 3, Sonicaid Oxford Instruments. Peak frequency of the internal carotid is 7.2 kH_3 equivalent to a 75% stenosis. The common and external signal have no end-peak frequency.

probe was used to insonate the common carotid, external carotid and internal carotid arteries (Fig. 4). In particular the probe was carried carefully beyond the distal arteriotomy, the sight of a possible flap. Change of frequency at this level was noted with great care. If there was any doubt the arteriotomy would be re-opened. The technique of endarterectomy used was to 'overpass' the distal site of endarterectomy, so it was most unlikely that a flap would occur. A tacking suture was used extremely seldom and practically not at all. Completion on-table arteriogram was not performed in any of these patients; instead, a satisfactory Doppler assessment was performed at surgery. The wound was then closed over a suction drain and the skin suture was completed with subcutaneous prolene. A plastic dressing was used to cover the wound of the subcuticular prolene suture which would allow for immediate postoperative Doppler assessment in the event of symptoms, or assessment in 24 hours under normal circumstances.

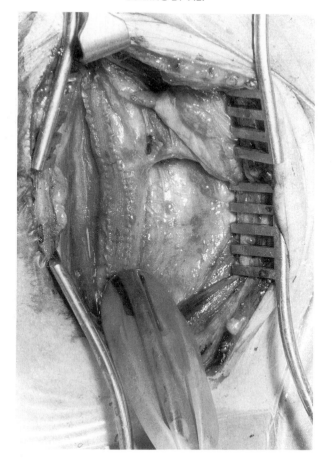

Fig. 4.   Continuous wave frequency (velocity) analysis of patched carotid bifurcation at operation using a Doppler probe in a sterile sleeve.

Postoperative assessment

Asymptomatic patients were assessed 24 hours after surgery by continuous wave frequency analysis (Fig. 5) and colour duplex scan (Fig. 6). It is instructive to compare continuous wave frequency analysis before surgery (Fig. 2) and after surgery (Fig. 5) and preoperative duplex scanning (Fig. 3) and postoperative duplex scanning (Fig. 6).

RESULTS

Of the 118 patients duplex imaging was easily achieved in 109 instances and eight of the remaining nine were successfully assessed by a continuous wave Doppler frequency analysis. In these eight no significant abnormality was detected. However, one patient could not be imaged due to oedema and calcification of vessels.

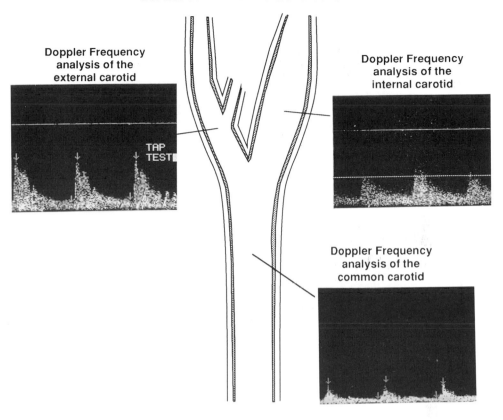

Doppler Frequency analysis of the external carotid

Doppler Frequency analysis of the internal carotid

Doppler Frequency analysis of the common carotid

Fig. 5. Continuous wave frequency (velocity) analysis 24 hours after operation. Vasoflow 3, Sonicaid Oxford Instruments. Internal carotid peak frequencies is now normal (2.2 kH$_3$).

Symptoms suggesting neurological instability occurred in four postoperative patients shortly after surgery and duplex scanning was performed in the recovery room. Of these, on three occasions it was suspected that a thrombus was developing at the carotid bifurcation and the patients were heparinized, re-explored and a shunt inserted. Thrombus was found and removed and the arteriotomy closed with a Dacron patch. The patients had an uneventful recovery with a normal scan at 24 hours and no neurological deficit. The fourth patient developed a stroke and was unfit for re-exploration and had a significant internal carotid stenosis despite the fact that a patch had been used. This patient must have had an abnormality at the time of operation which was missed by the Doppler pencil probe at surgery. The remaining 114 patients were scanned at 24 hours since they were asymptomatic. One female patient was found to have a 55% common carotid stenosis and a male patient to have a 70% distal internal carotid asymptomatic stenosis. It was suspected that these could be technical problems which could have been detected at the time of operation but were missed by pencil Doppler scan continuous wave frequency analysis assessment. No other patient had a stenosis > 10% in the internal carotid artery but 12 patients had mild stenosis of 25–45% in the common carotid artery found 24 hours after surgery.

At 3 months, some new stenoses had occurred. Of the original 118 patients, 99 have been followed for 9 months and all have remained asymptomatic. In Table 1, patients 1 and 2 represent those whose stenoses were noted 24 hours after the operation and these stenoses remained unchanged at 3 months. The remaining six can truly be said to have developed a restenosis. As can be seen from Table 1 those restenoses have occurred largely in the internal carotid artery, thus the >50% stenosis rate at 3 months is 8%, but two patients had these lesions from the operation and so the true restenosis rate at 3 months is 6% and all asymptomatic.

DISCUSSION

No patient in this series of 118 consecutive patients was found to have an unexpected thrombus through overnight thrombosis of an internal carotid artery before surgery. Thus at operation this problem was avoided and the practice of duplex scanning immediately before and on the day of operation for severe stenosis is to be supported. Of the four patients with neurological instability in the recovery room immediately after surgery, three were explored and crescentic thrombus was found to be lying in the carotid bifurcation as suggested on the duplex scan. These patients were re-explored, heparinized and a shunt inserted and the arteriotomy closed with a Dacron patch. Full patency was achieved at 24 hours and 3 months and there were no lasting neurological deficits. The fourth patient had a stroke and was too sick for re-operation and the technical problem detected by duplex scan was subsequently confirmed by arteriography. Duplex scan through the plastic dressing performed in the recovery room is thus an excellent procedure and this part of our protocol is certainly to be supported on this evidence.

Two asymptomatic stenoses were found at 24 hours (patients 1 and 2 shown in Table 1). It can be argued that these patients are successes staying asymptomatic with no evidence that they will restenose further or cause further symptoms and so it could be said that they are cured. Nevertheless, these two patients had a significance stenosis left behind at the time of operation as did the one patient who had a stroke. In other words three patients of 118 (2.6%) had inadequate assessment

Table 1. Eight out of 99 patients developed stenoses of >50% between operation and 3 months later. Patients 1 and 2 had residual operative stenoses (2%) and 3–8 developed restenoses within the 3-month period (6%)

Patient	Sex	Dacron patched at operation	% Stenosis of common carotid	% Stenosis of internal carotid	Time of detection
1	F	Yes	55	10	At 24 h, unchanged at 3 months
2	M	No	10	70	At 24 h, unchanged at 3 months
3	M	No	20	60	First seen at 3 months
4	F	No	25	70	First seen at 3 months
5	F	No	10	50	First seen at 3 months
6	M	No	15	60	First seen at 3 months
7	M	No	20	80	First seen at 3 months
8	M	No	45	85	First seen at 3 months

on the operating table after the arteriotomy was closed and before the operation was completed. It is clear that these problems should have been detected at operation. Operative arteriography as suggested by Mannick *et al.*, this volume, pp. 259–262, may have spotted these problems. Equally, it is possible that duplex scan at the time of surgery would have detected these abnormalities. On the contrary, it is relevant that abnormality associated with stroke occurred only in one of 118 patients (0.8%) and this is difficult to improve upon. On-table arteriography has been recommended in the past.[3,4] Perioperative duplex scanning has also been recommended (see pp. 253–258, Myhre *et al.*[5]). Continuous wave Doppler analysis supported by Thompson in his description of standards in endarterectomy in this volume (pp. 149–156), and others have recommended that this is the optimal on-table assessment.[6,7]

It is clearly a good idea to scan at 24 hours as suggested in this protocol and we find that the plastic dressing and subcuticular suture are very suitable for this purpose. Accordingly we can be certain that true restones have occurred in six of the eight patients with >50% stenosis found at 3 months. As a result of the 24-hour scan, the two asymptomatic patients with residual stenoses can be subtracted from the eight, leaving six with true restenosis (normal at 24 hours, stenosed at 3 months). This is important in trying to achieve better standards. It is quite inappropriate to attribute restenosis to technical problems which were indeed present at the time of operation. These should be picked up before the wound is closed by an on-table assessment since, when found at 24 hours, it is too late.

We are certain that some early restenosis does occur, and that not all problems are technical problems of stenosis being left at operation. This is important to recognize in order that we can study factors associated with this unwanted restenosis process that occurs so early in the period after operation. The factors associated with such restenosis are described by Powell *et al.*, pp. 45–52, this volume.

REFERENCES

1. Cuming R, Perkin GD, Greenhalgh RM: Urgent carotid surgery. *In* Emergency Vascular Surgery, Greenhalgh RM, Hollier LH (Eds). London/Philadelphia: W B Saunders, pp. 145–156, 1992
2. Courbier R (Ed.): Basis for a Classification of Cerebral Arterial Disease. Amsterdam: Excerpta Medica, 1985
3. Courbier R, Sousseran J-M, Reggi M *et al.*: Routine intraoperative carotid angiography: its impact on operative morbidity and carotid stenosis. J Vasc Surg 3: 343–350, 1986
4. Scott SM, Sethi GK, Bridgeman AH: Perioperative stroke during carotid endarterectomy: the value of intraoperative angiography. J Cardiovasc Surg 23: 353–358, 1982
5. Lane RJ, Appleberg M: Realtime intraoperative angiosonography after carotid endarterectomy. Surgery 92: 5–9, 1982
6. Klotter H-J, Ganstaller G, Gronninger J *et al.*: Intraoperative sonographic nach endarterectomy der arteria carotis. Chirgurie 55: 339–342, 1984
7. Sandmann W, Kniemeyer H, Perroneau P: Carotid bifurcation Doppler spectrum analysis at surgery. *In* Diagnostic Techniques and Assessment Procedures on Vascular Surgery, Greenhalgh RM (Ed.). London: Grune & Stratton, pp. 123–127, 1985

New Imaging Modalities: Magnetic Resonance and Computed Tomographic Angiography
Is conventional angiography still needed?

Evan H. Dillon, Bert C. Eikelboom and Maarten van Leeuwen

Magnetic resonance angiography (MRA) and computed tomographic angiography (CTA) are two recently developed non-invasive techniques which can be used to produce images of the carotid artery. These two techniques have been developed to yield the angiographic overview which Doppler fails to provide but without the risks and costs of conventional angiography. This chapter will review these two procedures and discuss their potential for replacing carotid angiography.

MAGNETIC RESONANCE ANGIOGRAPHY

Magnetic resonance angiography can be performed by taking advantage of either of two different phenomena resulting in two different types of MRA: phase contrast and time of flight (TOF) imaging.[1] While phase contrast imaging has been applied to the evaluation of carotid disease, better success has been achieved by the use of TOF sequences. Both two-dimensional (2-D) and three-dimensional (3-D) TOF sequences can be used to produce MR angiograms. Three-dimensional TOF sequences have the advantage of higher resolution but result in poorer contrast in areas of slow velocity. Two-dimensional TOF sequences yield lower resolution but higher contrast in areas of compromised flow. Perhaps the best success can be achieved by performing both sequences in the same patient.[2] The only disadvantage of performing both is the increase in image acquisition time with a resultant increase in cost.

The most important consideration in deciding whether or not to perform an MR angiogram is the reliability of the resulting information. Masaryk et al. compared 3-D TOF MRA with selective carotid arteriography and reported no significant difference in the ability of the two techniques to depict stenoses[3] (Fig. 1). However, most other reports have indicated that MRA may not be as reliable as initially expected, primarily due to signal loss in areas of abnormal flow (Fig. 2).

Kido et al. compared phase contrast and transverse TOF images to arch aortography and reported that MRA correctly classified 35% of stenoses,[4] but resulted in a discrepancy of one stenosis category in 38% and two or more categories in 26%. Both overestimation and underestimation of the stenoses were observed.

Several authors have compared 2-D TOF sequences with angiography. Riles reported that MRA correctly classified 52% of stenoses.[5] It tended to result in an overestimation of the degree of stenosis, but in three cases indicated severe stenosis in carotid arteries which were found to be occluded on angiography. Litt reported an overall agreement between MRA and conventional angiography of 70% for one observer and 56% for a second observer.[6] However, a correct diagnosis of occlusion

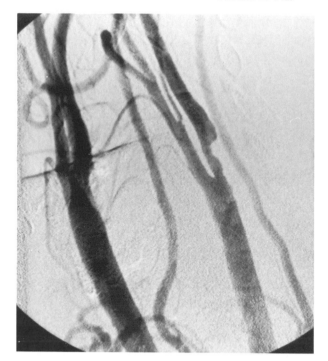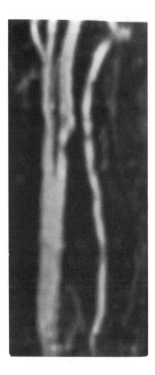

Fig. 1. MRA *vs* angiography in moderate stenosis. A (left): Aortic arch injection demonstrates moderate stenosis of the proximal left internal carotid artery. B (right): Two-dimensional TOF MRA demonstrates essentially the same degree of stenosis.

using MRA was observed in only 29% for the first observer and 25% for the second observer. Buijs reported a correlation between MRA and conventional angiography of 62% for one observer and 76% for a second observer.[7] Overestimation was also observed in that study: 50% of the vessels which were moderately stenosed on conventional angiography appeared to be severely stenosed on MR images.

Anderson used both 2-D and 3-D TOF sequences and compared the results with conventional angiography.[2] MRA and conventional angiography correlated in 64% of cases. In the other cases, the MRA results differed by only one category and usually resulted in an overestimation of the stenosis.

Comparison of these various results is made difficult by the different MRA techniques, but the overall results are less promising than initially expected as MRA has a particular tendency to result in an overestimation of the degree of stenosis. Even in normal patients, the carotid bulb appears flattened due to signal loss in the normal area of reversed blood flow[2,6] (Fig. 3). Additionally, the difficulty of distinguishing between severe stenosis and occlusion, as observed in the studies discussed above, is especially problematic since this differentiation is crucial for surgical planning. While future advances may improve the results of MRA, it does not currently appear to provide the reliable information needed to guide surgical intervention.

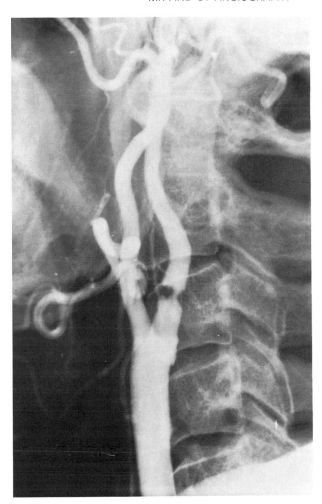

Fig. 2. MRA *vs* selective angiography in severe stenosis. A (left): Selective carotid injection demonstrates a short segment of severe stenosis in the carotid bulb. B (right): Two-dimensional TOF MRA demonstrates an apparent discontinuity at the site of the stenosis, and the stenotic segment appears much longer and more severe than on the angiogram.

COMPUTED TOMOGRAPHIC ANGIOGRAPHY

Computed tomographic angiography (CTA) is the newest non-invasive technique for vascular imaging. In fact, it is so new that the results of its application in carotid imaging have not yet been published. However, the authors of this chapter, in conjunction with others at this institution, are actively involved in investigating the application of this technique to carotid disease, and the preliminary results will be reported in this chapter.

Computed tomographic angiography refers to the production of angiographic images by means of three-dimensional reconstruction of CT images of vascular

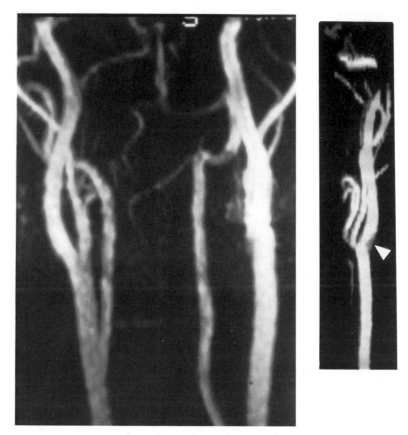

Fig. 3. Two-dimensional TOF MRA in normal volunteers. A (left): The carotid bifurcation is well demonstrated, but the carotid bulb appears more flattened than expected for a normal carotid artery. B (right): The normal area of reversed flow is decreased in signal relative to the rest of the carotid artery (arrow).

anatomy. In order to perform CTA, three pieces of equipment must be available: a slip-ring CT scanner, a mechanical injector for contrast administration, and an independent workstation with a 3-D reconstruction programme. A slip-ring CT scanner is required for CTA since it is able to acquire numerous, thin, overlapping CT sections in a short period of time (i.e. less than 1 min). At this institution, a CT scanner capable of performing 50 rotations in 50 seconds is used (Tomoscan SR-HP, Philips Medical Systems, Best, The Netherlands). A table speed of 3 mm/s allows imaging of 15 cm in 50 s. The data from these rotations are reprocessed to yield 150 3-mm thick slices each overlapping 2 mm with each adjacent slice. The concentration of intra-arterial contrast material is maintained at a high level throughout the acquisition by injecting 120 ml of intravenous contrast material at a rate of 2 ml/s via an antecubital vein. After acquiring the CT images, the data is transferred to the independent workstation for 3-D reconstruction.

The most crucial step in performing accurate CTA is defining the Hounsfield density range which will be recognised by the reconstruction programme as representing vessel lumen, a process known as segmentation. If the minimum segmentation level is set too low, a stenosis will appear to be less severe than it does on conventional angiography, and if it is set too high, the stenosis will appear more severe than on conventional angiography. Thus, a quantitative and operator-independent means of determining the minimum segmentation level must be used. The maximum segmentation level is less crucial and is set so that cortical bone is excluded from the segmentation range. Using this technique, a 3-D angiographic projection of both carotid arteries can be produced in just over 1 hour. The CT data acquisition requires less than 1 min, and the CT scanner requires an additional 15 min to display the images. The segmentation and reconstruction process currently requires approximately 45 min. While the entire process takes longer than a conventional angiogram, it eliminates the costs of in-patient observation and the risks of vascular injury or stroke associated with angiography.

Given the advantages of CTA, the main question, of course, is its accuracy in presenting the carotid anatomy. As mentioned above, the results presented herein are very preliminary. During 1993, a number of research papers describing this technique will probably appear. The results will no doubt vary, but the most important issue in assessing these results will be attention to the method by which the segmentation levels were determined in each paper.

To date, at this institution, 74 carotid arteries (37 patients) have been examined using CTA (Fig. 4). Only one CTA was unsuccessful due to artefact produced by swallowing. A variety of carotid diseases have been imaged including atherosclerotic disease, aneurysm, pseudoaneurysm, dissection, and glomus tumour. Overall,

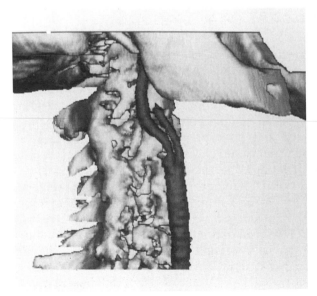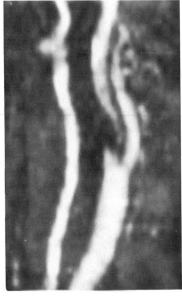

Fig. 4. Computed tomographic angiography *vs* magnetic resonance angiography. A (left): The CTA demonstrates approximately 50% diameter reduction in the proximal right internal carotid. B (right): Two-dimensional TOF MRA demonstrates an apparent discontinuity in the right carotid, and the stenosis appears more severe and much longer.

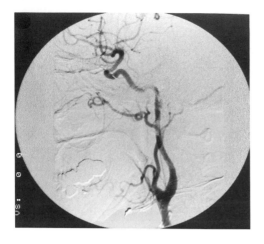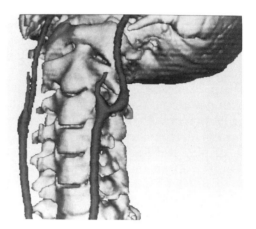

Fig. 5. Normal bifurcation. The left carotid bulb has a similar appearance in both the selective angiogram (A, left) and the CTA (B, right) without the flattening often seen with MRA.

the images provided by CTA have been comparable with those provided by conventional angiography (Figs 5, 6).

Most of our studies have been performed for preoperative assessment of carotid stenosis. Seventeen carotid arteries have been evaluated with CTA for which a corresponding selective carotid angiogram was available for comparison (Fig. 7); CTA correctly classified the stenosis in 14 (82%) and was one category less severe in three (18%).

IS ANGIOGRAPHY STILL NEEDED?

Moore maintains that ultrasound (US), in conjunction with a history and physical examination, provides sufficient preoperative information in most patients.[8] Other authors, including Geuder, report that additional imaging evaluation is needed prior to surgical intervention.[9] Since US has been demonstrated to be an accurate technique in evaluating the carotid bifurcation, what further information is to be provided by an additional imaging study? The answer is twofold: confirmation of the US diagnosis and evaluation of the remainder of the carotid circulation.

Confirmation of the US diagnosis adds a level of confidence to preoperative planning since US is operator dependent and may be inaccurate in assessing stenoses in tortuous vessels or in recognizing a pseudoocclusion.[10-11] As discussed above, most reports indicate that MRA is not highly reliable in evaluating the stenosis since it tends to result in an overestimation of both the length and severity of the stenosis. In contrast, the preliminary results from the CTA research reported herein suggest that CTA is more accurate than MRA in assessing stenoses in the bifurcation and internal carotid artery. If these results are confirmed in future studies, then CTA would appear to meet the first requirement for an additional imaging study.

An additional imaging study should also provide information regarding the remainder of the carotid circulation. Most important to surgical planning is assessment

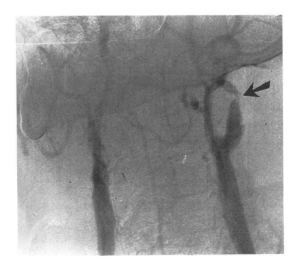

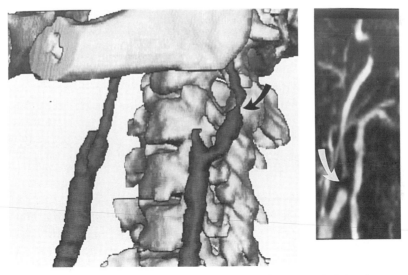

Fig. 6. Stenosis of left internal carotid. A (upper): Aortic arch injection angiogram demonstrates approximately 70% diameter reduction in the left internal carotid at the distal end of the bulb. B (lower left): The CTA demonstrates essentially the same degree of stenosis. C (lower right): Two-dimensional TOF MRA demonstrates an apparent discontinuity, and the stenosis appears longer and more severe.

of the course and configuration of the extracranial carotid artery with particular attention to visualization of tandem stenotic lesions or loops or kinks of the carotid artery. Both MRA and CTA are capable of providing this overview of the circulation. However, CTA may prove to be accurate since MRA may suffer from signal loss due to in-plane flow in carotid loops and due to turbulent flow in tandem stenotic lesions.

Information regarding the origin of the common carotid artery may also be desired before surgery. In routine clinical use, neither CTA nor MRA provides information

DILLON *ET AL.*

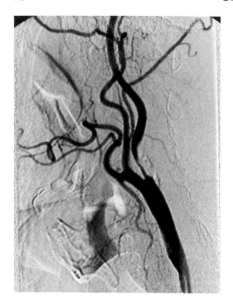 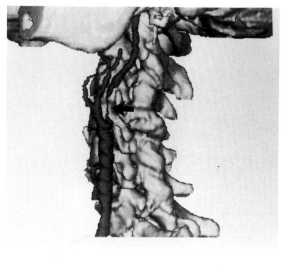

Fig. 7. Severe stenosis in the proximal left internal carotid is visible on both the selective angiogram (A, left) and the CTA (B, right).

about the origin of the great vessels. At this level, CTA is hampered by artefact from the inflowing contrast material in the superior vena cava. This artefact can be eliminated by groin or lower extremity injection of the contrast, but such an injection is not routinely performed. Magnetic resonance angiography has a limited field of view, and imaging of the aortic arch region would double the acquisition time. However, as Moore reports, occlusive disease of the arch vessels can often be detected by a careful physical assessment, and in those patients, angiography or a special CTA or MRA study could be requested.[8]

Finally, information regarding the intracranial carotid circulation may be useful in preoperative planning. MRA offers the possibility of imaging this portion of the carotid circulation but often suffers from signal loss at the level of the foramen lacerum. To date, in our experience, CTA has not been reliable in imaging the carotid siphon. However, the presence of an intracranial stenosis may not alter the surgical plan if a significant bifurcation stenosis is also present.

In conclusion, routine use of one of these two non-invasive studies, CTA or MRA, may provide sufficient complementary information to the US evaluation to allow surgical planning without the risks and costs of angiography. Angiography may then be reserved for patients in whom arch disease is suggested by physical assessment or in whom intracranial disease is suggested by the lack of correlation between the symptomatology and the degree of extracranial carotid stenosis.

ACKNOWLEDGEMENTS

The MRA images shown in the accompanying figures were provided by Peter Buijs MD, of the Department of Diagnostic Radiology, University Hospital Utrecht,

Utrecht, The Netherlands; and by Mike Merriam MD, of the Department of Diagnostic Radiology, Yale University School of Medicine, New Haven, CT, USA.

REFERENCES

1. Chien D, Edelman RR: Basic principles and clinical applications of magnetic resonance angiography. Sem Roent 27: 53–62, 1992
2. Anderson CM, Saloner D, Lee RE et al.: Assessment of carotid artery stenosis by MR angiography: comparison with X-ray angiography and color-coded Doppler ultrasound. AJNR 13: 989–1003, 1992
3. Masaryk AM, Ross JS, DiCello MC et al.: 3DFT MR angiography of the carotid bifurcation: potential and limitations as a screening examination. Radiology 179: 797–804, 1991
4. Kido DK, Barsotti JB, Rice LZ et al.: Evaluation of the carotid artery bifurcation: comparison of magnetic resonance angiography and digital subtraction arch aortography. Neuroradiology 33: 48–51, 1991
5. Riles TS, Eidelman EM, Litt AW et al.: Comparison of magnetic resonance angiography, conventional angiography, and duplex scanning. Stroke 23: 341–346, 1992
6. Litt AW, Eidelman EM, Pinto RS: Diagnosis of carotid artery stenosis: comparison of 2DFT time-of-flight MR angiography with contrast angiography in 50 patients. AJNR 12: 149–154, 1991
7. Buijs PC, Klop RBJ, Eikelboom BC et al.: Carotid bifurcation imaging: magnetic resonance angiography compared to conventional angiography and Doppler ultrasound. European J Vasc Surg (pending publication).
8. Moore WS, Ziomek S, Quinones-Baldrich WJ et al.: Can clinical evaluation and noninvasive testing substitute for arteriography in the evaluation of carotid disease? Ann Surg 208: 91–94, 1988
9. Geuder JW, Lamparello PJ, Riles TS, Giangola G, Imparato AM: Is duplex scanning sufficient evaluation before carotid endarterectomy? J Vasc Surg 9: 193–201, 1989
10. Erickson SJ, Mewissen MW, Foley WD: Stenosis of the internal carotid artery: assessment using color Doppler imaging compared with angiography. Am J Roent 152: 1299–1305, 1989
11. Steinke W, Kloetzsch C, Hennerici M: Carotid artery disease assessed by color Doppler flow imaging: correlation with standard Doppler sonography and angiography. AJNR 11:259–266, 1990

Cerebral Blood Flow Measurements in Carotid Artery Disease

Torben V. Schroeder

Measurement of cerebral blood flow (CBF) in man has been possible for as long as carotid endarterectomy has been a therapeutic option,[1,2] and indeed CBF studies seem relevant in this connection. Several issues are of interest, among other things the importance of haemodynamic factors in the pathogenesis and treatment of carotid artery disease. Cerebral blood flow might also determine tolerance for carotid cross-clamping during preoperative balloon occlusion or during surgery. Finally, CBF measurements could assess a possible haemodynamic effect of carotid surgery. Still, the technique has never gained widespread popularity among vascular surgeons. Inherent technical difficulties, as well as the obvious rationale for performing carotid surgery have probably limited the interest, particularly in North America, where the number of carotid endarterectomies increased considerably during the 1970s and 1980s. The negative result of the international multicentre study on external carotid/internal carotid (EC/IC) bypass surgery as well as the narrowing of indications for carotid surgery with the recent publication of three randomized studies have contributed to an increased interest in assessing the cerebral perfusion in connection with carotid artery disease.[3-6]

At Rigshospitalet, University of Copenhagen, we have been interested in cerebral haemodynamics in carotid artery disease for more than two decades.[7-12] This experience, together with a summary of the recent literature, form the basis for this review of the value of CBF in carotid artery disease, with special emphasis on the preoperative identification of haemodynamic insufficiency and the effect of carotid endarterectomy on cerebral perfusion.

PATHOPHYSIOLOGICAL ASPECTS OF CAROTID ARTERY DISEASES

During recent years there has been considerable disagreement about the pathogenetic mechanism of focal cerebral ischaemic attacks associated with carotid stenosis. A theory of cerebral vasospasm was succeeded by a concept of haemodynamic insufficiency,[13] and today embolization from the atheromatous carotid lesion is considered the primary mechanism. The haemodynamic concept has not been rejected, but is considered responsible for probably less than 10%, depending on the population under investigation.

A 'haemodynamically significant stenosis' is defined as that degree of arterial constriction which produces a fall in blood pressure and flow distal to the stenosis. In the carotid artery this degree of stenosis is reached when the diameter of the artery is reduced by 50–70%, beyond which flow is increasingly restricted. While a stenosis greater than 50% is a necessary condition for haemodynamic compromise, it is not sufficient. The decreased flow contributed through the one carotid artery may be fully compensated by collateral circulatory pathways. Figure 1 shows connected values of the degree of carotid stenosis and the intraoperatively measured internal to common carotid artery (ICA/CCA) pressure ratio. A marked reduction of perfusion pressure of 25% or more was observed in 13/24 (57%) patients with stenoses >70%, whereas all patients with stenoses ≤70% had less pronounced, if any, reductions of perfusion pressure. These data are in accordance with previous studies.[14,15] Thus, a significant reduction of cerebral perfusion pressure may be expected in approximately half of those patients considered candidates for carotid surgery by the standard of today, i.e. >70% stenosis. In this context it should be realized, that the severity of the stenosis, in any individual patient, does not permit an estimate of the haemodynamic state of the brain.

If perfusion pressure is reduced, CBF may still be maintained by an autoregulatory dilation of resistance vessels and by increasing cerebral blood volume (CBV) as well as the CBV/CBF ratio (Fig. 2).[10,16,17] When the capacity for vasodilation is exceeded, autoregulation fails, and CBF falls. In this situation the ability to react to other vasoactive stimuli is impaired. Thus, the normal flow increase with hypercapnia may be attenuated or abolished. In cases of focal reduction of perfusion pressure, flow may even decrease due to a steal phenomenon.[9] Also, a reduction of systemic blood pressure, that normally has no effect on cerebral perfusion, may further reduce CBF. Metabolism may still be maintained below the lower limit of autoregulation by compensatory increase of oxygen extraction fraction (OEF). If perfusion pressure continues to fall the energy demands of the brain may no longer be fulfilled and clinical evidence of dysfunction will occur. Unless the circulation is restored rapidly, permanent tissue damage may result.

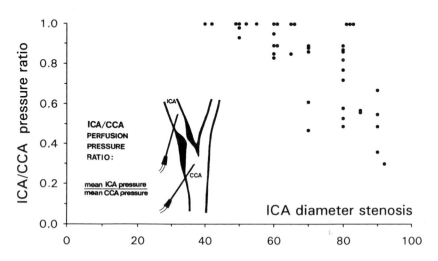

Fig. 1. Degree of internal carotid artery stenosis related to the ratio of internal to common carotid artery (ICA/CCA) mean blood pressure in 42 patients who underwent carotid endarterectomy (Sillesen & Schroeder, unpublished data).

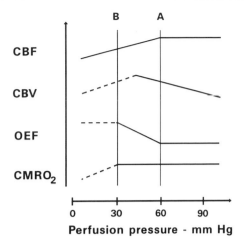

Fig. 2. Compensatory response of cerebral blood flow (CBF), cerebral blood volume (CBV), oxygen extraction fraction (OEF) and cerebral oxygen metabolism ($CMRO_2$), as cerebral perfusion pressure falls. When vasodilation is maximal, autoregulation fails (A). The point of maximal oxygen extraction is indicated (B). Redrawn from Powers.[16]

PREOPERATIVE DETERMINATION OF THE HAEMODYNAMIC STATE

Direct measurements of baseline CBF alone may not identify haemodynamic failure.[18,19] A reduced flow focally or in the hemisphere may be the result of a restricted blood supply, causing a state of critically reduced perfusion pressure. More often, though, it is caused by a decreased metabolic demand of the brain due to infarction. The latter may be distinguished by the presence of infarction on a CT scan. However, as many as 50% of patients with clinical symptoms of a supratentorial stroke have no evidence of a cerebral infarction on CT.[9] Also infarction may occur in low perfusion pressure territory. To make matters worse, CBF measurements are hampered by a high degree of variability, physiological as well as methodological.[20,21] Though variability may be reduced by considering the side-to-side asymmetry, significant differences can be shown only in groups of patients, whereas individual data are not convincingly correlated with clinical findings.

For determination of the haemodynamic state of the brain two modalities have emerged, both based on the reflections presented in Fig. 2. The first, and most frequently employed, consists of paired CBF measurements, one at baseline conditions and the second during a strong cerebral vasodilator stimulus.[22-42] Vasodilation can be induced by intravenous acetazolamide or by CO_2 inhalation. In a dose of 1 g, acetazolamide, a carbonic anhydrase inhibitor, induces a vasodilation similar to that seen during inhalation of 5–6% CO_2.[9,43] The more severe the occlusive disease, the lower the vasoreactivity. Alternatively, the systemic blood pressure can be lowered using an antihypertensive drug, like trimetaphan or labetalol, that does not affect cerebral resistance,[44] or using lower body negative pressure[45] (Fig. 3). The paired measurements can be made by several techniques including 133-Xenon clearance studied with either stationary detectors[10] or a tomographic method.[9] Positron emission tomography (PET) may also be used for this purpose.[38]

In experimental studies unilateral carotid occlusion had no effect on baseline CBF, whereas a markedly reduced flow response to 5% CO_2 inhalation was observed in the hemisphere ipsilateral to the occlusion.[46,47] Several of the above referenced clinical studies have correlated the extent of cerebrovascular occlusive disease with a reduced response to CO_2. Groups of patients show significantly impaired CO_2 reactivity ipsilateral to high-grade stenosis or occlusion, but with few exceptions the wide range of CO_2 reactivity makes individual interpretation difficult, if not impossible. In normal subjects of any age there is a wide range for both resting and vasoactivated CBF. Thus the lower 95% confidence intervals for vasodilated CBF overlap the upper 95% confidence intervals for resting CBF, limiting the usefulness of CBF determination alone.[31]

The variability may be reduced considerably by using the patients as their own controls by comparing CBF reactivity in a region of interest (ROI) or in the one hemisphere with that of the symmetrical hemisphere.[20,21,31] Thus, instead of using the hemispheric flow increase to vasodilation, the change in side-to-side asymmetry has proved more reliable for identification of patients with low perfusion pressure.[28] Figure 4 shows the result of the vasodilatory test related to the relative perfusion pressure (ICA to CCA pressure ratio). Forty-eight of 53 (91%) patients with unilateral stenosis greater than 50% could be classified correctly as having a reduction of perfusion pressure above or below 25%, respectively, whereas 15 of 20 (75%) patients with bilateral severe stenoses were classified correctly, giving an overall accuracy of 89%. Since the method when on a difference between hemispheric perfusion, the least convincing results were expected in cases where both hemispheres were haemodynamically compromised.

In this non-tomographic technique several tissue layers are superimposed upon each other and stationary detectors are less suitable for the detection of focal flow reduction. The three-dimensional approach as applied in single-photon emission computed tomography (SPECT) improves the possibility of detecting focal areas of impaired vasoreactivity, indicating local severe reduction of perfusion pressure.[49] Our results obtained with stationary detectors have been confirmed using 133-Xenon and SPECT.[30,48] In a study directly comparing the two methods, the side-to-side asymmetries were excellently correlated, although the static detectors quantitatively detected only 60–80% of the asymmetry disclosed tomographically.[50] Using SPECT, with one of the recently developed tracers that cross the blood–brain barrier, has enabled imaging of the distribution of cerebral perfusion.[37,40–43,51,52] This method allows for relative CBF determinations, whereas the absolute CBF level can not be measured. Except for the degree of occlusive disease, none of these studies have included quantitative parameters, like perfusion pressure, that allows for an assessment of the haemodynamic compromise. Norrving et al.[26] first described a close relationship between the hypercapnic CBF response and the anatomical pattern of collateral supply: patients with reversal of ophthalmic flow had impaired vasoreactivity. Other observations have shown that inverted flow in the periorbital arteries reflect a reduction of perfusion pressure of at least 10–20 mgHg.[15] A study by Hasegawa et al.[42] showed that five patients with posturally provoked or

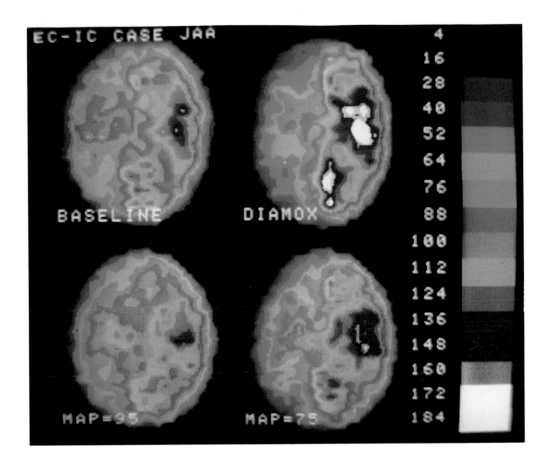

Fig. 3. Patient with left sided internal carotid artery occlusion investigated with Xe-133 single photon emission computer tomography (SPECT). Top left: baseline. Top right: 20 min after 1 g acetazolamide. Bottom left: baseline at MAP 95 mmHg. Bottom right: MAP reduced to 75 mmHg by means of lower body negative pressure. Following acetazolamide as well as after MAP reduction flow is redistributed, causing a steal in the left hemisphere, most pronounced in the middle cerebral artery territory. Illustration provided by courtesy of Sissel Vorstrup, MD, DMSc, Department of Neurology, Rigshospitalet.

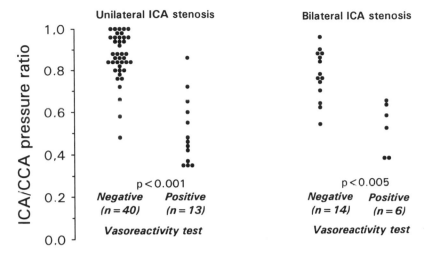

Fig. 4. Outcome of preoperative CBF vasodilator test related to the ratio of internal to common carotid artery (ICA/CCA) mean blood pressure measured during carotid surgery in 53 patients with unilateral and 20 patients with bilateral tight internal carotid artery (ICA) stenosis. Data from Schroeder.[10]

fluctuating deficits, considered to be of haemodynamic origin, belonged to the group of 20 (out of 51) patients who had a reduced vasodilatory capacity. Other observations question the possibility of identifying patients with low perfusion pressures, based on the symptomatic neurological profile.[53]

Studies of the middle cerebral artery flow velocity by transcranial Doppler may give similar information provided cerebral vasodilation does not include the proximal part of the middle cerebral artery. However, results have been equivocal.[34,39]

The second strategy for determining the haemodynamic state of the cerebral perfusion involves simultaneous determination of CBF and CBV in the resting brain. As mentioned above (Fig. 2) the CBV/CBF ratio, being equivalent to the mean transit time for erythrocytes through the cerebral vessels, will increase as cerebral perfusion pressure approaches the lower limit of autoregulation. Both CBF and CBV can be determined with either SPECT or PET. The use in PET of paired, opposed scintillation counters minimizes the contribution of scattered photons. Another advantage of positron emission tomography involves the possibility of studying OEF and metabolism. Gibbs et al.[17] first reported on combined measurements of CBF, CBV and OEF, suggesting that the CBV/CBF ratio was a reliable indicator of the haemodynamic reserve in cerebrovascular occlusive disease. However, results were only applicable in groups of patients, not in individuals. Later, Powers et al.[54] provided evidence in a series of 19 patients with unilateral haemodynamically significant carotid artery disease. The CBV/CBF ratio was increased in 12 patients of whom four also had increased oxygen extraction fraction, reflecting a more severe haemodynamic impairment. These findings were closely related to the angiographic collateral pattern, i.e. the middle cerebral artery territory was supplied from the ophthalmic and/or meningeal collaterals. Similar results have been reported in smaller groups of patients.[55,56] In another study from St Louis,[57] 32 patients with severe ICA stenosis/occlusion, transient symptoms and normal brain CT were examined to investigate whether focal haemodynamic impairment existed in the arterial borderzone regions of the brain. In contrast to a previous, though much smaller study,[58] no evidence of borderzone haemodynamic impairment was found. Thus the positron emission technology has increased the knowledge of cerebral haemodynamics, though results are not always easy to interpret. Moreover, the high costs and the short lived positron emitters, necessitating an on-site cyclotron, hamper the spread of this method.

HAEMODYNAMIC EFFECT OF CAROTID ENDARTERECTOMY

Since the first study[59] in 1963 a number of invasive, as well as non-invasive, studies have been performed at various times following surgery.[7,35,41,48,60–67] Most CBF studies have considered only baseline conditions, which may be normal in spite of severe functional incapacity, whereas a vasoactive stress test has the potential to unmask the haemodynamic effect of a localized lesion. The conclusions reached have ranged from unchanged CBF to marked improvement. In most of these studies, results have been related to the degree of vessel obstruction. As can be expected, the most pronounced increase in CBF was observed among patients with severe stenosis of the operated vessel, severe stenosis in combination with contralateral occlusion, or in patients who had no measurable ICA flow prior to endarterectomy. These cases probably represent some of the most haemodynamically compromised patients. Moreover, some of these studies were performed immediately after surgery. The flow increase may therefore be a result of the temporary hyperaemia shown by some patients,[48,66,68–70] in all probability related to temporary defective cerebral autoregulation.[12] When groups of patients are studied months after surgery no change in baseline CBF is observed.[48,66,35] In a study of 32 uncomplicated carotid endarterectomies we related the postoperative CBF to the cerebral perfusion pressure measured intraoperatively.[65] Only in six patients did baseline CBF improve, and all patients had a significant reduction of perfusion pressure. Another eight patients who also had low perfusion pressures showed no such postoperative improvement. Similar postoperative CBF increase has been reported in single patients presenting marked pressure reduction.[50,63] Boysen et al.[5] demonstrated that the effect of surgery was to redistribute the blood supply to the hemisphere from previously adequate collateral pathways back to the ipsilateral carotid artery. Similar results have been reported by Gratzl et al.[35] using common carotid Doppler flow measurements. In most cases of decreased baseline CBF focally or in one hemisphere, surgery has no effect, suggesting the presence of irreversible ischaemic tissue damage.[62] This conclusion is given further support by CBF studies after EC-IC bypass surgery. Though the CBF level had increased from 3–15%, when measured weeks to months postoperatively, later recordings showed a return of CBF to the preoperative level or even lower.[9,71–73]

Using acetazolamide, a clear correlation was found between the improvement in perfusion reserve, in terms of change in interhemispheric CBF asymmetry after vasodilation, and the degree of haemodynamic impairment, as evaluated by the ICA/CCA pressure ratio[65] (Fig. 5). A significant postoperative improvement in vasoreactivity was found in 11 of 14 patients with severe stenoses and a reduction in perfusion pressure ratio of at least 20%. Conversely, no improvement occurred in 18 patients with no, or only minor, reduction of pressure ratio, irrespective of the degree of ICA stenosis. These results have later been reproduced using stationary detectors as well as tomographic methods, i.e. vasoreactivity is improved or normalized by carotid endarterectomy in nearly all patients that preoperatively had reduced reactivity.[35,41,48,66]

No postendarterectomy PET results are available, although data are available after EC-IC bypass procedures. As expected, decreased OEF and CBV/CBF ratio without changes in metabolism have been observed by some. Others have reported less interpretable findings, such as increased metabolism without changes in OEF, occurring in some cases bilaterally although only one carotid artery was diseased.[16,55,74] Though some of the results are convincing, more data are needed, especially following carotid endarterectomy, before definite conclusions can be drawn.

CLINICAL IMPLICATIONS

Based on the above data it seems reasonable to conclude that an improvement of baseline CBF may be expected only in a few patients, and only in patients with marked reduction of perfusion pressure. In the majority of patients, who have no, or only minor, pressure gradients across the stenosis, even if it be severe, minimal

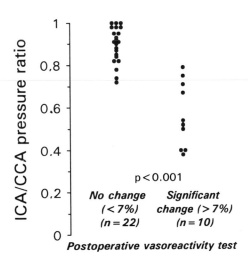

Fig. 5. Postoperative change in 32 patients of CBF vasodilator test related to the ratio of internal to common carotid artery (ICA/CCA) mean blood pressure measured during carotid surgery. Redrawn from Schroeder et al.[65]

changes in CBF are to be expected. In agreement with the conclusion stated by Boysen (1973),[8] the main haemodynamic effect of endarterectomy is an increase in ICA flow. This indicates a redistribution of cerebral perfusion, since collateral flow is reduced in parallel to the increase in ICA flow.

A state of reversible reduced CBF, as detected with available methods, is present in only a few patients. The concept of an ischaemic penumbra, a state of ischaemia allowing the neurons to survive though not to exert their proper function, is undoubtedly a rare occurrence.[75] The limits for such a state are very narrow in terms of CBF level and duration. The chances are that a flow reduction is either insufficient for symptoms to occur, or is so severe as to eventually cause irreversible tissue damage. Concomitant with revascularization of a penumbra area, baseline CBF should at least regionally increase. However, an increase in baseline CBF can not *per se* be taken as evidence of restored neuronal function. While improvement of neurologic status by an increase in baseline CBF thus is a rare occurrence, psychological studies have provided substantial evidence of postoperative intellectual improvement related to the laterality of the operation.[64,76] The improved intellectual performance, however, could not be related to an increase in CBF.[64] Instead it is suggested that it is caused by the cessation of repeated microembolisms.

A substantial proportion, maybe 50%, of patients considered eligible for carotid surgery by the standard of today, i.e. symptomatic >70% ICA stenosis, will have a significant reduction in cerebral perfusion pressure distal to the occlusive lesion. This state of hypoperfusion will manifest itself as a decreased vasoreactivity or an increased sensitivity to a drop in systemic perfusion pressure. Though an immediate beneficial effect of increased perfusion reserve is not apparent in most cases, it has generally been assumed that an exhausted perfusion reserve makes the brain tissue more susceptible to the effect of embolism or reduction of systemic perfusion pressure.[61] More than any other event, the negative outcome of the multicentre EC-IC bypass study triggered this debate and that of whether the subgroup of patients with reduction in perfusion pressure distal to a symptomatic arterial lesion are more likely to benefit from surgery. The issue has been addressed in an animal model.[77] Middle cerebral artery ligature was performed in two groups of rats, in one preceded by ICA occlusion, simulating the effect of extracranial arterial disease. In the examined rats ICA occlusion lowered the distal ICA pressure by 50%. Infarct size, measured 4 days later, was significantly larger in those rats that had ICA occlusion prior to MCA occlusion. Only few clinical data exist: two small longitudinal studies have not been able to demonstrate a relationship between cerebral haemodynamics, assessed with PET, and the subsequent occurrence of stroke.[78,79] In a 1-year follow-up study, none of 21 patients with symptomatic severe occlusive carotid disease causing abnormal haemodynamics developed relevant stroke.[78] In another study of 23 similar patients who underwent EC-IC bypass surgery, three suffered ipsilateral ischaemic stroke during the first postoperative year, giving little evidence to suggest that haemodynamic evaluation can identify a group of patients who would benefit from EC-IC bypass.[79] While data regarding the relationship of cerebral haemodynamics to stroke risk are questionable, though limited, there is positive evidence that these patients carry a greater risk of perioperative complications.[80] Correction of a chronic low perfusion pressure by carotid endarterectomy may result in a pronounced hyperaemia, thought to be related to temporary failure or readjustment of cerebral autoregulation.[10,12,80,81] This postendarterectomy hyperperfusion may in some cases lead to cerebral oedema and haemorrhage, a complication also described following resection of cerebral arteriovenous malformations.[82]

CONCLUSION

Cerebral blood flow measurement in carotid artery disease has been possible for several decades, but has mainly been used as a research tool due to the difficulty in performing it as well as its methodological shortcomings. Recent advances have made it possible to evaluate regional cerebral haemodynamics in individual patients. These measurements have provided new insight into the pathogenesis of cerebral ischaemia as well as preliminary observations regarding the relationship of cerebral haemodynamics to symptoms and prognosis. Further investigations will decide whether this information becomes of importance for future indications for carotid endarterectomy.

REFERENCES

1. Kety SS, Schmidt CF: The determination of cerebral blood flow in many by use of nitrous oxide in low concentrations. Am J Phys 143: 53–66, 1945
2. Eastcott HGH, Pickering GW, Rob CG: Reconstruction of internal carotid artery in a patient with intermittent attacks of hemiplegia. Lancet ii: 994, 1954
3. EC/IC Bypass Group: Failure of extracranial arterial bypass to reduce the risk of ischemic stroke. Results of an international randomized trial. N Engl J Med 313: 1191–1200, 1985
4. European carotid surgery trialists' collaborative group: MCR European carotid trial: interim results for symptomatic patients with severe (70–99%) or with mild (0–29%) carotid stenosis. Lancet 337: 1235–1243, 1991
5. North American symptomatic carotid endarterectomy trial collaborators: Beneficial effect of carotid endarterectomy in symptomatic patients with high-grade carotid stenosis. N Engl J Med 325: 445–453, 1991
6. Mayberg MR, Wilson E, Yatsu F et al.: Carotid endarterectomy and prevention of cerebral ischemia in symptomatic carotid stenosis. JAMA 266: 3289–3294, 1991
7. Engell HC, Boysen G, Ladegaard-Pedersen, Henriksen H: Cerebral blood flow before and after carotid endarterectomy. Vasc Surg 6: 14–19, 1972
8. Boysen G: Cerebral hemodynamics in carotid surgery (Thesis). Acta Neurol Scand 49: 1–84, 1973
9. Vorstrup S: Tomographic cerebral blood flow measurements in patients with ischemic cerebrovascular disease and evaluation of vasodilatory capacity by the acetazolamide test (Thesis). Acta Neurol Scand 77 (Suppl 114): 1–48, 1988
10. Schroeder TV: Hemodynamic significance of internal carotid artery disease (Thesis). Acta Neurol Scand 77: 353–372, 1988
11. Sillesen H: Diagnosis and hemodynamic evaluation of internal carotid artery stenoses by Doppler ultrasound (Thesis). Naerum: Bruel & Kjaer A/S 1–58, 1990

12. Jørgensen L, Schroeder TV: Defective cerebrovascular autoregulation after carotid endarterectomy. Eur J Vasc Surg 1993 (in press)

13. Crawford ES, DeBakey ME, Blaisdell FW, Morris GC, Fields WS: Hemodynamic alterations in patients with cerebral arterial insufficiency before and after operation. Surgery 48: 76–96, 1960

14. Ricotta JJ, Fiore WM, Holen J et al.: Definition of extracranial carotid disease: comparison of oculopneumoplethysmography, continuous wave Doppler angiography and measurement at operation. In Progress in Stroke Research Vol. 2, Greenhalgh RM, Rose CF (Eds). London: Pitman, pp. 91–102, 1983

15. Sillesen H, Schroeder T, Buchardt Hansen HJ: Hemodynamic evaluation of the cerebral circulation by periorbital Doppler examination and CBF measurements in carotid artery disease. Neurol Res 1988: 10: 57–60, 1988

16. Powers WJ: Cerebral hemodynamics in ischemic cerebrovascular disease. Ann Neurol 29: 231–240, 1991

17. Gibbs JM, Leenders KL, Wise RJS, Jones T: Evaluation of cerebral perfusion pressure reserve in patients with carotid artery occlusion. Lancet i: 182–186, 1984

18. Teasdale G, Mendelow D: Cerebral blood flow measurements in clinical neurosurgery. J Cereb Blood Flow Metabol 1: 357–359, 1981

19. Yonekura M, Austin G: Comparison of regional cerebral blood flow in TIA patients with and without occlusion or stenosis of major vessels. Neurol Res 7: 149–152, 1985

20. Blauenstein UW, Halsey JH, Wilson EM, Wills EL, Risberg J: 133-xenon inhalation method. Analysis of reproducibility: some of its physiological implications. Stroke 8: 92–102, 1977

21. Schroeder T, Holstein P, Lassen NA, Engell HC: Measurement of cerebral blood flow by intravenous xenon-133 technique and a mobile system. Reproducibility using the Obnst model compared with total curve analysis. Neurol Res 8: 237–242, 1986

22. Schieve JF, Wilson WP: The influence of age, anesthesia and cerebral arteriosclerosis on cerebral vascular reactivity to carbon dioxide. Am J Med 15: 171–180, 1953

23. Fieschi C, Agnoli A, Galbo E: Effects of carbon dioxide on cerebral hemodynamics in normal subjects and in cerebrovascular disease studied by carotid injection of radioalbumin. Circ Res 13: 436–447, 1963

24. Dyken ML, Campbell RL, Frayser R: Cerebral blood flow, oxygen utilization, and vascular reactivity. Internal carotid artery complete occlusion versus incomplete occlusion with infarction. Neurology 20: 1127–1132, 1970

25. Tuteur P, Reivich M, Goldberg HI et al.: Transient responses of cerebral blood flow and ventilation to changes in $PaCO_2$ in normal subjects and patients with cerebrovascular disease. Stroke 7: 584–590, 1976

26. Norrving B, Nielsson B, Risberg J: rCBF in patients with carotid occlusion. Resting and hypercapnic flow related to collateral pattern. Stroke 13: 154–162, 1982

27. Bullock R, Mendelow AD, Bone I et al.: Cerebral blood flow and CO_2 responsiveness as an indicator of collateral reserve capacity in patients with carotid artery disease. Br J Surg 72: 348–351, 1985

28. Schroeder T: Cerebrovascular reactivity of acetazolamide in carotid artery disease. Neurol Res 8: 231–236, 1986

29. Brown M, Wade JPH, Bishop CCR, Russell RWR: Reactivity of the cerebral circulation in patients with carotid occlusion. J Neurol Neurosurg Psych 49: 899–904, 1986

30. Vorstrup S, Boysen G, Brun B, Engell HC: Evaluation of the regional cerebral vasodilatory capacity before carotid endarterectomy by the acetazolamide test. Neurol Res 9: 10–18, 1987

31. Sullivan HG, Kingsbury TB, Morgan ME et al.: The rCBF response to Diamox in normal subjects and cerebrovascular disease patients. J Neurosurg 67: 525–534, 1987

32. Keyeux A, Laterre C, Beckers C. Resting and hypercapnic rCBF in patients with unilateral occlusive disease of the internal carotid artery. J Nucl Med 29: 311–319, 1988

33. Chollet F, Celsis P, Clanet M et al.: SPECT study of cerebral blood flow reactivity after acetazolamide in patients with transient ischemic attacks. Stroke 20: 458–464, 1989
34. Piepgras A, Schmeidek P, Leinsinger G et al.: A simple test to assess cerebrovascular reserve capacity using transcranial Doppler sonography and acetazolamide. Stroke 21: 1306–1311, 1990
35. Gratzl O, Rem J, Mueller HR, Radue EW, Mueller-Brandt J: Cerebral blood flow and common carotid flow in neurologically asymptomatic carotid endarterectomy patients. Neurol Res 12: 26–28, 1990
36. Cavestri R, Radice L, Ferrarini F et al.: CBF side-to-side asymmetries in stenosis–occlusion of internal carotid artery. Relevance of CT findings and collateral supply. Ital J Neurol Sci 12: 383–388, 1991
37. Brushnell DL, Gupta S, Barnes WE et al.: Evaluation of cerebral perfusion reserve using 5% CO_2 and SPECT neuroperfusion imaging. Clin Nucl Med 16: 263–267, 1991
38. Levine RL, Dobkin JA, Rozental JM, Satter MR, Nickles RJ: Blood flow reactivity to hypercapnia in strictly unilateral carotid disease: preliminary results. J Neurol Neurosurg Psych 54: 204–209, 1991
39. Vorstrup S, Zbornikova V, Sjöholm L, Skoglund L, Ryding E: CBF and transcranial Doppler sonography during vasodilatory stress tests in patients with common carotid artery occlusion. Neurol Res 14: 31–38, 1992
40. Burt RW, Witt RM, Cikrit DF, Reddy RV: Carotid artery disease: Evaluation with acetazolamide-enhanced Tc-99m HMPAO SPECT[1]. Radiology 182: 461–466, 1992
41. Cikit DE, Burt RW, Dalsing MC et al.: Acetazolamide enhanced single photon emission computed tomography (SPECT) evaluation of cerebral perfusion before and after carotid endarterectomy. J Vasc Surg 15: 747–754, 1992
42. Hasegawa Y, Yamaguchi T, Tsuchiya T, Minematsu K, Nishimura T: Sequential change of hemodynamic reserve in patients with major cerebral artery occlusion or severe stenosis. Neuroradiol 34: 15–21, 1992
43. Olesen J: Cerebral blood flow methods for measurement regulation, effects of drugs and changes in disease. Acta Neurol Scand 50 (Suppl 57): 1–130, 1974
44. Strandgaard S. Cerebral ischemia caused by overzealous blood pressure lowering. Dan Med Bull 34 (Suppl 1): 5–7, 1987
45. Vorstrup S, Schmidt JF, Waldemar G, Haase J, Paulson OB: Identification of hemodynamic patients for EC-IC bypass surgery. In Stimulated Cerebral Blood Flow. Schmiedek P, Einhäupel K, Kirsch LM (Eds). Berlin: Springer-Verlag, pp. 171–174, 1992
46. Sengupta D, Harper M, Jennet B: Effect of carotid ligation on cerebral blood flow in baboons. 1. Response to altered arterial pCO_2. J Neurol Neurosurg Psych 36: 736–741, 1973
47. DeLey G, Nshimyumuremyi J-B, Leusen I: Hemispheric blood flow in the rat after unilateral common carotid occlusion: Evolution with time. Stroke 16: 69–73, 1985
48. Russell D, Dybevod S, Kjartansson O et al.: Cerebral vasoreactivity and blood flow before and 3 months after carotid endarterectomy. Stroke 21: 1029–1032, 1990
49. Lassen NA, Henriksen L, Paulson O: Regional cerebral blood flow in stroke by 133-xenon inhalation and emission tomography. Stroke 12: 284–288, 1981
50. Schroeder T, Vorstrup S, Lassen NA, Engell HC: Noninvasive xenon-133 measurements of cerebral blood flow using stationary detectors compared with dynamic emission tomography. J Cereb Blood Flow Metabol 6: 739–746, 1986
51. Lassen NA, Hennksen L, Holm S et al.: Cerebral blood flow tomography. Xenon-133 compared to isopropyl-amphetamine-iodine-123. J Nucl Med 24: 17–21, 1983
52. Holm S, Andersen AR, Vorstrup S et al.: Dynamic SPECT of the brain using a lipophilic technetium-99m complex, PnAO. J Nucl Med 26: 1129–1134, 1985
53. Schroeder T, Utzon NP, Aabech J et al.: Carotid artery disease and low cerebral perfusion pressure: symptomatology, operative risk and outcome. Neurol Res 12: 35–40, 1990
54. Powers WJ, Press GA, Grubb RL, Gado M, Raichle ME: The effect of hemodynamically significant carotid artery disease on the hemodynamic status of the cerebral circulation. Ann Int Med 106: 27–35, 1987
55. LeBlanc R, Tyler JL, Mohr G et al.: Hemodynamic and metabolic effects of cerebral revascularization. J Neurosurg 66: 529–535, 1987

56. Baron JC, Bousser MG, Rey A: Reversal of focal "misery-perfusion syndrome" by extra-intracranial arterial bypass in hemodynamic cerebral ischemia. Stroke 12: 454–459, 1981
57. Carpenter DA, Grubb RL, Powers WJ: Borderzone hemodynamics in cerebrovascular disease. Neurol 40: 1587–1592, 1990
58. Leblanc R, Yamamoto YL, Tyler JL: Borderzone ischemia. Ann Neurol 22: 707–713, 1987
59. Adams JE, Smith MC, Wylie EJ, Leake TB, Halliday B: Cerebral blood flow and hemodynamics in extracranial vascular disease: Effect of endarterectomy. Surgery 53: 449–455, 1963
60. Waltz AG, Sundt TM, Michenfelder JD: Cerebral blood flow during carotid endarterectomy. Circulation 4: 191–196, 1972
61. Sundt TM, Sharbrough FW, Piepgras DG et al.: Correlation of cerebral blood flow and electroencephalographic changes during carotid endarterectomy with results of surgery and hemodynamics of cerebral ischemia. Mayo Clin Proc 56: 533–543, 1981
62. Vorstrup S, Hemmingsen R, Henriksen L et al.: Regional cerebral blood flow in patients with transient ischemic attacks studied by xenon-133 inhalation and tomography. Stroke 14: 903–910, 1983
63. Vorstrup S, Engell HC, Lindewald H, Lassen NA: Hemodynamically significant stenosis of the internal carotid artery treated with endarterectomy. J Neurosurg 60: 1070–1075, 1984
64. Hemmingsen R, Mejsholm B, Vorstrup S et al.: Carotid surgery, cognitive function, and cerebral blood flow in patients with transient ischemic attacks. Ann Neurol 2: 13–19, 1986
65. Schroeder T, Sillesen H, Engell HC: Hemodynamic effect of carotid endarterectomy. Stroke 18: 204–209, 1987
66. Bishop CCR, Butler L, Hunt T, Burnard KG, Browse NL: Effect of carotid endarterectomy on cerebral blood flow and its response to hypercapnia. Br J Surg 74: 994–996, 1987
67. Maurer AH, Siegel JA, Comerata AJ, Morgan WA, Johnson MH: SPECT quantification of cerebral ischemia before and after carotid endarterectomy. J Nucl Med 31: 1412–1420, 1990
68. Sundt TM: The ischemic tolerance of neural tissue and the need for monitoring and selective shunting during carotid endarterectomy. Stroke 14: 93–98, 1983
69. Schroeder T, Holstein P, Engell HC: Hyperperfusion following endarterectomy. Stroke 15: 758, 1984
70. Schroeder T, Sillesen H, Sørensen O, Engell HC: Cerebral hyperperfusion following carotid endarterectomy. J Neurosurg 66: 824–829, 1987
71. Bishop CCR, Burnand KG, Brown M, Russell RR, Browse NL: Reduced response of cerebral blood flow to hypercapnia: restoration by extracranial–intracranial bypass. Br J Surg 74: 802–804, 1987
72. Halsey JH, Morawetz RB, Blauenstein UW: The hemodynamic effect of STA-MCA bypass. Stroke 13: 163–167, 1982
73. Tanahashi N, Meyer JS, Rogers RL et al.: Long term assessment of cerebral perfusion following STA-MCA by-pass in patients. Stroke 16: 85–91, 1985
74. Samson Y, Baron JC, Bousser MG et al.: Effects of extra–intracranial arterial bypass on cerebral blood flow and oxygen metabolism in humans. Stroke 16: 609–616, 1985
75. Astrup J, Siesjo BK, Symon L: Thresholds in cerebral ischemia—the ischemic penumbra. Stroke 12: 723–725, 1981
76. Jacobs LA, Ganji S, Shirley JG, Morell RM, Brinkman SD: Cognitive improvement after extracranial reconstruction for the low flow-endangered brain. Surgery 93: 683–687, 1983
77. Sillesen H, Nedergaard M, Schroeder T, Buchardt Hansen HJ: Middle cerebral artery occlusion in presence of low perfusion pressure increases infarct size in rats. Neurol Res 10: 61–63, 1988
78. Powers WJ, Tempel LW, Grubb RL: Influence of cerebral hemodynamics on stroke risk: One-year follow-up of 30 medically treated patients. Ann Neurol 25: 325–330, 1989
79. Powers WJ, Grubb RL, Raichle ME: Clinical results of extracranial–intracranial bypass surgery in patients with hemodynamic cerebrovascular disease. J Neurosurg 70: 61–67, 1989
80. Schroeder T, Sillesen H, Boesen J, Laursen H, Soelberg Sørensen P: Intracerebral hemorrhage after carotid endarterectomy. Eur J Vasc Surg 1: 51–60, 1987
81. Bernstein M, Flemming JFR, Deck JHN: Cerebral hyperperfusion after carotid endarterectomy: A cause of cerebral hemorrhage. Neurosurgery 15: 50–56.80, 1984
82. Spetzler RF, Wilson CB, Weinstein P et al.: Normal perfusion pressure breakthrough theory. Clin Neurosurg 25: 651–672

Intra-arterial Arch Digital Subtraction Angiography

Nigel Barrett, David M. Nott, James McIvor, Rachel Cuming,
G. David Perkin, John Wade and Roger M. Greenhalgh

INTRODUCTION

The annual incidence of stroke in the UK is between one and two per thousand of the population.[1] Up to 75% of the warning symptoms preceding stroke are related to lesions in the extracranial circulation, usually in association with carotid arteriosclerosis, and in two-thirds of patients with symptoms of cerebrovascular insufficiency, the lesions are surgically accessible. For these reasons much attention is currently focussed on the diagnostic evaluation of the extracranial carotid system where early diagnosis may lead to successful early treatment.

Referral of patients suspected of having extracranial arterial disease for neurovascular investigation by the Charing Cross Regional Vascular Service is via four routes. Patients may present directly to the neurologist with symptoms of either transient ischaemic attacks (TIA), reversible ischaemic neurological deficit, amaurosis fugax, evolving stroke, frank stroke or non-focal symptoms such as blackouts, migraines and dizziness. Secondly, patients with asymptomatic bruits discovered on routine clinical examination by General Physicians are usually referred directly to the neurologist for assessment. Thirdly, General Practitioners have access to a comprehensive referral service for non-invasive carotid scanning as part of the government's policy to prioritize reduction in strokes and finally, patients are referred from other hospitals having had angiography delineating operable extracranial disease.

LIMITATIONS OF ANGIOGRAPHY

Although angiography permits complete assessment of the cerebrovascular circulation and is often indicated for patients in whom surgical correction of a carotid lesion is planned, it has several limitations as a screening test for patients at risk for stroke. Angiography does not permit inspection of a true cross-section of a vessel and is limited in its ability to identify intraplaque haemorrhage and ulceration. This has cast some doubt on the value of angiography as the gold standard with which new non-invasive methods should be compared. Also, angiography is accompanied by 2–13% incidence of minor complications such as haematoma and transient neurological deficits and major complication rates including stroke and death of 0.2–0.7%. The risk of complications is greater in patients with symptomatic cerebrovascular disease[2] and in those with difficulty in selective cathterization of vessels arising from the aortic arch.[3] Other factors relevant to risk are the volume of the contrast medium, duration of the procedure, age of the patient (the dividing age being 40), the disease process (risk being higher in patients with vascular disease or subarachnoid haemorrhage than those with tumour), and the experience of the radiologist. Indeed, in a previous study from this centre, a single radiologist performing most of the techniques of selective extracranial angiography had a major long-term complication rate of 2.2% following selective carotid catheterization.[4] In view of the high morbidity associated with angiographic methods, alternative approaches to image the carotid circulation have been investigated.

DIGITAL SUBTRACTION ANGIOGRAPHY

With the introduction of digital subtraction angiography (DSA), by administering the contrast intravenously it was possible to obtain images of the carotid bulb. The principle of digital subtraction angiography is the production of an image showing only the vessels that have been opacified by removing the overlying bone and soft tissue. This is performed electronically by obtaining an image before contrast is injected and then an image with contrast in the vessels while the patient is in the same position and then subtracting the second image from the first, to give a processed image of the opacified vessel lumens free of any bone or soft tissue structures.[5] In theory, this would be an ideal method because it would avoid all problems associated with arterial puncture and the potential complications that can occur with the injections of contrast materials. However, for the carotid artery, it proved to be very disappointing because of the lack of diagnostic quality in up to 20% of the studies. Movement artefacts degraded the image and even minor movements such as breathing or swallowing caused significant artefacts. Poor cardiac output also limited the usefulness of intravenous (IV) DSA as less concentrated contrast reached the aortic arch and main branches due to a decreased stroke volume.[6] This was overcome by placing a catheter directly into the arterial tree and opacifying it directly (intra-arterial digital subtraction angiography (IA DSA)) and had the advantage of reducing motion artefact since there was less time between the image acquisition, but it did have the added disadvantage of requiring an arterial puncture and manipulation of the catheter near the origin of the artery to be opacified.

The principal threat to quality DSA imaging arises from two problems that are seldom encountered with conventional angiography. The first of these is simultaneous opacification of all the cervical and intracranial vessels. This results frequently in the overlapping of the bifurcation vessels and also overlap with the vertebral artery. In order to separate these vessels to allow proper assesment, multiple views with proper positioning are of absolute importance. The second problem is misregistration artefacts secondary to motion. Since absolute agreement between the mass image and subsequent images chosen for subtraction is essential, any motion after establishing the image mass will result in artefact. This requires a cooperative patient to minimize major motion artefact. However, even minor motion, such as pulsatile vessel wall movement, will introduce streak artefacts if sufficient plaque calcification is present.[7] Swallowing is less easily controlled and is a source of frequent artefacts.

DUPLEX SCANNING AND DIGITAL SUBTRACTION ANGIOGRAPHY

With the advent of duplex scanning, which is non-invasive, free of risk and has no contraindications, the extracranial carotid system is well suited for investigation.

Because of the problems of conventional angiography carried out by selective bilateral common carotid injections with biplanar views, Eikelboom *et al.* combined the use of intravenous digital subtraction angiography with duplex scanning.[8] Results showed that duplex scanning had a sensitivity of 96% and specificity of 88% and IV DSA a sensitivity of 96% and specificity of 91%. When both of these studies were combined, if compared with angiography, a positive predictive value of 100% and negative predictive value of 98% were achieved. These results helped to influence the decision to operate or not to operate which was felt could be safely based on duplex scanning and IV DSA; conventional angiography was preferable if duplex scanning and IV DSA disagreed.

We and others[9] felt that IV DSA did not provide images of satisfactory quality since less concentrated contrast reached the aortic arch and its branches; this problem would be compounded if the patient had a decreased stroke volume. To improve the imaging, therefore, catheters were placed in the right atrium using a superior vena cava route. However, this was not without significant risk and mediastinal extravasation occurred in 0.13% of procedures[10] and a case of cardiac tamponade produced by the catheter rupturing the pericardial cavity has been reported.[11] This procedure was not without morbidity and appeared as invasive as catheterizing the arch.

INTRA-ARTERIAL DIGITAL SUBTRACTION ANGIOGRAPHY

Improved quality of imaging might therefore be improved by placing a catheter directly into the arterial tree and opacifying it directly (IA DSA). This has the advantage of reducing motion artefact as there is less time between administration of contrast and image acquisition, but it does have the added disadvantage of needing an arterial puncture and manipulation of the catheter near the origin of the artery to be opacified.

METHODS

We have performed IA DSA in a consecutive series of 235 patients at Charing Cross Hospital. Each patient was initially seen by a consultant neurologist prior to angiography to document the ischaemic event and to identify any persisting disability. Amaurosis fugax presented in 19% of the patients, while the majority (57%) of patients presented with transient ischaemic attacks, transient stroke (6%), and 19% with established stroke with a good clinical recovery. Intra-arterial flush DSA was performed using the femoral route in 227 patients (97%); when the femoral was not possible, the axillary route was used in eight (3%). Examinations were performed under a combination of local anaesthetic and intravenous sedation. A 5 F pigtail catheter was placed in the ascending aorta and serial digital angiograms were obtained by injecting 40 ml of non-ionic contrast media through the catheter using a mechanical pump injector. Oblique views of the aortic arch to show the origins of the great vessels (Fig. 1) followed by three views of the neck vessels are routinely performed. These views are anterior–posterior and right and left

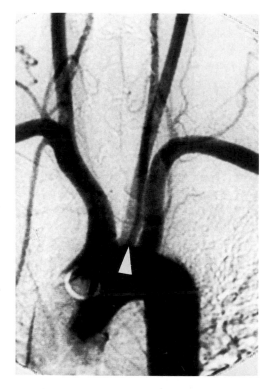

Fig. 1. Right posterior oblique projection showing the origin of the great vessels. The left vertebral artery is seen arising from the arch (arrow).

oblique views of the carotid arteries to image the carotid bifurcations (Figs 2, 3, 4). If there was vessel overlap then steeper angles of obliquity were added to the examination to show the vessel of interest, free of overlying vessels. The examination was completed by performing an angled down frontal view which showed the larger intracerebral vessels and would exclude a visible aneurysm (Fig. 5), and a lateral oblique view to show the carotid siphon, disease in which may preclude the patient from carotid endarterectomy. The patients were discharged either on the same day or on the following day unless immediate surgery was performed. A record was made of any complications.

RESULTS

Every study produced adequate diagnostic images from the aortic arch to the proximal carotid siphon. However, the technique did not allow for adequate identification of disease within the cranium. No repeat procedures were necessary because of technical failures and the use of an axillary route did not significantly increase the complication rate. In 39 patients (17%) there was at least one occluded

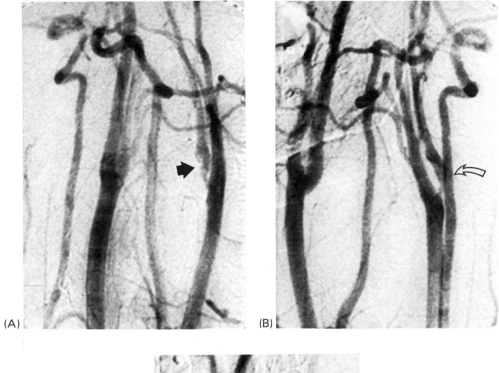

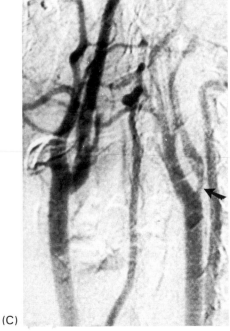

Fig. 2. (A) Left posterior oblique projection (18 degree) showing irregularity of the left internal carotid artery (arrow). (B) Right posterior oblique projection (18 degree) showing the left internal carotid artery projection over the left vertebral artery. (C) Right posterior oblique projection (25 degree) showing the left internal carotid artery free of the vertebral artery and confirms that it is markedly narrowed (arrow).

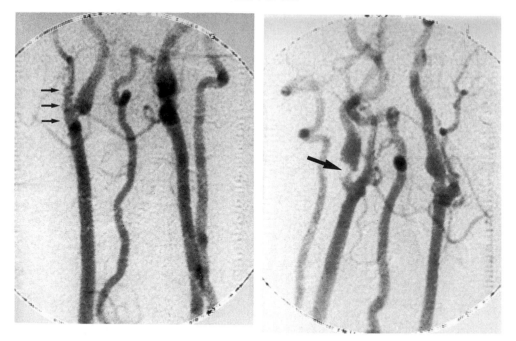

Fig. 3A. Right posterior oblique projection (18 degree) in which overlap at the right carotid bifurcation marks the right internal carotid stenoses seen in Fig. 3B.

Fig. 3B. Left posterior oblique projection (18 degree) of the same patient showing the significant right internal carotid artery stenosis (arrow).

artery, 94 patients (40%) had a stenosis of 50–99%, 42 (18%) had a stenosis of 25–49%, and 60 (24%) had less than 25% stenosis. There were no deaths and no major long-term neurological morbidity. Six patients (2.5%) experienced TIAs, of which three were in the form of amaurosis fugax. In five cases the attacks were repetitions of all the patients' original symptoms. All these have resolved within 24 hours. There were no major systemic complications. Three known angina sufferers reported transient chest pain. Two skin rashes, probably related to the contrast injection, were observed and groin haematoma or oozing from the puncture site were noted in 22 (9.3%), all of which resolved spontaneously.

DISCUSSION

The neurological complication rate in this study is substantially lower than the figures quoted in almost all selective arterial studies of the cerebral vessels.[13] Retrospective studies may only report minor neurological complications but it is unlikely that a permanent neurological deficit could have been missed in this series. The reduction in morbidity using the present technique is likely to be the consequence of the small diameter catheter remaining confined to the aortic arch rather than being introduced into the carotid vessels. The examination can be tailored to the patient studied, with further views being added if the standard views do not show the vessels clearly;

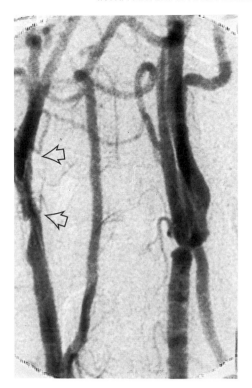

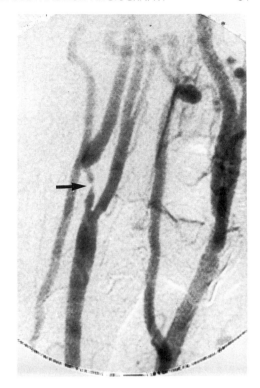

Fig. 4A. Right posterior oblique projection showing overlap of right carotid vessels.

Fig. 4B. Left posterior oblique projection of the same patient showing 90 degree stenosis of right internal carotid artery.

it has the added advantage of allowing selective catheterization of a vessel if required to obtain the necessary preoperative information. However, this was not necessary in this study.

There is no doubt that as the technology of the digital systems improve so will the image resolution of intravenous studies, but until those images are consistently as accurate as intra-arterial studies, flush angiography will remain the method of choice for opacifying the carotid arteries at this institution.

It is interesting to speculate also that as the technology of duplex scanning is also improving hand in hand with the expertise of the technicians that perform the scans the capacity to replace angiography exists. Indeed there are some vascular surgeons who will operate on the basis of a scan alone. In our experience we feel that angiography is necessary in order to confirm occlusions (duplex scanning is less sensitive to low flow rates) and to detect intracranial lesions such as high grade stenoses in the carotid siphon.

Patients who present with low grade stenoses in the carotid bulb may be rescanned by duplex ultrasound at intervals of 6 months and, if progression of the disease is noted and patients become candidates for surgery, then IA DSA is performed. The recent introduction of peroperative Doppler ultrasound can also be used to examine the middle cerebral artery through the relatively sonolucent window of the temporal

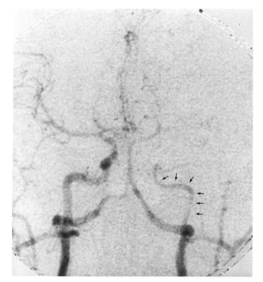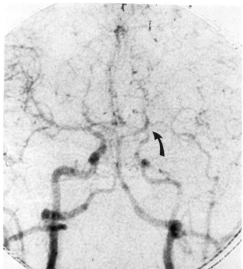

Fig. 5A. The same patient as shown in Fig. 2. There is delayed filling of the intra-cerebral circulation of the left internal carotid artery.

Fig. 5B. Delayed images showing occlusion of the left middle cerebral artery (arrow).

bone and changes in flow patterns on peroperative trial occlusion of the ipsilateral carotid artery can enable shunting to be selective and may help to reduce the morbidity of shunt related complications.

In conclusion, we feel that arch angiography with selective catheterization carries too high a morbidity to make it beneficial for routine use. Indeed, when the two studies were compared, there was a significantly higher morbidity ($p=0.03$) with selective angiography compared with IA DSA. Thus the absence of any major neurological deficit makes IA DSA combined with duplex scanning the methods of choice for preoperative examination of the extracranial arterial tree at the present time.

REFERENCES

1. Ellis MR, Greenhalgh RM: Management of asymptomatic carotid bruit. J Vasc Surg 5: 869–873, 1987
2. Faught E, Trader SD, Hanna GR: Cerebral complications of arteriography for transient ischaemia and stroke: Prediction of risk. Neurology 29: 4–15, 1979
3. Olivecrona H: Complications of cerebral angiography. Neuroradiology 14: 175–181, 1977
4. McIvor J, Stiener TJ, Perkin GD *et al.*: Neurological morbidity or arch and carotid arteriography in cerebrovascular disease. The influence of contrast medium. Br J Radiol 60: 117–122, 1987
5. Curry TS, Dowdey JE, Murray RC: Christensen's Physics of Diagnostic Radiology, 4th edn, Pennsylvania, USA: Lea and Febiger, pp. 392–431, 1990
6. Dawson P: Digital subtraction angiography — a critical analysis. Clin Radiol 39: 474–477, 1988

7. Brodie WR, Enzmann DR, Deutsch LS *et al.*: Intravenous carotid angiography using line scanned digital radiography. Radiology 139: 297, 1981
8. Eikelboom BC, Ackerstaff RGA, Moll FL, de Vries AR: Accuracy and usefulness of combined Duplex scanning and digital subtraction angiography. *In* Progress in Stroke Research Vol. 2, Greenhalgh R, Rose CF (Eds), pp. 178–185. London: Pitman 1982
9. McReary JA, Schellhas KP, Brant-Zawadski M, Norman D, Newton TH: Outpatient DSA in cerebrovascular disease using transbrachial arch injection. Am J Roent 145: 941–947, 1985
10. Pinto RS, Manuell M, Kricheff H: Complications of digital intravenous angiography: Experience in 2488 cerviccranial examinations. Am J Roent 143: 1295–1299, 1984
11. Gallant MJ, Studley JG: Delayed cardiac tamponade following accidental injection of non-ionic contrast medium into the pericardium. Clin Radiol 41: 139–140, 1990
12. Hankey GJ, Warlow CP, Sellar RJ: Cerebral Angiographic risk in mild cerebro-vascular disease. Stroke 21: 209–222, 1990

INDICATIONS FOR
CAROTID SURGERY

Indications for Carotid Endarterectomy According to Presenting Clinical Symptoms

Samuel R. Money and Larry H. Hollier

Stroke continues to be a leading cause of death in the USA and Western Europe. The mortality rate from stroke in the USA is approximately 75 per 100 000 population.[1] The annual current incidence of stroke is approximately 200 per 100 000.[1] The incidence of stroke increases with age up to approximately 1400 per 100 000 in males who are 75–84 years of age.[2] The economic burden of stroke is enormous and rapidly escalating. In a study it was found that the cost of a stroke in a male victim between the ages of 35 and 54 amounts to approximately $200 000 per patient in 1982 health care dollars.[3] Because of the factors outlined above, the timely identification of patients with carotid bifurcation disease who are amenable to surgical treatment that could reduce the incidence of severe strokes is quite important.

Recently, much progress has been made in the use of randomized clinical trials to determine the exact role of carotid endarterectomy under specific circumstances.[4-6] However, these clinical trials provide only limited information. They are unable to provide data regarding a wide range of potential clinical indications, although they have been able to determine indications for certain basic clinical situations. To fill in this gap, many clinicians base their impressions upon practical interpretations of these clinical trials and also upon personal experience. This chapter will use both the few clinical trials that have been published, and the clinical experience of our clinic with a wide experience in carotid surgery to provide a brief outline of indications for carotid endarterectomy based on the presenting clinical symptoms and angiographic findings of the patient. Additionally, we have modified the tables and information published by the Rand Corporation that were developed to provide ratings of appropriateness for carotid endarterectomy.[7]

The decision to operate on a patient for carotid disease should be based upon a careful assessment of relative risks. Surgical risks associated with carotid endarterectomy must be considered, but also one must consider the risks to the patient of not operating. Thus, one compares the natural history of stroke and death for a given clinical situation (stroke, transient ischaemic attack, amaurosis fugax, asymptomatic stenosis) and angiographic finding (mild stenosis, high-grade stenosis, deep ulceration, etc.) with the risk of surgery in that individual, taking into account the medical risk factors. If the surgical risk of carotid endarterectomy is low in relation to a high risk of stroke without operating, than clearly the benefits of carotid endarterectomy as a low risk strategy may be worthwhile. The converse, however, is also true, if morbidity and mortality of the procedure are excessive and they outweigh the natural history of the untreated or the non-operated lesion, then surgery should be avoided.

In a report by the Ad Hoc Committee on Carotid Surgery Standards of the Stroke Council of the American Heart Association, some guidelines for morbidity and

Table 1. Maximum acceptable 30-day mortality[a] and 30-day morbidity due to stroke associated with carotid endarterectomy[a]

Asymptomatic stenosis	< 3%
Transient ischaemic attack	<−5%
Ischaemic stroke	< 7%
Recurrent carotid disease after previous carotid endarterectomy	<10%

[a]Mortality should not exceed 2%

mortality due to stroke in the perioperative carotid endarterectomy period have been reviewed (Table 1).[8] Table 2 lists the expected long-term risk of stroke (CVA) and transient ischaemic attack (TIA) for patients who present with the various clinical situations.[9–13]

Thus, based on relative risks, patients who are asymptomatic but yet have a high-grade stenosis should undergo carotid endarterectomy if the procedure can be performed with a combined perioperative mortality and stroke morbidity of less than 3%. Patients who have transient ischaemic attacks should have the procedure performed if it can be carried out with morbidity and mortality of less than 5%. Patients who have had an ischaemic stroke and have recovered from the stroke should generally undergo a carotid endarterectomy if the morbidity and mortality can be kept below 7%. Patients who need to undergo a carotid endarterectomy for recurrent disease should have the procedure performed if the major morbidity and mortality can be kept below 10%. Basically, this defines most of our patient population. The morbidity and mortality for each category obviously vary from institution to institution.

TRANSIENT ISCHAEMIC EVENTS

Patients can present with multiple symptoms which can be divided into various basic categories. The first category covers those patients who present with transient episodes of lateralizing dysfunction such as amaurosis fugax (AF) or transient ischaemic attacks (TIA). These events produce a temporary loss of vision in one eye or one-sided sensory dysfunction or loss of motor function. These resolve usually within minutes but, by definition, may take up to 24 hours to reverse. Classical teaching suggests these are totally reversible and patients are left with no permanent neurologic damage; however, newer imaging techniques have demonstrated that what is clinically called a TIA may actually be associated with accumulative and permanent loss of neuronal tissue.[4] The pathogenesis of TIAs is usually thromboembolic in

Table 2. Risk of future neurological events based on presenting symptoms

Clinical presentation	Incidence of TIA/stroke (%)
Asymptomatic stenosis	
>50%[9]	23
>75%[10]	30
Transient ischaemic attack/amaurosis[11]	36
Previous stroke[12]	42
Recurrent symptoms after ipsilateral endarterectomy[13]	54

origin; they generally occur when platelet aggregates, cholesterol crystals, or plaque debris embolize to the cerebral circulation (Figs 1A, B and 2). Indications for surgery in these patients are multiple. Scientific evidence clearly supports operation in patients with a TIA and ipsilateral carotid lesion of greater than 70%.[4] The North American Symptomatic Carotid Endarterectomy trial which will be discussed in this

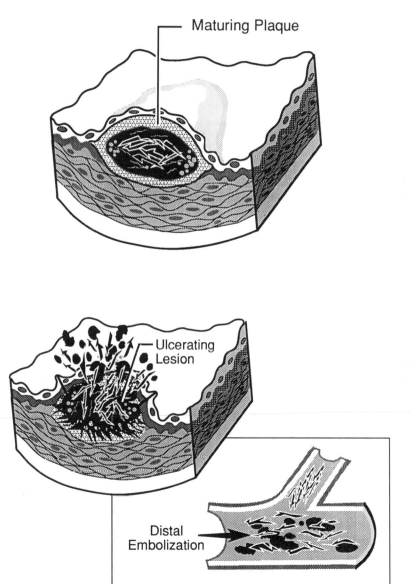

Fig. 1A (upper) and B (lower). Schematic diagram of plaque maturation, degeneration, and embolization as the aetiology of TIAs and stroke.

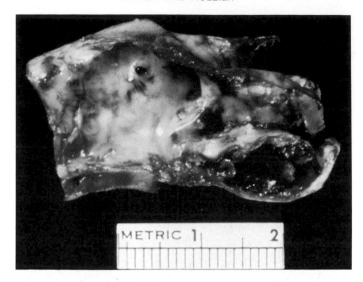

Fig. 2.   Operative photograph of a carotid plaque demonstrating the degeneration similar to that diagrammed in Fig 1B. Note the focal ulceration and the central plaque haemorrhage.

volume, in the chapter by Barnett, supports carotid endarterectomy over medical therapy for patients with a greater than 70% stenosis and TIAs or amaurosis fugax referable to the stenotic side.[4]

Patients with a single TIA who demonstrate an ipsilateral 50–69% stenosis and a large ulcer present in the plaque, we believe, should also undergo carotid endarterectomy (Fig. 3). Patients who have a 50–69% stenosis and a small ulcer should also undergo carotid endarterectomy if the operative mortality and stroke morbidity are below 5%[8] (Table 3).

Patients with multiple TIAs, and especially crescendo TIAs appear to have increased risk of stroke and should be treated aggressively. Obviously, patients with an ipsilateral stenosis of greater than 70% and multiple TIAs should undergo carotid endarterectomy and patients with 50–69% stenosis and a large ulcer, we believe, should also undergo a carotid endarterectomy. In the patients with multiple TIAs and a 50–69% stenosis on the affected side who have even small ulceration evident should also undergo a carotid endarterectomy if medical risks are acceptable. This is especially true in centres where the combined stroke, morbidity, and mortality of carotid endarterectomy is less than 5–7%.[8] However, there is serious question as to the benefit of surgery in patients with lesser stenosis, i.e. 30–49%. Patients who present with new onset of multiple TIAs and are found on investigation to have an ipsilateral carotid artery that is acutely occluded probably should also be considered for carotid endarterectomy, regardless of whether the contralateral carotid has significant disease or not. It is our belief that in this situation the symptoms usually occur due to thromboembolism from the fresh thrombus propagating cephalad in the carotid artery, and therefore treatment should be carotid endarterectomy. In sharp contrast to this, patients who have a chronically occluded carotid artery should not undergo operation.

In summary, patients with transient ischaemic attacks should be operated on if the ipsilateral side has stenosis of 50–99%. The indication for surgery becomes

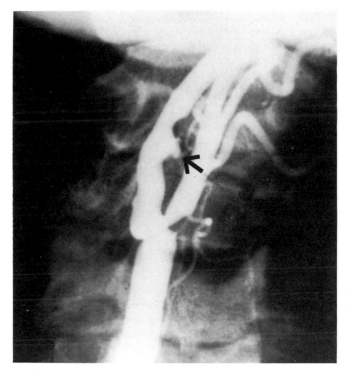

Fig. 3. Angiogram of patient with transient ischaemic attacks from an ulceration in a mildly stenotic plaque.

Table 3. Transient ischaemic attack/amaurosis fugax appropriateness of operating ipsilaterally if angiography shows

	Low surgical risk	Elevated surgical risk	High surgical risk
Ipsi. = chronically occluded Contra. = any degree	−	−	−
Ipsi. − 1–49% Contra. = any degree	−	−	−
Ipsi. = 50–69%, smooth Contra. = any degree	+	−	−
Ipsi. = 50–69%, ulcerated Contra. = any degree	+ +	+	+
Ipsi. = 70–99% Contra. = any degree	+ + +	+ + +	+ +
Ipsi. = deep ulcer Contra. = any degree	+ + +	+ +	+

Ipsi. = degree of stenosis of ipsilateral artery.
Contra = degree of stenosis of contralateral artery.
+ + + = highly indicated; + + = acceptable if surgeon has low morbidity for CEA; + = acceptable, but controversial; − = inappropriate, or medical treatment preferred.

significantly stronger with the presence of severe ulceration of the plaque. In addition, we believe that patients with multiple TIAs who present early with an acutely occluded carotid artery should undergo surgery.

FAILURE OF MEDICAL MANAGEMENT

There are a group of patients with TIAs who have been under medical care for their symptoms. These patients may have been treated with a host of medications but most often aspirin has been used.[15] A percentage of these patients fail medical treatment and clearly should be considered candidates for surgical therapy. Obviously those patients who have an internal carotid stenosis of greater than 70% should be operated on. In addition, patients who are under medical treatment and have a 50–69% stenosis with or without ulceration and continue to have symptoms of recurrent TIAs should be operated upon. We believe these patients are treatment failures of medical therapy and therefore would be more likely to benefit from surgical therapy. There is a grey zone of patients, those who are on medical therapy, have an ipsilateral stenosis of 40–50%, and continue to have TIAs. If ulceration is clearly present, we believe good risk patients probably should also undergo surgical intervention, although it is the patients in this group in whom the indications for surgery are not clear cut. Again, in a centre with very low morbidity and mortality from carotid artery surgery, these patients would likely benefit from carotid endarterectomy.

With the recent reports of the success of carotid endarterectomy in symptomatic patients,[4] a new class of patients to evaluate becomes evident, namely the patients who were successfully treated by aspirin previously. These patients may have had one or more bouts of TIAs and have had their symptoms controlled by taking aspirin. It is our belief that if a stenosis of greater than 70% is present in these patients, they should undergo a prophylactic carotid endarterectomy even though they may now be asymptomatic. The evidence for this is not as strong as for patients who have not been treated or have failed medical therapy, but it is our belief that these patients will do well in the long term undergoing prophylactic carotid endarterectomy.

ESTABLISHED STROKE

The decision to consider surgical treatment in a patient who has suffered a stroke obviously depends on the extent of neurologic dysfunction. Patients who have resolved their neurologic deficit or who have mild deficits remaining should be evaluated. If a spectramine perfusion scan suggests that they have additional brain tissue at risk, they should be strongly considered for an appropriately timed carotid endarterectomy (Fig. 4). We believe that patients should be excluded if they have a significantly altered level of consciousness or if they are totally limited functionally by their neurologic deficit. In addition, patients who are unstable or whose symptoms show deterioration should not be considered as surgical candidates.

If a patient suffers a mild stroke and the diagnostic evaluation defines ipsilateral carotid disease that is believed to be the cause of the stroke, carotid endarterectomy should be performed (Table 4). Optimally, the operation should be deferred until the

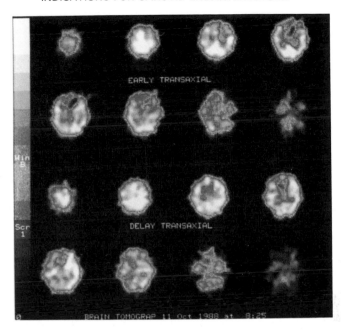

Fig. 4. Spectramine scan of the brain demonstrating delayed uptake of radioisotope in a large segment of one hemisphere, suggesting severe ischaemia that is potentially reversible by revascularization.

patient has achieved their maximal level of recovery from the initial stroke. Multiple different clinical papers suggest that surgical therapy in this patient population can improve the quality of life and the risk of recurrent stroke can also be decreased when compared with patients treated non-operatively.[16-17]

The timing of surgical intervention in patients after stroke is an important issue. Patients who have sustained a cerebral infarct are believed to have residual brain tissue at high risk for further injury; however, patients who undergo a carotid endarterectomy in the presence of acute stroke can suffer increased morbidity and mortality.[8] It is our treatment policy that patients who have a mild deficit that has resolved can undergo early operation if the CT scan suggests only minor cerebral injury. The patient who has a mild deficit that has not resolved completely or is still improving should undergo carotid endarterectomy after a minimum of 4–6 weeks. We believe that a prudent approach is to avoid early carotid endarterectomy following a major established stroke. Although numerous reports have suggested that carotid endarterectomy may be safely performed within the first 10–14 days after a stroke, this is not our preference. We believe that an approach that allows the patient 4–6 weeks to stabilize following a completed stroke is best.

ASYMPTOMATIC STENOSIS

The following group of patients that will be discussed are those who are asymptomatic of neurologic deficit on the side with the carotid lesion. These patients basically fit

Table 4. Prior cerebrovascular accident with good function appropriateness of operating ipsilaterally if angiography shows

	Low surgical risk	Elevated surgical risk	High surgical risk
Ipsi. = chronically occluded Contra. = any degree	−	−	−
Ipsi. = 1–49% Contra. = any degree	−	−	−
Ipsi. = 50–69%, smooth Contra. = any degree	+	−	−
Ipsi. = 50–69%, ulcerated Contra. = any degree	+ +	+	−
Ipsi. = 70–99% Contra. = any degree	+ + +	+ +	+
Ipsi. = deep ulcer Contra. = any degree	+ +	+	−

Ipsi. = degree of stenosis of ipsilateral artery.
Contra = degree of stenosis of contralateral artery.
+ + + = highly indicated; + + = acceptable if surgeon has low morbidity for CEA; + = acceptable, but controversial; − = inappropriate, or medical treatment preferred.

into four different classes. The first class consists of those patients who have carotid bruits. The presence of a bruit does not necessarily correlate with the presence of a high-grade carotid stenosis. Patients with a 20% carotid stenosis are just as likely to have a bruit as patients with a 90% carotid stenosis.[18] In addition, carotid bruits often merely reflect more proximal cardiac murmurs. A bruit, of itself, has no relevance in the decision to perform carotid endarterectomy. Such decisions can only be made on the basis of severity of internal carotid artery stenosis. The second class consists of those patients who have had a previous carotid endarterectomy on a symptomatic side but also have contralateral disease. A fair percentage of patients who undergo a carotid endarterectomy for symptomatic disease on one side will demonstrate significant disease on the contralateral side. A third class of patients are those who have had a TIA or stroke on one side and, as part of a workup for the neurologic symptoms, are found to have a significant stenosis on the uninvolved side. The fourth class of patients, that are discussed in this volume, in the chapter by Wolfe, are those patients who are found to have carotid stenosis during the course of their evaluation before other surgical procedures or during a routine medical evaluation.

Regardless of how the stenosis is found, we believe the treatment of asymptomatic carotid stenosis depends on the extent of the stenosis and the character of the plaque (Table 5). Patients who present with a 70% stenosis despite the presence of limited disease on the contralateral side should undergo carotid endarterectomy. It is our belief that in centres which perform a large number of carotid endarterectomies in which results in this group of patients demonstrate morbidity and mortality of less than 3%, this procedure should be performed. In addition, patients with lesser stenosis but with large ulcers present in the plaque, also should undergo surgery.

In summary, patients in good medical condition with symptomatic or asymptomatic lesions resulting in 70% or greater stenosis, should clearly undergo carotid endarterectomy.

Table 5. Asymptomatic appropriateness of operating ipsilaterally if angiography shows

	Low surgical risk	Elevated surgical risk	High surgical risk
Ipsi. = occluded Contra. = any degree	–	–	–
Ipsi. = 1–49% Contra. = any degree	–	–	–
Ipsi. = 50–69%, ulcerated Contra. = any degree	+	–	–
Ipsi. = 70–99% Contra. = any degree	+ +	+ +	–
Ipsi. = deep ulcer Contra. = any degree	+ +	+	–

Ipsi. = degree of stenosis of ipsilateral artery.
Contra = degree of stenosis of contralateral artery.
+ + = acceptable if surgeon has low morbidity for CEA; + = acceptable, but controversial;
– = inappropriate, or medical treatment preferred.

There are also many other clinical situations which warrant carotid endarterectomy which we have attempted to outline in this chapter. As stated previously, by minimizing perioperative mortality and stroke rate in patients undergoing endarterectomy, it is our belief that this procedure offers a distinct advantage in reducing the incidence of long-term disability from cerebrovascular accidents.

REFERENCES

1. McDowell FH, Caplan LR (Eds): Cerebrovascular Survey Report 1985. For the National Institute of Neurological and Communicative Disorders and Stroke. Public Health Service, Bethesda, MD: National Institutes of Health.
2. Moore WS, Mohr JP, Najafi H et al.: Carotid endarterectomy: Practice guidelines. J Vasc Surg 15: 469–479, 1992
3. Wolf PA, O'Neal A, D'Agostino RB et al.: Declining mortality not declining incidence of stroke: The Framingham study. Stroke 20: 158, 1989
4. North American Symptomatic Carotid Endarterectomy Trial Collaborators: Beneficial effect of carotid endarterectomy in symptomatic patients with high-grade carotid stenosis. N Engl J Med 325: 445–453, 1991
5. European Carotid Surgery Trialists Collaborative Group: MRC European Surgery trial: Interim results for symptomatic patients with severe (70–99%) or with mild (0–29%) carotid stenosis. Lancet 337: 1235–1243, 1991
6. Mayberg MR, Wilson ES, Yatsu F et al.: Carotid endarterectomy and prevention of cerebral ischemia in symptomatic carotid stenosis. JAMA 266: 3289–3294, 1991
7. Merrick NJ, Fink A, Brook RH et al.: Indications for selected medical and surgical procedures—A literature review and ratings of appropriateness. Carotid Endarterectomy. Santa Monica, California. May 1986
8. Beebe HG, Clagett GP, DeWeese JA et al.: Assessing risk associated with carotid endarterectomy. Special Report AHA Stroke Council Carotid Endarterectomy Risk. Stroke 20: 314–315, 1989
9. Long JB, Lynch TG, Hobson RW: Asymptomatic carotid stenosis. In Wilson SE, Veith FJ, Hobson RW, Williams RA (Eds). Vascular Surgery: Principles and Practice. New York: McGraw-Hill, 581–591, 1987

10. Hobson RW: Asymptomatic carotid stenosis: Current diagnosis and management. Perspect Vas Surg 1988
11. Whisnant JP, Matsumoto N, Elveback LR: Transient cerebral ischemic attacks in a community; Rochester, Minnesota 1955–1969. Mayo Clin Proc 48: 194–198, 1973
12. Sacco RL, Wolf PA, Kannel WB *et al.*: Survival and recurrence following stroke. Stroke 13: 290–295, 1982
13. Das MB, Hertzer NR, Ratliff NB *et al.*: Recurrent carotid stenosis. A five year series of 65 reoperations. Ann Surg 202: 28–35, 1985
14. Powers WJ, Grubb RL, Raichle ME: Physiological responses to focal cerebral ischemia in humans. Ann Neurol 16: 546–552, 1984
15. UK-TIA study group. United Kingdom transient ischemic attack aspirin trial—interim results. Br Med J 227: 995–996, 1988
16. Piotrowski JJ, Bernhard VM, Rubin JR *et al.*: Timing of carotid endarterectomy after acute stroke. J Vasc Surg 11: 45–51, 1990
17. McCullough JL, Mentzer RM Jr, Harman PK *et al.*: Carotid endarterectomy after a completed stroke: Reduction in long-term neurologic deteriorization. J Vasc Surg 2: 7–14, 1985
18. Chambers BR, Norris JW: The case against surgery for asymptomatic carotid stenosis. Stroke 15: 964–967, 1984

The Management of Asymptomatic Carotid Disease in Patients who Require Coronary Artery Bypass

G. L. Gilling-Smith and J. H. N. Wolfe

There is at present no hard evidence that carotid endarterectomy reduces the risk of stroke in patients with asymptomatic but haemodynamically significant disease of the internal carotid artery (Fig. 1). However, if these patients require coronary revascularization, many surgeons advocate carotid endarterectomy before cardiac surgery in order to reduce the risk of cerebral hypoperfusion during the period of hypotension that is inevitable with cardiopulmonary bypass and thus the risk of perioperative stroke.

This intuitive approach relies on several assumptions: first that patients with coexistent carotid and coronary artery disease are at increased risk of stroke during coronary artery bypass; second, that perioperative stroke in such patients results primarily from a reduction in cerebral blood flow and that the incidence of

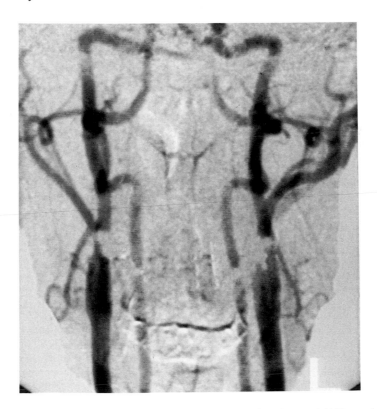

Fig. 1. Carotid angiogram (DSA) showing tight stenoses of both carotid bifurcations. (Dept Radiology, St Mary's Hospital, London).

postoperative neurological deficit can therefore be reduced by prophylactic carotid endarterectomy and third that any reduction in the incidence of perioperative stroke can be achieved without significant increase in morbidity or mortality consequent upon performance of additional surgery in these 'high risk' arteriopaths.

PREVALENCE OF CAROTID DISEASE IN PATIENTS UNDERGOING CARDIAC SURGERY

The reported prevalence of carotid disease in patients undergoing cardiac surgery varies with the method and completeness of preoperative evaluation. A carotid bruit may be found in up to 7% of these patients[1,2] but is an unreliable guide to the presence or severity of disease at the carotid bifurcation. A bruit may originate from the proximal common or external carotid artery while haemodynamically significant disease of the bulb or internal carotid artery may remain silent. Thus, on duplex examination, Barnes et al.[3] found significant disease in only 37% of carotid arteries in which a bruit was heard but noted that only 27% of stenoses were associated with a bruit.

When non-invasive techniques are employed to screen patients before cardiac surgery, the reported prevalence of carotid disease varies between 2.3 and 17.6%.[1,3,4-8] This variation reflects not only the different sensitivities and specificities of the techniques employed but also variation in the definition of 'haemodynamic significance' and differences between the populations studied.

Turnipseed et al.[4] found significant carotid disease in 11.7% of 170 patients examined with Doppler and spectral analysis while, on duplex scanning, Breslau et al.[5] found more than 50% stenosis of the carotid bifurcation in 17.6% of 102 patients. However, both of these studies included symptomatic patients and in neither was angiographic confirmation obtained. Barnes et al.[3] found asymptomatic stenoses in 12.3% of 324 patients screened with duplex but did not define the severity of stenosis and did not confirm their findings with angiography. In contrast, Balderman et al.[1] screened 500 patients with oculoplethysmography (OPG) and found significant carotid disease in only 18 (3.6%). Angiography revealed only one false positive but two patients were found to have contralateral disease that had been missed on OPG.

More recently, Brener et al.[6] reported the results of a much larger prospective study of 4047 patients scheduled to undergo cardiac surgery. The prevalence of significant carotid disease was only 2.3% when patients were examined by OPG but increased to 5.2% when Doppler and spectral analysis were employed. Angiographic confirmation was obtained in all patients with a positive OPG but in only half the patients with a positive Doppler examination. Employing both OPG and duplex scanning, Faggioli et al.[7] found asymptomatic high grade (>75%) stenoses in 8.7% of 539 patients examined before cardiac surgery but they noted that the prevalence of carotid disease increased with age, being significantly greater in patients over 60 (11.3%) than in younger patients (3.8%). Other investigators have noted this increased prevalence with age and in a study of 1087 patients over 65, Berens et al.[8] found a greater than 50% stenosis on duplex scanning in 17.1% of patients scheduled for cardiac surgery. However, this included both symptomatic and asymptomatic lesions and the prevalence fell to 6% when only high grade stenoses (>80%) or occlusions were included.

Thus occult haemodynamically significant disease of the internal carotid artery may be found in between 5 and 10% of patients scheduled for cardiac surgery and is more common in older patients.

THE INCIDENCE OF STROKE AFTER CARDIAC SURGERY

Stroke occurs in 1–5% of patients who undergo cardiac surgery, with a significantly higher incidence being recorded by careful prospective evaluation of all patients undergoing surgery than by retrospective review of hospital records.[9] Thus in three large series,[10-12] retrospective review of almost 10 000 cases yielded a stroke incidence between 0.7 and 1.0%. However, in a detailed prospective study of 312 patients undergoing coronary artery bypass, Shaw et al.[13] recorded 15 perioperative strokes (4.8%) while a similar study of 421 patients at the Cleveland Clinic[14] identified 24 strokes in 22 patients (5.2%). Gardner et al.[15] noted that the incidence of perioperative stroke increased with age. In a prospective study of 3816 patients undergoing coronary artery bypass, the incidence of stroke was only 1.3% in patients who were less than 60 years of age but rose to 6.3% in patients over 70 and 8% in patients over 75.

A variety of mechanisms have been proposed to explain the relatively high incidence of neurological deficit during and immediately after cardiac surgery, including embolization of atheroma during manipulation and clamping of the ascending thoracic aorta[16] and release of left ventricular thrombus during manipulation of the heart,[17] a complication that is particularly likely in patients who have previously suffered a myocardial infarction.[14] Cardiopulmonary bypass is also associated with formation of platelet aggregates,[18] activation of complement[19] and microembolization of air and fat.[13] However, these features are common to all patients who undergo cardiac surgery while only a minority experience major neurological deficit. Furthermore, such mechanisms do not for the most part explain the occurrence of stroke during the early postoperative period. Although the majority of published series do not define the temporal relationship between stroke and surgery, it is clear that some patients do not develop a neurological deficit until several hours or even days after cardiac surgery. In one series,[13] 20% of perioperative strokes developed after the third postoperative day while in another, 70% of strokes in patients with a positive OPG developed more than 48 h after surgery.[20] Thus, although Johnsson et al.[21] found no reduction in cerebral blood flow during cardiopulmonary bypass in patients with haemodynamically significant disease of the extracranial carotid arteries, it is difficult to believe that such patients are not at risk during episodes of postoperative hypotension.

THE INCIDENCE OF PERIOPERATIVE STROKE IN PATIENTS WITH CAROTID ARTERY DISEASE

While the risk of perioperative stroke is undoubtedly increased in patients with carotid disease who also have a history of ipsilateral hemispheric stroke or transient ischaemic attack (TIA),[10,15] the evidence for an increased stroke risk in patients with *asymptomatic* disease is less convincing.

In a prospective study of 324 patients who underwent coronary artery bypass, Barnes *et al.*[3] found no significant difference in the incidence of perioperative stroke between patients with asymptomatic but haemodynamically significant disease of the carotid bifurcation (2.5%) and patients in whom no disease could be found on duplex scanning (1.4%). However, in a retrospective review of 234 patients screened with OPG, Kartchner and McRae[20] recorded seven perioperative strokes in 41 patients with a positive OPG (17%) compared with only two strokes in 161 patients with a negative OPG (1.2%). They concluded that a positive OPG was a reliable predictor of perioperative stroke but unfortunately did not differentiate between symptomatic and asymptomatic patients.

In a larger prospective study of over 4000 patients undergoing cardiac surgery, Brener *et al.*[6] found a significantly increased incidence of perioperative stroke in patients with carotid disease: compared with an incidence of only 1.9% in patients without evidence of carotid disease, the stroke incidence was 5.1% in 59 patients with uncorrected unilateral or bilateral carotid stenoses, 13.8% in 29 patients with unilateral carotid occlusion and 20% in five patients who had both a stenosis and contralateral occlusion. An association with bilateral disease was also noted by Fagioli *et al.*:[7] in a retrospective review of 539 patients, they recorded four strokes in 28 patients (14.3%) with asymptomatic high grade stenoses on duplex scanning compared with only five strokes in 492 patients (1%) without evidence of significant disease. Two of the strokes occurred in patients with bilateral stenoses. These investigators also noted that the incidence of perioperative stroke increased with age, but remarked that even in these elderly patients the majority of strokes occurred in those with high grade stenoses.

There is thus at least circumstantial evidence that the risk of stroke during cardiac surgery is increased in patients with asymptomatic disease of the extracranial carotid arteries, particularly if this is bilateral or associated with contralateral occlusion. Furthermore, the risk of stroke in such patients would seem to increase with increasing age. However since the majority of reports do not differentiate between hemispheric and non-hemispheric strokes or relate the occurrence of stroke to disease of the ipsilateral or contralateral carotid artery, it is impossible to estimate how often a stroke might have been prevented by prophylactic endarterectomy.

IS THE INCIDENCE OF STROKE REDUCED BY CAROTID ENDARTERECTOMY?

This question can only be answered by prospective randomization of all patients who are found on preoperative screening to have asymptomatic but haemodynamically significant disease of the extracranial carotid arteries. Unfortunately, surgeons have in general been reluctant to randomize patients, preferring instead to rely on their own clinical judgment or the often anecdotal reports of others. Such a study would of course present formidable logistical problems. For every 1000 patients who undergo coronary artery bypass, less than 100 will have significant carotid disease and less than 10 of these will sustain a perioperative stroke. To show a statistically significant difference in the incidence of stroke between patients who underwent prophylactic carotid endarterectomy and those who did not, one would therefore need to recruit several thousand patients. This would almost certainly require the participation of several large centres and analysis of data would therefore be complicated by the inevitable introduction of uncontrolled variables.

In a retrospective review of 234 patients who underwent major cardiac or vascular surgery, Kartchner and McRae[20] identified 73 patients with a positive preoperative OPG. Thirty of these had undergone carotid endarterectomy before cardiovascular surgery and none had sustained a perioperative neurological deficit. In contrast, there were seven strokes among 41 patients (17%) who had undergone cardiovascular surgery alone. Unfortunately the indications of carotid endarterectomy were not reported in this non-randomized study while both symptomatic and asymptomatic patients were included.

Furlan and Craciun[22] retrospectively studied 144 patients who underwent coronary artery bypass in the presence of uncorrected but haemodynamically significant disease of the internal carotid artery. One hundred and fifteen patients had bilateral carotid stenoses and underwent carotid endarterectomy at the same time as coronary artery bypass. The contralateral stenosis remained uncorrected and served as a control. A further 29 patients with unilateral (18) or bilateral (11) carotid stenoses underwent coronary bypass without endarterectomy. The authors documented six perioperative infarcts (5.2%) in 115 cerebral hemispheres distal to carotid stenoses that had been corrected prior to coronary revascularization compared with only two infarcts (1.9%) in 106 hemispheres distal to stenoses that were not corrected. One infarct (2%) occurred in 49 hemispheres that were ipsilateral to complete occlusions of the internal carotid artery. They concluded that the risk of ipsilateral hemispheric stroke during coronary artery bypass was not reduced by prophylactic endarterectomy of haemodynamically significant disease. However, this study included both symptomatic and asymptomatic patients and their mean age was only 59 years.

Furthermore, in a later report from the same institution, Hertzer et al.[23] documented a significantly lower incidence of stroke in 71 patients with asymptomatic carotid disease who were randomly assigned to undergo synchronous combined carotid endarterectomy and coronary artery bypass than in 58 patients assigned to carotid endarterectomy after cardiac surgery. Mortality was similar in both groups (4.2% and 5.2% respectively) but there were significantly more strokes in the group undergoing staged operations (13.7%) than in those undergoing combined procedures (2.8%). However, half of these strokes occurred after delayed carotid endarterectomy and the stroke incidence after isolated cardiac surgery (6.9%) was not significantly greater than after synchronous combined operations. Thus, while this data may suggest an increased stroke risk if carotid endarterectomy is performed within a few days of coronary artery bypass, it does not support synchronous combined surgery in patients with asymptomatic carotid disease.

Brener et al.[6] found no significant difference in the incidence of perioperative neurological deficit when they compared 57 patients with carotid disease who underwent synchronous combined carotid and cardiac surgery (8.8%) with 64 patients who underwent cardiac surgery alone (6.2%). However, this non-randomized prospective study included a historical bias since combined procedures were performed more frequently during the first 3 years of the study while isolated procedures were performed almost exclusively during the latter 3 years. Further-more, closer inspection of the data reveals a marked difference between patients with patent carotid arteries (even if both were stenosed) and those with stenosis contralateral to an occlusion. If these groups are considered separately, the incidence of stroke was less after combined carotid and cardiac surgery (0 and 14% respectively) than after cardiac surgery alone (5.1% and 20%). However, irrespective of the surgery performed, stroke occurred significantly more frequently in patients with an occluded carotid artery. Whatever the flaws of this study, it clearly demonstrates the risks of cardiac surgery in the presence of an occluded carotid artery.

Schultz et al.[24] retrospectively compared 62 patients with *symptomatic* carotid disease who underwent both carotid endarterectomy and coronary bypass (46 staged, 16 synchronous) with 50 patients who had *asymptomatic* carotid bruits and haemodynamically significant stenosis on OPG or duplex scanning but underwent only coronary revascularization. They found no significant difference in operative mortality or incidence of perioperative stroke. Mortality was significantly higher (6.5 and 7.2% respectively) than in a random group of 200 patients who underwent isolated coronary artery bypass (1.5%) but these patients had a better clinical and cardiac status than patients with coexisting carotid disease. There were two perioperative strokes in the group who underwent both carotid endarterectomy and coronary artery bypass and both involved the ipsilateral hemisphere. In contrast, only one patient in the group with uncorrected carotid disease sustained a perioperative neurological deficit and this was a TIA which involved the contralateral hemisphere. It is difficult to refute the authors' claim that prophylactic endarterectomy would be unlikely to have reduced the incidence of neurological deficit in these patients since the single TIA was apparently unrelated to disease of the carotid artery. However, the incidence of neurological deficit during follow-up was significantly higher in this group. Seven patients (15%) sustained hemispheric strokes (four) or TIAs (three) during follow-up and six of these were ipsilateral to the uncorrected carotid stenosis. In contrast, only two patients (3.4%) who underwent both carotid and cardiac surgery sustained late strokes and only one of these involved the ipsilateral hemisphere. An increased incidence of late neurological events in patients with uncorrected carotid stenoses was also noted by Barnes et al.[25] but they remarked that such patients rarely presented with a completed stroke.

There has only been one study comparing isolated cardiac surgery with cardiac surgery *after* carotid endarterectomy in patients with asymptomatic disease of the carotid bifurcation. In a retrospective review of 539 patients screened with both OPG and duplex scanning, Faggioli et al.[7] identified 19 patients with asymptomatic high grade stenoses (including five with stenoses contralateral to an occluded carotid artery) who underwent carotid endarterectomy before coronary artery bypass. None experienced a perioperative neurological deficit. In contrast, 28 patients with asymptomatic high grade stenoses or unilateral occlusions underwent 'unprotected' cardiac surgery. Four developed hemispheric strokes ipsilateral to an uncorrected stenosis. Interestingly, all strokes developed between 2 and 9 days after operation. Unfortunately patients were not randomized and the numbers are too small to reach any firm conclusions regarding the benefit of prophylactic carotid endarterectomy.

There is thus little evidence to support prophylactic carotid endarterectomy in patients with asymptomatic stenoses who require cardiac surgery. There is some evidence to suggest that patients with bilateral stenoses or stenosis and contralateral occlusion may benefit from carotid surgery, particularly if they are elderly, but for the time being the decision to offer prophylactic endarterectomy remains a matter for clinical judgment. It may be that the results of ongoing trials into the management of asymptomatic carotid disease will render this question obsolete but it is perhaps more likely that this difficult problem will remain unresolved.

TIMING OF COMBINED OPERATIONS: SYNCHRONOUS *VS* STAGED

Myocardial infarction is the most important cause of perioperative death in patients undergoing carotid endarterecomy[26] and is significantly more frequent in patients with coexisting coronary artery disease.[27] There is thus an argument for performing synchronous combined carotid and cardiac surgery (in those patients thought to require both) so as to reduce the risk of cardiac death during or after isolated carotid endarterectomy in patients scheduled for staged procedures.[28,29] Although a number of reports attest to the relative safety of this approach,[30-32] none has yet demonstrated any clear advantage in patients with stable cardiac disease and many centres continue to recommend staged operations (carotid endarterectomy before cardiac surgery) in these patients.[33]

CONCLUSIONS

The risk of stroke during cardiac surgery is undoubtedly increased in patients with asymptomatic but haemodynamically significant disease of the internal carotid artery, particularly if this is bilateral or associated with contralateral occlusion. Carotid endarterectomy can be performed without significant increase in either morbidity or mortality but there is no good evidence that this will reduce the incidence of perioperative stroke and the management of these patients must therefore remain a matter for clinical judgment.

Our cardiac surgeons do not routinely screen for asymptomatic carotid disease and refer patients only if a bruit is noted on preoperative examination. These patients undergo careful neurological evaluation, duplex scanning and computed tomographic (CT) imaging of the brain. We generally perform prophylactic carotid endarterectomy in patients with haemodynamically significant stenoses of both internal carotid arteries or those with stenosis and contralateral occlusion (Fig. 2). We occasionally offer carotid endarterectomy to patients with evidence of silent ipsilateral hemispheric infarcts on CT or to those with a tight unilateral stenosis and evidence of poor collateralization through the Circle of Willis.

We prefer to perform carotid endarterectomy 7–10 days before cardiac surgery but occasionally perform synchronous combined procedures in patients with unstable angina or significant left main stem disease who are considered to be at increased risk of perioperative myocardial infarction. In these cases, endarterectomy is

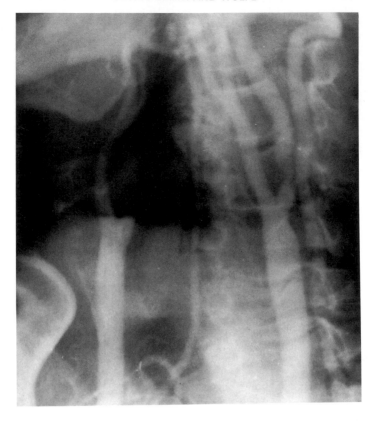

Fig. 2. Carotid angiogram (lateral oblique view) showing stenosis of the left internal carotid artery and occlusion of the right internal carotid artery. (Dept Radiology, St Mary's Hospital, London).

performed during saphenous vein harvest and prior to median sternotomy. In order to ensure haemostasis, we do not close the cervical wound until the patient is off bypass and heparin has been reversed.

REFERENCES

1. Balderman SC, Gutierrez IZ, Makala P, Bhayana JN, Gage AA: Non-invasive screening for asymptomatic carotid artery disease prior to cardiac operation. Experience with 500 patients. J Thorac Cardiovasc Surg 85: 427–433, 1983
2. Ivey TD: Combined carotid and coronary disease—a conservative strategy. J Vasc Surg 3: 687–689, 1986
3. Barnes RW, Liebman PR, Marszalek RN, Kirk CL, Goldman MH: The natural history of asymptomatic carotid disease in patients undergoing cardiovascular surgery. Surgery 90: 1075–1083, 1981
4. Turnipseed WD, Berkoff HA, Belzer FO: Postoperative stroke in cardiac and peripheral vascular disease. Ann Surg 192: 365–367, 1980
5. Breslau PJ, Fell G, Ivey TD et al.: Carotid arterial disease in patients undergoing coronary artery bypass operations. J Thorac Cardiovasc Surg 82: 765–767, 1981

6. Brener BJ, Brief DK, Alpert J: The risk of stroke in patients with asymptomatic carotid stenosis undergoing cardiac surgery: a follow up study. J Vasc Surg 5: 269–279, 1987
7. Faggioli GL, Curl GR, Ricotta JJ: The role of carotid screening before coronary artery bypass. J Vasc Surg 12: 724–731, 1990
8. Berens ES, Kouchoukos NT, Murphy SF, Wareing TH: Preoperative carotid artery screening in elderly patients undergoing cardiac surgery. J Vasc Surg 15: 313–323, 1992
9. Sotaniemi KA: Cerebral outcome after extracorporeal circulation: comparison between prospective and retrospective evaluations. Arch Neurol 40: 75–77, 1983
10. Jones EL, Craver JM, Michalik RA et al.: Combined carotid and coronary operations: when are they necessary? J Thorac Cardiovasc Surg 87: 7–16, 1984
11. Lee MC, Geiger J, Nicoloff D, Klassen AC, Resch JA: Cerebrovascular complications associated with coronary artery bypass procedure. Stroke 10: 107–109, 1979
12. Bojar RM, Najafi H, Delaria GA, Serry C, Goldin MD: Neurological complications of coronary revascularisation. Ann Thorac Surg 36: 427–432, 1983
13. Shaw PJ, Bates D, Cartlidge NEF et al.: Early neurological complications of coronary artery bypass surgery. Br Med J 291: 1384–1387, 1985
14. Breuer AC, Furlan AJ, Hanson MR et al.: Central nervous system complications of coronary artery bypass graft surgery: prospective analysis of 421 patients. Stroke 14: 682–687, 1983
15. Gardner TJ, Horneffer PJ, Manolio TA, Hoff SJ, Pearson TA: Major stroke after coronary artery bypass surgery: changing magnitude of the problem. J Vasc Surg 3: 684–687, 1986
16. McKibbon DW, Bulkley BH, Green WR, Gott VL, Hutchins GM: Fatal cerebral atheromatous embolisation after cardiopulmonary bypass. J Thorac Cardiovasc Surg 71: 741–745, 1976
17. Breuer AC, Franco I, Marzewski D, Soto-Velasco J: Left ventricular thrombi seen by ventriculography are a significant risk factor for stroke in open heart surgery. Ann Neurol 10: 103–104, 1981
18. Addonizio VP, Smith JB, Strauss JF, Colman RW, Edmunds LH: Thromboxane synthesis and platelet secretion during cardiopulmonary bypass with bubble oxygenator. J Thorac Cardiovasc Surg 79: 91–96, 1980
19. Chenoweth DE, Cooper SW, Hugh TW et al.: Complement activation during cardiopulmonary bypass. N Engl J Med 304: 497–503, 1981
20. Kartchner MM, McRae LP: Carotid occlusive disease as a risk factor in major cardiovascular surgery. Arch Surg 117: 1086–1088, 1982
21. Johnsson P, Algotsson L, Ryding E, Stahl E, Messeter K: Cardiopulmonary perfusion and cerebral blood flow in bilateral carotid artery disease. Ann Thorac Surg 51: 579–584, 1991
22. Furlan AJ, Craciun AR: Risk of stroke during coronary artery bypass graft surgery in patients with internal carotid artery disease documented by angiography. Stroke 16: 797–799, 1985
23. Hertzer NR, Loop FD, Beven EG, O'Hara PJ, Krajewski LP: Surgical staging for simultaneous coronary and carotid disease: a study including prospective randomisation. J Vasc Surg 9: 455–463, 1989
24. Schultz RD, Sterpetti AV, Feldhaus RJ: Early and late results in patients with carotid disease undergoing myocardial revascularisation. Ann Thorac Surg 45: 603–609, 1988
25. Barnes RW, Nix ML, Sansonetti D: Late outcome of untreated asymptomatic carotid disease following cardiovascular operations. J Vasc Surg 2: 843–849, 1985
26. Hertzer NR, Lees CD: Fatal myocardial infarction following carotid endarterectomy. Ann Surg 194: 212–218, 1981
27. Ennix CL, Lawrie GM, Morris GC: Improved results of carotid endarterectomy in patients with symptomatic coronary disease: an analysis of 1546 consecutive carotid operations. Stroke 10: 122–125, 1979
28. Bernhard VM, Johnson WD, Peterson JJ: Carotid artery stenosis: association with surgery for coronary artery disease. Arch Surg 105: 837–840, 1972
29. Hertzer NR, Loop FD, Taylor PC, Beven EG: Staged and combined surgical approach to simultaneous carotid and coronary vascular disease. Surgery 84: 803–811, 1978

30. Hertzer NR, Loop FD, Taylor PC, Beven EG: Combined myocardial revascularisation and carotid endarterectomy. J Thorac Cardiovasc Surg 85: 577–589, 1983
31. Babu SC, Shah PM, Singh BM et al.: Coexisting carotid stenosis in patients undergoing cardiac surgery: indications and guidelines for simultaneous operations. Am J Surg 150: 207–211, 1985
32. Cambria RP, Ivarsson BL, Akins CW et al.: Simultaneous carotid and coronary disease: safety of the combined approach. J Vasc Surg 9: 56–64, 1989
33. Perler BA, Burdick JF, Minken SL, Williams GM: Should we perform carotid endarterectomy synchronously with cardiac surgical procedures? J Vasc Surg 8: 402–409, 1988

Amaurosis Fugax, Risk Factors and Difference from Transient Ischaemic Attack

J. Buth, Gier, P. van Eerten, H. Hillen, J. Berendes, F. Lammers and C. Legein

In many surgical series that evaluate cerebrovascular reconstruction amaurosis fugax is considered combined with transient ischaemic attacks (TIA).[1-3] This may not be appropriate since the pathogenesis, natural history and the long-term results in patients with amaurosis fugax may differ from those with TIA. For example, in a recent survey of the Oxfordshire Community Stroke Project, late stroke rates in a group with TIA were better than those in patients with minor ischaemic strokes.[4] However, the difference in prognosis could be explained by the favourable prognosis of patients with amaurosis fugax among those with TIA. After eliminating the amaurosis fugax patients from the analysis, the risks of future stroke in the groups with TIA and minor stroke were similar. It is apparent that epidemiologic studies can be interpreted better if the data of the distinct diagnostic categories are considered.

The clinical picture of amaurosis fugax is characterized by episodes of monocular loss of vision with a sudden onset. This may involve a part or the entire field of vision. These attacks, which are painless, usually last for a few seconds or minutes, but rarely longer than 30 minutes. The usual mechanism of amaurosis fugax is embolic occlusion of the ophthalmic artery or its direct branch, the central retinal artery, that supplies blood to the retina. Visual loss occurs when the retinal bed becomes ischaemic. In amaurosis fugax the emboli quickly break up with resolution of the symptoms. If emboli do not disperse, retinal infarction with permanent loss of vision results. Carotid bifurcation disease is the most frequent single cause of transient retinal ischaemia, although vascular lesions anywhere upstream from the ophthalmic artery may produce emboli. In this review the outcome of conservative therapy and carotid endarterectomy for amaurosis fugax as reported in the literature will be outlined. In addition, a clinical series from our own institution will be presented and the results discussed.

AETIOLOGY OF TRANSIENT VASCULAR MONOCULAR BLINDNESS

Several causes of retinal ischaemia resulting in amaurosis fugax have been identified. These are detailed in a recent publication by the Amaurosis Fugax Study Group[5] and will be summarized here. Microemboli from the arteriosclerotic, stenotic or ulcerative carotid artery are the most frequent cause. Because of this ominous mechanism, amaurosis fugax is often considered a harbinger for future strokes and complete blindness caused by embolic central retinal arterial occlusion. Less frequently, cardiac valve abnormalities, aneurysms and myocardial infarction may cause embolization to the eye. Other sources for emboli may be in the great supra-aortic vessels, or the carotid siphon. If the internal carotid arteries are occluded embolization via the external carotid artery to the eye may occur.[6] Moreover, haemodynamic insufficiency because of extensive arteriosclerotic extracranial occlusive arterial disease may cause hypoperfusion of the retina. Cardiac failure, hypovolaemia, hyperviscosity of the blood and systemic diseases like lupus erythematosis may also produce ocular symptoms due to low perfusion pressure. Amaurosis fugax in patients under 45 years old was not found to be associated with smoking nor the use of oral anticonceptives.[7] However, many recent reports indicate a strong link between antiphospholipid antibodies and amaurosis fugax in young adults.[8-10] Finally in a substantial proportion of patients amaurosis fugax will be idiopathic.

DIFFERENTIAL DIAGNOSIS

Disorders that are important for the differential diagnosis are giant cell arteritis and vasospasm caused by retinal manifestations of migraine. Both conditions are characterized by headache or ipsilateral orbital pain. In the differential diagnosis homonymus haemianopsia caused by posterior optic chiasma processes also has to be considered.

Other syndromes that initially may be mistaken for amaurosis fugax should be ruled out. These conditions, which often result in permanent loss of vision either complete or partial, are:

    1. central ophthalmic artery or branch ophthalmic artery occlusions (Fig. 1) (often of embolic nature);

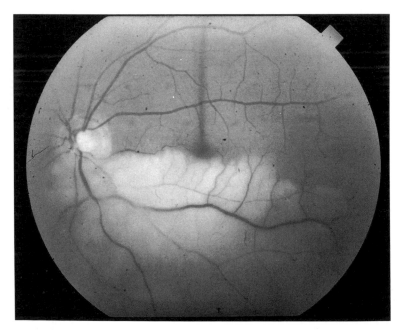

Fig. 1. Photograph of ocular fundus with branch retinal artery occlusion with area of retinal infarction.

2. the 'chronic ocular ischaemic syndrome', characterized by venous stasis retinopathy, retinal artery narrowing, rubeosis iridis with neovascularization or ischaemic glaucoma.[11-14]

Although several descriptions exist, this is not a clearly defined complex of syndromes. There is a fairly distinct relation between these conditions and the presence of extracranial cerebrovascular disease or narrowing of the ophthalmic artery branches;[12,15]

3. ischaemic optic neuropathy, caused by occlusion of the posterior ciliary arteries[16];
4. embolization of cholesterol crystals from the carotid bifurcation to the retina.

These emboli, that are characterized by a bright, yellow and glistening appearance can be observed by fundoscopy. These so-called Hollenhorst plaques have long been considered a warning sign for impending stroke or retinal infarction.[17] However, in recent reports it has been suggested that the presence of Hollenhorst plaques incidentally found at ophthalmic examination only was weakly related to later impairment of vision or the chance of ipsilateral TIA or stroke.[18,19]

RISK FACTORS IN AMAUROSIS FUGAX

Although amaurosis fugax is a disturbing symptom, most often the attacks are of short duration and are not very frequent.[20] The importance of recognizing amaurosis fugax is mainly that it is a marker of generalized atherosclerosis and cerebrovascular disease in particular. Poole and Ross Russell, in a study of 110 medically treated patients with amaurosis fugax, found a 6-year cumulative death rate of 21%, a figure similar to that in TIA patients.[21] Similarly, no differences were found in late mortality following carotid endarterectomy in amaurosis fugax and TIA groups.[22]

The annual stroke risk after onset of symptoms in conservatively treated amaurosis fugax patients is 2% overall, four times as high as in the normal population. However, when co-existing carotid artery narrowing or occlusion is present the stroke-rate is significantly higher.[21] Even moderate carotid artery narrowing is associated with an increased stroke-rate. This risk was 6.5% in patients with 0–19% carotid stenoses and 9.1% in 20–49% stenoses after a mean follow-up of 3 years.[23] The finding that the severity of carotid stenosis in conservatively treated patients with TIA (including amaurosis fugax) is directly related to the stroke-risk was recently confirmed in the European Carotid Surgery Trial.[2]

Retinal infarction resulting in permanent partial or complete blindness is a typical risk for the patient with amaurosis fugax. The annual rate for this sequela in medically treated series is approximately 3%.[21,24-26] On the other hand, retinal infarction often develops without warning symptoms. Only 16–25% of the patients with central, or branch retinal artery occlusion experienced episodes of amaurosis fugax prior to the permanent visual loss.[14,27] Nevertheless, episodes of transient blindness are an urgent indication for evaluation and treatment.

DIAGNOSTIC EVALUATION AND TREATMENT OPTIONS

To save time the work-up of these patients should be multidisciplinary from the beginning. Patients with amaurosis fugax initially are referred most often to an ophthalmologist. His examination will include fundoscopy not only to assess the presence of hypertensive or diabetic retinopathy but also to look for signs of retinal emboli and ischaemia. Cholesterol emboli can be distinguished visually from platelet-fibrin aggregates. Fluorescein angiography is an accessory method that can be used to demonstrate retinal arterial or venous thrombosis with or without infarction. Ocular pressures are measured to rule out glaucoma as a cause of complaints with vision. An internist performs a physical examination and evaluates blood chemistry and haematology values, parameters of the coagulation system and the lipid metabolism. If the patient is younger than 45 years or has a family history of thromboembolic events at an early age, screening for antiphospholipid antibodies, homocystinuria and anti-thrombi III deficiency is performed. A neurologist will look for signs of cerebral infarction and may request electroencephalography and computed tomography to identify a silent stroke. Duplex examination serves a critical role in avoiding unnecessary angiography. It is now generally recognized that duplex scanning has an excellent accuracy in the identification of significant cervical carotid artery lesions when compared with angiography.[28] In addition complete internal carotid artery occlusion can be discriminated reliably from stenoses.[29] The newer colour-flow imaging technique enhances the B-mode picture of the vessels and simplifies the examination.

If duplex scanning indicates no carotid bifurcation abnormalities, the possibility of a cardiac source for embolism must be evaluated by echocardiography. Identification of proximal arch venal lesion may require angiography. Transcranial Doppler examination may be used to assess the presence of narrowing at the level of the carotid siphon. If a 70% stenosis of the internal carotid artery is identified, angiographic confirmation is required. Recently criteria to discriminate stenoses of greater than 70% diameter reduction from smaller lesions have been refined.[30] If the duplex examination indicates a minor to moderate narrowing (<50% diameter reduction), antiplatelet therapy with aspirin is the most widely used treatment. Anticoagulants either prescribed alone or combined with platelet aggregation inhibiting medication are reserved for symptoms that are refractory to aspirin alone. Careful management of general atherosclerotic risk factors as the control of hypertension, diabetes mellitus and hyperlipidaemia, should be maintained by the department of internal medicine and/or the patients' General Practitioner. Patients are strongly advised to stop smoking. There is uncertainty about the therapeutic management of patients with 50–70% carotid stenoses. Additional factors such as whether there is an ulcerated aspect of the lesion, severity of the amaurosis fugax attacks and the patients' age and operating risk may be considered to determine what management to follow.

PATIENT SERIES

Combined evaluation of amaurosis fugax patients by internists, ophthalmologists, neurologists and vascular surgeons has been practised in the Catharina Hospital,

Eindhoven, The Netherlands since 1985. The publication of the recommendations for diagnostic and therapeutic management by the Amaurosis Fugax Working Group, which laid a strong emphasis on a multispeciality approach, caused us to evaluate retrospectively our own results in patients referred between 1985 and 1990. Only patients with a complete duplex examination of the carotid arteries were considered in this study. There were 97 patients of whom 65 had received medical treatment (MT) as described above. Thirty-two had undergone carotid endarterectomy (CE) and medical therapy (Table 1). Only patients with classic amaurosis fugax attacks were considered. Patients with symptoms caused by migraine or retinal artery or vein occlusion were excluded from this review. For the grading of carotid lesions we used the duplex criteria as developed by the group of the University of Washington.[28]

The characteristics and risk factors in patients with MT and CE are compared in Table 2. Previous cerebrovascular symptoms such as TIAs, strokes or vertebrobasilar symptoms occurred much more often in patients eligible for carotid endarterectomy. Similarly, previous cardiac or peripheral vascular symptoms were observed more often in the CE group. Dizziness, TIAs and stroke concomitant with the presenting amaurosis fugax as well as abnormalities established with the neurologic examination were found more often in the CE category. In contrast, abnormalities at fundoscopy were found with similar frequency in both treatment groups.

As expected, the majority of operated lesions were severe stenoses (>80% diameter reduction), whereas only two had a lesion of less than 50% diameter reduction (Table 3). These latter lesions were ulcerated. Conservative treatment was elected in a few significant lesions because of medical reasons or because of complete occlusion.

The recurrence rate of cerebrovascular symptoms during follow-up was comparable in both treatment categories (Table 4). In contrast, the rate of patients free of new cardiac and peripheral vascular symptoms combined was greater in patients receiving MT alone than in CE patients, i.e. 92% compared with 76% at 3 years of follow-up respectively (Fig. 2). If cardiac, peripheral vascular symptoms and death are considered as a combined end-point the differences were even greater, with at 3 years, 90% free of events in the MT group and 68% in the CE group ($p=0.004$).

These observations confirm previous observations that carotid endarterectomy reduces effectively the risk of stroke in the category with significant carotid artery disease to a level comparable with the rate seen in patients with mild carotid artery lesions, treated medically. However, the rate of new cardiac and peripheral vascular

Table 1. Characteristics in 97 patients with amaurosis fugax

Variable	No. of patients (%)
Average duration of symptoms months (range)	2.4 (0–72)
Average number of amaurosis fugax episodes (range)	2.3 (1–10)
Median age years (range)	64 (35–91)
Sex	
male	54 (56)
female	43 (44)
Therapeutic management	
medical treatment	65 (67)
carotid endarterectomy	32 (33)

Table 2.   Characteristics and risk factors in patients with MT and CE

Variable	Medical treatment (n = 65) % of patients	Carotid endarterectomy (n = 32) % of patients
Previous cerebrovascular symptoms	3	41
Previous cardiovascular symptoms	23	44
Previous peripheral vascular symptoms	6	22
Hypertension	48	41
Diabetes mellitus	2	25
Smoking	46	33
Concomitant cerebral symptoms	8	58
Neurologic, EEG or CT abnormalities	5	34
Fundoscopy abnormalities	26[a]	25

[a]Three patients had Hollenhorst plaques.

symptoms during follow-up is higher in the operatively treated category, possibly reflecting a more advanced stage of atherosclerosis.

AMAUROSIS FUGAX; DIFFERENCES FROM TIA

In most epidemiologic carotid artery studies amaurosis fugax is combined with TIA groups; 14–20% of all TIA patients have amaurosis fugax, as was observed in two large community studies.[4,31] However, the actual prevalence of amaurosis fugax may be as much as twice as high because this symptom is not as alarming as a hemispheric TIA, especially for elderly people.[31]

Several studies comparing amaurosis fugax and TIA have demonstrated distinct differences in pathogenesis, natural history and long-term results after carotid endarterectomy. Bernstein and Dilley found in twelve collected series that stenosis of the ipsilateral carotid artery was strongly associated with amaurosis fugax.[22] An average of 50% of the patients studied had significant carotid artery disease. Selection factors may account for a somewhat low 35% of significant carotid lesions in our series. The use of duplex as a non-invasive screening test may have resulted in an increased number of patients without significant extracranial vascular disease. Nevertheless the prevalence of extracranial carotid disease in patients with TIA is considerably lower and ranges from 30 to 50%.[32-34] In one series comparing angiographic studies, patients presenting with amaurosis fugax showed a predominance

Table 3.   Severity of carotid artery stenosis ipsilateral to side of amaurosis fugax

Management	< 15% No. of patients (%)	15–49% No. of patients (%)	50–79% No. of patients (%)	80–99% No. of patients (%)	Occlusion No. of patients (%)
Medical treatment (n = 65)	50 (51)	7 (11)	1 (2)	3 (5)	4 (6)
Carotid endarterectomy (n = 32)	—	2 (6)	3 (9)	27 (84)	—

[a]Percentage diameter reduction.

Table 4. Occurrence of cerebrovascular symptoms during follow-up

Symptoms	Medical treatment (n = 65) No. of patients	Carotid endarterectomy (n = 32) No. of patients
Amaurosis fugax	8 (12)	1 (3)
TIA	3 (5)	2 (6)
CVA	2 (3)	2 (6)
All symptoms	13 (20)	5 (16)

of extracranial carotid disease, whereas intracranial vessel disease was more common in TIA patients.[33] The hypothesis from these authors was that amaurosis fugax in most cases is caused by emboli from the carotid system, whereas hemispheric TIAs are caused by more heterogeneous mechanisms.

An important study by Grigg and associates presented a provocative hypothesis on the pathogenesis of transient monocular blindness.[35] These authors postulated that showers of small emboli resulting in multiple silent minute infarctions, detectable on CT as atrophy, would be the mechanism by which amaurosis fugax is produced. Because of these small size platelet aggregates, these emboli do not produce hemispheric symptoms, but only symptoms in the very sensitive retina. In TIA and stroke the pattern may be different in that larger emboli produce larger symptomatic hemispheric infarctions. This may suggest that different emboli are formed in different types of arterial lesions. This theory can be used to replace the common idea of laminar blood flow and selective embolization in the carotid and ophthalmic artery system. More clinical and cerebral imaging data are needed to confirm this theory.

Natural history studies indicate a lower annual stroke rate in patients with amaurosis fugax compared with 5–10% reported in patients with TIA. In combined series, stroke rates of approximately 2% per year following the onset of the eye symptoms have been reported.[21,24,32,34] Most of these studies however do not relate the risk of stroke

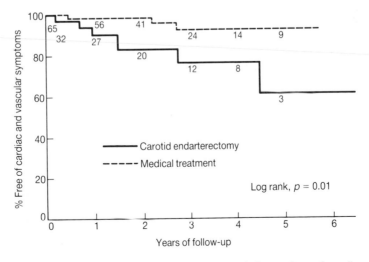

Fig. 2. Cumulative percentage of patients with amaurosis fugax free of cardiac or peripheral vascular symptoms during follow-up.

with the severity of the carotid bifurcation disease. Poole and Ross Russell observed an annual stroke rate approaching 5% per year in patients with significant carotid stenosis, which is 10 times as high as in amaurosis fugax patients with normal angiograms.[21] Other studies have also suggested a relatively high incidence of stroke with severe carotid disease.[24,36] Bernstein and Dilley concluded from this that amaurosis fugax, if combined with significant carotid disease perhaps had a greater propensity for later stroke than hemispheric ischaemic episodes.[22] In addition, these authors demonstrated superior late results of carotid endarterectomy in patients with amaurosis fugax compared with patients operated for TIA in the same period. Considering the high stroke rate in untreated high grade carotid lesions with ocular transient ischaemia, this condition appears to be a particularly favourable indication for carotid endarterectomy.

CONCLUSION

The diagnostic evaluation in amaurosis fugax is optimally performed with a team including a neurologist, an internist, an ophthalmologist and a vascular surgeon. High quality duplex scanning is mandatory in all patients because temporary loss of vision due to extracranial carotid artery disease is the most frequent single cause of amaurosis fugax. If non-invasive testing shows a stenosis with a diameter reduction greater than 70%, carotid endarterectomy is usually indicated since medical treatment alone carries a high risk of stroke and retinal infarction. If the internal carotid artery is completely occluded or if lesions are absent or non-significant, surgery is not indicated. In these cases, antiplatelet aggregation therapy and management of associated risk factors for vascular disease are the mainstays of management.

REFERENCES

1. Fields WS, Maslenikow V, Meyer J: Joint study of extracranial arterial occlusions. J Am Med Ass 211: 1973–2003, 1970
2. European Carotid Surgery Trialists' Collaborative Group: MRC European carotid surgery trial: interim results for symptomatic patients with severe (70–90%) or with mild (0–29%) carotid stenosis. Lancet 337: 1235–1243, 1991
3. North American symptomatic carotid endarterectomy trial collaborators: Beneficial effect of carotid endarterectomy in symptomatic patients with high-grade carotid stenosis. N Engl J Med 325: 445–453, 1991
4. Dennis MS, Bamford JM, Sandercock PAG, Warlow CP: A comparison of risk factors and prognosis for transient ischemic attacks and minor ischemic strokes. The Oxford community stroke project. Stroke 20: 1494–1499, 1989
5. The Amaurosis Fugax Study Group: Current management of amaurosis fugax. Stroke 21: 201–208, 1990
6. Cote R, Barnett HJM, Taylor DW: Internal carotid occlusion: A prospective study. Stroke 14: 898–906, 1983
7. Tippin J, Corbett JJ: Amaurosis fugax and ocular infarction in adolescents and young adults. Ann Neurol 26: 69–77, 1989
8. Digre KB. Amaurosis fugax associated with antiphospholipid antibodies. Ann Neurol 25: 228–232, 1989
9. Valesini G, Priori R, Luan FL, Falco M, Balsano F: Amaurosis fugax and antiphospholipid antibodies. Lancet 336: 374, 1990

10. Hess DC: Stroke associated with antiphospholipid antibodies. Stroke 23 suppl. 1: 1,23–28, 1992
11. Young LHY, Appen RE: Ischemic oculopathy. A manifestation of carotid artery disease. Arch Neurol 38: 358–361, 1981
12. Berguer R: Idiopathic ischemic syndromes of the retina and optic nerve and their carotid origin. J Vasc Surg 2: 649–653, 1985
13. Rubin J, McIntyre KM, Lukens MC, Plecha EJ, Bernhard VM: Carotid endarterectomy for chronic retinal ischemia. Surg Gyn Obstetr 171: 497–501, 1990
14. Kirschner RL, Green RM, Searl SS, DeWeese JA: Ocular manifestations of carotid artery atheroma. J Vasc Surg 2: 850–853, 1985
15. Jorgenson R, Towne JB, Kay M, Bandyk G: Monocular ischemia. The influence of carotid atherosclerosis versus primary ocular disease on prognosis. Surgery 104: 507–511, 1988
16. Eagling EM, Sanders MD, Miller SJH: Ischemic papillopathy. Clinical and fluorescein angiographic review of forty cases. Br J Ophthalmol 58: 990–1008, 1974
17. Hollenhorst RW: Ocular manifestations of insufficiency or thrombosis of the internal carotid artery. Trans Am Ophthalmol Soc 56: 474–506, 1958
18. Bunt TJ: The clinical significance of asymptomatic Hollenhorst plaque. J Vasc Surg 4: 559–562, 1986
19. Schwarcz TH, Eton D, Ellenby MI et al.: Hollenhorst plaques: Retinal manifestations and the role of carotid endarterectomy: J Vasc Surg 11: 635–641, 1990
20. Ross Russell RW: Observations on the retinal blood vessels in monocular blindness. Lancet ii: 1422–1428, 1961
21. Poole CJM, Ross Russell RW: Mortality and stroke after amaurosis fugax. J Neurol Neurosurg Psychiatry 48: 902–905, 1985
22. Bernstein EF, Dilley RB: Late results after carotid endarterectomy for amaurosis fugax. J Vasc Surg 6: 333–340, 1987
23. Torem S, Rossman ME, Schneider PA et al.: The natural history of amaurosis fugax with minor degrees of internal carotid artery stenosis. Ann Vasc Surg 4: 46–51, 1990
24. Marshall J, Meadows S: The natural history of amaurosis fugax. Brain 91: 419–434, 1968
25. Hooshmand H, Vines FS, Lee HM, Grindal A: Amaurosis fugax: Diagnostic and therapeutic aspects. Stroke 5: 643–647, 1974
26. Parkin PJ, Kendall BE, Marshall J, McDonald WI: Amaurosis fugax some aspects of its management. J Neurol Neurosurg Psychiatry 45: 1–6, 1982
27. Wilson LA, Warlow CP, Ross Russell RW: Cardiovascular disease in patients with retinal artery occlusion. Lancet i: 292–294, 1979
28. Taylor DC, Strandness DE: Carotid artery duplex scanning. J Clin Ultrasound 15: 635–644, 1987
29. Mattos MA, Hodgson KJ, Ramsey DE, Barkmeier LD, Sumner DS: Identifying total carotid occlusion with colour flow duplex scanning. Eur J Vasc Surg 2: 204–210, 1992
30. Moneta GL, Edwards JM, Lee RW et al.: Correlation of North American Symptomatic Carotid Endarterectomy Trial definition of 70–99% internal carotid stenosis with duplex criteria. J Vasc Surg 15: 1063–1064, 1992
31. Andersen CU, Marquardsen J, Mikkelsen B et al.: Amaurosis fugax in a Danish community. A prospective study. Stroke 19: 196–199, 1988
32. Mohr JP: Transient ischemic attacks and the prevention of strokes. N Engl J Med 299: 93–95, 1978
33. Harrison MJG, Marshall J: Arteriographic comparison of amaurosis fugax and hemispheric transient ischaemic attacks. Stroke 16: 795–797, 1985
34. Hurwitz BJ, Heyman A, Wilkinson BE, Haynes CS, Utley CM: Comparison of amaurosis fugax and transient cerebral ischemia: A prospective clinical and arteriographic study. Ann Neurol 18: 698–704, 1985
35. Grigg MJ, Papadakis K, Nicolaides AN et al.: The significance of cerebral infarction and atrophy in patients with amaurosis fugax and transient ischemic attacks in relation to internal carotid artery stenosis: A preliminary report. J Vasc Surg 7: 215–222, 1988
36. Pfaffenbach DD, Hollenhorst RW: Morbidity and survivorship of patients with embolic cholesterol crystals in the ocular fundus. Am J Ophthalmol 75: 66–72, 1973

TIMING OF CAROTID SURGERY

Cerebral Oximetry in Carotid Endarterectomy and Acute Stroke

Ian M. Williams and Charles McCollum

Carotid endarterectomy is now practised by over 110 surgeons in the UK performing a total of over 1400 operations each year or 24 per million.[1] In the USA, the comparable rate is 360 carotid endarterectomies per million per year: a total of 72 000 per year. Prior to the publication of European and North American carotid surgery trials in symptomatic patients it was not clear whether surgeons in the UK were performing too few or USA surgeons performing too many carotid procedures. The results of these two studies with definite reduction in stroke following carotid endarterectomy in patients with stenoses in excess of 70% suggests that many more carotid endarterectomies will be done in the future.[2,3]

Cerebral protection during carotid clamping is of paramount importance in carotid endarterectomy. In the absence of an adequate measure for cerebral perfusion and oxygen delivery the use of shunting has been little better than arbitrary. Of the 110 surgeons in a UK survey, 38% always used a shunt, 59% sometimes or rarely used one, and 3% never used one.[4]

Of the surgeons who occasionally used a shunt, nearly 60% made their decision based on the stump or back pressure following external and common carotid clamping, 11% used electroencephalographic changes as their criteria for shunting and 4.6% performed the procedure under local anaesthetic. The remaining 18% used other non-specified criteria to decide when to shunt or not.

The need for a reliable measure of cerebral perfusion is perhaps even greater in the diagnosis of acute stroke. Cerebrovascular accidents now account for approximately 11% of all deaths throughout Europe and the USA. Many more people are severely debilitated and as a result lose their independence in the declining years of their lives. Computed tomographic (CT) scanning and, more recently, nuclear magnetic resonance imaging have allowed precise diagnosis of brain lesion so that we now recognize that over two-thirds of such strokes are due to cerebral infarction with the majority of these due to extracranial arterial disease.

Although our main research effort should be directed towards the diagnosis and prophylactic treatment of conditions leading to stroke there remains the opportunity to limit the severity of stroke if ischaemic brain could be identified. To date, only positron emission tomography allows us to identify the high extraction of oxygen from circulating blood that is typical of ischaemic yet still viable brain. We now need a method which is more accessible if we are to identify those patients with acute stroke in whom restoration of blood flow may rescue ischaemic brain tissue and improve subsequent neurological function.

MEASURES OF CEREBRAL PERFUSION

Electroencephalography (EEG) is still used in cerebral monitoring and reflects the electrical activity of the cerebral cortex which is derived from the postsynaptic potentials. When cerebral oxygenation falls with a fall in the cerebral blood flow of 20 ml per 100 g brain per minute then there will be a slowing of the EEG with reduced frequency and lower amplitude waves. Below 15 ml per 100 g brain per minute the EEG becomes flat.[5] These criteria may be used to trigger intervention to prevent further cerebral ischaemia. Principally, EEG detects changes in the superficial layers of the cortex and hence may fail to detect significant deeper subcortical or internal capsular ischaemia. Direct measurements of cerebral blood flow may be performed by using Xenon washout techniques.[6,7] These techniques which are particularly sensitive to the superficial cortical blood flow may ignore deeper ischaemic areas and hence are not suitable for continuous monitoring of cerebral perfusion.

Transcranial Doppler may be used to measure middle cerebral artery blood flow during surgery.[8-12] This is completely non-invasive and continuously monitors the linear velocity in the middle cerebral artery throughout the operative period. It is still not a reliable measure of cerebral perfusion as the quality of collateral blood flow within the brain substance cannot be assessed and high velocity readings would be detected where the middle cerebral artery is narrowed by disease. The Doppler probe is placed on the ipsilateral side to the carotid endarterectomy over the temporal bone above the zygomatic arch and 1 cm anterior to the tragus of the ear. Doppler probe position profoundly affects the middle cerebral signal.[13] There are no widely agreed criteria for shunting based on transcranial Doppler velocity.

INDICATIONS FOR CAROTID SHUNTING

Back pressure measurement was first proposed by Moore and Hall as an index to the use of a shunt.[14] The recommended safe pressure before shunting is necessary has been reported throughout a range from as low as 25 mmHg up to 70 mmHg.[15-20] Back or stump pressure readings are also influenced by anaesthetic agents, disease in the Circle of Willis, cerebral resistance, intracranial pressure and the systemic arterial blood pressure.

Although a carefully inserted shunt should carry very little risk there are disadvantages in a policy of always shunting:
1. A small calibre or diseased internal carotid artery may cause difficult insertion of the shunt with resulting intimal damage or dissection.
2. Difficulty visualizing the proximal and distal limits of the plaque during endarterectomy.
3. A theoretical risk of plaque embolization or air/thrombus emboli during insertion or removal.
4. Peri shunt thrombosis.
5. Kinking or impinging directly on the artery wall during the procedure.
6. Malposition or malfunction.

The decision to shunt or not could also be influenced by the degree of stenosis in the contralateral carotid artery as a complete occlusion may sway a surgeon into prophylactic shunting. We previously exercised a policy of selectively inserting a Javid shunt whenever the internal carotid stump pressure falls rapidly towards 50 mmHg or was non-pulsatile, without waiting for final equilibration. If a shunt is not used, a clearer operative field and easier access to the distal edge of the intimal plaque is afforded allowing a complete endarterectomy to be performed under direct vision.

The blood supply to the brain is derived from the carotid and vertebral arteries, with extensive intracranial anastomoses via the Circle of Willis. Normally there is little collateral blood supply within the brain substance. Attempts to identify collaterals within the brain by arteriography only show anatomical abnormalities up to the Circle of Willis and fail to give useful information on the redistribution of blood flow due to disease or following cross-clamping the carotid artery. These existing techniques give information about arterial blood velocity, carotid artery back pressure and the cerebral electrical activity, but none provided reliable data on the adequacy of cerebral perfusion or oxygenation.

NEAR INFRA-RED CEREBRAL OXIMETRY

Cerebral oximetry is a non-invasive method of continuously monitoring the intracerebral oxygen saturation using spectroscopy of reflected near infra-red light with an optimal wavelength maximally to penetrate human tissues.[21-27] The wavelength chosen penetrates the human head to a depth of approximately 2.5 cm. The brain contains approximately 600–1000 mg haemoglobin/100 g tissue and the attenuation of infra-red light can be attributed to the well characterized light absorbing chromophores oxy- and deoxyhaemoglobin.[26] The attenuated light is reflected in a parabola and the instrument measures the oxygen saturation within the compartment being measured (Fig. 1).[28] The instrument we employ is the Cerebral Oximeter INVOS 3100 (Somanetics Corp., Troy, MI, USA). The light source is a broad band high intensity light and the infra-red light it generates is directed through filters to generate small discrete wavebands in the near infra-red spectrum (650–1100 nm).

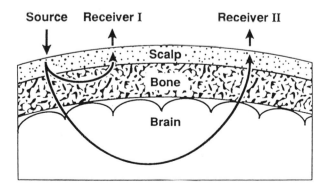

Fig. 1.   Parabolic reflection of attenuated infra-fred light to sensors.

The probe consists of the light source transmitter and two light receiving sensors. These are situated 10 and 25 mm from the light source. The transmitter and two sensors are encased within an adhesive, flexible plastic holder providing easy attachment to the scalp. The sensor nearer to the transmitter detects photons which have passed through the scalp and cranium; the farthest sensor detects photons which passed through both the superficial tissues and cerebral substance. At a 10 mm separation between source and sensor, photons can penetrate up to 7.0 mm and at 30 mm separation approximately 25 mm of tissue penetration occurs. The probe can monitor continuously information from a cerebral blood volume of approximately 1.0 ml.[25] Hence the oximeter's processor then uses the shallow signal to correct the deeper signal removing the effects of extracerebral absorption. The corrected signal is then processed to produce a number reflecting oxygen saturation of the haemoglobin in the microvasculature of the measured region of the brain.

The accuracy of reflected near infra-red light spectroscopy was validated by differential uptake when a small bolus of the infra-red attenuating tracer indocyanine green was injected into the internal carotid artery whilst the external carotid artery was occluded. Infra-red spectroscopy was carried out and a series of measurements was then made with the transit of the infra-red absorber through the cerebral vasculature calculated. The superficial channel showed no significant increase in optical density, but the deep channel showed a time-related increase in optical density consistent with the flow into and out of the cerebral vasculature, thus showing the selectivity of the sensory probes.[26]

Between 70 and 75% of the blood volume within the brain substance is venous and cerebral oximeter readings correlate closely with the oxygen saturation of blood in the jugular bulb. Hence the reading obtained is also a measure of the oxygen extraction of cerebral blood after it has passed through the cerebral microcirculation.

CEREBRAL OXIMETRY IN CAROTID SURGERY

During carotid endarterectomy the cerebral oximetry probe was placed on the forehead on the side ipsilateral to surgery (Fig. 2). The transcranial Doppler (TCD) was also secured and focused on the middle cerebral artery just before indication of anaesthesia so that baseline measurements might be recorded. During surgery the arterial CO_2 was maintained at 36–40 mmHg to reduce the changes in cerebral vascular tone. We have now performed 22 elective endarterectomies with the above system of monitoring (Fig. 3). Once the common, external and internal carotid arteries were mobilized, the carotid back pressure (stump pressure) was recorded following clamping of the external and common carotid arteries. We performed 22 elective endarterectomies with the above system of monitoring; in 12 shunting was required, based on the fall in the stump pressure.

The mean (SE mean) percentage cerebral saturation of oxygen (CsO_2) was 71.7% (1.8%) immediately prior to cross-clamping with a corresponding mean TCD velocity in the middle cerebral artery of 41.2 cm/s.[3,7] On applying the cross-clamp the mean fall in CsO_2 was 2.71 (0.88)% which compares with a fall of 28.0 (4.5) cm/s in mean TCD velocity. The mean fall in the TCD mean velocity in patients with a fall in CsO_2

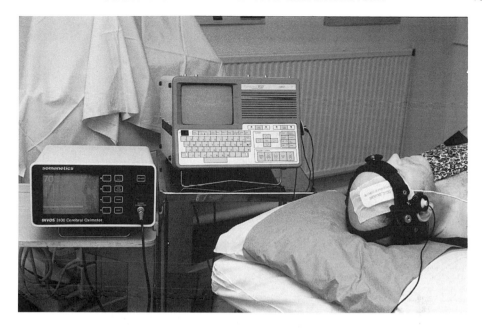

Fig. 2. Cerebral oximeter + transcranial Doppler probes in position.

of less than 5% was 29 cm/s (52.5%), which compares with a fall of 67 cm/s (83.1%) when the fall in CsO_2 was >5% ($p<0.01$) (Fig. 4).

A significant linear relationship was found between the changes in the two measures on cross-clamping ($r=0.62$, $p=0.002$) (Fig. 5). Calculated from the line of best fit on this correlation, patients experiencing a fall of 5% or more in the CsO_2 would show a fall of at least 38 cm/s in the mean TCD velocity. The mean stump pressure was 48.82 (16.53) and a significant correlation was found between the stump pressure and the mean TCD velocity following carotid cross-clamping ($r=0.533$, $p=0.005$).

Throughout surgery, the within patient changes in CsO_2 correlated significantly with the changes in the TCD mean velocity ($r=0.25$, $p=0.0013$) and with the arterial blood pressure ($r=0.406$, $p<0.001$).

Two patients showed no change in the oximetry reading on cross-clamping the common carotid artery despite marked falls in TCD flow velocity. This may have been due to loss of the TCD signal by disturbing the Doppler probe or to collateral blood flow redistributing blood to the ipsilateral hemisphere other than through the middle cerebral artery. Oximetry readings which fall more than 5% on application of the cross-clamp indicate poor collaterals unable to meet the metabolic demands of the brain resulting in increased oxygen extraction.

Transcranial Doppler measures blood flow in a single artery whereas the cerebral oximeter measures oxygenation extraction in the total blood volume of a small area of the brain. Our results demonstrate that a fall in the middle cerebral artery flow velocity does not always result in a drop in CsO_2 due to pre-existing collaterals supplies or newly recruited collaterals.[28] However, there was a close relationship between more significant falls in CsO_2 and changes in the middle cerebral blood flow on the TCD. The stump pressure correlated only poorly with the CsO_2.

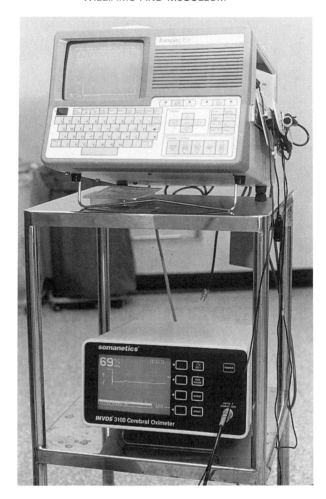

Fig. 3. Cerebral oximeter + transcranial Doppler monitors in theatre easily visualized by the anaesthetist and surgeon.

CEREBRAL OXIMETRY IN ACUTE STROKE

In many patients suffering acute cerebral infarction the initial symptoms may not be devastating but may progressively deteriorate or fluctuate with time. Fluctuating neurological signs clearly indicate that there is an ischaemic area of viable brain which must therefore be capable of recovery. In such cases, increased oxygen extraction has been demonstrated in large areas of the brain by positron emission tomography. The oxygen extraction ratio increases immediately postinfarct associated with the decreased blood flow. With time, this ratio decreases and gradually approaches normality.[29]

The use of the oximeter in the monitoring of acute strokes is very much in its infancy. We have assessed acute stroke patients with both the TCD and the cerebral

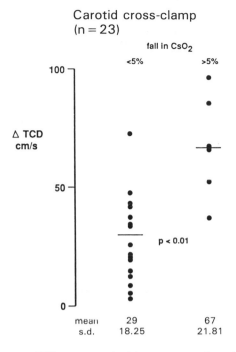

Fig. 4. Change in the mean TCD compared with a greater or less than 5% drop in the cerebral oxygenation.

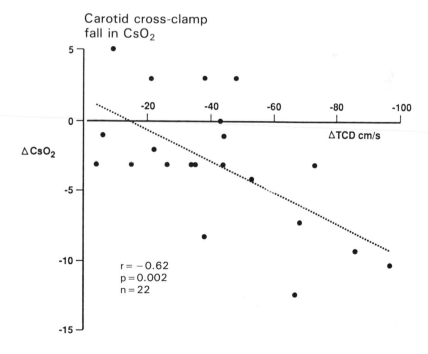

Fig. 5. Change in mean TCD compared with the change in CsO_2 on carotid cross-clamping.

oximeter. All patients with acute stroke underwent CT scanning to rule out haemorrhage and to localize the anatomical region of the infarct. Duplex scanning of their carotid arteries and transcranial Doppler measurements of the middle cerebral arteries was also performed.

The cerebral oximetry probe was initially positioned over the ipsilateral forehead ignoring the anatomical location of the infarct as demonstrated by the CT scan. Our early results in seven acute stroke patients demonstrated that the CsO_2 over the frontal lobes remains constant following a cerebrovascular accident.

As an example, a 56-year-old man was admitted to a neighbouring hospital with a 7-day history of intermittent weakness in his right leg and arm; however on the day of admission this weakness became far worse. A duplex scan of his carotid arteries showed a complete occlusion of his left internal carotid artery and a 95% stenosis on the right. CsO_2 was 66% over the frontal lobe and remained unchanged over the ensuing 3 days. The mean TCD velocity in the middle cerebral artery was 23 cm/s on the right and 14 cm/s on the left. These were repeated on the following 3 days and showed no significant changes. His condition continued to worsen and ultimately he was left with a dense right hemiparesis. His TCD mean velocities consistently demonstrated reduced flow on the left side compared with the right.

Another patient aged 46 years was admitted with uncontrolled hypertension and with fluctuating neurological signs. He was diagnosed as having coarctation of the aorta and the oximetry probe was placed onto his right frontal area. During the night there was a sudden drop in the oximetry tracing from 64% to 51% and subsequently a further decline over 3 hours to only 36%. A subsequent CT scan revealed a massive subarachnoid haemorrhage. On TCD, we found difficulty identifying the middle cerebral arteries which appeared to have a peak flow of only 18 cm/s. From now on we intend to measure CsO_2 over the appropriate region of the brain as demonstrated by the CT scan. This may give us a better indication of the cerebral oxygenation over the actual infarct site.

THE FUTURE POTENTIAL OF CEREBRAL OXIMETRY

We have demonstrated that the cerebral oximeter may be used in monitoring perfusion of the brain during carotid surgery. Although it does take 30–60 seconds for the CsO_2 to fall following cross-clamping, the oximeter is relatively inexpensive and very easy to use. Transcranial Doppler has the advantage of immediately detecting changes in the velocity of middle cerebral blood flow on cross-clamping, but requires considerable technical expertise with the continuous risk of probe displacement during surgery resulting in a deterioration or complete loss of the signal. Experience of both instruments has demonstrated to us that the surgeon may take a little longer than previously thought in reaching a decision on shunting. Furthermore, we now believe that he can afford to take greater care over flushing the artery and absolutely ensuring that embolization does not occur as he has at least 4–5 minutes before cerebral oxygen saturation falls to a critical level. If other units have a similar experience with this instrument, cerebral oximetry may become the optimal method of monitoring perfusion of the brain during carotid surgery. We do not yet have sufficient information on the potential of cerebral oximetry in diagnosing treatable ischaemia of the brain during acute or progressing stroke.

Light reflective cerebral oximetry clearly may have wide ranging applications beyond those of assessing patients with cerebrovascular disease. It offers, for the first time, the opportunity to monitor continuously the perfusion and oxygenation of brain tissue using a simple and inexpensive instrument. Potential applications include the monitoring of patients on intensive care, undergoing major surgery such as cardiopulmonary bypass and following head injury. The combination of transcranial Doppler giving information on the cerebral blood flow and a measure of cerebral blood oxygen saturation giving an indication of oxygen extraction offers new opportunities in understanding the pathophysiology of brain injury due to either ischaemia or hypoxia.

REFERENCES

1. Murie JA, Morris PJ: Carotid endarterectomy in Great Britain and Ireland: trends and current practice. Br J Surg 78: 397–400, 1991
2. European Carotid Surgery Trialists Collaborative Group: MRC European Carotid Surgery Trial: interim results for symptomatic patients with severe (70–99) or with mild (0–29%) carotid stenosis. Lancet 337: 1235–1241, 1991
3. North American Symptomatic Carotid Endarterectomy Trial Collaborators: Beneficial effect of carotid endarterectomy in symptomatic patients with high grade stenosis. N Engl J Med 325: 445–453, 1991
4. Naylor AR, Bell PRF, Ruckley CV: Monitoring and cerebral protection during carotid endarterectomy. Br J Surg 79: 735–741, 1992
5. O'Sullivan K, Cunningham AJ: Intraoperative cerebral ischaemia. Br J Hosp Med 42: 286–296, 1989
6. Sundt TM: Correlation of cerebral blood flow measurements and continuous electroencephalography during carotid endarterectomy and risk–benefit ratio of shunting. In Cerebral Blood Flow: Physiologic and Clinical Aspects, Woods J (Ed.). New York: McGraw Hill, pp 679–692, 1987
7. Gibbs JM, Wise RJ, Legg NJ: Positron emission tomography studies in acute stroke and in patients with carotid occlusion: pathophysiology of cerebral ischaemia and diminished perfusion reserve. In Progress in Stroke Research Vol. 2, Greenhalgh RM, Rose FC (Eds). London: Pitman Medical, pp 214–226, 1983
8. Aaslid R, Markwalder TM, Nomes H: Noninvasive transcranial Doppler ultrasound recording of flow velocity in the basal cerebral arteries. J Neurosurg 57: 769–774, 1982
9. Padayachee TS, Gosling RG, Bishop CC et al.: Transcranial Doppler assessment of cerebral collateral during carotid endarterectomy. Br J Surg 74: 260–262, 1987
10. Padayachee TS, Gosling RG, Bishop CC et al.: Monitoring middle cerebral artery blood velocity during carotid endarterectomy. Br J Surg 73: 98–100, 1986
11. Bernstein EF: Role of transcranial Doppler in carotid surgery. Surg Clin N Am 70: 225–234, 1990
12. Chiesa R, Minicucci F, Melissano G et al.: The role of transcranial Doppler in carotid artery surgery. Eur J Vasc Surg 6: 211–216, 1992
13. Bass A, Krupski WC, Schneider PA et al.: Intraoperative transcranial Doppler: Limitations of the method. J Vasc Surg 10: 549–553, 1989
14. Moore WS, Hall AD: Carotid artery back pressure. A test of cerebral tolerance to temporary carotid occlusion. Arch Surg 99: 702–710, 1969
15. Naylor AR, Wildsmith JAW, McClure J et al.: Transcranial Doppler monitoring during carotid endarterectomy. Br J Surg 78: 1264–1268, 1991

16. Jorgensen LG, Schroeder TV: Transcranial Doppler for detection of cerebral ischaemia during carotid endorterectomy
17. Gnander DA, Wang N, Comunale FL, Reile DA: Carotid artery stump pressure: how reliable is it in predicting the need for a shunt? Ann Vasc Surg 3: 313–317, 1989
18. Hays RJ, Levinson SA, Wylie EJ: Intraoperative measurement of carotid back pressure as a guide to operative management of carotid endarterectomy. Surgery 72: 953–960, 1972
19. Browse NL, Ross-Russel AO: Carotid endarterectomy and the Javid shunt: the early results of 215 consecutive operations for transient ischaemic attacks. Br J Surg 71: 53–57, 1984
20. Archie JP. Technique and clinical results of carotid stump back pressure to determine selective shunting during carotid endarterectomy. J Vasc Surg 13: 319–327, 1991
21. Brazy J, Lewis DV, Mitruck MH et al.: Non-invasive monitoring of cerebral oxygenation in pre-term infants: Preliminary observations. Paediatrics 75: 217–225, 1985
22. McCormick PW: Measurement of regional cerebrovascular haemoglobin oxygen saturation in cats using optical spectroscopy. Neurol Res 13: 65–70, 1991
23. Frost EAM: Cerebrovascular disease. Curr Opin Anaesthesiol 4: 639–644, 1991
24. McCormick PW: Monitoring cerebral oxygen delivery and hemodynamics. Curr Opin Anaesthesiol 4: 657–661, 1991
25. McCormick PW, Stewart M, Goetting MG et al.: Regional cerebrovascular oxygen saturation measured by optical spectroscopy in humans. Stroke 22: 596–602, 1991
26. McCormick PW, Stewart M, Goetting MG et al.: Noninvasive cerebral optical spectroscopy for monitoring cerebral oxygen delivery and haemodynamics. Critical Care Med 19: 89–97, 1991
27. McCormick PW, Stewart M, Dujovny M et al.: Clinical application of diffuse near infrared transmission spectroscopy to measure cerebral oxygen metabolism. Hospimedics 39–47, 1990
28. Schridner PA: Transcranial Doppler in the management of extracranial vascular disease: Implications in diagnosis and monitoring. J Vasc Surg 7: 223–231, 1988
29. Charlesworth D, Underwood CJ: The measurement of carotid artery back pressure. An unresolved problem. In Progress in Stroke Research Vol. 2, Greenhalgh RM, Rose FC (Eds). London: Pitman Medical, pp 392–398, 1983

Emergency Carotid Surgery with Positive Computed Tomographic Scan

Paolo Fiorani, Enrico Sbarigia, Francesco Speziale, Maurizio Taurino, Marco Colonna, Alfonso Pannone and Gilnardo Novelli

INTRODUCTION

Emergency carotid endarterectomy has been recommended by some surgeons for an unstable lesion (tight internal carotid artery stenosis, floating thrombus or ulcerative plaque) presenting as progressing stroke or crescendo transient ischaemic attacks (TIA).[1-3] Nevertheless a recent cerebral infarct detected by computed tomographic (CT) scan has generally been considered a contraindication to urgent revascularization. Many surgeons believe that in this condition, it is worth delaying carotid endarterectomy for at least 4–6 weeks, accepting the risk of new strokes which may occur.[4] Dosik *et al*.[5] reported that such strokes occur in up to 21% of cases and these risks may be more preferable to submitting a patient to surgery which carries greater risks from revascularization.[6-8]

This arbitrary delay in performing carotid endarterectomy after known CT-confirmed infarct results from the concern that surgery may convert an 'ischaemic' into a 'haemorrhagic' infarct. This belief is based on earlier reported experience[6-8] of patients with acute stroke who subsequently underwent operation. The Joint Study of Extracranial Arterial Occlusion also documented the uselessness of emergency revascularization of patients with acute stroke (including profound deficit or coma) and carotid occlusion.[9]

In spite of this scepticism and concern over the value of urgent carotid endarterectomy for acute stroke, some reports of success in selected cases have re-kindled interest in this topic.[1] More recently good results have been reported for the surgical treatment of crescendo TIA and progressing stroke and those with documented acute cerebral infarct confirmed by CT scan. These series have reported low operative morbidity and mortality rates.[3,10,11]

In 1986 Pritz described three patients each with a normal level of consciousness, mild to moderate neurological deficit, a small cerebral infarct and ipsilateral severe stenosis of the internal carotid artery. Surgery in each case did not cause either a worsening of clinical symptoms or detectable changes on CT scanning.[12] In some circumstances therefore, by selecting the appropriate patient, surgery may be justified. We report our experience in patients who fall into this category.

CASE 1

Male: 65 years old

A left-handed man was admitted to the neurology emergency unit with an acute transient left hemiparesis with aphasia, anisocoria (R > L), left hemianopia and a mild VII cranial nerve deficit. A CT scan performed on admission did not show signs of cerebral infarction or any mass. The patient underwent duplex scanning of the carotid arteries which revealed a right internal carotid artery stenosis >50%. Transcranial Doppler sonography showed no significant asymmetry between the intracranial vessels on both sides, and digital subtraction angiography confirmed an 80% stenosis of the internal carotid artery. The patient's neurological condition improved significantly within the first hours following admission. However, the next day a sudden worsening of the left hemiparesis and aphasia were observed. A further CT scan was performed which showed no new changes. On the recommendation of the neurologist an urgent carotid endarterectomy was performed under local anaesthesia and continuous EEG monitoring. A shunt was used during carotid clamping. Throughout surgery invasive systemic blood pressure monitoring helped to maintain the patient in a normotensive state (130–80 mmHg). Some hours after the operation a significant improvement of the left hemiparesis and aphasia was noted while left hemianopia and the mild VII cranial nerve deficit remained unchanged. A CT scan performed 24 hours after the operation showed enhanced perfusion of previously ischaemic right basal ganglia and occipital area.

The patient's neurological status remained unchanged.

CASE 2

Male: 74 years old

A hypertensive right-handed patient underwent right carotid endarterectomy and resection of an abdominal aortic aneurysm 9 years previously. On admission he presented with transient right monoparesis and aphasia. A CT scan showed a small (1 cm) parietotemporal ischaemic area with signs of blood enhancement (Fig. 1). Duplex scanning of the carotid arteries detected a tight left internal carotid artery stenosis (>90%) with a floating thrombus in the residual lumen.

Transcranial Doppler sonography revealed a slight asymmetry (left <30% right) between the middle cerebral arteries with satisfactory diastolic flow. Immediate anticoagulant therapy with heparin was initiated, but after 12 hours, because of instability and worsening symptoms, a left carotid endarterectomy under local anaesthetic was performed. Cross-clamping was employed during surgery. No deterioration of the monoparesis and no change in the EEG was detected. An internal shunt was used. During the operation and in the postoperative period systemic blood pressure was carefully monitored. The operation was successful and there was a progressive improvement of both the monoparesis and the aphasia. A CT scan performed on the second postoperative day did not show any sign of intracranial haemorrhage (Fig. 2). The patient was discharged on the sixth postoperative day with a mild right monoparesis.

CASE 3

Male: 49 years old

A young right-handed hypertensive man was admitted to the neurological intensive care unit with left hemiparesis and facial weakness. An earlier CT scan showed

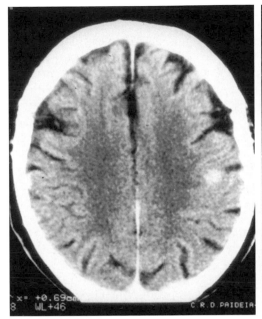 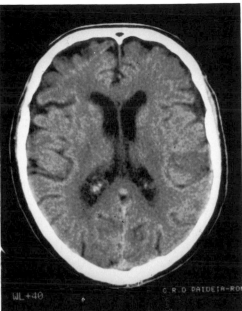

Fig. 1. Case 2: Preoperative CT scan showing small parietotemporal ischaemic area with blood enhancement.

Fig. 2. Postoperative CT scan 48 hours after carotid endarterectomy: no signs of haemorrhage into the infarct after reperfusion.

hypodensity of the right basal ganglia. Duplex scanning of the carotid arteries revealed an occlusion of the right internal carotid. Transcranial Doppler sonography demonstrated a relevant asymmetry of the right middle cerebral artery (<60% left). Marked hypoperfusion of the right temporal lobe was demonstrated by single-photon emission tomography (SPECT). Immediate fibrinolytic therapy was instituted with intravenous recombinant tissue plasminogen activator. One hour later, a second SPECT showed a reduction of the hypoperfusion of the temporal lobe, and duplex scanning of the carotid arteries confirmed recanalization of the right carotid bifurcation, where a tight internal carotid lesion (>80% was evident). Transcranial Doppler sonography showed a reduction of the asymmetry of the middle cerebral arteries (right <35% of the left).

A CT scan performed on the following day (Fig. 3) showed a haemorrhage into the ischaemic area. Nevertheless the hemiparesis improved progressively. Three days later a further CT scan demonstrated partial reabsorption of the haemorrhage (Fig. 4), whilst the neurological deficit continued to improve. Ten days after the stroke, despite CT evidence of a slight infarction, it was decided to perform carotid endarterectomy under local anaesthetic. No intraoperative cerebral ischaemia occurred and no shunt was used. Also in this patient systemic blood pressure was carefully monitored and maintained at between 120–80 mmHg. There were no postoperative complications. On the third postoperative day a further CT scan was performed (Fig. 5) and no evidence of infarction was observed. The patient was discharged on the sixth postoperative day with improvement of the left hemiparesis but persistence of a mild facial weakness.

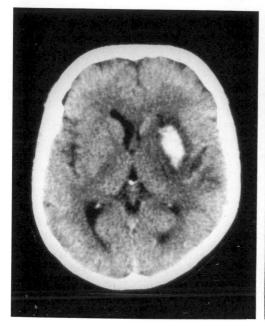

Fig. 3. Case 3: Preoperative CT scan (after rTPA infusion) with evident blood enhancement in the right. In spite of this extended haemorrhage neurological symptoms were improving.

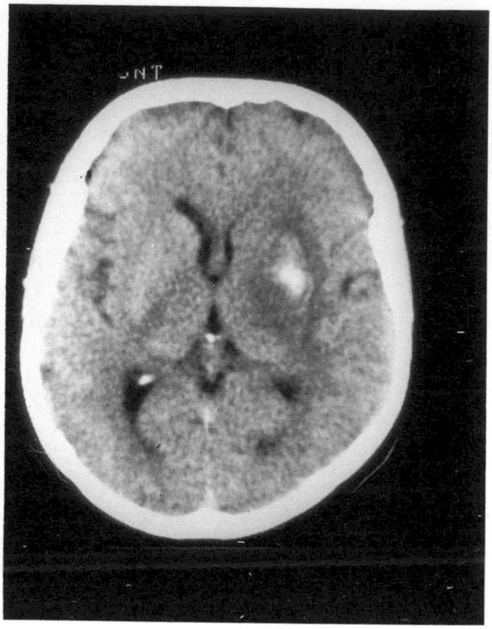

Fig. 4. Case 3: CT scan of the same patient 3 days later. Partial regression of the haemorrhage is evident.

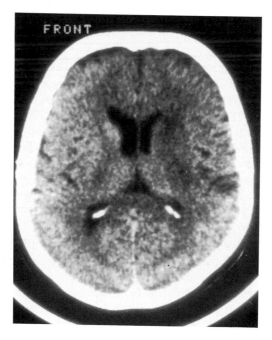

Fig. 5. Case 3: Postoperative CT scan (3 days after operation). No signs of bleeding into the ischaemic area.

CASE 4

Male: 79 years old

A right-handed patient was admitted after a right monoparesis with forearm paraesthesiae. After some time the clinical symptoms relieved completely. A duplex scan showed a bilateral internal carotid artery stenosis more severe on left side (>90%). A CT scan showed an old left parasagittal parietal infarct. The patient was scheduled for left carotid endarterectomy. Whilst awaiting surgery a further right monoparesis occurred and a CT scan confirmed a recent small parietal infarct. Duplex scanning did not reveal any modification of the left internal carotid stenosis and transcranial Doppler sonography did not show any significant asymmetry between the intracranial vessels. On the contrary a transcranial Doppler evaluation with acetazolamide test showed absence of autoregulation of the left hemisphere (no response to vasodilating stimulus to acetazolamide), confirming the patient to be at high risk of reperfusion. Five days after the previous neurologic symptoms the patient underwent a left carotid endarterectomy under local anaesthetic. Cross-clamping did not cause ischaemia and no shunt was therefore employed. There were no postoperative complications. A CT scan performed on the third postoperative day did not show any sign of deterioration and the patient was discharged on the sixth postoperative day.

DISCUSSION

Despite some clinical differences (two progressing strokes and two minor recent strokes) the four patients exhibited common features: acute mild to moderate cerebral ischaemia, severe unstable internal carotid artery lesions, and three showed a small cerebral infarct with enhancement on CT scan. Only the first patient did not show signs of cerebral infarction on early CT scan. In this patient the early endarterectomy improved intracerebral perfusion with an equivalent improvement of the neurological status. The positive effect was probably attributable to the reperfusion of the ischaemic penumbra with regression of most of the neurological symptoms.[13,14] Only a small portion of the involved cerebral tissue was already affected by an irreversible ischaemia which resulted in persistent left haemianopia. This early experience gave us the opportunity to re-evaluate the indications concerning urgent carotid endarterectomy, and especially to question the validity of delaying surgery in patients in whom CT scanning reveals recent acute cerebral infarction.

The general conviction among surgeons with regard to the necessity to delay revascularization of an acute cerebral infarction derives from earlier reported experiences. The disappointing results of the Joint Cooperative Study[9] on emergency revascularization as well as others[6–8] were probably the result of inappropriate indications for surgery. These series included patients with coma, or profound and long-lasting neurological deficit, and even with cervical internal carotid occlusions. Moreover no data were available on the anatomical status of the acute brain ischaemia. Introduction of neuroimaging techniques such as cerebral CT scanning has improved our understanding of this condition. The presence of an ischaemic infarct was always believed to be an absolute contraindication to emergency or urgent revascularization because of the assumed very high risk. Delay was considered necessary to permit a stabilization of the cerebral lesion and particularly of the capillary bed. During the first weeks, it has been supposed that important changes occur in the infarcted area: a reparative scarring process that is characterized by proliferation of a new dense capillary network. Consequently, enhancement of a cerebral infarct on CT is considered a high risk situation for urgent surgery. For this reason a delay of 4–6 weeks before revascularization is generally recommended.[4] Nevertheless, during this waiting period the neurologic impairment may progress to a more severe and lasting deficit. Millikan reported 204 patients with progressing stroke: after 14 days only 12% were normal, 74% had developed moderate or severe neurologic deficits, and 14% died.[15] Mentzer reported an unfavourable outcome in a series of 26 patients: in 66% (severe deficit) 15% died, and only 19% recovered or retained a mild deficit.[16]

Equally the natural history of early mild strokes can be unfavourable. Dosik *et al.*[5] reported that during a delay of 4–6 weeks for operation, a second stroke occurred in 21% of patients, and hence, some experiences reported in the literature suggest that urgent carotid endarterectomy may have a limited place and improve outcome.[1-3,10]

Many reports on CT-confirmed brain infarct have described bleeding in an ischaemic area on the fourth or fifth day after stroke in 40–50% of patients irrespective of whether or not they have been submitted to anticoagulant therapy.[17-19] It has been assumed that such bleeding into the infarct has been the result of reperfusion caused by spontaneous reopening of an occluded vessel, or via collateral pathways from leptomeningeal arteries.[20]

We did not observe in any of our patients a deterioration of clinical status due to progression of the ischaemic infarct to a haemorrhage. We conclude therefore that the criteria we have selected for the timing and performance of endarterectomy appear to be those most important to obtaining satisfactory results from urgent reperfusion of an acute brain ischaemic infarct. These findings agree with a larger series described in another centre.[3]

REFERENCES

1. Goldstone J, Moore WS: A new look at emergency carotid artery operations for the treatment of cerebrovascular insufficiency. Stroke 9: 599–602, 1978
2. Fiorani P, Pistolese GR, Speziale F *et al.*: Stroke in evolution and crescendo transient ischemic attack. *In* Indications in Vascular Surgery, Greenhalgh RM (Ed.). London, Philadelphia: WB Saunders, 1987
3. Cuming R, Perkin GD, Greenhalgh RM: Urgent carotid surgery. *In* Emergency Vascular Surgery, Greenhalgh RM, Hollies LH (Eds). London, Philadelphia: WB Saunders, 1992
4. Giordano JM, Trout HH, Kozloff L, De Palma RG: Timing of carotid endarterectomy after stroke. J Vasc Surg 2: 250–254, 1985
5. Dosik SM, Whalen RC, Gale SS: Carotid endarterectomy in the stroke patient: Computerized axial tomography to determine timing. J Vasc Surg 2: 214–219, 1985
6. Wylie EJ, Hein MF, Adams JE: Intracranial hemorrhage following surgical revascularization for treatment of acute strokes. J Neurosurg 21: 212–215, 1964
7. Breutman ME, Fields WS, Crawford ES, DeBackey ME: Cerebral hemorrhage in carotid artery surgery. Arch Neurol 9: 458–467, 1963

8. Rob CG: Operation for acute completed stroke due to thrombosis of internal carotid artery. Surgery 65: 962–965, 1969

9. Blaisdell WF, Clauss RH, Goldbraith JG, Imparato AM, Wylie EJ: Joint study of extracranial arterial occlusion IV a review of surgical considerations. J Am Med Assoc 209: 1889–1895, 1969

10. Piotrowsky JJ, Bernhard VM, Rubin JR *et al.*: Timing of carotid endarterectomy after acute stroke. J Vasc Surg 11: 45–52, 1990

11. McIntyre KE, Goldstone J: Carotid surgery for crescendo TIA and stroke in evolution. *In* Cerebrovascular Insufficiency, Bergan JJ, Yao JST (Eds). New York: Grune & Stratton, 1983

12. Pritz MB: Carotid endarterectomy after recent stroke: preliminary observations in patients undergoing early operation. Neurosurgery 19: 604–609, 1986

13. Astrup WF, Siesjo BK, Symon L: Threshold in cerebral ischemia: The ischemic penumbra. Stroke 12: 723, 1981

14. Olsen TS, Larsen, Herning M *et al.*: Blood flow and vascular reactivity in collaterally perfused brain tissue. Evidence of an ischemic penumbra in patients with acute stroke. Stroke 14: 332, 1983

15. Millikan CH, McDowell FH: Treatment of progressive stroke. Prog Cardiovasc Dis 22: 396, 1980

16. Mentzer RM, Finkelmeier BA, Crosby IK: Emergency carotid endarterectomy for fluctuating neurologic deficit. Surgery 89: 60, 1981

17. Bozzao L, Angeloni U, Bastianello S *et al.*: Early angiographic and CT findings in patients with hemorrhagic infarction in the distribution of the middle cerebral artery. Am J Neuroradiol 12: 115–121, 1991

18. Sherman DG, Hart RG: Cerebral embolism study group. Brain hemorrhage in embolic stroke. *In* Central nervous system control of the heart. Stober T, Schmrijk K, Ganten D, Sherman DG (Eds). Boston: Martinus Nijhoff, pp. 249–253, 1986

19. Okada Y, Yamaguchi T, Minematsu K: Hemorrhagic transformation in cerebral embolism. Stroke 20: 598–603, 1983

20. Pessin MS, Teal PA, Caplan LR: Hemorrhagic infarction: guilt by association? Am J Neuroradiol 12: 1123–1126, 1991

TECHNIQUES OF CAROTID SURGERY

Standard Carotid Endarterectomy

Jesse E. Thompson

Carotid endarterectomy is the procedure most frequently employed in the operative treatment of cerebral ischaemic syndromes due to atherosclerotic disease. Clinical considerations determine the indications and contraindications for operation. The principal indication is transient cerebral ischaemia since strokes can be prevented and troublesome episodes of ischaemia are largely abolished.

Technical considerations are of the utmost importance in carotid endarterectomy since the limits of tolerance to temporary occlusion of the blood supply to the brain may be quite narrow. Safety factors must be employed which will eliminate in most instances the occurrence or aggravation of neurological deficits. Any method of carotid endarterectomy should carry low mortality, few complications, satisfactory immediate and long-term anatomical results, and good functional results relative to cerebrovascular insufficiency. The technique to be described has evolved over a period of 35 years and has proved safe and reliable. It involves the routine use of a temporary inlying bypass shunt.[1]

The operation is performed under light general anaesthesia. The head is turned away from the side to be operated upon and placed on a rubber ring (Fig. 1). The shoulders are elevated slightly using a folded sheet but there should be no undue extension of the neck. An oblique incision is made along the anterior border of the sternocleidomastoid muscle, curving medialward at its lower end, centred over the bifurcation of the common carotid artery, and curved slightly inferior to the lobe of the ear at the upper end.

Adequate exposure of the common carotid and of the internal and external carotid divisions is essential. The carotid sinus area is infiltrated with 1% lidocaine to prevent hypotension and bradycardia. The artery is freed completely including division of the carotid sinus plexus if necessary.

One must avoid injury to the mandibular branch of the facial nerve and the vagus, hypoglossal and superior laryngeal nerves. A small branch of the external carotid artery, supplying the sternocleidomastoid muscle, usually passes over the hypoglossal nerve holding it down as a sling. This small artery should be ligated and divided to free the hypoglossal nerve from the external and internal carotid divisions. Though rarely necessary, the superior thyroid artery may be ligated and divided to facilitate dissection and exposure. An umbilical tape is first placed around the external carotid artery. Umbilical tapes are then placed around the common and internal carotid arteries and segments of No. 16 French rubber catheters are threaded over the tapes to act as tourniquets.

The occluding plaque is usually located at the bifurcation of the common carotid and extends a short distance into the internal carotid (Fig. 2). The distal internal carotid is ordinarily soft and thin-walled and is freed up for at least 1 cm beyond the palpable distal end of the plaque. Utmost gentleness is used throughout

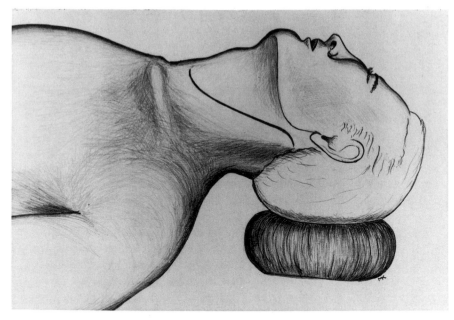

Fig. 1. Position of patient's head on the table and location of incision for carotid endarterectomy. (From Thompson JE: Carotid endarterectomy with shunt. *In* Mastery of Surgery, Vol. II, Nyhus LM, Baker RJ (Eds). Boston: Little, Brown and Co., 1992. Reproduced with permission.)

manipulation and the artery is simply palpated, never squeezed, since platelets, thrombi or atherosclerotic debris may break off and embolize intracranially.

When satisfactory exposure is obtained, systemic heparinization is effected with 3500–5000 units of heparin. The external carotid is occluded with a bull-dog clamp and heparinized locally with 10 ml of a solution containing 100 units of heparin per ml. The common carotid is then clamped proximally with an angled vascular clamp.

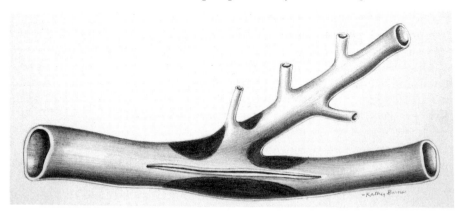

Fig. 2. Site of the linear arteriotomy. (From Thompson JE, Garrett WV: Thrombo-obliterative disease of the vessels of the aortic arch. *In* Hardy's Textook of Surgery, 2nd edn, Hardy JD (Ed). Philadelphia: JB Lippincott, 1988. Reproduced with permission.)

The distal internal carotid is occluded with a soft bull-dog clamp and a linear arteriotomy is made from the common carotid into the internal carotid beyond the distal extent of the plaque (Fig. 2). It is important that the internal carotid be opened beyond the plaque and that the entire extent of plaque be visualized in order to facilitate the succeeding steps of the operation. A plastic catheter shunt is then inserted into the distal internal carotid and the artery allowed to back flow (Fig. 3). The proximal end of the plastic shunt is then placed into the common carotid lumen and the umbilical tapes with rubber tourniquets are made snug (Figs 4 and 5). Cerebral blood flow is thus restored through the shunt. This step of the operation requires from 45 to 90 seconds.

The average size shunt which fits the distal internal carotid is a No. 10 French plastic catheter about 9 cm in length. A No. 8 or No. 12 catheter may be used as a shunt if the artery is smaller or larger than usual. The internal diameter of the No. 10 catheter used is 2.5 mm. With normal levels of blood pressure this shunt carries approximately 125 ml of blood per minute. Experience has shown that this is adequate flow during the period required for endarterectomy.

With the intraluminal shunt in place one may endarterectomize the vessel without undue haste (Fig. 6). The appropriate plane is entered with a fine pointed haemostat or other dissector and the plaque dissected from the common carotid, the bifurcation, first portion of the external carotid and that portion of the internal carotid containing the plaque (Fig. 7). The distal end of the plaque in the internal carotid usually feathers off quite smoothly leaving only thin intima above, which should not be disturbed. Small bits of debris may be lifted out with forceps or flushed out with saline. It is of the utmost importance that the distal extent of the endarterectomy be visualized so that no large pieces of intima be left to dissect distalward and produce a postoperative occlusion. Occasionally it is advisable to secure the distal intima with a few interrupted stitches to prevent dissection. 6–0 polyester sutures serve well to

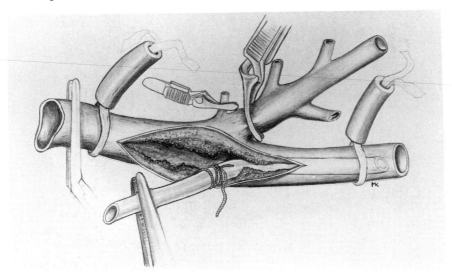

Fig. 3. Insertion of shunt into the internal carotid artery. (From Thompson JE: Carotid endarterectomy with shunt. *In* Mastery of Surgery, Vol. II, Nyhus LM, Baker RJ (Eds). Boston: Little, Brown and Co, 1992. Reproduced with permission.)

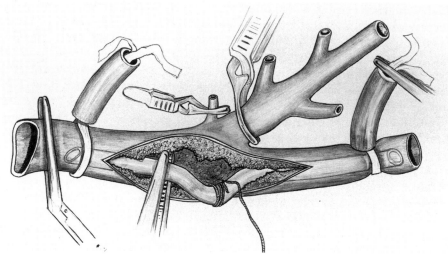

Fig. 4.   Insertion of the shunt into the common carotid artery. (From Thompson JE: Carotid endarterectomy with shunt. *In* Mastery of Surgery, Vol. II, Nyhus LM, Baker RJ (Eds). Boston: Little, Brown and Co, 1992. Reproduced with permission.)

tack down the intima as well as to close the arteriotomy. It is also important to endarterectomize carefully the origin of the external carotid since this artery is an important source of blood supply to the brain (Fig. 8).

The arteriotomy is then closed with running sutures of 6–0 polyester beginning at each end (Fig. 9). Immediately prior to placing the final three or four sutures the common carotid and internal carotid are clamped and the shunt removed. The vessels are then flushed. The final sutures are quickly placed and tied. At this point the internal carotid is allowed to back flow and is then re-clamped.

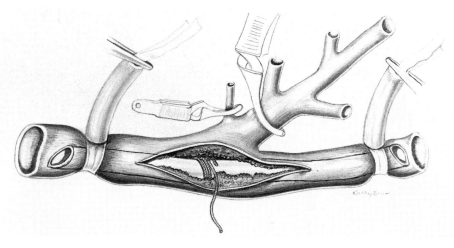

Fig. 5.   Shunt in place, flow restored. (From Thompson JE: Carotid endarterectomy with shunt. *In* Mastery of Surgery, Vol. II, Nyhus LM, Baker RJ (Eds). Boston: Little, Brown and Co, 1992. Reproduced with permission.)

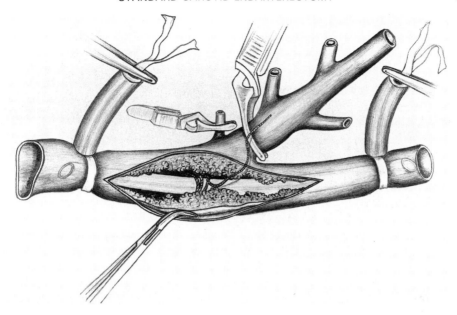

Fig. 6. Beginning the endarterectomy. (From Thompson JE: Carotid endarterectomy with shunt. *In* Mastery of Surgery Vol. II, Nyhus LM, Baker RJ (Eds). Boston: Little, Brown and Co, 1992. Reproduced with permission.)

Clamps are removed from the external carotid and common carotid arteries and flow restored into the external carotid allowing any debris or air to be flushed into it rather than into the internal carotid. The clamp is then removed from the internal carotid and flow restored to the brain. The occlusion time during this final step is from 1 to 2 minutes. The heparin is then reversed with protamine, if necessary (Fig. 10).

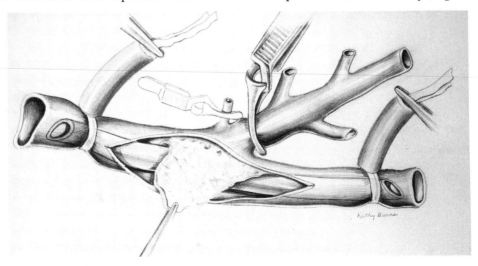

Fig. 7. Removing the plaque. (From Thompson JE, Garrett WV: Thrombo-obliterative disease of the vessels of the aortic arch. *In* Hardy's Textbook of Surgery, 2nd edn, Hardy JD (Ed). Philadelphia: JB Lippincott, 1988. Reproduced with permission.)

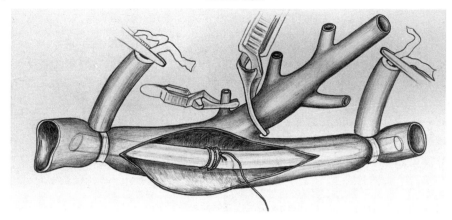

Fig. 8.   Endarterectomy completed. (From Thompson JE: Carotid endarterectomy with shunt. *In* Mastery of Surgery, Vol. II, Nyhus LM, Baker RJ (Eds). Boston: Little, Brown and Co, 1992. Reproduced with permission.)

One may vary the technique of arteriotomy closure by using a thin-blade partially occluding clamp to include the unfinished portion of the suture line after the shunt is removed. In this way cerebral blood flow is quickly re-established and the suture line is then completed (Fig. 11).

If one is concerned about completeness of endarterectomy or the quality of pulsation in the internal carotid following restoration of flow, arteriograms may be performed on the operating table. Some surgeons perform this step routinely, but the author has not found its routine use necessary. A sterile Doppler probe is useful in this regard.

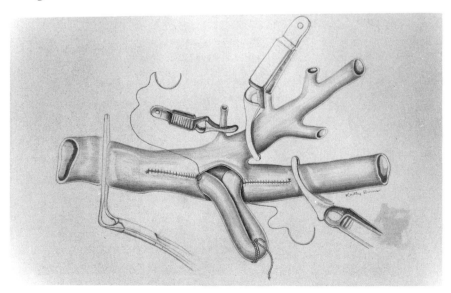

Fig. 9.   Removing the shunt. (From Thompson JE, Garrett WV: Thrombo-obliterative disease of the vessels of the aortic arch. *In* Hardy's Textbook of Surgery, 2nd edn, Hardy JD (Ed). Philadelphia: JB Lippincott, 1988. Reproduced with permission.)

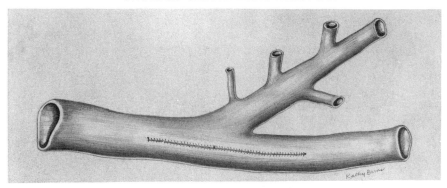

Fig. 10. Completed arteriotomy closure. (From Thompson JE, Garrett WV: Thrombo-obliterative disease of the vessels of the aortic arch. *In* Hardy's Textbook of Surgery, 2nd edn, Hardy JD (Ed). Philadelphia: JB Lippincott, 1988. Reproduced with permission.)

It is rarely necessary to use a patch graft for closure of the arteriotomy, but if the artery is quite small a patch graft of autologous vein or prosthetic material may be used (Fig. 12).

The wound in the neck is then closed anatomically in two layers with interrupted sutures of fine cotton. A small rubber drain is brought out of the lower end of the wound and is removed 24 hours postoperatively. Bilateral operations when necessary are done in separate stages about a week apart to avoid complications of laryngeal oedema, transient hypoglossal paresis, and cerebral oedema.

It is important that adequate levels of blood pressure be maintained during operation and in the immediate postoperative period. The most satisfactory way to achieve this is to administer 500–1000 ml of lactated Ringer's solution during the operation and postoperatively. Vasopressors are occasionally necessary even when adequate fluids have been given. Routine postoperative heparinization is not used.

The technique may vary depending upon variation in pathology. If the plaque is a long one and extends quite far distally a longer arteriotomy is necessary as is

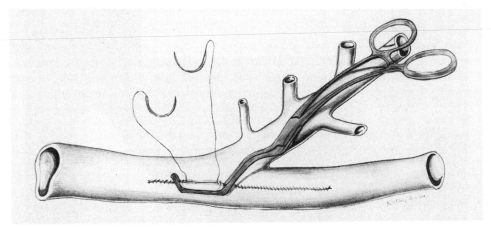

Fig. 11. Alternative method of arteriotomy closure. (From Thompson JE, Garrett WV: Thrombo-obliterative disease of the vessels of the aortic arch. *In* Hardy's Textbook of Surgery, 2nd edn, Hardy JD (Ed). Philadelphia: JB Lippincott, 1988. Reproduced with permission.)

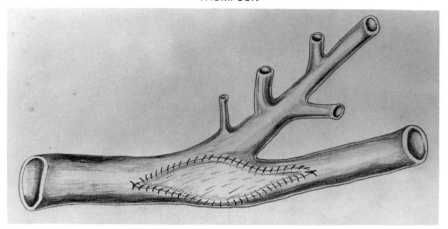

Fig. 12.   Arteriotomy closure with patch graft.

a longer shunt. At times it is prudent to close the distal portion of the arteriotomy and move the shunt proximalward before completing the endarterectomy at the common carotid bifurcation. Occasionally one finds a plaque in the common carotid a centimeter or so proximal to the bifurcation. In this case the arteriotomy may be extended proximally, as it is important to remove this plaque as well.

Rarely one encounters patients with bilaterally occluded internal carotid arteries which cannot be opened by operation. Under these circumstances it is important that patency of the external carotid arteries be maintained, and endarterectomy of the orifices of these arteries may be necessary to improve collateral cerebral blood flow. The shunt technique is easily adapted to endarterectomy of the external carotid arteries.

The technique as described depicts carotid endarterectomy with the aid of a temporary inlying shunt, which is the most reliable method for cerebral support. Some surgeons use the shunt routinely in all partially occlusive lesions, some use it selectively based on an assessment of cerebral collateral circulation, while a few rarely if ever use it. Those who advocate selective shunting rely on the criterion of inadequacy of cerebral collateral circulation. Some test the patient under local anaesthesia and use a shunt if temporary clamping cannot be tolerated. Others, using general anaesthesia, insert a shunt if internal carotid artery stump pressure is below 50–55 Hg or if EEG changes occur upon carotid clamping. In the hands of experienced operators, comparable results may be obtained using selective shunting.

REFERENCE

1. Thompson JE: Carotid endarterectomy. *In* Vascular Surgical Techniques, An Atlas, 2nd edn, Greenhalgh RM (Ed). London: WB Saunders, pp. 83–88, 1989

Carotid Endarterectomy with Selective Shunting and Selective Patching

R. M. Greenhalgh, Rachel Cuming, Stephen D. Blair and G. David Perkin

A retrospective review of our total experience of carotid surgery allows an analysis of results of standard carotid endarterectomy according to presenting symptoms as recommended by Thompson in this volume, pp. 149–156. Postoperative stroke rate including 30-day perioperative stroke, totalled postoperative ipsilateral and contra-lateral strokes can be analysed as can mortality and restenosis rate. For the whole period, a protocol of selective shunting has been performed as previously described.[1] The technique used is a standard carotid endarterectomy technique as described by Thompson in this volume and more fully elsewhere.[2] As recommended by Thompson, in the early days, a patch was seldom used and vein patch was favoured. Rupture of vein patch was subsequently reported[3] and inappropriate excess dilatation of the carotid bulb by vein patch was also reported.[4] In addition there were favourable reports in terms of restenosis when a Dacron patch was used[3] and since 1988, a protocol involving prospective selective Dacron patching is described for these patients for a little over 3 years.

CAROTID SURGERY WITH SELECTIVE SHUNTING

A total experience of 356 patients is described and the presenting symptoms are given in Fig. 1. By far the commonest indication was amaurosis fugax, 66 (18.5%) and transient ischaemic attack (TIA), 167 (46.9%). Nevertheless there were a significant number of patients operated upon who already had an established stroke

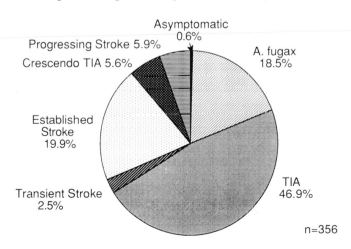

Fig. 1. Presenting symptoms of the whole series of 356 consecutive patients.

and made a good recovery, 71 (19.9%). A further nine (2.5%) had had a transient stroke and two (0.6%) were asymptomatic. Additionally, more than 10% of the series were operated upon for urgent indications. The majority (246 of the patients) were male, a ratio of 7 : 3 with an average age of 66.3±8.6 years. A minority of patients were non-smokers, 50 (14%), the rest were current smokers, 111 (31%) or ex-smokers, 196 (55%). History of symptomatic coronary artery disease with myocardial infarction or angina was found in 126 (35.4%), peripheral arterial disease in 150 (42.1%), treatment for hypertension 171 (48.8%) and diabetes in 38 (10.7%).

The patients were all selected for surgery by a consultant neurologist and investigated before operation with colour duplex scan, computed tomographic (CT) scan and arch flush angiogram.

Standard carotid endarterectomy was performed under general anaesthetic. Before clamping of the carotid artery, a stump pressure reading was achieved as previously described.[1] A Javid intraluminal shunt was used for cerebral protection, if the stump pressure was less than 50 mmHg or if the wave form of the internal carotid artery was flat.[1] If during the performance of measurement of stump pressure the pressure was above 50 mmHg with a pulsatile wave form from the internal carotid then shunting was not performed. Several times it was not required even when operating for progressing stroke as previously described.[5] Stroke rate after carotid endarterectomy for all indications in 356 patients is shown in Fig. 2a. The stroke rate for all is exactly similar from 1 month postoperation (1.8% per year) over 5 years but there were expected differences relative to presenting symptoms in terms of 30-day stroke rates: for TIA and amaurosis fugax (2.4%), established stroke (7.0%), progressing stroke (10.0%) and crescendo TIA (37.3%).

Mortality after carotid endarterectomy for the whole series is given in Fig. 2b. Mortality in patients after carotid endarterectomy is similar when the operation is performed for various indications (5.7% per year) over 5 years.

Restenosis of greater than 50% and greater than 25% diameter reduction has been followed for 5 years using colour code duplex scanning (Fig. 3). As can be seen, a restenosis rate of >50% at 12 months was 8.7% and >25% at 12 months was 29%. At 60 months or 5 years the >50% stenosis rate was 17% and the >25% stenosis rate was 59%. In this experience patching was not performed in 265 patients and Dacron patch was performed in 73 and vein patching in 18. A Javid shunt was used for 186 (52%) of patients. Stroke rate irrespective of indications but according to shunting and no shunting only is given following carotid endarterectomy in Fig. 4. As can be seen there is no difference in stroke rate when selective shunting is performed according to this protocol.

SELECTIVE DACRON PATCHING ACCORDING TO CAROTID DIMENSIONS

With an experience of a restenosis of >50% of 16.9% for 5 years in 356 patients, this was similar to restenosis rates quoted by others.[6,7] As this has been achieved as described above without the use of patch in 74% of the series, there was some reluctance to accept that patching could significantly lower restenosis rates. Dacron patch was favoured to avoid complications of rupture of vein patch[3] and excess dilatation and increased thrombogenicity.[4] A knitted Dacron patch was selected as

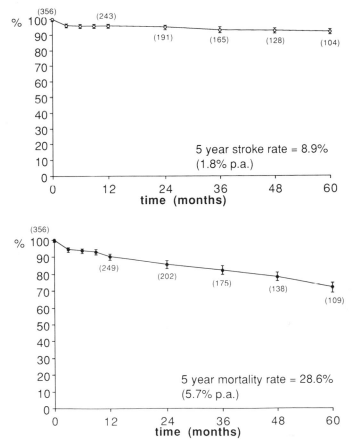

Fig. 2. a (upper): Stroke rate including perioperative ipsilateral and contralateral established strokes after operation for the whole series of 356 patients. b (lower): Mortality after carotid endarterectomy including 30 days operative mortality for the whole series of 356 patients.

this would be unlikely to stretch. A diameter of 5 mm Dacron patch was selected to be used on all small carotid arteries (Fig. 5). As can be seen in the figure, for a small carotid artery, closure without patch would tend to narrow particularly the internal carotid artery no matter how carefully sewn with tiny sutures and fine suture material. Nevertheless even for a small artery, after endarterectomy in almost every case, the flow would be increased and by removal of the stent of atheroma the elastic remaining vessel could be expected to dilate somewhat. It is by no means certain that by non-use of a patch the artery would be narrowed in every case after endarterectomy. For a large artery, clearly there are instances where a patch is not required, as this would lead to excessive dilatation and a capacious carotid bulb so large as to encourage the deposition of thrombus through the production of a somewhat aneurysmal dilatation. A 5 mm Dacron patch was selected as optimal for small arteries on the basis that during the anastomoses, if 1 mm bites were taken on each side, each suture line takes up 1 mm of Dacron and 1 mm of artery, a total of 4 mm lost in the circumference. A Dacron patch would therefore increase the

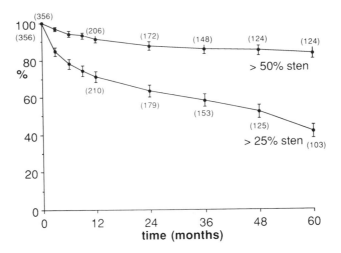

Fig. 3. Restenosis rates for the whole series of 356 patients. At 5 years >50% restenosis occurred in 17% and >25%, restenosis in 59%.

circumference by 1 mm in total rather than decrease it. This would more closely reconstruct the carotid bifurcation with similar dimensions to those that it had originally. A large carotid artery closed directly without patch might produce a little narrowing but this should not be any serious disadvantage. The question to be decided is what size of carotid artery should be used in determining the need for patch. A decision would need to be made at operation. Metal calipers were used to measure the diameter of the common carotid (CC), internal carotid bulb (ICB), and distal internal carotid artery (ICD) as shown in Fig. 6. On a purely arbitrary basis it was decided to insert a patch if the distal internal carotid artery measured 5 mm or less by caliper at operation.

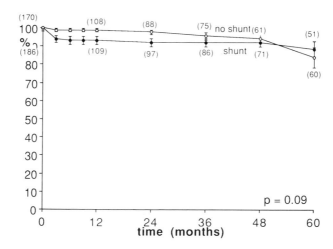

Fig. 4. Stroke rate compared for 356 patients with relation to use of shunt (186) or no shunt (170). There is no significant difference at any stage.

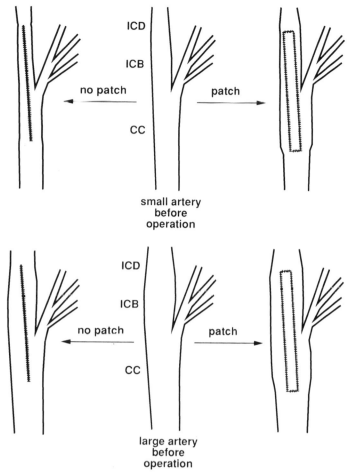

Fig. 5.   Indications for Dacron patching. CC = common carotid; ICB = internal carotid bulb; ICD = distal internal carotid.

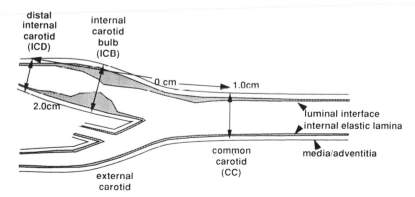

Fig. 6.   Duplex diameter measurements of the common and internal carotid artery. Diameters measured before and after operation by colour code duplex scan and calipers: a) common carotid (CC), b) internal carotid bulb (ICB), c) distal internal carotid (ICD).

PATIENT SERIES

A total of 94 patients have been operated upon according to this protocol and 45 received a 5 mm Dacron patch and 49 did not. Presenting symptoms for patched and non-patched patients are similar as shown in Fig. 7. Of the patched patients, 67% were male and of the non-patched 65% were male. Risk factors in both groups are given in Fig. 8. As can be seen there is a similar incidence of diabetes, treatment for hypertension, coincidence of symptomatic peripheral arterial disease and symptomatic coronary arterial disease for the patched and non-patched patients. Before surgery, colour duplex scan was performed and the maximum external diameter of the common carotid internal carotid bulb and distal internal carotid were measured so that they could be compared with the immediate postoperative dimension by duplex scan. At operation a metal caliper was used to measure maximum external diameter at the three sites. For an internal carotid measuring 5 mm or less, a Dacron patch was performed in 45 patients. Shunting was performed according to stump pressure as

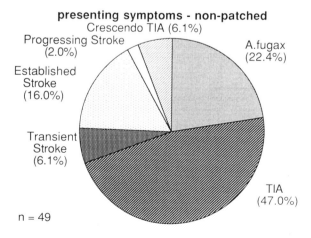

Fig. 7. Presenting symptoms for patched and non-patched patients.

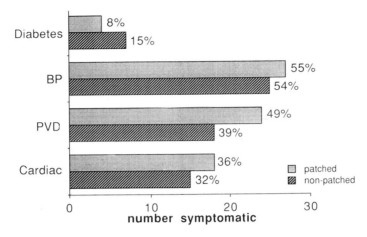

Fig. 8. Risk factors for patched and non-patched patients.

previously described.[1] After closure of the arteriotomy, carotid dimensions were measured by caliper once again. Similar measurements of maximum external diameter were made by colour duplex scan before and 24 hours after operation.

RESULTS

In Table 1, maximum external measurements by caliper and ultrasound before and after reconstruction are given for patched and non-patched patients. The distal internal carotid (ICD) diameter is significantly smaller before operation in patched

Table 1. Maximum external measurements before and after reconstruction

	Patched carotids (n = 45) arterial diameters (mm)				
	Caliper		Ultrasound	
	preop	postop	preop	postop
CC	9.2 ± 1.0	9.8 ± 1.0	9.5 ± 1.5	10.3 ± 1.4
ICB	6.9 ± 1.2	7.5 ± 1.2	8.5 ± 1.4	8.8 ± 1.7
ICD	4.6 ± 0.78	5.3 ± 0.5	5.8 ± 0.8	6.3 ± 1.0

	Non-patched carotids (n = 49) arterial diameters (mm)				
	Caliper		Ultrasound	
	preop	postop	preop	postop
CC	9.4 ± 1.1	9.1 ± 1.1	9.3 ± 1.1	9.1 ± 1.3
ICB	8.5 ± 1.6	7.5 ± 1.4	9.0 ± 1.2	7.9 ± 0.9
ICD	5.6 ± 0.6	5.4 ± 0.5	6.4 ± 1.1	5.8 ± 0.6

The distal internal carotid (ICD) diameter is signficantly smaller before operation in patched carotids ($p < 0.001$). The common carotid (CC) and distal internal carotid diameters are increased significantly by patching ($p < 0.05$, $p < 0.01$). The internal carotid bulb (ICB) and distal internal carotid diameters are decreased significantly in non-patched carotids ($p < 0.01$, $p < 0.01$).

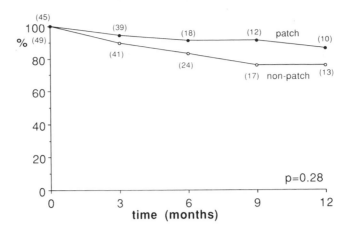

Fig. 9. Incidence of >50% restenosis in patched (14%) and non-patched (24%) patients at 12 months.

carotids ($p < 0.001$). The common carotid (CC) and distal internal carotid diameters are increased significantly by patching ($p < 0.05$, $p < 0.01$). The internal carotid bulb (ICB) and distal internal carotid diameters are decreased significantly in non-patched carotids ($p < 0.01$, $p < 0.01$).

The occurrence of >50% restenosis over the first 12 months is shown in Fig. 9 for patched and non-patched patients and there is no significant difference, 13.8% for patched and 24.1% non-patched patients. Bearing in mind that the patched patients started off with a narrow carotid artery, patching has certainly not disadvantaged these patients who were presumably at a higher risk of restenosis. Freedom from stroke in patched and non-patched patients at 30 days, 3, 6, 9, 12 and 24 months respectively is identical in the follow-up so far. Symptoms of TIA or stroke in association with >50% restenosis has occurred rarely in this series, one of 45 (2.2%) patched and one of 49 (2.0%) unpatched patients.

DISCUSSION

It must be remembered that patching and non-patching was not decided by random allocation of this series and patching was performed for narrower carotid diameters. Therefore in no sense were the groups similar to each other. Nevertheless, a similar incidence of carotid restenosis has been achieved by patching the smaller diameter patients and not patching the larger diameter patients. The incidence of symptoms associated with restenosis is very small indeed and in this series symptoms associated with >50% stenosis only occurred in one of 45 (2.2%) patched patients and one of 49 (2.0%) unpatched patients over 12 months. In the total series of 356 patients, symptoms of TIA or stroke occurred in patients with >50% stenosis in only three (13.6%) of patients with >50% stenosis (0.8% of whole series) over 5 years. The problem of restenosis associated with symptoms is relatively unimportant and when it has occurred we have treated the patient with platelet inhibitory therapy and not reoperated. Asymptomatic restenosis is a benign condition and there is a good argument in favour of not scanning patients repeatedly after carotid endarterectomy but awaiting symptoms, and these occur extremely rarely as has been seen. Use of selective 5 mm Dacron patching for smaller diameter carotid arteries has produced results of recurrent stenotic problems at least as good as patients with larger diameters in which no patch was required after complete endarterectomy.

REFERENCES

1. Greenhalgh RM: Carotid endarterectomy. *In* Vascular Surgical Techniques, Greenhalgh RM (Ed.), London: Butterworth, pp 41–48, 1984
2. Thompson JE: Carotid endarterectomy: *In* Vascular Surgical Techniques: An Atlas, Greenhalgh RM (Ed.), London/Philadelphia: W B Saunders, pp 83–88, 1989
3. Eikelboom BC, Ackerstaff RGA, Hoeneveld H *et al.*: Benefits of carotid patching. A randomized study. J Vasc Surg 7: 240–247, 1988
4. Meek AC, Cuming R, Greenhalgh RM: Carotid restenosis. *In* The Maintenance of Arterial Reconstruction, Greenhalgh RM, Hollier LH (Eds). London/Philadelphia: W B Saunders, 279–287, 1991
5. Cuming R, Perkin GD, Greenhalgh RM: Urgent carotid surgery. *In* Emergency Vascular Surgery, Greenhalgh RM, Hollier LH (Eds). London/Philadelphia: W B Saunders, pp. 145–156, 1992
6. Bartlett FF, Ropp JH, Goldstone J *et al.*: Recurrent carotid stenosis: operative strategy and late results. J Vasc Surg 5: 452–456, 1987
7. Pierce GE, Utopoulos JI, Holcomb MA *et al.*: Incidence of recurrent stenosis after carotid endarterectomy determined by digital subtraction angiography. Am J Surg 148: 848–853, 1984

Blood Flow in Carotid Shunts

Jonathan D. Beard

INTRODUCTION

There is still much controversy concerning the use of a shunt during carotid endarterectomy. Proponents argue that the routine use of a shunt allows time for a more thorough endarterectomy because of continued cerebral perfusion[1] and that intraoperative monitoring by EEG,[2] cerebral blood flow measurement,[3] or transcranial Doppler[4] may be dispensed with. Those who do not use shunts claim that there is a risk of embolization of air or atheromatous debris[5] or intimal damage during shunt insertion. However, this risk can be minimized by selection of a shunt that is small enough to fit easily into the internal carotid artery[6] and by careful flushing.[7] Selective shunting based upon the measurement of internal carotid artery stump pressure has been advocated[8] but recently its accuracy in predicting those patients at risk of stroke during cross-clamping, has been questioned.[9]

The arguments surrounding the use of carotid shunts tend to ignore the most important point that the presence of a shunt is no guarantee that the brain is being adequately perfused.[10] Despite much work on cerebral blood flow during carotid endarterectomy,[11] little attention has been paid to the measurement of blood flow through different types of carotid shunt. There is evidence that even a relatively large diameter shunt may act as a greater than 75% stenosis[12] and the purpose of this project was to determine whether currently available shunts could deliver an adequate flow of blood.

Three separate studies were performed. In the first experiment blood flow through eight different carotid shunts was measured in the laboratory on a hydraulic test rig. Two carotid shunts; the 32 cm, 17/10 French Javid shunt[13] and the 32 cm, 10 French Pruitt Inahara shunt[14] were selected for the clinical studies because of differences in their flow rates and handling characteristics. In the second study, carotid blood flow was measured preoperatively with a Doppler flowmeter during 25 carotid endarterectomies before, during and after shunting. This study confirmed the differences in shunt blood flow and the third study examined whether these differences affected cerebral blood flow. This consisted of a randomized study of the Javid and Pruitt shunts during 32 carotid endarterectomies using transcranial Doppler monitoring of the middle cerebral artery blood flow velocity.

SHUNT FLOW STUDY

The blood flow through eight different carotid shunts was measured in the laboratory on a hydraulic test rig. The shunts tested were the 13 cm, 10, 12 and 14 French USCI straight intraluminal shunts the 32 cm, 10 French Pruitt straight extraluminal shunt,[14] the 12 cm, 17/10 French Brenner tapered intraluminal shunt,[15] the 32 cm, 17/10 French Javid tapered extraluminal shunt[13] and two 25 cm, straight extraluminal shunts made from 8 and 10 French PVC umbilical catheter tubing (Portex, UK).

The hydraulic test rig consisted of a constant pressure head tank filled with citrated whole human blood with a packed cell volume of 45% and a peristaltic pump delivering a pulsatile blood flow of variable pressure (Fig. 1). The blood flow through each shunt was measured with a previously calibrated 0.25″ Nycotron cannulating electromagnetic flow probe and blood pressure with a Gould P231D pressure transducer proximal to the shunt. The tubing distal to the shunt had a large internal diameter (7.5 mm) and was as short as possible (10 cm), so that the mean pressure proximal to the shunt was effectively equal to the pressure gradient across the shunt. The mean blood pressure (BP) was increased from 20 to 120 mmHg in 20 mm increments and the mean of five blood flow measurements recorded at each step.

RESULTS

The results of the blood flow measurements are shown in Fig. 2. Most shunts had adequate flows of more than 200 ml/min but the 10 French USCI and Pruitt shunts delivered less than 100 ml/min for a mean pressure of 80 mmHg across the shunt. The 10 French catheter shunt delivered more than 200 ml/min for the same external diameter and even the 8 French catheter performed better than the two commercially available 10 French shunts. The measured flow rates were approximately 25% lower than the theoretical flow rates calculated from Poiseuilles' Formula:

$$Q = \frac{(P_1 - P_2)\ 60\ \pi\ R^4}{8\mu L}\ \text{ml/min}$$

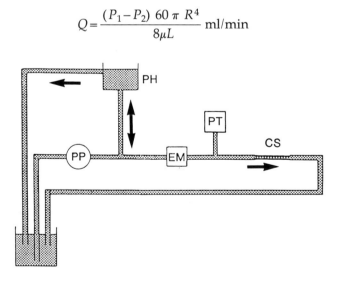

Fig. 1. Hydraulic test rig consisting of a constant pressure head tank (PH) filled with citrated blood and a peristaltic pump (PP). Blood flow through each carotid shunt (CS) was measured with an electromagnetic flowmeter (EM) and blood pressure with a pressure transducer (PT).

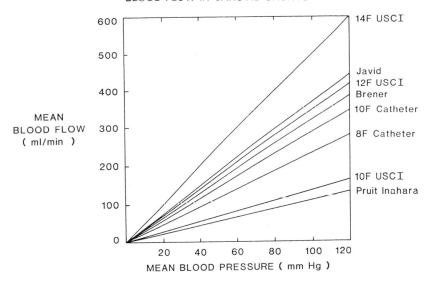

Fig. 2. Mean blood flow against mean blood pressure gradient across the shunt for the 8 carotid shunts tested. F = French (external circumference in mm).

Where Q = blood flow $P_1 - P_2$ = pressure gradient across the shunt, R = radius of the shunt lumen, μ = viscosity of blood and L = length of the shunt. The likely reasons for the lower flows recorded experimentally were the pulsatile nature of the blood flow which probably resulted in some turbulence, and the high viscosity of blood at room temperature. Poiseuilles' Formula is only valid for continuous laminar flow and a viscosity of 0.04 Poise was used in the formula which is the viscosity of blood at 37° Centigrade.[16]

The reason for the differences between the three 10 French shunts is shown in Fig. 3. Although all three have the same external circumference of 10 mm the 10 French catheter shunt has a much thinner wall and hence a larger internal diameter. According to Poiseuilles' Formula, flow Q is proportional to the radius R^4 and therefore a small increase in the internal radius leads to a marked increase in flow.

$$Q = \frac{(P_1 - P_2)\, \pi\, 60\, R^4}{8\,\mu l} = KR^4 \text{ ml/min}$$

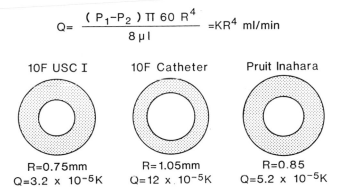

Fig. 3. Cross-sections of the three 10 French carotid shunts demonstrating the thinner wall of the 10 French catheter resulting in a larger internal radius (R) and hence higher flow (Q).

In the case of the 10 French catheter this increase is more than double that of the Pruitt shunt and nearly four times that of the French USCI shunt per unit length but as the USCI shunt is only half the length the increase is only double. The purpose of the thick wall of the 10 French USCI and Pruitt shunts is to prevent kinking and the thickness of the Pruitt shunt is further increased by the inflatable latex balloon used to retain the shunt in the carotid artery.

The blood flow potential of all the small calibre straight shunts was limited by the lack of a taper which takes advantage of the larger calibre of the common carotid artery as found in the Javid and Brenner shunts (Fig. 4). On the basis of these results, the Javid and Pruitt shunts were selected for comparison in the subsequent clinical studies. These two were chosen because of the large difference in their flow rates with the Javid delivering over 250 ml/min compared with less than 100 ml/min for the Pruitt at a mean pressure of 80 mmHg. The Pruitt rather than the 10 French USCI or catheter shunts was chosen because of the difficulty of holding these shunts in the opened carotid artery. Despite tight slings these simpler shunts had a tendency to dislodge, especially from the common carotid artery whereas the inflatable balloons of the Pruitt shunt ensured good stability with no leakage.

CAROTID FLOW STUDY

Carotid blood flow during carotid endarterectomy was measured in 25 consecutive patients. All patients except one were symptomatic, with transient ischaemic attacks or amaurosis fugax in 18 and recovered stroke in six. There were 19 men and 6 women with a median age of 72 (range 31–89 years).

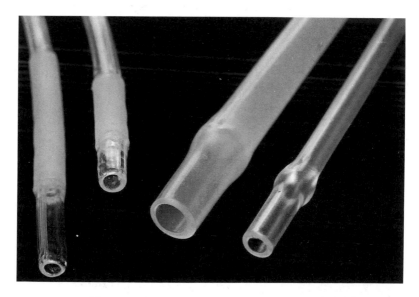

Fig. 4. Proximal and distal ends of the Pruitt (left) and Javid (right) shunts. The tapered Javid shunt takes advantage of the larger diameter of the common carotid artery but it has a thick wall. The Pruitt shunt has no taper and although the wall is thinner, the balloons add to the overall thickness.

All patients were investigated preoperatively by grey scale duplex scanning and selective carotid arteriography in three projections to confirm the duplex findings and measure the degree of stenosis.[17] The arteriographic measurements of the internal carotid diameter were made at the narrowest part of the stenosis and at the normal poststenotic part. The percentage degree of stenosis was calculated as the ratio of these two measurements. The median ipsilateral internal carotid artery stenosis was 85% (range 30–99%) and the median stenosis of the contralateral internal carotid artery was 30% (range 0–100%). Only one contralateral internal carotid was occluded and the status of the vertebral arteries was not documented.

After dissection of the carotid bifurcation, blood flow measurements were performed using a Doppler ultrasound flowmeter,[18] developed by the author (Opdop, Scimed UK). The volume flow in the common carotid artery was measured and the proportion of blood flow up the internal carotid artery calculated by measuring the common carotid flow again, with the external carotid artery clamped. Twelve patients were shunted with a Pruitt shunt and 13 with a Javid shunt. The shunt selection was not randomized but was based on the preference of the two surgeons performing these operations. Shunt blood flow as measured using the Doppler flowmeter positioned on the shunt (Fig. 5). At completion of the endarterectomy, common carotid artery flow was again measured with the external carotid artery open and then clamped. Blood pressure was maintained at or above the preoperative systolic value for each patient and this was helped by routine use of lignocaine to block the carotid sinus.[19] End tidal carbon dioxide concentration was kept within normal limits throughout the procedure.[20] The internal carotid artery stump pressure was also measured before shunting.

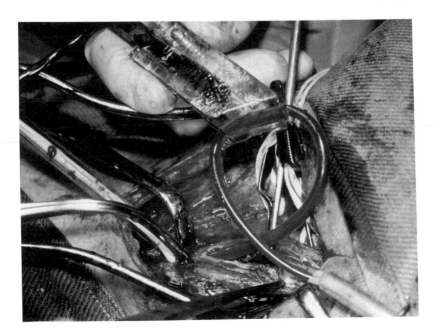

Fig. 5. Doppler ultrasound flowmeter (Opdop) measuring blood flow through a Javid shunt during carotid endarterectomy.

Table 1. Carotid blood flow measured with the Doppler flowmeter before and after 25 carotid endarterectomies (median and range). Statistical analysis: Wilcoxon signed Rank Test

	Before endarterectomy ml/min	After endarterectomy ml/min	p
Common carotid	216 (95–400)	250 (166–350)	0.002
Internal carotid	86 (20–254)	176 (125–280)	0.001
External carotid	94 (26–247)	66 (16–110)	0.001
IC flow > EC flow	13/25	25/25	

RESULTS

The common carotid blood flow and the proportion flowing up the internal and external carotid arteries before and after endarterectomy are summarized in Table 1. Following endarterectomy there was a significant increase in both total common carotid and internal carotid blood flow mirrored by a similar decrease in external carotid flow. Before endarterectomy the proportion of flow up the internal carotid artery was greater than that up the external carotid artery in 13 of 25 cases and following endarterectomy in all 25. There was a good correlation between the percentage stenosis of the internal carotid artery and its blood flow prior to endarterectomy (Spearman rank correlation $p < 0.001$, Fig. 6). However, flow was still significant even in the presence of a 90% stenosis with a flow of greater than 120 ml/min recorded in one case. There was a weak correlation towards higher flow up the external carotid artery in those patients with a severe stenosis of the internal

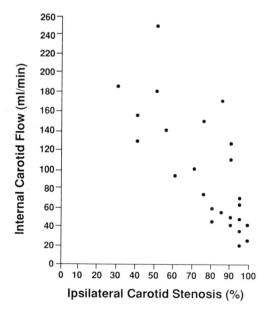

Fig. 6. Correlation between the percentage stenosis of the internal carotid artery and its blood flow prior to endarterectomy. (Spearman Rank Correlation: $p < 0.001$.)

carotid artery. This suggests that the external carotid artery may act as an important collateral supply to the brain in the presence of a severe internal carotid artery stenosis. This might also explain the fall in external carotid flow following endarterectomy, although another reason could be damage to the external carotid artery due to incomplete endarterectomy.[21] There also appeared to be an association between common carotid flow and the degree of contralateral carotid disease but there were insufficient contralateral high grade stenoses for analysis. The collateral theory would also explain this phenomenon.

There was a wide variation in shunt blood from 32 ml/min up to 250 ml/min (median 92 ml/min). There was no correlation between shunt flow and mean arterial blood pressure or internal carotid artery stump pressure measured prior to insertion of the shunt (median 55 mmHg, range 32–78). Blood flow in the Javid shunts was significantly higher than in the Pruitt shunts, although there was no difference in the internal carotid artery blood flow and after shunting between the two groups (Fig. 7). In two cases where very low flows were recorded through a Pruitt shunt, it was changed for a Javid with improvement of flow from 34 to 79 ml/min and from 32 to 62 ml/min respectively (Fig. 8).

Studies during carotid endarterectomy[21] and in monkeys[22] have shown that cerebral blood flow below 15 ml/100 g brain tissue per minute results in paralysis of neuronal activity and permanent damage within 15–30 min. This implies a carotid shunt blood flow of at least 75 ml/min assuming an ipsilateral cerebral hemispheric weight of 500 g and no cross-cerebral circulation, either due to an incomplete Circle

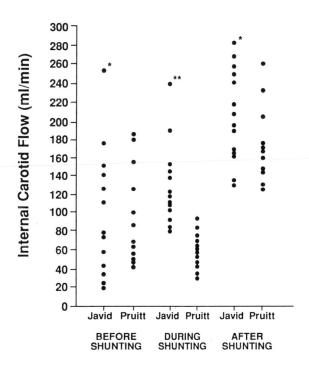

Fig. 7. Comparison of the internal carotid artery blood flow before, during and after shunting between the Javid and Pruitt groups. Mann Whitney U test: $*p > 0.05$, $**p < 0.001$.

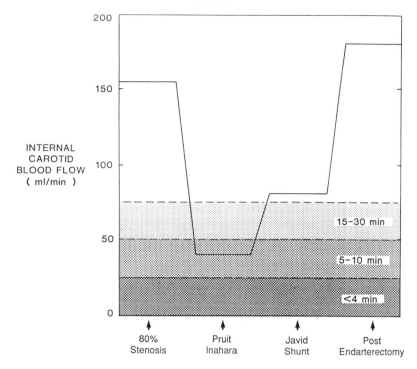

Fig. 8. Increase in internal and carotid blood flow after a Pruitt shunt was changed for a Javid shunt superimposed upon the theoretical cerebral tolerance assuming no collateral blood supply.

of Willis or disease of the other extracranial vessels. This level was not reached in a significant number of cases in the Pruitt shunt group. The presence of a high grade stenosis of the internal carotid artery might imply that an adequate collateral circulation already exists and this is used as a reason by some for not using a shunt. However, this study has demonstrated that significant internal carotid flow may exist in the presence of high grade stenosis, and that the external carotid artery may act as a significant collateral. This collateral flow is also lost when the artery is clamped during endarterectomy. Significant internal carotid flow in the presence of a high grade stenosis may be explained by the fact that the stenosis is often very short. Although shunts might be expected to perform better than a high grade carotid stenosis, they frequently do not as a result of their small internal diameter and relatively long length.

CEREBRAL FLOW STUDY

A prospective randomized trial of Javid v Pruitt shunts was undertaken to see whether the flow differences in the Second Study affected the mean middle cerebral artery velocity (MCAV) measured with transcranial Doppler. Thirty-five patients were considered for the study but three were not entered because no transcranial Doppler signal could be obtained. The median age of the 32 patients entered into the study was 61 years (range 37–76) and there were 22 men and 10 women. The indication for operation was recovered stroke in eight with the other 24 suffering from transient ischaemic attacks and/or amaurosis fugax.

Preoperative investigations consisted of a screening by colour Doppler scan followed by non-selective intra-arterial digital subtraction arch angiography. The percentage stenosis of the internal carotid artery was calculated by the same method described in the Second Study. The median ipsilateral internal carotid artery stenosis was 80% (30–100%) and the median contralateral internal carotid artery stenosis 60% (0–100%). The ipsilateral total occlusion (100%) on angiography was judged to be a 99% stenosis on colour Doppler scans before and after angiography and this was confirmed at operation. There were 11 contralateral total occlusions. There was excellent agreement between the percentage stenosis as judged by colour Doppler and angiography.[23] Patients with stenoses less than 70% had been randomized to surgery as part of the European Carotid Surgery Trial.

Transcranial Doppler monitoring was performed with a Transpect TCD (Medasonics, California, USA). A 2 MHz probe was positioned over the temporal window and the angle and depth of the pulsed Doppler beam adjusted for an optimum mean MCAV. The probe was then fixed using a headpiece (Fig. 9). The Doppler waveform was recorded every 5 min on the machine's memory and subsequently downloaded to the computer for automated analysis of the MCAV. Embolic events denoted by transient high pitched 'chirping' noises were also recorded.[24]

The anaesthetic technique was the same as in the Second Study. All patients were shunted with 16 randomized to receive a Javid shunt and 16 a Pruitt shunt. Carotid cross-clamping during shunt insertion and removal was never more than 3 min. A

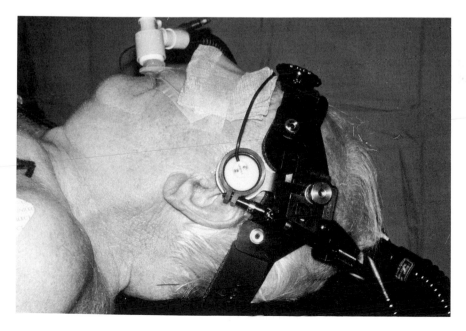

Fig. 9. 2 MHz transcranial Doppler probe held in position over the temporal window with a headpiece.

standard endarterectomy with vein patch repair was performed in all cases, except for three patients in whom the internal carotid artery after opening was also transposed downwards because of tortuosity, and one patient who received a PTFE patch because of a lack of suitable vein.

The mean MCAV was compared at five time periods during the course of the carotid endarterectomy: a baseline before insertion of the shunt; during carotid cross-clamping; after insertion of the shunt; just before removal of the shunt to exclude any shift; and at completion of the arterial repair following removal of the shunt. The change in mean MCAV for the group as a whole was analysed by the Wilcoxon signed Rank Test and at each time interval the difference between the mean MCAV in the Javid and Pruitt groups was analysed by the Mann Whitney U Test.

RESULTS

There was no difference in the baseline characteristics of the two groups in terms of age; sex ratio; indication for operation; and percentage stenosis of both the ipsilateral and contralateral internal carotid artery. In contrast to the direct carotid blood flow measurements in the Second Study, there was no correlation between the percentage stenosis of the ipsilateral internal carotid artery and the mean baseline MCAV (Fig. 10). This is probably explained by the collateral contribution from the ipsilateral external carotid artery plus the contralateral carotid system and vertebral arteries via the Circle of Willis.

For the group as a whole there was a highly significant reduction in the mean MCAV on carotid cross-clamping ($p < 0.001$), falling to zero in six cases (Fig. 11). Even in those cases where there was no reduction in mean MCAV, a frequent finding was a reduction in the power of the Doppler signal, indicating a decreased vessel diameter presumably due to a reduction in perfusion pressure. There was no correlation between the reduction in mean MCAV on clamping and the severity of the contralateral carotid disease. Once the shunt was inserted mean MCAV was restored to a level similar to that before shunting (Table 2). There was little change in

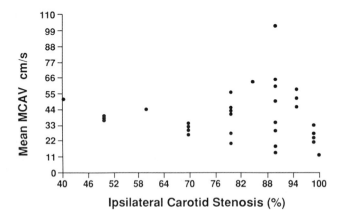

Fig. 10. Lack of correlation between mean MCAV prior to shunting and the percentage stenosis of the ipsilateral internal carotid artery.

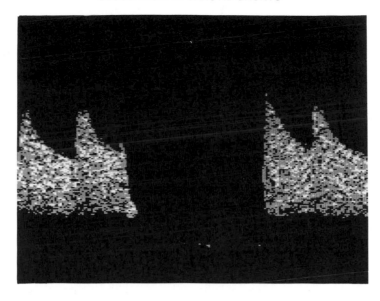

Fig. 11. Transcranial Doppler signal from the middle cerebral artery showing complete cessation of flow during carotid cross-clamping.

MCAV during the period of shunting whilst the endarterectomy was performed but after removal of the shunt and repair of the arteriotomy there was a significant increase in mean MCAV ($p < 0.001$). The finding of little change in mean MCAV before and during shunting is in agreement with the Second Study and confirms that cerebral perfusion is generally maintained, but not improved by the use of shunts which have the same haemodynamic effect as a severe stenosis, for the reasons previously outlined.

Figure 12 shows the mean MCAV values for the 16 patients in the Javid group, compared to the 16 patients in the Pruitt group for the five consecutive time periods. There was no significant difference between mean MCAV before shunting but during shunting the mean MCAV in the Pruitt group was significantly lower ($p < 0.1$). After removal of the shunt and repair of the arteriotomy there was again no difference between the two groups. This finding reinforces the message from the second study that the inferior flow rates obtained with the Pruitt shunt are reflected in impaired ipsilateral cerebral perfusion, as measured by transcranial Doppler.[26] There is now good evidence that a brain with pre-existing ischaemic damage and impaired

Table 2. Mean MCAV during carotid endarterectomy, for both the Javid and Pruitt groups combined, expressed as a median and range. Statistical analysis: Wilcoxon signed Rank test

Time period	Mean MCAV (cm/s)	p
Before shunting	38.3 (13.4–103)	< 0.001
Carotid clamping	20.0 (0–49)	< 0.001
Start of shunting	37.7 (11–70.8)	> 0.05
End of shunting	39.4 (11–80.4)	0.001
After shunting	51.8 (13–83)	

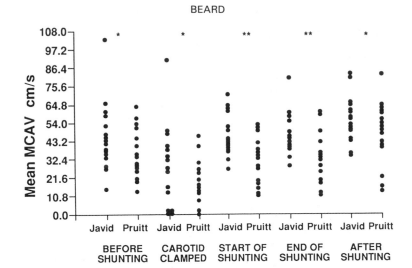

Fig. 12. Comparison of the mean MCAV between the Javid and Pruitt groups for the five time periods during carotid endarterectomy. Mann Whitney U test: $p > 0.05$, ** $p < 0.01$.

haemodynamic reserve, may be more susceptible to embolic or apparently innocuous decreases in cerebral perfusion pressure during carotid endarterectomy.[21,25,27] It is therefore important that cerebral perfusion during endarterectomy is not compromised by a shunt with an inadequate flow capacity, as this may reduce the margin for technical error.

Transcranial Doppler evidence of air emboli were observed in 13 patients during shunt insertion and this is a well recognized finding.[4,24] However, these were usually minor because of careful flushing of the shunt after insertion of the proximal end into the common carotid artery followed by back bleeding of the internal carotid artery during insertion of the distal end. A more significant problem was unrelated to shunt use and occurred at restoration of flow after completion of the arterial repair. This was noted in 18 patients, despite careful flushing of the arteriotomy prior to closure followed by initial release of flow up the external carotid artery. In fact, the most marked bursts of emboli occurred on releasing the external carotid artery in cases where there had been a severe stenosis of the internal carotid artery. This again clearly demonstrates that the external carotid artery may be an important source of collateral flow to the brain, and therefore also a source of emboli during carotid endarterectomy.[28] For this reason, it is important that the endarterectomy of the origin of the external carotid artery is also performed with care. There was no difference between the incidence of emboli between the two different shunts, except for the detection of emboli during shunting in two Javid shunts. This was found to be due to aspiration of air from the sidearm of the shunt due to the Venturi effect, despite the sidearm tap being closed. We now also flush the sidearm with blood prior to shunt insertion.

The relative advantages and disadvantages of the Javid and Pruit shunts in terms of haemodynamics, cost and handling characteristics are summarized in Table 3.

Subjectively, endarterectomy was easier to perform using the Pruitt shunt because of better flexibility and improved access to the distal internal carotid artery, whereas

Table 3. Advantages and disadvantages of the Javid and
Pruitt shunts

	Javid	*Pruitt*
Advantages	Higher flow	Good distal access
	Inexpensive	Less intimal damage?
	Reusable	Very flexible
Disadvantages	Less flexible	Low flow
	Clamp slippage	Expensive
	Poor distal access	Balloon problems

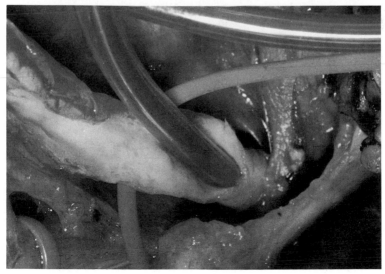

Fig. 13(a + b).   Comparison of surgical access to the distal internal carotid artery between
the Javid (upper) and Pruitt (lower) shunts.

access could be obscured by the Javid shunt because of the need for a clamp (Fig. 13). There was also concern that the Javid clamps could cause vessel injury[1] (Fig. 14), whereas the balloons on the Pruitt shunt appear to be less traumatic. The Javid clamp tended to slip on the thin distal internal carotid artery especially when the internal carotid artery had been completely divided because of tortuosity. This made control of the shunt position in the internal carotid artery extremely difficult. The proximal end of the Javid shunt also dislodged from the common carotid artery on one occasion because the clamp sprang apart. Once correctly placed, the Pruitt shunt tended not to dislodge but control was lost once when the distal balloon was punctured by the suture needle during closure of the arteriotomy. Transcranial Doppler monitoring also revealed defective flow in three cases when using a Javid shunt. Two of these occurred because the shunt had been inserted too far up the internal carotid artery and was impacting on the carotid syphon. This was simply corrected by partial withdrawal of the shunt. The other problem occurred during shunting due to inadvertent kinking and the Javid shunt certainly kinked more easily than the Pruitt.

There were one major and two minor strokes postoperatively. The major stroke was in the Javid group and developed 12 h postoperatively. Interestingly, it occurred in the patient that received a polytetrafluoroethylene (PTFE) patch and protamine had been given at the end of the operation to control stitch hole bleeding. A CT scan confirmed a large, ipsilateral cerebral infarct and it is possible that this was due to dislodgement of thrombus that had formed on the patch, although a duplex scan of the endarterectomy site showed no abnormality. The two minor strokes occurred in the Pruitt group: one of these was probably related to a prolonged burst of emboli heard on transcranial Doppler monitoring, when the

Fig. 14.   Possibility of vessel wall damage caused by Javid clamp.

external carotid artery was released. Both these strokes were extensions of existing deficits. Because of the low incidence of neurological deficit following carotid endarterectomy, a much larger randomized study than this would be required to show whether there was a significant difference in stroke rate between the Javid and Pruitt shunts.

SUMMARY

Many carotid shunts currently available do not provide an adequate flow of blood to guarantee cerebral perfusion, and in some cases perform worse than a 95% carotid stenosis. Although flow through the Pruitt shunt is inferior to the Javid, this is balanced by its superior handling characteristics.

Cerebral perfusion during endarterectomy should not be compromised as this may reduce the margin for technical error. The ideal shunt for maximal blood flow should be tapered like the Javid, but made of a material that is thin walled and kink-resistant. It should combine this with the flexibility and balloon system of the Pruitt shunt.

REFERENCES

1. Browse NL, Ross-Russell R: Carotid endarterectomy and the Javid shunt: The early results of 215 consecutive operations for transient ischaemic attacks. Br J Surg 71: 53–57, 1984
2. Callow AD, Matsumoto G, Baker D, Cossman D, Watson W: Protection of the high risk carotid endarterectomy patients by continuous electroencephalography. J Cardiovasc Surg 19: 55–64, 1978
3. Boysen G: Cerebral blood flow measurement as a safeguard during carotid endarterectomy. Stroke 2: 1–10, 1971
4. Padayachee TS, Gosling RG, Bishop CC, Burnand K, Browse NL: Monitoring middle cerebral artery blood flow velocity during carotid endarterectomy. Br J Surg 73: 98–100, 1986
5. Towne JB, Benhard VM: Neurologic deficit following carotid endarterectomy. Surg Gynaecol Obstet 154: 819–852, 1982
6. Bandyk DF, Thiele BL: Safe intraluminal shunting during carotid endarterectomy. Surgery 93: 260–263, 1983
7. Beezley MJ: Safer shunt insertion during carotid endarterectomy. J Vasc Surg 2: 607–609, 1985
8. Hunter GC, Sieffert G, Malone JM, Moorer WS: The accuracy of carotid back pressure as index of shunt requirements. Stroke 13: 319–326, 1982
9. Archer JP: Technique and clinical results of carotid stump back-pressure to determine selective shunting during carotid endarterectomy. J Vasc Surg 13: 319–327, 1991
10. Naylor AR, Bell PRF, Ruckley CV: Monitoring and cerebral protection during carotid endarterectomy. Br J Surg 79: 735–741, 1992
11. Sundt TM, Sharbrough FW, Piepglas DG et al.: Correlation of cerebral blood flow and electroencephalographic changes during carotid endarterectomy. Mayo Clin Proc 56: 533–543, 1981
12. Gee W, McDonald KM, Kaupp HA: Carotid endarterectomy shunting: Effectiveness determined by operative occular pneumoplethysmography. Arch Surg 114: 720–721, 1979
13. Javid H: Can surgery prevent stroke? Surgery 59: 1147–1153, 1966
14. Pruitt JC: 1009 Consecutive carotid endarterectomies using local anaesthesia, EEG and selective shunting with Pruitt–Inahara shunt. Contemp Surg 23: 49–58, 1983
15. Berner BJ, Brief DK, Alpert J, Parsonnet V: A T-shaped carotid shunt. Arch Surg 110: 1249–1250, 1975

16. McDonald DA: Blood Flow in Arteries, 2nd edn. London: Edward Arnold, pp. 55–70, 1974
17. Jeans WD, MacKenzie S, Bard RN: Angiography in transient cerebral ischaemia using the views of the carotid bifurcation. Br J Radiol 59: 135–142, 1986
18. Beard JD, Evans JM, Skidmore R, Horrocks M: A Doppler flowmeter for use in theatre. Ultrasound Med Biol 12: 883–889, 1986
19. Welch M, Tait WF, Durvans D, Carr HMH: Role of topical lignocaine during carotid endarterectomy. Br J Surg 79: 1035–1037, 1992
20. Markwalder TM, Gromilund P, Seiler RW, Roth F, Aashid R: Dependency of blood flow velocity in the middle cerebral artery on end-tidal CO_2 partial pressure: a transcranial Doppler study. J Cereb Bloodflow Metab 4: 368–372, 1984
22. Symon L: The relationship between CBDF, evoked potentials and the clinical features in cerebral ischaemia. Acta Neurol Scand 62: 175–190, 1980
23. Flanigan DP, Shuker JJ, Vogel M et al.: The role of carotid duplex scanning in surgical decision making. J Vasc Surg 2: 15–24, 1985
24. Spencer MP, Thomas GI, Nicholls SC, Savage LR: Detection of middle cerebral arterial emboli during carotid endarterectomy using transcranial Doppler ultrasonography. Stroke 21: 415–423, 1990
25. Naylor AR, Meerick MV, Ruckley CV: Risk factors for intra-operative neurological deficit during carotid endarterectomy. Eur J Vasc Surg 5: 33–39, 1991
26. Jorgansen L, Schroeder T: Detection of cerebral ischaemia during carotid endarterectomy using transcranial Doppler. Eur J Vasc Surg (in press), 1993.
27. Schroeder T: Haemodynamic significance of internal carotid artery disease. Acta Neurol Scand 77: 353–372, 1988
28. Naylor AR, Wildsmith JAW, McClure J, Jenkins A, McL, Ruckley CV: Transcranial Doppler monitoring during carotid endarterectomy. Br J Surg 78: 1264–1268, 1991

The Eversion Endarterectomy — A New Technique

D. Raithel and P. Kasprzak

With increasing frequency of carotid reconstructions the vascular surgeon is nowadays confronted much more with the problem of recurrent stenoses. The rate of restenosis reported in the literature ranges from 1.2% to 23.9%, depending on the study methods.[1-3] Only a few clinical episodes are associated with restenosis, the rate of reintervention was only 1.2–3.6%.[4,5] Routine carotid patch angioplasty has been introduced to prevent the phenomenon of restenosis.[6-10] Although routine patching clearly decreases the rate of restenoses, it does not eliminate the complications, and small randomized studies have not definitely answered these questions.[10-11]

Several clinical and technical factors also influence the development of recurrent carotid stenoses, but in some cases the aetiology of the recurrence remains unclear.

CAUSES FOR RESTENOSES

A variety of causal factors have been proposed for recurrent carotid stenoses. In our opinion, technical failure more frequently results in restenoses than systemic factors. Technical failures include clamp traumas, intimal and medial flaps, strictures at the distal end of the arteriotomy together with inadequate resection of the internal carotid artery (ICA) (Fig. 1).

Systemic factors such as smoking and hypercholesterolaemia cause new additional proximal and distal diseases and develop in the later follow-up period. Anastomotic neointimal hyperplasia is a common cause of restenoses and is mainly located at the end of the patch angioplasty.

In a series of approximately 6000 carotid endarterectomies performed at the Nuremberg Medical Centre between August 1984 and July 1991, we found 66 carotid restenoses. In this group the cause for restenosis in 27 cases was an inadequate resection of the elongated ICA.[12]

Because of the high rate of restenosis after conventional carotid endarterectomy and some technical problems encountered in the correction of the elongated ICA we have searched for new methods of carotid endarterectomy.[12-15] The eversion endarterectomy by transection of the common carotid artery (CCA) was first mentioned by DeBakey in 1959 and described by Etheredge in 1970.[16-17] However, by this method the assessment of the distal intima is uncertain, and elongation of the ICA is rarely optimally resectable.

In order to reduce the frequency of restenoses, we recommend the eversion endarterectomy of the ICA. This procedure allows an easier correction of an elongated or kinked ICA. In our patient population we found a carotid lesion in combination with a kinking in 37%.[12]

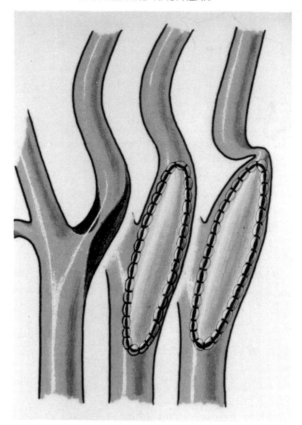

Fig. 1. Kinking of the ICA after conventional
endarterectomy with patch angioplasty.

MATERIAL AND METHODS

The difference between the operative technique of the eversion endarterectomy (EEA)
of the ICA and the technique of the conventional carotid endarterectomy is the fact
that an elongated ICA can be optimally and easily reconstructed by EEA. The
operative principle is as follows (Figs 2–6):

    oblique transection of the ICA from the CCA,
    EEA of the ICA,
    endarterectomy of the carotid bifurcation and external carotid artery (ECA),
    reimplantation of the ICA in the CCA,
    intraoperative angioscopy.

    This operative technique allows an optimal correction of elongated ICAs, and an
endoscopy after carotid endarterectomy is an alternative or adjunct to angiography
or sonography. Angioscopy allows identification of the intraluminal structures and
the postoperative anatomy.

    For angioscopy we use a flexible and controllable angioscope (Olympus Optical Ltd,
Tokio) with an outer diameter of 2.2–3.6 mm and an irrigation channel; it is connected

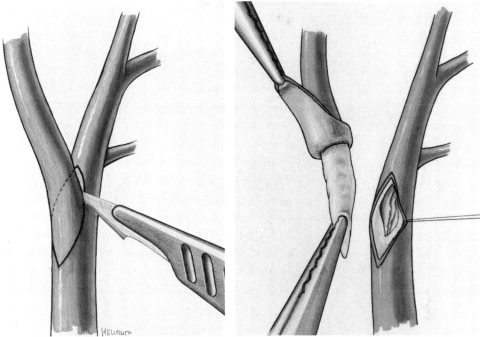

Fig. 2. Oblique transection of the ICA from the CAA.

Fig. 3. EEA of the ICA.

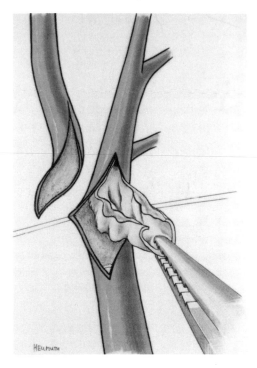

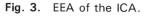

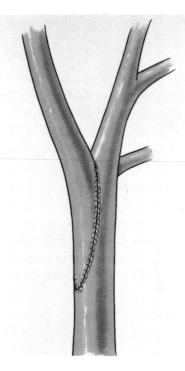

Fig. 4. Endarterectomy of the carotid bifurcation and ECA.

Fig. 5. Reimplantation of the ICA in the CCA.

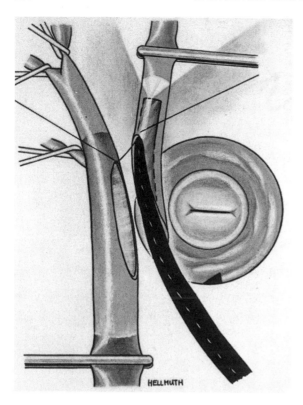

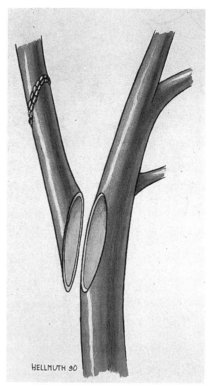

Fig. 6. Intraoperative angioscopy of the ICA.

Fig. 7. *'Ex-situ'* endarterectomy of the ICA.

to a video camera with a monitor and a recorder for photo-documentation.[19] If angioscopy shows a dissected intimal cylinder or plaque that reaches very far in the cranial direction, and if we suspect that this plaque could not be safely removed in the cranial direction, then we have the possibility of performing an *ex-situ* eversion endarterectomy (Fig. 7).

For this procedure, the ICA is cut off in the soft area further down, in the cranial direction, and then it is endarterectomized in an *ex-situ* way. Finally, the endarterectomized ICA segment is anastomosed termino-terminally, and reimplanted proximally to the CCA.

A technically easier method—at least for me—with very good late results is the possibility of interposing a polytetrafluoroethylene (PTFE) graft (6 mm in diameter) or a segment of the greater saphenous vein in carotido-carotidal position (Figs 8–9).

Our results with PTFE graft interpositions are very favourable, so these are used in nearly all problematical cases of eversion endarterectomy.

RESULTS

We have performed so far more than 2000 reconstructions by EEA (Fig. 10). The follow-ups done by Doppler sonography and angiography have proved EEA

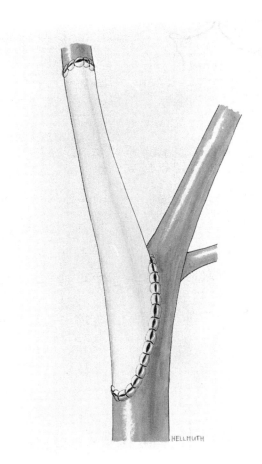

Fig. 8. Graft interposition (PTFE).

to be a method with significant advantages compared with direct closure or patch angioplasty.

From 1 August 1984 through 31 July 1992, 7084 carotid reconstructions were carried out at the Department of Vascular Surgery, Nuremberg Medical Centre. The study comprised 67.1% men and 32.9% women with a mean age of 67.4 years.

Conventional carotid endarterectomies were performed in 3552 cases, and 169 of them were done by direct closure, 3145 by patch, and 238 by patch angioplasty only. In 2714 patients we performed an eversion endarterectomy. The other 818 procedures were partial resections of the ICA, retrograde common carotid endarterectomies etc.

The perioperative morbidity was 2.3% (1.1% permanent and 1.2% transient neurologic deficit). The operative mortality in the total group was 1.3%.

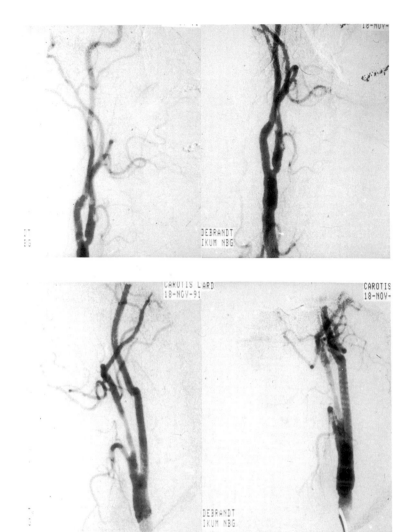

Fig. 9. Postoperative angiogram 1 year after PTFE interposition in ICA
position on both sides.

Comparing the conventional endarterectomy and the eversion endarterectomy,
we had a combined morbidity and mortality in the first group of 3.8%, and in the
second group of 2.5%. This difference was not statistically significant.

The mean clamping time in the group of conventional endarterectomy was
17.2 minutes (9–63 min), in the group of eversion endarterectomy 14 minutes
(8–24 min).

A group of 122 patients who had undergone operation between November 1985
and October 1988 was followed-up. Restenosis was defined as a greater than 50%
diameter reduction by duplex scanning. During a mean follow-up of 28 months,

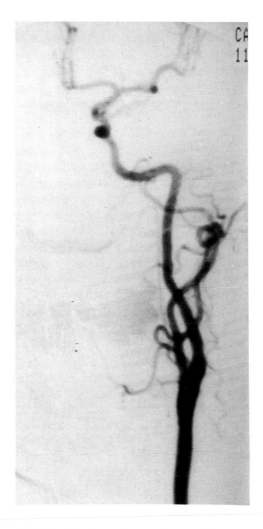

Fig. 10. Postoperative angiogram 2½ years after eversion endarterectomy of the ICA.

the rate of restenosis was 1.9%.[14] One restenosis was a clamping injury, and one was due to an intimal flap in the ICA. The cumulative stroke-free survival rate was 84% after 3 years.

DISCUSSION

After conventional carotid endarterectomy we had a 50% restenosis rate of 12.3% after 3 years measured by Doppler sonography.[12] After eversion endarterectomy, however, we found no more than two restenoses (1.9%) after a mean follow-up of

28 months. Of course this low rate of restenosis after EEA has to be verified by further follow-ups and randomized studies.

In a retrospective comparative study of 212 eversion endarterectomies versus 156 classic endarterectomies of the ICA, Kieny et al. found the following results: the first group showed a restenosis over 50% in only 1.9% (one occlusion and two restenoses), and in the second group the restenosis rate was 13.5% in the same follow-up period.[18] The follow-up was done by Doppler sonography and angiography.

These and our results show that the EEA is a procedure with a low perioperative morbidity and mortality, and we can expect a lower restenosis rate in the follow-up periods.

The intraoperative quality control by angiography, angioscopy or Doppler sonography will lead to an additional reduction of technical failures. Using angioscopy, intimal flaps can be easily verified: of 191 reconstructions carried out by EEA and examined by angioscopy in a consecutive series, 19% of the ICAs or ECAs were revised because angioscopy showed this to be necessary.[19] We believe that these lesions cannot be demonstrated by angiography, therefore angioscopy will provide us with additional information about the luminal surface.

Compared with intravascular sonography which requires quite a lot of experience and is time-consuming, angioscopy is emerging as a fast method with a relatively low risk for the patient. Furthermore, sonography requires a much longer clamping time than angioscopy. Analysing our results achieved by eversion endarterectomy, we found the following advantages:

> no patch material required,
> the occlusion time of the carotid artery is shorter than in the case of a classic endarterectomy with direct or patch closure,
> the correction of an elongated ICA is easily carried out by a shifted reimplantation which, in effect, lowers the origin of the ICA from the CCA and stretches the ICA.

Due to our many years of experience with the eversion endarterectomy we hold the view that a distal luminal control done by angioscopy is necessary in order to discover or verify intimal flaps or dissections, which would lead to reocclusions with consecutive stroke. Angioscopy itself is an easy procedure. The introduction of new devices such as:

> small calibre (<2 mm) angioscopes,
> ready-to-plug-in video set-ups, and
> disposable angioscopes

have made angioscopy a fast method with relatively low risk to the patient.

CONCLUSIONS

1. the EEA of the ICA is a safe operative procedure with a low perioperative morbidity and mortality and a low restenosis rate of 1.9% after 28 months.

2. The EEA allows a complete endarterectomy while maintaining the original diameter of the vessel.
3. The elongated ICA can be stretched by shifted reimplantation, in order to avoid an impending postanastomotic kinking.
4. No patch material is necessary (low infection rate).
5. The EEA has a shorter occlusion time compared with the classical endarterectomy.
6. The intraoperative angioscopy allows an optimal control of the distal intimal flap, reduces the perioperative risk and contributes considerably to the favourable operative results.

REFERENCES

1. Bernstein EF, Torem S, Dilley RB: Clinical significance of carotid restenosis. *In* Current Critical Problems in Vascular Surgery, Vol. 2, Veith FJ (Ed.). St Louis: Quality Medical Publishing, pp. 421–425, 1990
2. Nitzberg RS, Mackey WC, Prendiville E *et al.*: Long-term follow-up of patients operated on for recurrent carotid stenosis. J Vasc Surg 13: 121–127, 1991
3. Atnip RG, Wengrovitz M, Gifford RRM *et al.*: A rational approach to recurrent carotid stenosis. J Vasc Surg 11: 511–516, 1990
4. Rosenthal D, Archie JP, Garcia-Rinaldi R *et al.*: Carotid patch angioplasty: Immediate and long-term results. J Vasc Surg 12: 326–333, 1990
5. Ten Holter JBM, Ackerstaff RGA, Thoe Schwartzenberg GSW *et al.*: The impact of vein patch angioplasty on long-term surgical outcome after carotid endarterectomy. J Cardiovasc Surg 31: 58–64, 1990
6. Archie JP: Prevention of early restenosis and thrombosis-occlusion after carotid endarterectomy by saphenous vein patch angioplasty. Stroke 17: 901–904, 1986
7. Hertzer NR, Beven EG, O'Hara PJ, Krajewski LP: A prospective study of vein patch angioplasty during carotid enarterectomy. Ann Surg 206: 628–634, 1987
8. Deriu GP, Ballotia E, Bonavina L *et al.*: The rationale for patch graft angioplasty after carotid endarterectomy: early and long-term follow-up. Stroke 15: 972–979, 1984
9. Awad IA, Little JR: Patch angioplasty in carotid endarterectomy: advantages, concerns and controversies. Stroke 20: 717–722, 1989
10. Eikelboom BC, Ackherstaff RGA, Hoenveld H *et al.*: Benefits of carotid patching: a randomized study. J Vasc Surg 7: 240–246, 1988
11. Clagett GP, Patterson CB, Fisher DF Jr *et al.*: Vein patch versus primary closure for carotid endarterectomy. J Vasc Surg 9: 213–223, 1989
12. Raithel D: Optimum technique for carotid redo surgery. *In* Current Critical Problems in Vascular Surgery, Vol. 4, Veith FJ (Ed.). St Louis: Quality Medical Publishing, pp. 438–443, 1992.
13. Kasprzak P, Raithel D: Eversion carotid endarterectomy. Technique and early results. J Cardiovasc Surg 30: 49, 1989
14. Kasprzak P, Raithel D: Eversionsendarteriektomie der Arteria carotis interna. Angio 12: 1–8, 1990
15. Raithel D: New techniques in the surgical management of carotid-artery lesions. Surgical Rounds 13: 53–60, 1990
16. DeBakey ME, Crawford ES, Cooley DA, Morris JC Jr: Surgical considerations of occlusive disease of innominate, carotid, subclavian and vertebral arteries. Ann Surg 149: 690–710, 1959
17. Etheredge SN: A simple technique for carotid endarterectomy. Ann Surg 120: 275–278, 1970
18. Kieny R, Hirsch D, Seiller C, Thiranos JC, Petit H: Les resténoses après endarteriéctomie carotidienne par éversion et réimplantation. (in press)
19. Raithel D, Kasprzak P: Angioscopy after carotid endarterectomy. Ann Chir Gyn 81: 192–195, 1992

Single Stage Coronary Artery Bypass Grafting and Carotid Endarterectomy

P. R. F. Bell

Asymptomatic carotid artery occlusive disease occurs in 10% of patients undergoing coronary artery bypass grafting (CABG).[1] The perioperative stroke rate in these asymptomatic patients is no different from all patients undergoing CABG (<3%).[2] In contrast, symptomatic or high grade (>70%) carotid stenoses (Fig. 1) are present in 2–4% of patients undergoing CABG and the majority of neurological complications following cardiopulmonary bypass occur in this group.[3] The association between high grade stenosis and stroke after CABG is well documented with stroke rates of 9.2% and 8.9% in two series.[3,4] In the same way a carotid artery stenosis is a well known marker of myocardial ischaemia and 50% of these patients have coronary artery disease.[5] With these points in mind the problem therefore is how to treat these cases in order to minimize stroke and myocardial events. With the publication of the European[6] and NASCET[7] trials there is little disagreement that patients who are symptomatic and have stenoses in excess of 70% should have a carotid endarterectomy. The question is should they have this done before, at the same time as, or after CABG grafting?

For patients with an asymptomatic stenosis, attitudes vary but in the UK surgery is not normally undertaken. The current approach to patients who have a high grade stenosis and are due to have a CABG for myocardial ischaemia remains controversial. Should these patients have a carotid endarterectomy if CABG grafting is needed and if so when should it be done? In the absence of controlled, randomized studies these questions remain impossible to answer.

Because of the risk of myocardial ischaemia as a major cause of morbidity and mortality, it has been our policy in Leicester to carry out synchronous CABG grafting and carotid endarterectomy in all patients who have symptomatic lesions in excess of 70% stenosis, unilateral asymptomatic lesions >70%, bilateral lesions >70% (the dominant side is the one operated on) and in all patients with occlusion on one side and a severe stenosis >70% of the contralateral artery. This series consists of 30 patients.

PATIENTS

There were ten symptomatic patients who had a duplex scan (Fig. 2) performed and this was the only investigation done on the carotid artery. Unless there is evidence on the scan of proximal or distal disease it is not our policy to carry out angiography routinely. The remaining 20 patients were asymptomatic and were diagnosed because of the presence of a loud bruit discovered on routine examination prior to CABG. Duplex scanning was again the sole preoperative investigation in these patients. From

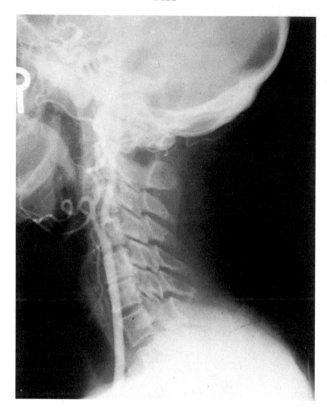

Fig. 1. Angiogram showing severe carotid stenosis.

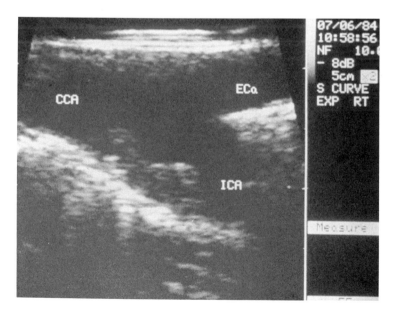

Fig. 2. Duplex scan showing stenosis and an echolucent lesion.

the cardiac point of view, three patients had unstable angina, 23 were asymptomatic but found to have an ischaemic ECG after exercise and four had additional procedures such as aortic or mitral valve replacements.

All patients with symptoms were placed on aspirin 150 mg/day once the lesion was diagnosed but asymptomatic cases were usually not treated. The aspirin was stopped in all patients one week prior to CABG grafting in view of the haemorrhagic complications this causes in such patients.

OPERATIVE TECHNIQUE

The patient was anaesthetized with appropriate support, bearing in mind the condition of the coronary arteries. Prior to going on bypass and while the long saphenous vein was being removed, the carotid artery was exposed with the patient cleansed and draped for bypass grafting of the coronary artery should this become urgently necessary. The carotid vessels were carefully exposed and a Pruitt shunt inserted in all cases after giving 5000 units of heparin. None of the patients were monitored. After completion of the endarterectomy, with fixation of the distal intimal flap where necessary, the defect in the carotid artery was closed with the upper portion of the long saphenous vein as a patch (Fig. 3). Once this had been done, haemostasis was secured and the wound loosely closed around a swab for complete closure later after the CABG had been performed and heparin reversed.

In our experience the endarterectomy has not added significantly to the time of the procedure, it is usually completed before the legs have been sutured after removal of the long saphenous vein. When the endarterectomy is finished the patient is immediately placed on bypass for CABG.

RESULTS

In this series of 30 patients there have been two perioperative deaths (6.7% mortality) due to severe myocardial problems. There was one perioperative stroke which

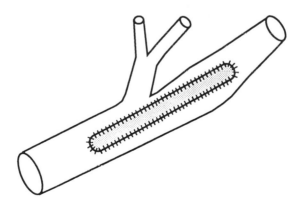

Fig. 3.   In all cases the arteriotomy was closed with a vein patch.

occurred on the contralateral side in a patient with bilateral disease. Two patients have suffered transient perioperative strokes, one due to haemorrhage following excessive anticoagulation and the other in a patient with contralateral occlusion where the shunt was kinked. All three of these recovered completely. One patient had a permanent stroke and died at 6 weeks. This gives an ipsilateral transient stroke rate of 10%, a contralateral transient stroke rate of 3% and a permanent stroke rate of 3%.

DISCUSSION

The correct method of treating these patients remains unanswered. Two recent publications have suggested that a staged procedure in patients who have high grade stenoses produces good results.[8,9] For asymptomatic cases we still do not know if a carotid endarterectomy is required at all. In patients who have symptomatic disease there is less controversy about the need for surgery to both systems but the question is when should it be done. There are no controlled studies to help us make the right decision. For synchronous procedures there is even disagreement about the order of the events. If the CABG is done first on bypass and the carotid second, better results have been claimed than if the CABG follows carotid endarterectomy.[10] The average mortality for synchronous procedures is 5.6% and the average permanent stroke rate 6.3%.[5] In our series the total mortality has been 10% but only two were due to myocardial ischaemia (6.7%). The permanent stroke rate was 3% but there were a number of transient events, one contralateral, which were caused by over anti-coagulation or shunt kinking. In a series of 250 non-CABG patients, our permanent stroke ratio has been 2%. It is likely that our results can be improved by the use of intraoperative monitoring with transcranial Doppler to assess the cerebral circulation throughout the combined procedure and afterwards in the recovery area.

At present the availability of data on the importance of high grade asymptomatic lesions, the question of whether or not an operation should be performed in these cases remains unresolved. It may be that unilateral asymptomatic lesions of whatever severity should probably be left alone. Bilateral severe lesions are again difficult but patients with occlusion on one side and a significant lesion on the other should also probably have a carotid endarterectomy of the stenosed side. Symptomatic lesions >70% should have a carotid endarterectomy but exactly when to do it remains controversial. There are obviously high risk cases and a randomized study has to be done before we can answer the question which patients undergoing CABG should have a CE and when should it be done. Such a trial would need to be multicentre because of the large number of patients needed and the variables involved.

REFERENCES

1. Hart RG, Eaton JD: Management of cervical bruits and carotid stenosis in preoperative patients. Stroke 14: 290–297, 1983
2. Barnes RW, Nix ML, Sansonetti D et al.: Late outcome of untreated asymptomatic carotid disease following cardiovascular operations. Surgery 2: 843–848, 1985

3. Brener BJ, Bruf DK, Alpert J *et al.*: The risk of stroke in patients with asymptomatic carotid stenosis undergoing cardiac surgery. A follow up study. J Vasc Surg 5: 269–277, 1987
4. Hertzer NR, Loop FD, Beven EG *et al.*: Surgical staging for simultaneous coronary and carotid disease: A study including prospective randomisation. J Vasc Surg 9: 455–463, 1989
5. Bernstein EF: Staged versus simultaneous carotid enarterectomy in patients undergoing cardiac surgery. J Vasc Surg 15: 870–871, 1992
6. MRC European Carotid Surgery Trial: Interim results for symptomatic patients with severe (70–99%) or mild (0–29%) carotid stenosis. Lancet 337: 1236–1242, 1991
7. NASCET. Beneficial effect of carotid endarterectomy in symptomatic patients with high grade carotid stenosis. N Engl J Med 325: 445–453, 1991
8. Suy R, Nevelsteen A, Sergeant P *et al.*: Combined myocardial and cerebral revascularisation. J Cardiovasc Surg 33 (Suppl 28): 1992
9. Newman DC, Hicks RG: Combined coronary artery surgery/carotid endarterectomy. The last resort. J Cardiovasc Surg 33 (Suppl 28): 1992
10. Minami K, Morshuis M, Moczulski J *et al.*: Simultaneous revascularisation for coronary and carotid stenosis using cardiopulmonary bypass for both procedures. J Cardiovasc Surg 33 (Suppl 28): 1992

Mandibular Subluxation for Exposure of the Distal Internal Carotid Artery

Calvin B. Ernst, Christos Dossa and Alexander D. Shepard

INTRODUCTION

The first report of successful carotid reconstruction for atherosclerotic occlusive disease, performed by Eastcott and Rob on 19 May 1954, appeared in the Lancet in 1954.[1] Although not reported until 1975, DeBakey performed the first successful carotid endarterectomy on 7 August 1953.[2] Over the ensuing four decades, the technical aspects of carotid endarterectomy have been refined and have become standardized; this is reflected in the over 100 000 carotid endarterectomies performed in the USA in 1985.[3] Less well standardized is exposure and reconstruction of the distal internal carotid artery (ICA), considered by some to be inaccessible. No doubt this perceived inaccessibility relates to obscuration of the distal internal carotid artery by the mandible and overlying neuromuscular structures. Also, because of the rarity of lesions involving the mid and distal segments of the ICA, such carotid exposure is seldom performed; it is a requirement in only about 5% of patients treated by the Vascular Surgery Division at the Henry Ford Hospital.

LESIONS REQUIRING DISTAL ICA EXPOSURE

Distal ICA lesions are defined as those cephlad to a line between the tip of the mastoid process and the angle of the mandible, projected on a lateral carotid arteriogram, as suggested by the Joint Study of Extracranial Arterial Occlusion.[4]

Practically all lesions requiring ICA reconstruction involve the bifurcation of the common carotid artery and proximal ICA, are atherosclerotic in origin, and are easily accessible. Conversely, lesions requiring distal ICA repair are rarely atherosclerotic. These include fibromuscular dysplastic stenoses and kinks, aneurysms either true, false, or mycotic, and ICA injuries. Management of arterial complications of radiation therapy and excision of benign and malignant neoplasms may also require distal ICA exposure for arterial reconstruction or ligation. Correction of these distally situated lesions is often impossible using standard ICA exposure techniques. Although over 95% of atherosclerotic carotid bifurcation lesions are readily exposed, some may extend into the mid and distal ICA. Under such circumstances, complete removal of such extensive disease may require distal ICA exposure. Distal ICA exposure may also be required when managing recurrent occlusive lesions, resulting from either atherosclerosis or fibrodysplasia.

The purpose of this chapter is to describe a technique to facilitate distal ICA exposure realizing that such exposure is uncommonly required but when it is, the ability to obtain distal ICA exposure facilitates the technical aspects of the operation for the surgeon and safety for the patient.

TECHNIQUES OF DISTAL INTERNAL CAROTID EXPOSURE

A variety of techniques have been suggested to facilitate distal ICA exposure.[5–14] Some require resection of bone, and are time consuming, complicated, and may be deforming or disabling. Such techniques involve three anatomic approaches in the neck: posterolateral, anterolateral, and lateral.

Posterolateral exposure of the distal ICA requires muscles to be resected with or without mastoid process excision and facial nerve manipulation.[11,12]

Anterolateral approaches to the distal ICA require a variety of osteotomies through the angle, body, or horizontal ramus of the mandible.[5,6,10,13,14] These osteotomies are time consuming and require mandibular wiring and maxillomandibular interdental fixation during healing.

The lateral approach utilizes temporary mandibular subluxation. Fry and Fry were the first to allude to this technique when reporting on management of distal ICA injuries.[9] They employed bilateral mandibular subluxation stabilized by interdental arch bar fixation, a time consuming process. This technique was modified by Fisher and his colleagues by substituting circummandibular-transnasal wiring for arch bar fixation.[8] This modification requires four blind passages of a dental awl through the mouth and nose to secure a transnasal-circummandibular 24 gauge stainless steel wire. This may result in bleeding complications in up to 17% of patients from injuries to facial and lingual vessels.

Temporary unilateral mandibular subluxation translocates the vertical ramus of the mandible 2 cm forward (Figs 1 and 2). This manoeuvre transforms the triangular operative field into a rectangular one by widening the critical apex. The additional apical exposure provided by this manoeuvre facilitates distal ICA dissection to within 1–2 cm of the base of the skull. This position must be maintained during distal ICA exposure and carotid reconstruction; hence, the various fixation techniques.

A new technique, developed by the Division of Vascular Surgery at the Henry Ford Hospital, appears safer, simpler, and less invasive than those previously described. It has been employed in 26 of 520 patients undergoing carotid artery reconstruction over a 6-year period. Indications included carotid endarterectomy (19), carotid body tumour excision (2), repair of carotid gunshot wound (2), repair of postendarterectomy false aneurysm (2), and repair of a true aneurysm (1).

TECHNIQUE OF TEMPORARY IPSILATERAL MANDIBULAR SUBLUXATION

Subluxation manoeuvres are performed in cooperation with an oral surgeon. Preoperative panorex X-rays are obtained to define the quality of dentition and localize the mental foramena. Antibiotics are given to cover oral flora. Nasotracheal general anaesthesia is required to permit placement of intraoral fixation hardware. After inducing adequate general anaesthesia, two different techniques to maintain ipsilateral temporomandibular joint (TMJ) subluxation are used depending upon

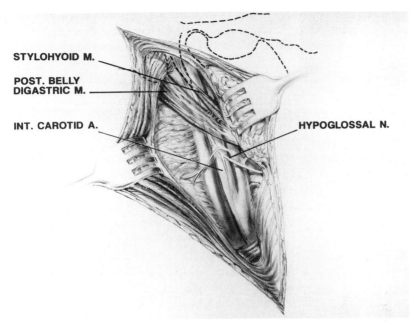

Fig. 1. Exposure of right carotid bifurcation through a standard cervical incision. Structures at apex of triangle obscure the distal internal carotid artery. Note normal configuration of the temporomandibular joint (dotted lines).

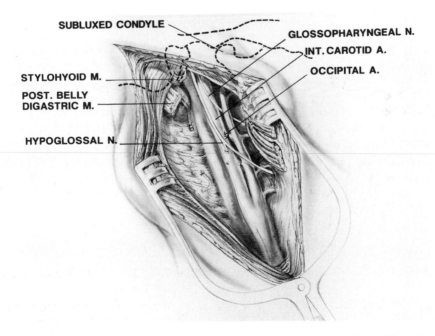

Fig. 2. Exposure of right carotid bifurcation after unilateral mandibular subluxation. The structures overlying the distal internal carotid artery have been divided. Note the subluxed mandibular condyle (dotted lines) converts the apex of the operative field from a triangular to a rectangular configuration.

presence or absence of healthy teeth. In dentate patients the subluxation position is held by Ivy loop interdental diagonal wiring of an ipsilateral mandibular cuspid or bicuspid tooth to a contralateral maxillary bicuspid or cuspid tooth using 25 gauge stainless steel wire.

In oedentulous patients stabilization is obtained by intermaxillary-mandibular wiring around two 3/32 inch Steinmann pins. After painting the oral cavity with an antiseptic solution, one pin is drilled into the ipsilateral mandible through the oral mucosa 2 cm posterior to the midline, anterior to the mental foramen, and midway between the inferior mandibular border and crest of the alveolar ridge. The pin is inserted until the tip is felt beneath the lingual oral mucosa but not through it. The second pin is drilled into the contralateral maxilla through the oral mucosa 2 cm posterior to the midline and 1 cm above the maxillary alveolar ridge until the tip is felt beneath the palatal mucosa. Each pin is cut so that 1–2 cm protrude and then a length of 25 gauge stainless steel wire is looped diagonally between the two protruding pins. After placing the diagonal wire loosely, the ipsilateral mandible is subluxed by gently pulling the jaw forward and toward the opposite side. It is important to avoid TMJ dislocation because this damages the joint cartilage and capsule (Fig. 3). The diagonal wire is then twisted tight enough to maintain a firm subluxation position. Total time for achieving subluxation and stabilization requires approximately 10–15 minutes.

After cleansing and draping the neck, a longitudinal incision is made along the anterior border of the sternocleidomastoid muscle (SCM). Occasionally, slight retroauricular extension of the skin incision is required. The parotid gland is not transected but mobilized anteriorly. The SCM is mobilized and retracted posteriorly,

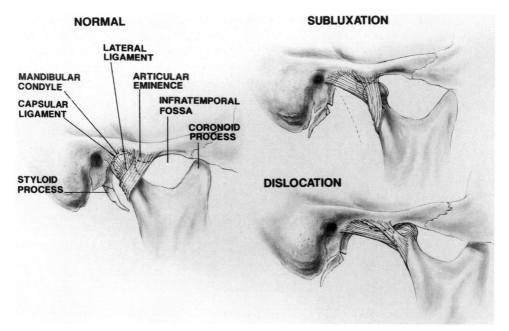

Fig. 3. Temporomandibular joint anatomy demonstrating subluxation and dislocation positions. Dislocation causes overstretching of joint capsular elements.

the carotid sheath is entered and the common, external, and proximal internal carotid arteries are dissected. After the vagus, hypoglossal, and glossopharyngeal nerves are identified, dissection of the ICA proceeds toward the base of the skull. The carotid sinus mechanism is preserved when possible. It is important to note that temporary mandibular subluxation distorts the normal anatomy of the apex of the anterior cervical triangle. The hypoglossal nerve and posterior belly of the digastric muscle are pulled anteriorly and assume a horizontal and more cephlad position than under normal circumstances.

Division of the posterior belly of the digastric muscle and the styloglosus, stylopharyngeus, and stylohyoid muscles exposes the underlying distal ICA. If necessary, the styloid process can be excised following division of the mastoid insertion of the SCM. The SCM must be incised with care to avoid injury to the underlying spinal accessory nerve. Excision of the styloid process is rarely required, however.

Following carotid reconstruction, the wires and pins are removed and the mandibular condyle is slipped back into place, a process requiring no more than 2–3 minutes.

Postoperatively, the patient is permitted to eat the following morning. No special restrictions are imposed. Prior to discharge and again 6 weeks after discharge the patient is reevaluated by an oral surgeon as well as a vascular surgeon.

COMMENT

Distal ICA exposure was adequate in all 26 patients studied. Three patients had transient TMJ pain which subsided within 72 hours of operation. No instances of bleeding, infection, malocclusion, or dental injury occurred. Seven patients had temporary cranial nerve deficits, not related to the subluxation, which resolved within 4 months. One had permanent dysfunction of cranial nerves IX, X, and XII following enbloc excision of a malignant carotid body tumour. All but two patients resumed eating the day after operation. No episodes of early or late TMJ dysfunction were encountered.

Exposure of the distal ICA may prove challenging even for the most experienced surgeon. This is particularly true under urgent or emergent circumstances. Temporary ipsilateral mandibular subluxation facilitates exposure of all but the distal 1 cm of the ICA before it enters the skull. Such exposure permits management of the majority of ICA lesions.

The method described is suitable for all patients regardless of dentition. In our experience, distal ICA exposure has not required mandibular osteotomy procedures. Although need for ipsilateral temporary mandibular subluxation may be required for only 3–5% of carotid endarterectomies, knowledge of such exposure facilitates difficult ICA operations and thereby enhances the safety of these procedures.

REFERENCES

1. Eastcott HHG, Pickering GW, Rob CG: Reconstruction of internal carotid artery in patient with intermittent attacks of hemiplegia. Lancet ii:994–996, 1954
2. DeBakey ME: Successful carotidendarterectomy for cerebrovascular insufficiency. Arch Surg 233:1083–1085, 1975

3. Ernst CB, Rutkow IM, Cleveland RJ, *et al.*: Vascular surgery in the United States. Report of the Joint Society for Vascular Surgery-International Society for Cardiovascular Surgery on Vascular Surgical Manpower. J Vasc Surg 6:611–621, 1987

4. Blaisdell WF, Clauss RH, Galbraith G, *et al.*: Joint study of extracranial arterial occlusion. J Am Med Assoc 209:1889–1895, 1969

5. Batzdorf U, Gregorius FK: Surgical exposure of the high cervical carotid artery: Experimental study and review. Neurosurg 13:657–660, 1983

6. Dichtel WJ, Miller RH, Feliciano DV, *et al.*: Lateral mandibulotomy: A technique of exposure for penetrating injuries of the internal carotid artery at the base of the skull. Laryngoscope 94:1140–1144, 1984

7. Dossa C, Shepard AD, Wolford DG, *et al.*: Distal internal carotid exposure: A simplified technique for temporary mandibular subluxation. J Vasc Surg 12:319–325, 1990

8. Fisher DF, Clagett GP, Parker JI, *et al.*: Mandibular subluxation for high carotid exposure. J Vasc Surg 6:727–733, 1984

9. Fry RE, Fry WJ: Extracranial carotid artery injuries. Surgery 88:581–587, 1980

10. Larsen PE, Smead WL: Vertical ramus osteotomy for improved exposure of the distal internal carotid artery: A new technique. J Vasc Surg 15:226–231, 1992

11. Purdue GF, Pellegrini RV, Arena S: Aneurysms of the high internal carotid artery: A new approach. Surgery 89:268–270, 1981

12. Shaha A, Phillips T, Scalea T, *et al.*: Exposure of the internal carotid artery near the skull base: The posterolateral anatomic approach. J Vasc Surg 8:618–622, 1988

13. Welsh P, Pradier R, Repetto R: Fibromuscular dysplasia of the distal cervical internal carotid artery. J Cardiovasc Surg 22:321–326, 1981

14. Wylie EJ, Ehrenfeld WK: Extracranial Occlusive Cerebrovascular Disease. Diagnosis and Management. Philadelphia: WB Saunders, p. 192, 1970

A Prospective Randomized Study of Local and General Anaesthetic

Rabbe Takolander

Pharmacological therapy combined with carotid endarterectomy is the method of choice to prevent stroke in symptomatic patients with ipsilateral carotid artery stenosis of 70% or more of the diameter.[1] In the long-term stroke frequency is low i.e. some 1% per year for patients who undertake the operation without problems.

It is thus of utmost importance to make the operation as safe as possible. The greatest problem during surgery consists of emboli in connection with exposing the vessels or emboli or postoperative occlusions due to intimal flaps. One source for intimal tear leading to a flap is the indwelling shunt used during operation to protect the brain from ischaemia during clamping of the carotid artery. There is a small group, 5–10% of the patients, who need the shunt. It has been shown that patients with contralateral occlusion and those with a preoperative stroke are in need of a shunt more often than other patients.[2] In choosing the other candidates for shunting a great number of methods have been used: stump pressure, rCBF measurements, EEG, transcranial Doppler alone or together with evoked potential response, jugular vein O_2 tension, and subjectively estimated quality of the back bleeding from the stump; all this concerns those patients being operated on under general anaesthetic (GA).

For local anaesthetic (LA) on the other hand, the patient may be neurologically monitored during the clamping of the carotid artery. A shunt need be applied only in cases of neurological dysfunction.

Local anaesthetic has been used for carotid surgery since the 1960s and Spencer and Eiseman[3] are of the opinion that only by having the patient awake and alert can the surgeon determine the safety of temporary occlusion of the internal carotid artery and then decide whether the patient needs a shunt or not. It has been postulated that LA is cheaper, less stressing for the patient and gives a faster operation. Several authors have also shown that a shunt is needed in significantly lower numbers in those patients operated under LA compared with those under GA.

However, given the choice, most surgeons are said to opt for GA. Furthermore, several patients are reluctant to undergo carotid surgery under LA.

There are also some disadvantages with LA. If the procedure is prolonged due to difficulties of any kind, the patient may become agitated. Furthermore, under LA the patient is anxious resulting in a higher level of sympathetic tonus[4] which is not comfortable. For the surgeon it may be distressing to perform a tricky operation on an anxious patient who may have problems lying calmly on the operating table.

But GA also has its pros and cons. During GA there are better possibilities to control the airway and to provide anaesthetics which lower the metabolic demand of the brain (e.g. isoflurane). Furthermore a sleeping patient does not disturb the surgeon and in cases where high dissection is anticipated GA may be better.

Several reports have also shown that there are equally good results with both forms of anaesthetic. In order to make a comparison between local and general anaesthetic with special emphasis on complications (stroke and mortality) and the need for intraoperative shunting, a randomized study was performed at Malmö General Hospital, University of Lund[5] during the years 1985–1987 since at that time no such randomized study could be found in the literature.

THE RANDOMIZED STUDY

Material

During the two years of the study 114 consecutive patients with carotid artery stenoses requiring operation were asked to participate in the randomized trial and 125 carotid operations were performed in these patients. On 14 occasions patients were not randomized for different reasons (Table 1). Of those originally randomized to LA eight were finally operated under GA for different reasons: changed consent in three, occurrence of preoperative angina in two, conversion to atrial fibrillation before induction of the LA in two cases and in one case due to failing anaesthesiological resources. There were no statistical differences between the groups as to indications, age, sex, presence of hypertension, coronary artery disease or diabetes mellitus. A 'second operation', i.e. an operation on a carotid artery on the side opposite to an earlier operated carotid, was more common ($p < 0.05$) among patients randomized to LA (16%) than in the group of patients randomized to GA (4%).

The median age in the LA group was 66 (47–88) years and in the GA group the median age was 63 (40–77) years. Both groups were premedicated with pethidin-dixyracin or fentanyl–droperidol.

Local anaesthetic was accomplished with a cervical block (Figs 1,2) using 20 ml 0.25% bupivacain accompanied by a 20–40 ml skin infiltration of the operative area with 0.5% mepivacin with adrenaline (5 µg/ml). No glomus caroticum blockade was

Table 1.   Unrandomized patients

Unwilling to participate	4
Ongoing heparin infusion	2
Serious chronic cerebral insuffiency	2
Extremely uneasy during previous LA	1
Randomization miss	1
Anxiety, angina	1
Previous allergic reaction to local analgesics	1
Simultaneous operation for aortic aneurysm	1
Emergent operation	1
Total:	14

LA: local anaesthesia.
From Eur J Vasc Surg 3: 503–509, 1989, with permission.

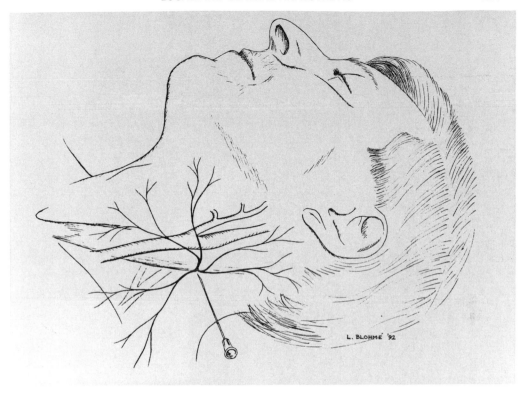

Fig. 1. The superficial nerve block. The needle is inserted some 2 cm in front of the posterior border of the sternomastoid muscle at the midpoint between the clavicle and the basis of the skull.

used. The induction of general anaesthetic was performed with thiopenthal (3–5 mg/kg bodyweight) and anaesthesia was maintained with isoflurane and nitrous oxide together with intravenously administered fentanyl (0.2–0.4 mg totally). After induction the skin in the operative area was infiltrated with ~40 ml 0.25% bupivacain with adrenaline (5 μg/ml).

Criteria for using a shunt

In the LA group an intraoperative shunt was used if any evidence of neurological deterioration was seen during 1-min test clamping or later during the procedure. In the GA group a shunt was used whenever possible in all patients with reversible or permanent strokes and whenever the stump pressure was lower than 50 mmHg (systolic) in patients with vertebrobasilar ischaemia and if lower than 25 mgHg in all other patients. The Pruitt-Inahara shunt was used and during shunting the patients were heparinized. All patients received 1000 ml dextran 40 during the day of operation and 500 ml for each of the three following days.

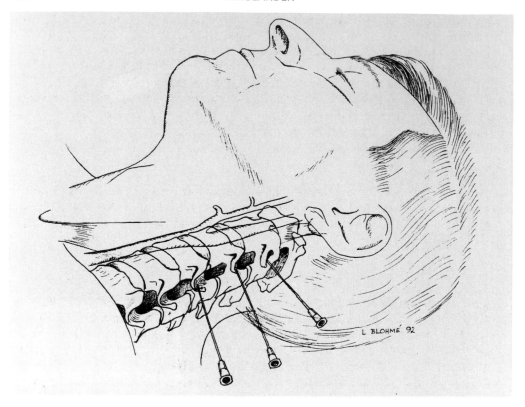

Fig. 2. Deep cervical block is accomplished by directing the needle against the transverse processes from behind the vessel structures and depositing the local anaesthetic where the nerves emerge. (Care must be taken to avoid the vertebral artery.)

Results

Mortality

Among the randomized patients one patient in the GA group died of sudden asystole 96 h after the operation—probably a coronary death. In the non-randomized group also one patient died due to myocardial infarction 7 h after operation.

Neurological defects

Neurological defects were seen in seven patients (Table 2). Of these, three patients in the LA group and two in the GA group were re-explored. Three LA patients and one GA patient had a thrombus removed. The remaining patient had a normal postoperative vessel without thrombus. Of those with a thrombus removed, one was

Table 2.   Perioperative neurological deficits

LA	GA	Non-randomized
4 (8.3%)	2 (3.6%) NS	1

LA: local anaesthesia; GA: general anaesthesia.

free from symptoms after reoperation, and the others suffered established strokes. Thus three patients in the LA group and one in the GA group suffered established strokes of minor degree. One patient in each group (as well as the non-randomized patient) were symptom-free in 2–3 days (reversible transient stroke).

The median time lapse from operation to discovered neurological deficit in the six patients who were included in the randomized groups was 3 h with a range of 1 to 9 h. There was no statistical difference in the interval to detection of stroke between the two groups (mean LA 1.75 h, GA 5.5 h).

Blood pressure during operation

Both at clamping and intraoperatively the blood pressure was higher in the LA group ($p<0.001$). Intraoperatively both the highest recorded intraoperative systolic as well as the lowest recorded intraoperative systolic pressure was significantly higher in the LA group ($p<0.001$) (Fig. 3).

The use of shunt

An indwelling shunt was used in five of the operations performed under LA and in 25 of the operations performed under GA. Thus a 10.4% shunt use in the LA group *vs* 45% in the GA group a highly significant difference ($p<0.001$). In the LA group two patients had symptoms during test clamping and three developed symptoms later on during clamping (Table 3). An additional patient had neurological symptoms at the end of the clamping period and was not shunted. In all patients the symptoms disappeared after restoration of flow (either shunting or declamping). Of the 26 stroke patients in the LA group, 20 were shunted whereas six (who had pressures below 50 mmHg) were not shunted for technical reasons. Five transient ischaemic attack (TIA) or Am Fugax patients were also shunted in this group of patients, three because of low stump pressures and two (with pressures >50 mmHg) for technical reasons in order to avoid extremely long clamping times.

If strict pressure criteria had been used in the LA group, ten patients would have been shunted and three of the patients who developed symptoms would not have been shunted. Indeed, when combining both pressure and the clinical state of the patients (preoperative stroke) for both groups, 29 in the GA group and 22 in the LA group of patients would have needed a shunt.

Myocardial infarction

There was one myocardial infarction in the GA group (fatal) and two in the LA group. Also one myocardial infarction occurred in the non-randomized group. All of these patients suffered from preoperative recognized coronary artery disease.

Further remarks

Postoperative bleeding, necessitating reoperation, occurred in one of the LA group and in six of the GA group. The operating time was the same in both groups (84/85 min).

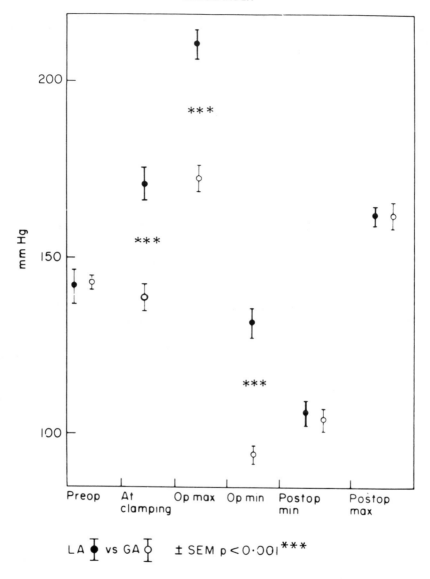

Fig. 3. Systolic blood pressure during carotid endarterectomy. From Ref. 5, with permision.

COMMENTS

There were no differences in stroke incidence or mortality between the two groups. From the beginning it was thought that big differences should be found and thus a fairly small material would be satisfactory. However, there were other lessons to be learned from this study which brought further understanding for both of the forms of anaesthetic.

No patient in the study had a stroke during the operation, indicating that no perioperative low flow infarction occurred. It is, however, possible that selective

Table 3. Development of neurological symptoms during LA

Indication for surgery	Stump pressure (systolic mmHg)	Time of occlusion (min)
Stroke	40	<1
Stroke	35	11
TIA	30	<1
TIA[a]	35	20
TIA	30	10
TIA[a]	35	18

[a]Systolic pressure drop of 20 mmHg immediately before symptoms developed.
Modified from Eur J Vasc Surg 3: 503–509, 1989, with permission

shunting in the GA group based on stump pressure criteria may have included patients who would not have been operated with a shunt, had they been operated on under LA because the blood pressure was higher in the LA group. But, as mentioned earlier, many shunts in the GA group were for pragmatic reasons. On the other hand the higher blood pressure in the LA group during the operation is probably reflected in the fact that if strict pressure criteria had been used, twice as many GA as LA patients would have been shunted.

However, although patients in the LA group had higher blood pressures during surgery, this was not reflected in higher stump pressures. The conclusion of this is that raising the systemic blood pressure must not necessarily lead to higher stump pressures which has been pointed out earlier[2] and moderate hypertension does not prevent cerebral ischaemia during carotid clamping in patients with critically impaired collateral function.[6] With a higher pressure during operation in these patients the cardiac risk rises.[7,8] With a restrictive use of at least phenylephrine during GA the occurrence of perioperative myocardial infarction appears to decrease.[9] Thus it seems to be a simple and safe way to evaluate the need for a shunt by monitoring the conscious patient, a fact that has been pointed out by several investigators.[2,3,10–20]

Some are of the opinion that regional anaesthesia is more for patients with coronary artery disease and in patients at risk of intolerance to cross-clamping e.g. those with clinical signs and/or cerebral sequelae.[21,22]

Usually a temporary clamping of 1 min is used in order to detect if the patient is in need of a shunt. However, in our study it was shown[5] that the 1 min clamping did not reveal all those patients in need of an intraoperative shunt and there were patients who still experienced a functional ischaemia after 20 min. Others have used a 5-min test clamping time satisfactorily.

One of the drawbacks with LA was clearly seen in this study. Four of the patients were unwilling to participate in the randomization because of fear of being operated under LA. Three patients changed their consent. Two developed severe angina before induction of the local anaesthetic and two converted to atrial fibrillation preoperatively. Several of the patients in the LA group were definitely anxious during the procedure. Others have also reported patient refusal in 10%.[23]

A fairly high percentage of the patients in the study showed signs of coronary artery disease (49%). It is thus understandable that angina pectoris and atrial fibrillation disturbed the study. Mental stress can cause angina in patients with coronary artery disease and data suggest that in atherosclerosis unopposed constriction caused by a local failure of endothelium-dependent dilation causes the coronary arteries to respond abnormally to mental stress.[24]

SYMPATHETIC ACTIVITY DURING LOCAL AND GENERAL ANAESTHESIA: A SPIN-OFF STUDY

On clinical grounds it was thus obvious that several patients experienced stress during their operation under local anaesthetic. In order to evaluate the state of affairs a spin-off study of sympathetic activity during the procedure was conducted.[4]

Three different groups of patients were studied: those who underwent the operation under 1) LA; 2) GA with skin infiltration (GAs); and 3) GA without skin infiltration (GAo).

If one disregards results concerning plasma-adrenaline which to some extent may have been biased at least during the first stages of anaesthesia and surgery by adrenaline given in the local anaesthetics both in the LA and GAs groups there was a significant rise in plasma noradrenaline in the LA group during anaesthesia and surgery (Fig. 4). The rate of noradrenaline release has been shown to parallel the rate of sympathetic nerve firing[25-27] and plasma noradrenaline activity in these cases may thus be used as an index of overall sympathetic activity.[28-30] Plasma

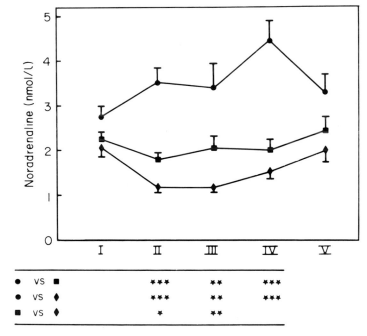

Fig. 4. Arterial plasma noradrenaline concentration in connection with carotid endarterectomy. I: 30 min before anaesthesia; II: After anaesthesia immediately before skin incision; III: After exposure of the carotid artery before clamping; IV: After declamping of the carotid artery; V: 1 h after surgery; ● local anaesthesia; ■ general anaesthesia with skin infiltration; ◆ general anaesthesia without skin infiltration. *$P<0.05$, **$P<0.01$, ***$P<0.001$. Mean ± SEM. From Ref. 4, with permission.

catecholamines were positively correlated to blood pressure and hypotensive reactions were mainly seen during GA and hypertensive reactions were only seen during LA.

From these studies it is clear that both types of anaesthetic have their disadvantages in patients with an increased risk for cardiovascular morbidity/mortality i.e. a risk patient is a risk patient.

PROS AND CONS

Perioperative hypertension in carotid surgery is usually best correlated with badly controlled preoperative hypertension. It has been shown that perioperative hypertension in connection with carotid endarterectomy has a shorter duration in patients operated under LA compared with those operated under GA.[31,32] It is believed that this would be related to the effects of GA, with increased sensitivity to, or release of, sympathomimetic hormones as a direct result of the anaesthetic agents. However, there is evidence of higher catecholamine levels in the LA group.[4]

When discussing pros and cons for local and general anaesthetic in carotid surgery one has to agree with Trop[33] who is of the opinion that the controversy is not local vs general anaesthetic but rather temporary indwelling shunt or not. If for a moment we disregard the question of shunting, then the discussion becomes dull and filled with personal preferences more than ever. But these preferences are intimately coupled with our concern for the protection of the brain during clamping.

The problem with our LA group would be the anxiety of the patient and if this could be mastered in a better way at least our concern at this point could be eliminated. With neuroleptics it is possible to overcome the anxiety of the patient and its triggering effect on the sympathoadrenal response but these may induce apnoea. In the present study only low doses of fentanyl (0.2–0.4 mg totally) were used. But even in higher doses (10 μg/kg bodyweight) fentanyl seems to be less damping on the sympathoadrenal response than e.g. enflurane.[34] In order to prevent increase in catecholamine concentrations and attenuate the circulatory response to surgical stress much higher doses are needed (100 μg/kg body weight) which has been administered in connection with GA.[35] However, it has been claimed that LA with neuroleptic supplement i.e. droperidol in increments of 0.1 mg to a total dose of 5 mg and fentanyl citrate in increments of 0.05 mg to a total dose of 0.3 mg is sufficient to overcome patient anxiety in connection with LA.[36]

COST-EFFECTIVENESS

In our study there were no differences in costs between the two forms of anaesthetic due to some simple facts. First of all LA per se was not allowed to influence the length of stay in hospital. Secondly, an anaesthesiologist was present all the time during all operations under LA and GA. Furthermore, there was no difference in the duration of the procedures with LA or GA.

Others have noticed both a longer stay in the intensive care unit (ICU) and in a regular hospital bed by the group of patients operated under GA. The longer ICU stay has been due to postoperative hypertension treated with intravenous nitroprusside.

In the series of Godin *et al.*[32] LA saved 54% in hospital room fees alone and in Gabelman's study[14] the savings with LA were reported to be 29% compared with GA. However, in socialized countries the savings may not be significant between the two groups.

CONCLUSIONS

Good results have been recorded with several different techniques in carotid surgery both with the patient conscious, or under general anaesthetic with differences in opinion regarding the specificity and sensitivity of monitoring techniques and what protective measures should be taken to avoid cerebral damage during the procedure.[37,38]

When discussing the pros and cons of LA and GA most of the discussion concerns how best to protect the brain during clamping—i.e. to use a shunt or not.

With the patient under LA the brain function may be monitored accurately and unnecessary shunts avoided. No other monitoring technique is as accurate, but many patients are reluctant to undergo carotid endarterectomy under LA and those undergoing it may show signs of anxiety with higher blood pressures recorded than during GA and a higher sympathoadrenal activity may be observed. Hypertensive periods may be longer among those patients operated under GA.

Equally good results have been accomplished with endarterectomy of the carotid arteries under GA and LA. Both techniques offer their pros and cons but neither outrules the other. Several authors have expressed their satisfaction with performing carotid endarterectomy under LA.

REFERENCES

1. ECST trialists' collaborative group. MRC European carotid surgery trial: interim results for symptomatic patients with severe (70–99%) or mild (0–29%) carotid stenosis. Lancet 337: 1235–1243, 1991
2. Imparato A, Ramirez A, Riles T, Mintzer R: Cerebral protection in carotid surgery. Arch Surg 117: 1073–1078, 1982
3. Spencer F, Eiseman B: Technique of carotid endarterectomy. Surg Gynecol Obstet 115: 115–117, 1962
4. Takolander R, Bergqvist D, Hulthén U, Johansson A, Katzman P: Carotid artery surgery. Local versus general anaesthesia as related to sympathetic activity and cardiovascular effects. Eur J Vasc Surg 4: 265–270, 1990
5. Forssell C, Takolander R, Bergqvist D, Johansson A, Persson N: Local versus general anaesthesia in carotid surgery. A prospective, randomised study. Eur J Vasc Surg 3: 503–509, 1989
6. Boysen G, Engell H, Henriksen H: The effect of induced hypertension on internal carotid artery pressure and regional cerebral blood flow during temporary carotid clamping for endarterectomy. Neurology 22: 1133–1144, 1972
7. Riles T, Kopelman I, Imparato A: Myocardial infarction following carotid endarterectomy: A review of 683 operations. Surgery 85: 249–252, 1979
8. Smith J, Roizen M, Cahalan *et al.*: Does anesthetic technique make a difference? Augmentation of systolic blood pressure during carotid endarterectomy: Effects of phenylephrine versus light anesthesia and of isoflurane versus halothane on the incidence of myocardial ischemia. Anesthesiology 69: 846–853, 1988

9. Modica P, Tempelhoff R, Rich K, Grupp R: Computerized electroencephalographic monitoring and selective shunting: Influence on intraoperative administration of phenylephrine and myocardial infarction after general anesthesia for carotid endarterectomy. Neurosurgery 30: 842–846, 1982

10. Agrifoglio G, Agus G, Bonalumi F, Costantini A, Crlesi R: The role of regional nerve block anesthesia for carotid endarterectomy: An experimental comparison with previous series with the use of general anesthesia and barbiturates for cerebral protection. Inter Angio 6: 365–369, 1987

11. Bosiljevac J, Farha S: Carotid endarterectomy: Results using regional anesthesia. Am Surg 46: 403–408, 1980

12. Connolly J: Carotid endarterectomy in the awake patient. Am J Surg 150: 159–165, 1985

13. Evans W, Hayes J, Waltke E, Vermilion B: Optimal cerebral monitoring during carotid endarterectomy: Neurologic response under local anaesthesia. J Vasc Surg 6: 775–777, 1985

14. Gableman C, Gann D, Ashworth C, Carney W: One-hundred consecutive reconstructions: Local versus general anaesthesia. Am J Surg 145: 477–481, 1983

15. Hafner C: Minimizing the risks of carotid endarterectomy. J Vasc Surg 1: 392–397, 1984

16. Hafner C, Evans W: Carotid endarterectomy with local anesthesia: Results and advantages. J Vasc Surg 7: 232–239, 1988

17. Luosto R, Ketonen P, Mattila S, Takkunen O, Eerola S: Local anaesthesia in carotid surgery. Scand J Thor Cardiovasc Surg 18: 133–137, 1984

18. Peitzman A, Webster M, Loubeau J-M, Grundy B, Bahnson H: Carotid endarterectomy under regional (conductive) anesthesia. Ann Surg 196: 59–64, 1982

19. Prough D, Scuderi P, Stullken E, Davis C: Myocardial infarction following regional anaesthesia for carotid endarterectomy. Can Anaesth Soc J 31: 192–196, 1984

20. Shifrin E, Gertler M, Anner H, Olshwang D, Levy P: Local anesthesia in carotid endarterectomy: an alternative method. Israel J Med Sci 21: 511–513, 1985

21. Becquemin J-P, Paris E, Valverde A, Pluskwa F, Mellière D: Carotid surgery. Is regional anesthesia always appropriate? J Cardiovasc Surg 32: 592–598, 1991

22. Bergeron P, Benichou H, Rudondy P et al.: Stroke prevention during carotid surgery in high risk patients (value of transcranial Doppler and local anesthesia). J Cardiovasc Surg 32: 713–719, 1991

23. Pick M, Taylor G: Selective shunting on the basis of carotid clamping under regional anaesthesia. Int Anesthesiol Clin 22: 129–135, 1984

24. Yeung A, Vekshtein V, Krantz D et al.: The effect of atherosclerosis on the vasomotor response of coronary arteries to mental stress. N Engl J Med 325: 1551–1556, 1991

25. Wallin B, Mörlin C, Hjelmdahl P: Muscle sympathetic activity and venous plasma noradrenaline concentrations during static exercise in normotensive and hypertensive subjects. Acta Physiol Scand 129: 489–497, 1987

26. Wallin B: Muscle sympathetic activity and plasma concentration of noradrenaline. Acta Physiol Scand 527 (suppl): 21–24, 1984

27. Brown G, Gillespie J: The output of sympathetic transmitter from the spleen of the cat. J Physiol 138: 81–102, 1957

28. Esler M, Hasking G, Willett I, Leonard P, Jennings G: Noradrenaline release and sympathetic nervous system activity. J Hypertens 3: 117–129, 1985

29. Bravo E, Tarazi R. Plasma catecholamines in clinical investigations: a useful index or a meaningless number? J Lab Clin Med 100: 155–160, 1982

30. Cryer P. Physiology and pathophysiology of the human sympathoadrenal and neuro-endocrine system. N Engl J Med 303: 436–444, 1980

31. Corson J, Chang B, Leopold P et al.: Perioperative hypertension in patients undergoing carotid endarterectomy: shorter duration under regional block anesthesia. Circulation 74 (Suppl I): I.1–I.4, 1986

32. Godin M, Bell W, Schwedler M, Kerstein M: Cost effectiveness of regional anesthesia in carotid endarterectomy. Am Surg 55: 656–659, 1989

33. Trop D: Con: Carotid endarterectomy: General is safer than regional anesthesia. J Cardiothor Anesth 1: 483–488, 1987

34. Hamberger B, Järnberg P-O: Plasma catecholamines during surgical stress: Differences between neurolept and enflurane anaesthesia. Acta Anaesthesiol Scand 27: 307–310, 1983

35. Klingstedt C, Giesecke K, Hamberger B, Järnberg P-O: High- and low-dose fentanyl anaesthesia: circulatory and plasma catecholamine responses during cholecystectomy. Br J Anaesth 59: 184–188, 1987

36. Slutzki S, Behar M, Negri M: Carotid endarterectomy under local anesthesia supplemented with neuroleptic analgesia. Surg Gynecol Obstet 170: 141–144, 1990

37. Ferguson G: Intra-operative monitoring and internal shunts: Are they necessary in carotid endarterectomy? Stroke 13: 287–289, 1982

38. Imparato A: How much can the risk of stroke be influenced by surgery? *In* Vascular Surgery, Issues in Current Practice, Greenhalgh RM, Jamieson CW, Nicolaides AM (Eds). London, New York: Grune & Stratton, 1986

Peripheral Nerve Injuries in Carotid Artery Surgery

C. Forssell, D. Bergqvist and S.-E. Bergentz

Injuries to the peripheral nerves have been less frequently studied than other complications in carotid artery surgery, especially in prospective studies. Reported frequencies of injuries vary from 3 to 80%.[1,2] The reasons for these variations are multifactorial and will be discussed later in this chapter.

Since the area surrounding the carotid bifurcation has a very elaborate anatomical structure it is not surprising that injuries to the nerves are common and carotid artery surgery is probably the surgical procedure most often complicated by nerve damage. A detailed knowledge of the surgical anatomy of the area and a meticulous surgical technique will help to prevent this irksome morbidity in otherwise successful carotid surgery.

FACIAL NERVE (VII)

The cervicofacial branch of the facial nerve has a mandibular branch which supplies the lower part of the orbicularis oris muscle. It exits from the parotid gland near its apex and swings just below the mandibular angle deep to the platysma. It continues parallel to and about 1 cm inferior to the mandibula and curves towards the corner of the mouth (Fig. 1).

Following injury the patient will experience weakness in the corner of the mouth and sometimes subsequent socially handicapping drooling or accidental biting of the lip leading to painful lacerations. The damage may be confused with a central facial paresis which, however, also involves the upper lip.

The importance of using a dorsally curved vertical incision or a more transverse incision to avoid this injury has been stressed by several authors.[3-6] Verta et al., however, mention[7] that transverse incisions may have served to increase the number of injuries to the hypoglossal and marginal mandibular nerve. Self-retaining retractors jamming the tissue between the wound and the jaw may also contribute to this injury. The head of the patient should not be turned too much as the nerve then will be more exposed to injury.

Damage is reported in a frequency of 0 to 6% in most studies[1,2,8-40] (Table 1) while in one old retrospective study the figure was as high as 11%.[20]

As with the other nerves described here, operations involving dissection towards the base of the skull carry a markedly increased risk of facial nerve injury. Sandmann et al.[37] and Sekhar et al.[38] report damage to this nerve in a frequency of 13 and 35%, respectively, in operations involving displacement of the mandible.

Most injuries to this nerve heal and symptoms resolve in a few days or weeks, and permanent damage from transection is rarely seen.

Table 1. Peripheral nerve injuries in carotid artery surgery

Author	No.	Year	p/r	Op	VII	IX	Xr	Xs	XI	XII	Phren	Aur	Cerv	Symp	Total
Hertzer	8	1980	p	240	2.5		5.8	2.1		5.4					15.8
Liapis	9	1981	p	40	5.0		27.0			20.0		7.5			[53]
Evans	10	1982	p	128		1.5	35.0			11.0					27.0
Astor	11	1983	p	133			5.9	1.3		5.8					14.3
Dehn	12	1983	p	43			25.0			5.0		60.0	69.0		30.0
Forssell	13	1985	p	162	0.6	1.2	3.1			10.5		6.8		1.2	16.7
Kitzing	14	1987	p	135			1.5			5.2					6.7
Downs	15	1987	p		4.0		4.0								12.0
Aldoori	2	1988	p	52	5.8		5.8			15.8		42.0	89.0		25.0
Forssell[a]		1992	p	665	0.3	0.3	1.2	0.5	0.2	10.7				0.3	11.4
Schmidt	16	1983	(p)	109	2.8		3.7			8.3					12.8
Weiss	17	1987	(p)	536	6.2	0.4	3.7			8.9		0.6			19.5
Rogers	1	1988	(p)	433	0.5	0.2	1.2			1.2					3.0
Rainer[c]	18	1966	r	148										0.7	4.8
DeWeese	19	1968	r	227						9.7					9.7
Ranson	20	1969	r	267			1.1			4.1				2.2	8.6
Matsumoto	21	1977	r	130	11.2					8.5					12.3
Bouchier-H	22	1979	r	72	1.5		2.3	1.4		8.3					12.5
Massey	23	1984	r	158	2.8		5.1			8.2					15.1
Koldsland[c]	24	1985	r	27	3.2					3.7					3.7
Krupski	25	1985	r	300	2.3		7.7			4.3		2.7		0.3	[17]
Das[d]	26	1985	r	65	3.0		1.5			6.2					11.0
Theodotou	27	1985	r	192	1.0		1.0			2.6					4.6
Rosenbloom	28	1987	r	2000		0.2									
Knight	29	1987	r	129	3.1		3.9			2.3					9.3
Tucker	30	1987	r	850					0.5						0.5
Fletcher	31	1988	r	142						4.2					7.7
Maniglia	32	1991	r	336	2.4		6.0			4.8	0.3				13.5
Brien	33	1991	r	100											10.0
DeBord	34	1991	r	324											3.1

Swedvasc[a]	35	1992	r	546				3.1	20.0	6.2
Fry[b]	36	1992	r	20						20.0
Fisher[e]	37	1984	r	24				4.2		4.2
Sandmann[e]	38	1984	r	31	12.5	50.0	21.9	9.4		65.6
Sekhar[e]	39	1986	r	29	34.5	44.8	44.8			?
Sundt[e]	40	1986	r	19		26.3				26.3
Hans[e]		1989	r	17		5.9				5.9

[a]Study not published.
[b]Carotid–subclavian bypass.
[c]Local anaesthesia.
[d]Operations for recurrent stenosis.
[e]Operations involving dissection near the base of the skull.
p/r Prospective/retrospective study.
(p) Prospective study without preoperative specialized laryngeal examination.
Figures are given in percentages of the number of operations in each study.
In the column for total there are percentages of operations with one or more cranial nerve injuries.
Figures in parens [ ] are estimated.

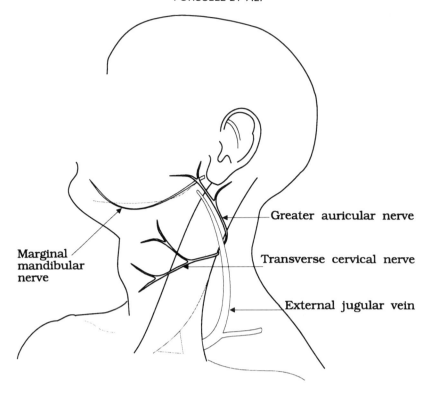

Greater auricular nerve

Marginal
mandibular
nerve

Transverse cervical nerve

External jugular vein

Fig. 1.

GLOSSOPHARYNGEAL NERVE (IX)

This nerve passes through the jugular foramen and descends laterally. Just below
the stylopharyngeal muscle it passes between the internal carotid artery and the
internal jugular vein lateral to the vagus nerve described below. It then continues
anteriorly under the cover of the hypoglossus muscle and crosses the middle
pharyngeal constrictor towards the base of the tongue (Fig. 2). The carotid sinus
nerve (nerve of Hering, nerve of deCastro) branches at the internal carotid artery
and descends to the carotid bulb. The pharyngeal plexus involves branches from
the ninth and tenth cranial nerve along with fibres from the superior cervical
sympathetic ganglion and supplies the complete motor and sensory innervation for
the pharynx.

The glossopharyngeal nerve provides sensory fibres for taste and sensation to the
posterior one-third of the tongue, pharyngeal mucosa, auditory tube and middle
ear. It also carries motor fibres to the laryngeal and pharyngeal elevators apart from
parasympathical fibres for the parotid gland. The carotid sinus nerve carries afferent
fibres from baro- and chemoreceptors in the carotid bulb.

The IXth nerve is normally not involved in the dissection for carotid endarterectomy,
unless it takes place towards the base of the skull. In high dissections damage to
the pharyngeal plexus may cause difficulties in swallowing.

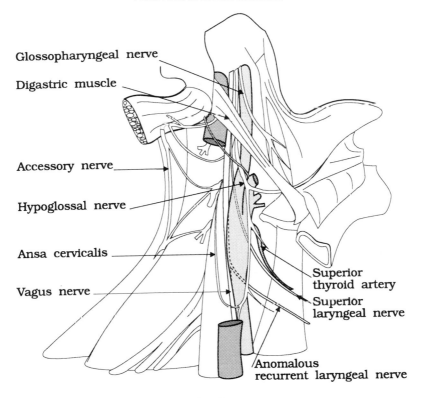

Glossopharyngeal nerve

Digastric muscle

Accessory nerve

Hypoglossal nerve

Ansa cervicalis

Vagus nerve

Superior
thyroid artery

Superior
laryngeal nerve

Anomalous
recurrent laryngeal nerve

Fig. 2.

Reports on damage to this nerve vary from 0 to 1.5% in prospective studies.[10,13,32] As with the VIIth nerve much higher frequencies are encountered after procedures involving high dissection and displacement of the mandible. Sandmann et al.[37] and Sekhar et al.[38] reported damage in 52 and 45%, respectively. It is also noteworthy that the contralateral nerves within the carotid sheath as well as the contralateral artery itself may be damaged in these operations.

In one study pharyngeal function has been examined with cineradiography before and after carotid surgery. Of 12 patients, five (42%) had pharyngeal dysfunction of which two were permanent.[41] These injuries were more common in patients operated on using a shunt, which may involve a more extensive dissection and traction.

Damage to the carotid sinus nerve may cause fluctuations in pulse and blood pressure. Hypertensive episodes during the operation may be avoided by infiltrating the carotid bifurcation with a local anaesthetic or by transecting the nerve. Postoperative baroreceptor function has been studied by several authors. Bove et al.[42] found a hypotensive postoperative response in 28% and a hypertensive response in 19%, and postoperative hypotension which seems to represent baroreceptor dysfunction was seen in 18%. Dehn and Angell-James[43] found no long-term effects on blood pressure while an increase in baroreceptor function was found in 32%, a decrease in 8% and no change in 60%. Hirschl et al.[44] found an increase in baroreceptor function in 50% of hypertensive patients after carotid endarterectomy while normotensive patients did not display any consistent postoperative blood pressure pattern. A paroxysm of hyptertension, headache and cutaneous flushing as a result of bilateral carotid sinus nerve damage has been reported in one case.[45]

In one patient chemoreceptor dysfunction after a bilateral carotid endarterectomy has been held responsible for postoperative respiratory depression,[46] while Vanmaele *et al.*[47] studied hypoxic ventilatory response after six bilateral carotid endarterectomies and found an increase in four, when special attention to preserve the carotid body was taken.

THE VAGUS NERVE (X)

The Xth cranial nerve exits the cranium through the jugular foramen, forms the ganglion nodosum and continues caudally posterolateral to the internal and common carotid artery in the groove towards the jugular vein within the carotid sheath. Anomalous position of the vagus nerve is not infrequent and in about 2% it may be found turning around the carotid artery on the anterior surface.[1,4]

The pharyngeal branches are given off at the superior end of the nodose ganglion. They form a plexus with branches from the glossopharyngeal nerve close to the pharyngeal wall.

The superior laryngeal nerve arises from the inferior end of the nodose ganglion and passes caudally medial to the carotid artery close to the pharyngeal wall. It divides within 2 cm into an external and an internal branch. The external branch, which is about 1–2 mm wide, has a great variation in its course towards the cricothyroid muscle and the laryngeal mucosa superior to the vocal cords which it innervates. In 70% it is bound within the visceral fascia while in 30% it is situated on the surface of the pretracheal fascia in close connection to the superior thyroid artery but mostly distinctly inferior to its origin. In 6%, however, the nerve lies anteriorly, following the artery[48] (Fig. 3). In distal bifurcations, the nerve can often be seen when the bifurcation is dissected free.

The recurrent laryngeal nerve is normally situated well away from the operative field. It branches from the medial fibres of the vagus nerve[49] in the mediastinum, on the left side around the ligamentum arteriosum and on the right side around the subclavian artery. The nerve passes to the larynx by way of the tracheoesophageal groove and may have an anomalous course directly to the larynx posterior to the carotid artery (Fig. 2).

Injury to the vagus nerve or its branches may occur at any level in the operating field during dissection or by improperly placed retractors. The vagus branches of the pharyngeal plexus carry motor fibres to the pharyngeal constrictors and injuries to these nerves will cause considerable dysphagia. Injuries to the superior laryngeal nerve are insidious with subtle symptoms which can be hard to detect. The voice becomes easily fatigued, lower pitched with a decreased range and is often coarse and husky. These symptoms are often transient but the injury may be permanent and disastrous to a person relying greatly on the use of his or her voice.[50,51]

Recurrent laryngeal nerve injury causes paralysis of all the ipsilateral intrinsic laryngeal muscles except for the aforementioned cricothyroid muscle and leaves the vocal cord in a median or paramedian position. This may be asymptomatic or cause

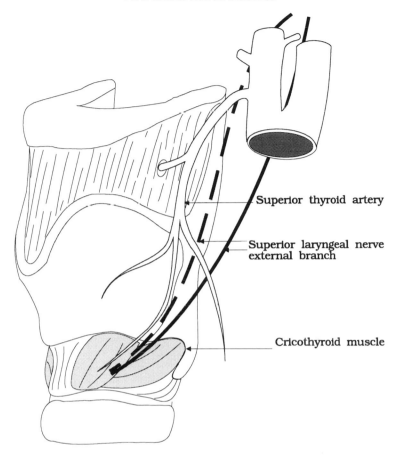

Superior thyroid artery

Superior laryngeal nerve
external branch

Cricothyroid muscle

Fig. 3.

hoarseness and loss of effective cough mechanism and/or dyspnoea. Bilateral injuries may cause life-threatening airway obstruction, and is one reason for not doing simultaneous bilateral surgery.

In redo-surgery or in patients with periarterial inflammation and fibrosis, meticulous technique during dissection is essential. If the plane of dissection is held adjacent to the artery, any injury to the vagus nerve or its branches can be avoided regardless of anatomical anomalies. Any dissection of the posterior aspect of the carotid bulb should be kept as close to the artery as possible so as not to damage the nerve.[4] Great care should also be taken when the superior thyroid artery is isolated and clamped.

Injuries to the superior laryngeal nerve may be missed if they are not actively looked for. Few injuries are reported in the literature and frequencies of damage vary in prospective studies from 0 to 2%.[8,13]

Reports on injuries to, or malfunction of, the recurrent laryngeal nerve show a markedly great variation in frequencies, in prospective studies from 3 to 35%.[9,10,13,14] This may in part be explained by the different approaches to pre- and postoperative examinations that have been taken in different institutions. The higher figures (27%,

35%) reported by Evans et al.[10] and Liapis et al.[9] were diagnosed by speech pathologists evaluating integrated speech functions by clinical examination and spectroanalysis of the voice, whereas examinations in the reports by Forssell et al.[13] and Kitzing et al.[14] were made by phoniatricians using voice recordings and stroboscopic light examination of the vocal cords. Evans and Liapis found a substantial frequency of preoperative pathology, whereas Forssell and Kitzing as well as Dehn and Taylor[12] found none. Voice changes pre- and postoperatively may have several causes and over- as well as underdiagnosis of structural nerve injuries are probably common. Recurrent nerve injuries may cause only mild symptoms and will be missed if postoperative hoarseness is used as the sole diagnostic tool, thus disqualifying retrospective studies in this field.[52] Furthermore, hoarseness may be due to oedema or haematoma of the vocal cords as a result of intubation, and endotracheal intubation has also been described to cause vocal cord paralysis.[53] A further implication is a mandatory preoperative examination before a staged bilateral carotid operation in order to avoid bilateral vocal cord paresis with disastrous consequences.

As with injuries to the VIIth and IXth cranial nerve, dissection near the base of the skull, and especially procedures involving displacement of the jaw, carries a markedly increased risk of vagus nerve injury. Sandmann et al.[37] and Sekhar et al.[38] reported 23 and 45%, respectively. Contralateral nerve injury has also been described as a result of jaw subluxation in carotid surgery.[36]

ACCESSORY NERVE (XI)

The XIth cranial nerve has a varied course after leaving the jugular foramen. It passes laterally and dorsally on the anterior surface of the levator scapulae muscle towards the upper part of the trapezius muscle which it innervates. In one-third it passes anteriorly and in two-thirds posteriorly in relation to the jugular vein before it passes through or dorsal to the sternocleidomastoid (SCM) muscle where it gives off motor branches (Fig. 2). The dorsal rami of the second, third and fourth cervical nerves join the nerve and contribute to the innervation of the lower part of the trapezius muscle, but if this contribution is merely proprioceptive or if these nerves carry motor function is a matter of controversy. Specific studies on the matter support the proprioceptive theory,[54] while clinical experience supports the latter.[55]

The nerve is not normally encountered in the surgical wound, which explains why injuries to this nerve are rare. Symptoms of injury are paralysis of the trapezius muscle, with a secondary dull ache, winged scapula at rest, inability to abduct the arm above the horizontal plane and in the long-term course paresis, anterior and inferior rotation of the shoulder girdle and muscle atrophy.[56] There may also be some degree of weakness in the SCM muscle.[57] Experience of these injuries is mostly from radical neck dissections where it is not uncommon[58] whereas in carotid surgery, this injury is described only 12 times in the literature.[23,30,32,59,60–62] None of the injuries were noted within 4 days of surgery, probably due to postoperative astenia in the patient or possibly because of late onset of damage due to oedema, haematoma or entrapment in scar tissue. Extensive stretch or traction during surgery have also been suggested as a potential mechanism of injury.

Accessory nerve injury is possibly more common when a shunt is used,[30] and as the nerve is situated superficially in the posterior triangle of the neck, the posterior approach to the carotid artery should carry an increased risk of damage to this nerve.

Most of the injuries will resolve within 2 months and will not need any treatment. When there is a permanent damage, however, attempts have been made to recover function by neurolysis, to correct any possible entrapment by scar tissue, or to perform a nerve transplant.[54]

HYPOGLOSSAL NERVE (XII)

The cranial nerve that is most commonly exposed during carotid surgery is the XIIth cranial nerve as it often crosses the internal and external carotid artery just distal to the level of the arteriotomy (Fig. 2). It passes through the hypoglossal canal medial to the internal carotid artery and passes dorsally to the artery and continues down anteriorly between the internal carotid artery and the jugular vein. It then curves medially just above the hyoid bone, anterior to the carotid vessels just inferior to the SCM branch of the external carotid artery which often arises from the occipital artery.[63] It then continues medially deep to the facial vein and under the tendon of the digastric muscle to the base of the tongue which it innervates with motor fibres. The course of the nerve itself is fairly constant while the relation to the carotid bifurcation varies greatly due to the varied location of the latter. The ansa cervicalis branches off from the XIIth nerve at the carotid bifurcation and forms an upper part of the cervical plexus. It contributes to motor innervation of the infrahyoidal muscles and may be divided with no functional consequence.

The XIIth cranial nerve often has to be mobilized in order to expose an adequate length of the internal carotid artery. It may be retracted after division of the ansa cervicalis and the sternocleidomastoid artery and vein as described above (Fig. 4).

A symptom of hypoglossal injury is ipsilateral paralysis of the muscles of the tongue, resulting in deviation of the outstretched tongue towards the affected side (Fig. 5). Unilateral paralysis is disturbing to the patient through difficulties in speech, mastication and swallowing. Most patients will find it difficult to transport soft food within the oral cavity. Some patients have to remove soft food from the vestibule with their fingers to their great embarrassment.[16] Bilateral injury is a potentially life threatening situation which may cause upper airway obstruction.[64] This is not often seen and only five cases are described, of which one needed tracheostomy.[65] Anaesthesiologists must be aware of this possibility since it may produce severe airway obstruction in the immediate postoperative period. For this reason a careful preoperative examination before a second contralateral operation must be made.

In a not yet published prospective study from our institution involving 656 operations hypoglossal injury was seen in 10.7%. The nerve was probably injured by retractors held too tight during a long time in the cranial part of the wound, while careful mobilization and retraction did not seem to increase the number of injuries. This frequency is in keeping with other studies (Table 1) but frequencies up to 20% have been reported.[9] Permanent injuries are rare, and function is usually recovered within 4–6 weeks.

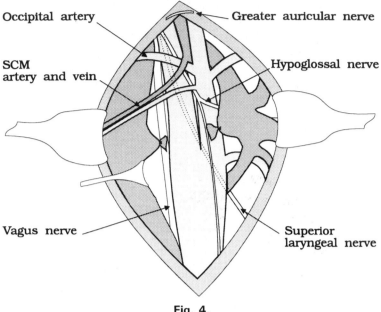

Fig. 4.

CERVICAL PLEXUS

The transverse cervical branch of the cervical plexus emerges from the cervical second and third root and turns around the lateral edge of the SCM muscle, deep to the platysma, to innervate the skin in the medial aspect of the neck (Fig. 1). Damage to this nerve is unavoidable when an oblique incision along the SCM muscle is used and produces anaesthesia medial to the incision. If a more transverse curved incision is used the nerve is less likely to be transected though the exposure of the artery is usually not as adequate as with a longitudinal incision.

The complaints from the patients vary from numbness to irritating hyperesthesia and painful sensations making shaving difficult in male patients. Most of these symptoms will subside within 6 months.

The greater auricular nerve, just as the transverse cervical nerve, is formed from the cervical plexus and supplies the earlobe and lateral part of the cheek with sensory fibres. It emerges just cranial to the transverse cervical nerve and runs cranial and parallel to the external jugular vein (Fig. 1). It may be severed or transected in the upper part of the incision especially if the incision is carried distally behind the ear and the parotid gland. Excessive traction or trauma to the greater auricular nerve may cause annoying numbness or severe pain in the earlobe and mastoid regions.[66]

Only two prospective studies have been made with special attention to these two nerves. They report 42 and 60% damage to the major auricular nerve and 69 and 89% to the transverse cervical nerve, respectively.[12,17] Most patients get used to the numbness in the affected areas but up to 20% will continue to complain bitterly of their symptoms.[12]

Fig. 5.

BRACHIAL PLEXUS

Injury to the brachial plexus during carotid surgery has been reported only once. The patient had an upper trunk palsy involving the suprascapular nerve with resulting weakness in the rhomboid, serratus anterior and supra- and infraspinatus muscles. This case also had involvement of the trapezius muscle, indicating a possible accessory nerve injury as well.

The fifth cervical root forms the upper trunk of the plexus and exits the girdle of neck muscles between the anterior and medial scalenus muscle just below the level of the carotid bifurcation. Since a buffering muscle lies between the root and the operating field, direct trauma to the nerve is not likely. The common mechanism of injury is overstretching of the plexus by unfortunate placing of the patient on the operating table with prolonged abduction of the arm or hyperextension of the neck with downward traction of the shoulder.[23] Most injuries are benign and resolve spontaneously within 6 months.

PHRENIC NERVE

Originating from the fourth and fifth cervical root this nerve forms from two branches just below the subclavian artery immediately lateral to the thyreocervical trunk. The main branch from the fourth root lies on the anterior border of the scalenus anterior muscle and may be injured in procedures involving bypass reconstructions from the subclavian to the carotid artery and possibly in reconstructions of the proximal part of the vertebral artery (Fig. 6). Four cases of phrenic nerve palsy have been reported after subclavian–carotid bypass[35] though without respiratory impairment. This injury could have serious consequences in patients already compromised in their respiratory function and the possibility of phrenic nerve damage should be kept in mind when this kind of surgery is performed.

CERVICAL SYMPATHETIC PLEXUS

Arising from the upper thoracic spine, the postganglionic fibres form the cervical sympathetic chain located deep to the carotid vessels under a thin layer of fascia.

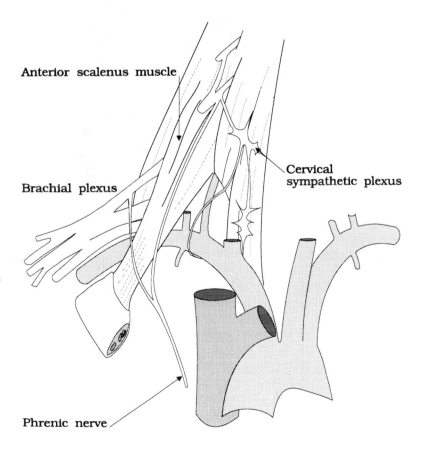

Fig. 6.

Efferent impulses are transmitted to the dilatator pupillae muscle and the levator palpebrae as well as to the cerebral vessels. Injury will cause Horner's syndrome with miosis and ptosis or sometimes more subtle changes as episodic miosis. This injury is not often reported and in the available literature only 10 cases are described.[13,18,20,25] The changes in the pupillary movements may be subtle and easily overlooked but may be more common than these studies suggest. A prospective study at our institution concerning neuroophthalmologic changes before and after carotid surgery is now performed in order to examine this.

COMMENTS

Injuries to nerves surrounding the operating field of carotid artery surgery are common and in all but few cases avoidable. Most of the injured nerves will have a normal function within weeks to months, thus indicating blunt trauma as a mechanism of injury. Less frequently, damage is inflicted through transection, electrocautery or nerve entrapment in ligatures with resulting permanent injuries (Table 3).

The frequency of nerve injury varies a great deal between different studies (Table 1). Several reasons for these differences may be found.

Many of the series have small sample sizes and for reason of statistical variance different results are produced.

Retrospective studies tend to underestimate the number of injuries for reasons mentioned earlier. This is most pronounced in damage to the vagus branches and the glossopharyngeal nerve, where asymptomatic injuries are common. Careful examination of the laryngeal and pharyngeal function pre- and postoperatively is the only way to accurately appraise the function of these nerves.

Some investigators include damage to the superficial sensory nerves and some do not. Since the frequency of these injuries probably is quite high this is one obvious reason for part of the differences.

Standards for reporting injuries vary, and some investigators use the number of damaged nerves in relation to the number of operations as a measure while others use the number of patients with injuries. Since multiple injuries are not uncommon this may have an influence on results (Table 2).

Surgical technique would seem important, causing nerve damage and as in other surgical procedures a 'learning curve' may exist. Three studies cast light on this presumption with partly conflicting results. Krupski et al.[25] examined 300 operations performed by three categories of surgeons with various experience and found no difference in the frequency of nerve injury, perhaps depending on the relatively small

Table 2. Multiple nerve injuries

Author	No.	Year	p/r	Op	1	2	3
Hertzer	8	1980	p	240	10.4	1.7	0.4
Aldoori	2	1988	p	52	23.1	1.9	
Forssell	13	1985	p	162	16.7	2.5	0.6
Forssell[a]		1992	p	667	10.3	0.7	0.1
Krupski	25	1985	r	300	18.0	1.0	

[a]Unpublished.
p/r Prospective/retrospective study.

Table 3. Permanent nerve injuries

Author	No.	Year	p/r	Op	VII	IX	Xr	XI	XII	Aur	Cerv	Symp
Weiss	17	1987	(p)	536	2.3/45.0		0.6/15.0		2.6/30.0			
Hertzer	8	1980	p	240	0.4/9.1		0.8/14.3		0.8/15.4			
Astor	11	1983	p	133			3.0/28.6		3.0/25.0			
Aldoori	2	1988	p	52						9.6/22.7	15.3/17.4	
Forssell[a]		1992	p	667			0.1/12.5		0.1/1.4			
Krupski	25	1985	r	300	0.6/28.6		2.7/34.8		0.6/15.4	2.7/100		0.3/100
Das[b]	26	1985	r	65			1.5/100					
Tucker	30	1987	r	850				0.1/25.0				
Maniglia	32	1991	r	336	0.3/12.5		3.0/50.0	0.3/100				
Sandmann[c]	37	1984	r	31	3.1/25.0		3.1/14.3		0.3/6.3			
Sekhar[c]	38	1986	r	29	13.8/40.0	3.5/7.7						
Sundt[c]	39	1986	r	19		26.3/20.0	31.0/69.0					

Figures are given as: percentages of operations with a permanent nerve injury/the percentage of nerve injuries that were permanent.
[a]Study not published.
[b]Operations for recurrent stenosis.
[c]Operations involving dissection near the base of the skull.

number of operations. Kitzing *et al.*[14] compared results in our institution during two periods and found a significantly lower rate of injuries during the second period (23.5%, 7.4% $p<0.01$), indicating better results as experience was gained and awareness of the problem had increased. In a yet unpublished series of 665 operations performed at our institution there was a difference in injuries to cranial nerves between senior and junior surgeons (10.1% *vs* 17.9% $p<0.05$). There were still more injuries when a patch or a shunt was used, while postoperative haematoma or reoperation for bleeding had no such impact. The difference may be explained by longer duration of the surgical procedures involving more injuries which would indicate blunt trauma from retractors held tight and static for a long time or nerve dehydration as likely mechanisms of injury.

Operations involving dissection above the normal area for carotid endarterectomy as well as redo-surgery or arterial resections have been pointed out as risk factors for increased peripheral nerve morbidity. Operations for distal plaques do not necessarily have to be consistent with a high frequency of nerve injury as the studies by Hanns *et al.*[40] (5.9% injuries) and Fisher *et al.*[36] (4.2%) indicate. Other authors have reported higher frequencies, 20 to 67% injuries to the facial and vagus nerve in these situations.[37,38,39]

Operations for recurrent stenosis have a potential for an increased frequency of nerve injuries because of the difficulties involved with dissection in scarred tissue. In three studies involving a total of 99 reoperations nine patients with peripheral nerve injuries were reported, two of which were permanent.[26,67,68] This indicates that careful dissection and optimum handling of tissues, even in difficult situations, produce results that compare well with results of primary operations.

Procedures involving subclavian–carotid bypass, resection and additional procedures other than TEA and thus with a longer exposition to traction and compression are also accompanied by more nerve injuries.[16,35,67]

Awareness of the problem with peripheral nerve injuries is important and these injuries can be avoided to a great extent if certain measures are taken. A detailed knowledge of the surgical anatomy is essential for the surgeon as well as for the assistant. Careful handling of tissues and an atraumatic surgical technique with sharp dissection close to the arterial wall will lessen this risk. Retractors must be placed with great care not to jam the nerves and special care should be taken not to place them too deep in the tracheooesophageal groove or to pull too hard and static on rectractors held in the cranial part of the wound. Precise bipolar electrocautery and carefully placed ligatures are important parts of the surgical technique and special attention should be taken to the small vessels 'tethering' the hypoglossal nerve (Fig. 4). If bleeding occurs at this point, these vessels should not be grasped blindly with clamps. The hypoglossal nerve should be identified and if necessary carefully dissected away after division of the ansa cervicalis. If the digastric muscle has to be divided it must be held in mind that this nerve is at risk for injury.

REFERENCES

1. Rogers W, Root HD: Cranial nerve injuries after carotid artery endarterectomy. South Med J 81: 1006–1009, 1988

2. Aldoori MI, Baird RN: Local neurological complication during carotid endarterectomy. J Cardiovasc Surg (Torino), 29: 432–436, 1988

3. Thompson JE: Complications of carotid endarterectomy and their prevention. World J Surg 3: 155–165, 1979

4. Towne JB: Nonneurologic complications of carotid artery surgery. In Complications in Vascular Surgery, Bernhard VM, Town JB (Eds). London, New York: Grune & Stratton, pp. 235–244, 1980

5. Lusby RJ, Wylie EJ: Complications of carotid endarterectomy. Surg Clin N Am 63: 1293–1302, 1983

6. Bergqvist D: Peripheral nerve injuries associated with carotid endarterectomy. Semin Vasc Surg 4: 47–53, 1991

7. Verta MJ, Appelbaum EL, McClusky DA, Yao JST, Bergan JJ: Cranial nerve injury during carotid endarterectomy. Ann Surg 185: 192–195, 1977

8. Hertzer NR, Feldman BJ, Beven EG, Tucker HM: A prospective study of the incidence of injury to the cranial nerves during carotid endarterectomy. Surg Gynecol Obstet 151: 781–784, 1980

9. Liapis CD, Satiani B, Florance CL, Evans WE: Motor speech malfunction following carotid endarterectomy. Surgery 89: 56–59, 1981

10. Evans WE, Mendelowitz DS, Liapis C, Wolfe V, Florence CL: Motor speech deficit following carotid endarterectomy. Ann Surg 196: 461–463, 1982

11. Astor FC, Santilli P, Tucker HM: Incidence of cranial nerve dysfunction following carotid endarterectomy. Head Neck Surg 6: 660–663, 1983

12. Dehn TCB, Taylor GW: Cranial and cervical nerve damage associated with carotid endarterectomy. Br J Surg 70: 365–368, 1983

13. Forssell C, Takolander R, Bergqvist D et al.: Cranial nerve injuries associated with carotid endarterectomy. A prospective study. Acta Chir Scand 151: 595–598, 1985

14. Kitzing P, Bergqvist D, Gramming P et al.: Phoniastrische komplikationen und Hirnnervenschädingungen nach Carotisendarterectomie. Lecture at XIV kongress der union der Europäischen Phoniater, Dresden, 29–31 October 1987

15. Downs AR, Jessen M, Lye CR: Peripheral nerve injuries during carotid endarterectomy. Can J Surg 30: 22–24, 1987

16. Schmidt D, Zuschneid W, Kaiser M: Cranial nerve injury during carotid arterial reconstructon. J Neurol 230: 131–135, 1983

17. Weiss K, Kramár R, Firt P: Cranial and cervical nerve injuries: local complications of carotid artery surgery. J Cardiovasc Surg (Torino) 28: 171–175, 1987

18. Rainer GW, Feiler EM, Bloomqvist CD, McCrory CB: Surgical approach to carotid arterial insufficiency. Risks and results. Ann Thorac Surg 2: 640–648, 1966

19. DeWeese JA, Rob CG, Satran R et al.: Surgical treatment for occlusive disease of the carotid artery. Ann Surg 168: 85–94, 1968

20. Ranson HC, Imparato AM, Clauss RH, Reed GE, Hass WK: Factors in the mortality and morbidity associated with surgical treatment of cerebrovascular insufficiency. Circulation 39–40: 269–274, 1969

21. Matsumoto GH, Cossman D, Callow AD: Hazards and safeguards during carotid endarterectomy. Am J Surg 133: 458–462, 1977

22. Bouchier-Hayes D, De Costa A, Macogowan AL: The morbidity of carotid endarterectomy. Br J Surg 66: 433–437, 1979

23. Massey E, Heyman A, Haynes C, Fuchs J: Cranial nerve paralysis following carotid endarterectomy. Stroke 15: 157–159, 1984

24. Koldsland S, Solheim K, Vasli L, Vaagenes P, Lind B, Rösjö Ö, Kayed K: Carotisendarterektomi i lokalanestesi. Tiddskr Nor Laegeforen 105: 1070–1072, 1985

25. Krupski WC, Effeney DJ, Goldstone J et al.: Carotid endarterectomy in a metropolitan community: Comparison of results from three institutions. Surgery 98: 492–499, 1985

26. Das MB, Hertzer NR, Ratlif NB, O'Hara PJ, Beven EG: Recurrent carotid stenosis: a five year series of 65 reoperations. Ann Surg 202: 28–35, 1985

27. Theodotou B, Mahaley MS: Injury of the peripheral cranial nerves during carotid endarterectomy. Stroke 16: 894–895, 1985

28. Rosenbloom M, Friedman SG, Lamparello PJ, Riles TS, Imparato AM: Glossopharyngeal nerve injury complicating carotid endarterectomy. J Vasc Surg 5: 469–471, 1987
29. Knight FW, Yeager RM, Morris DM: Cranial nerve injuries during carotid endarterectomy. Am J Surg 154: 529–532, 1987
30. Tucker JA, Gee W, Nicholas GG, McDonald KM, Goodreau JJ: Accessory nerve injury during carotid endarterectomy. J Vasc Surg 5: 440–444, 1987
31. Fletcher JP, Morris GL, Little JM, Kershaw LZ: EEG monitoring during carotid endarterectomy. Aust NZ J Surg 58: 285–288, 1988
32. Maniglia AJ, Han DP: Cranial nerve injuries following carotid endarterectomy: an analysis of 336 procedures. Head Neck Surg 13: 121–124, 1991
33. Brien HW, Yellin AE, Weaver FA, Carroll BF: A review of carotid endarterectomy at a large teaching hospital. Am Surg 57: 756–762, 1991
34. DeBord JR, Marshall WH, Wyffels PL, Marshall JS, Humphrey P: Carotid endarterectomy in a community hospital surgical practice. Am Surg 5: 627–632, 1991
35. Fry WR, Martin JD, Clagett GP, Fry WJ: Extrathoracic carotid reconstruction: the subclavian–carotid artery bypass. J Vasc Surg 15: 83–88, 1992
36. Fisher DF, Clagett PG, Parker JI et al.: Mandibular subluxation for high carotid exposure. J Vasc Surg 1: 727–733, 1984
37. Sandmann W, Hennerici M, Aulich A, Kniemeyer H, Kremer KW: Progress in carotid artery surgery at the base of the skull. J Vasc Surg 1: 734–743, 1984
38. Sekhar LN, Schramm VL Jr, Jones NF et al.: Operative exposure and management of the petrous and upper cervical internal carotid artery. Neurosurgery 19: 967–982, 1986
39. Sundt TM Jr, Pearson BW, Piepgras DG, Houser OW, Mokri B: Surgical management of aneurysms of the distal extracranial internal carotid artery. J Neurosurg 64: 169–182, 1986
40. Hanns SS, Shah S, Hans B: Carotid endarterectomy for high plaques. Am J Surg 157: 431–434: 1989
41. Ekberg O, Bergqvist D, Takolander R, Uddman R, Kitzing P: Pharyngeal function after carotid endarterectomy. Dysphagia 49: 151–154, 1989
42. Bove EL, Fry WJ, Gross WS, Stanley JC: Hypotension and hypertension as consequences of baroreceptor dysfunction following carotid endarterectomy. Surgery 85: 633–637, 1979
43. Dehn TC, Angell-James JE: Long-term effect of carotid endarterectomy on carotid sinus baroreceptor function and blood pressure control. Br J Surg 74: 997–1000, 1987
44. Hirschl M, Hirschl MM, Magometschnigg D et al.: Arterial baroreflex sensitivity and blood pressure variabilities before and after carotid surgery. Klin Wochenschr 69: 763–768, 1991
45. Aksamit TR, Floras JS, Victor RG, Aylward PE: Paroxysmal hypertension due to sinoaortic baroreceptor denervation in humans. Hypertension 9: 309–314, 1987
46. Toung TJ, Sieber FE, Grayson RF, Derrer SA: Chemoreceptor injury as probable cause of respiratory depression after a simultaneous, bilateral carotid endarterectomy. Crit Care Med 18: 1290–1291, 1990
47. Vanmaele RG, De Backer WA, Willemen MJ et al.: Hypoxic ventilatory response and carotid endarterectomy. Eur J Vasc Surg 6: 241–244, 1992
48. Durham CF, Harrison TS: The surgical anatomy of the superior laryngeal nerve. Surg Gynecol Obstet Jan: 38–44, 1964
49. Michlke A: Rehabilitation of vocal cord paralysis. Studies using the vagus recurrent bypass anastomosis, type ramus posterior shunt. Arch Otolaryngol 100: 431–441, 1974
50. Faaborg-Andersen K, Jensen M: Unilateral paralysis of the superior laryngeal nerve. Acta Otolaryngol 57: 155–159, 1964
51. Droulias C, Tzinas S, Harlaftis N et al.: The superior laryngeal nerve. Ann Surg 42: 635–638, 1976
52. Breiss BF: Identification of specific laryngeal muscle dysfunction by voice testing. Arch Otolaryngol 66: 375–382, 1957
53. Holley SH, Gildea JE: Vocal cord paralysis after tracheal intubation. JAMA 215: 281–284, 1971
54. Andersson R, Flowers RS: Free grafts of the spinal accessory nerve during radical neck dissection. Am J Surg 118: 796–799, 1969
55. Saunders JR, Hirata RM, Jaques DA: Considering the spinal accessory nerve in head and neck surgery. Am J Surg 150: 491–494, 1985

56. Olarte M, Adams D: Accessory nerve palsy. J Neurol Neurosurg Psychiat 40: 113–116, 1977
57. Vastamäki M, Solonen K: Accessory nerve injury. Acta Orthop Scand 55: 296–299, 1984
58. Leipzig B, Suen JY, English JL, Barnes J, Hooper M: Functional evaluation of the spinal accessory nerve after neck dissection. Am J Surg 146: 526–530, 1983
59. Sarala PK: Accessory nerve palsy: An uncommon etiology. Arch Phys Med Rhabil 63: 445–446, 1982
60. Swann KW, Heros RC: Accessory nerve palsy following carotid endarterectomy. Report of two cases. J Neurosurg 63: 630–632, 1985
61. Persson NH, Bergqvist D: Accessory nerve injury after carotid endarterectomy. Case report. Eur J Surg 157: 221–222, 1991
62. Sweeney PJ, Wilbourn AJ: Spinal accessory (11th) nerve palsy following carotid endarterectomy. Neurology 42: 674–675, 1992
63. Dunsker SB: Complications of carotid endarterectomy. Clin Neurosurg 23: 336–341, 1971
64. Bageant TE, Tondini D, Lysons D: Bilateral hypoglossal nerve palsy following a second carotid endarterectomy. Anesthesiology 43: 595–596, 1975
65. Gutrecht JA, Jones HRJ: Bilateral hypoglossal nerve injury after bilateral carotid endarterectomy. Stroke 19: 261–262, 1988
66. Bryant MF: Complications associated with carotid endarterectomy. Am Surg 42: 665–669, 1976
67. Kazmers A, Zierler E, Huang TW, Pulliam CW. Reoperative carotid surgery. Am J Surg 56: 346–351, 1988
68. Edwards WH Jr, Edwards WH Sr, Mulherin JL, Martin R: Recurrent carotid artery stenosis. Resection with autogenous vein replacement. Ann Surg 209: 662–669, 1989

Preservation of Carotid Flow in Carotid Body Tumour Surgery

Aires A. B. Barros D'Sa

The significant reduction in the prohibitive mortality and morbidity which once accompanied the operative management of carotid body tumours (CBTs) is a product of painstaking preoperative preparation and meticulous surgery. Advances in vascular surgical techniques and improved operative skills, aided by precise and sophisticated preoperative radiological diagnosis have beneficially influenced outcome in recent years. The vascular surgeon, more than any other specialist, has a duty to play a leading role in treatment. Essential to fulfilling that function would be a reasonable amount of experience in carotid artery surgery, intraluminal shunting and vein graft replacement but, most importantly, a special interest in CBTs which will attract case referrals, allowing the vascular surgeon to acquire the necessary expertise and confidence.

In order to preserve carotid flow in carotid body tumour surgery we must recognize the background and pathology of carotid body tumours, establish a clear diagnosis and use the information obtained in planning surgery and in safely excising the tumour.

UNDERSTAND THE BACKGROUND

It is generally conceded that the cells of the carotid body migrate from the neural crest with the autonomic nervous system[1] to form the minute ovoid structure located at the bifurcation of the common carotid artery or, occasionally, on adjacent vessels,[2] deriving its blood supply directly from the origin of the external carotid artery. Afferent branches from the ninth and tenth cranial nerves, as well as the cervical sympathetic ganglia, innervate the carotid body.[3] The chemoreceptor tissue of the carotid body exerts a profound but incompletely understood influence on the homeostatic control of arterial blood gases and pH. Histologically the carotid body consists of 'zellballen' or nests of rounded Type I or chief cells containing dense granules potentially capable of synthesizing catecholamines[1] held together by Type II or sustentaculum cells.

Hyperplasia of carotid body tissue is classically observed in populations living at high altitudes and carries an increased risk of carotid body tumour formation.[4,5] Chronic obstructive pulmonary disease, as well as certain congenital cyanotic heart conditions, characterized by persistently high arterial pCO_2 and low arterial PO_2 levels, are known to cause carotid body hyperplasia[6,7] and are implicated in the pathogenesis of CBTs.[8,9]

RECOGNIZE THE PATHOLOGY OF CBT

Tumours of the chemoreceptor system, otherwise termed chemodectomas or non-chromaffin paragangliomas, are principally encountered as carotid body tumours but also rarely as tumours of the jugular bulb (glomus jugulare), the middle ear (glomus typanicum), the ganglion nodosum of the vagus nerve (glomus intravagale) and the aortic body. These tumours occur infrequently and in sporadic fashion in any age group but particularly during the sixth decade of life and slightly more commonly in females. About 5% of carotid body tumours are bilateral but when they occur in families the prevalence of bilaterality rises to 30%.[10,11] Hereditary transmission of CBTs occurs in an autosomal dominant fashion[12] but the degree of penetration is variable and remains unexplained. Siblings of patients with familial bilateral CBTs may present with bilateral glomus jugulare tumours which tend to be aggressive and seem to affect the older female.[13] In those CBTs which have a familial predisposition chemodectomas involving diverse areas of chemoreceptor tissue may co-exist as a multiple tumour syndrome.[14,15] Classified as APUDomas, CBTs have been allocated to the multiple endocrine neoplasia (MEN) Type II group but their position within this arrangement remains to be justified.[16] A hormone unique to the carotid body has yet to be identified, although catecholamine-secreting CBTs do occur but raised plasma and urine levels are only rarely observed.[17,18]

The CBT is a painless, usually unilateral firm 'potato' tumour 2–5 cm in diameter situated in the carotid triangle at the angle of the jaw. In its benign form it has a reddish-brown lobulated surface under which haemorrhagic areas may be apparent, a thin capsule sometimes incorporating adjacent cranial nerves. The tumour nodules may extend into the adventitia of the carotid vessels and only exceptionally into the media. The high vascularity of the tumour is enhanced by the presence of numerous curling adventitial vessels. The enlarging tumour draws additional blood supply from the superior thyroid, occipital, subclavian, vertebral and thyrocervical arteries.[19]

The Type I or chief cells show proliferation, nuclear pleomorphism and vesicular nuclei, attempting to maintain the 'zellballen' structure within a field of increased vascularity (Fig. 1). In aggressive tumours, the nerves, lymphatics and vessels at the periphery of the tumour are infiltrated. Separation of CBTs into conventionally accepted categories of benign, locally invasive or malignant metastasizing tumour, cannot be achieved on the basis of histological criteria alone.[20-22] Most CBTs are histologically benign, but reports of local malignancy ranging from 3% to 13.5% and of distant metastases in a further 3% have been documented.[20,23-25] An unusually high incidence of metastases of up to 23% was recorded in one report of long-term follow-up of patients.[26] Preliminary histology may be unreliable in establishing the invasive or malignant potential of a tumour. The burden of proof often rests on the discovery of a tumour metastatic deposit, always bearing in mind the fact that tumours within the chemoreceptor system may be multicentric and an apparent metastatic site may simply be another chemodectoma.[14,22]

The behaviour of a particular tumour in terms of the relative ease with which it is removed by the surgeon is not necessarily reflected in the histopathological report. An analysis of a series of CBTs in one centre by Shamblin et al.[20] served to grade these tumours according to the progressively increasing difficulties encountered in excising them and the corresponding rise in associated morbidity. Under Shamblin's classification, CBTs are divided into three groups according to the gross tumour–vessel relationships observed in each case: Group I localized tumour, Group II tumour adherent and partially surrounding the vessels, Group III tumour intimately

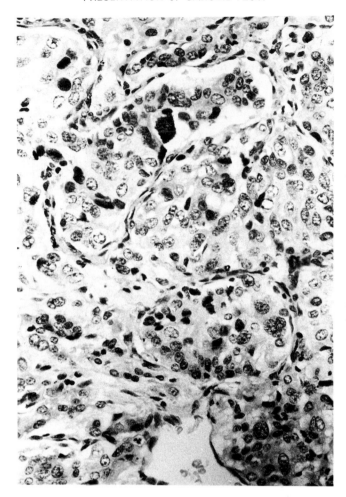

Fig. 1. Histopathology of a carotid body tumour (H & E stain, magnification ×400).

surrounding the vessels. The impressions at operation allow the surgeon to allocate a particular tumour to one of these three groups and to decide on the best surgical approach. While a majority of CBTs can be excised completely, leaving the carotid vessels intact, in the remainder tumour ablation is achievable only by removing a segment of artery in continuity with it.

SUSPECT POSSIBILITY OF CBT IN CLINICAL ASSESSMENT

The literature is replete with details of both complications and fatality associated with surgical intervention, a notoriety significantly enhanced by the failure of the clinician to entertain a clinical diagnosis of CBT when examining the patient.[20] The anatomical position of the tumour and its intrinsic characteristics, namely, its rich vascularity, the local pressure effects on surrounding anatomical structure, a capacity for local invasiveness and in a few cases the presence of a contralateral tumour, should arouse suspicion sufficient to stimulate a thorough examination of the head and neck as well as the cranial nerves.

Located at the angle of the mandible beneath the upper portion of the sternocleidomastoid muscle the CBT is a slow-growing, painless, non-tender laterally mobile mass (Fig. 2). Pain, if present, characterizes a rapidly enlarging tumour. Other features may be compressibility, pulsatility and the presence of a hum on auscultation. In a third of cases these tumours may be associated with cranial nerve palsies, predominantly involving the vagus and hypoglossal and to a lesser degree the glossopharyngeal and spinal accessory. Larger and more invasive tumours may involve the sympathetic nerve and the pharynx medially. Palpation, or some other external stimulus, may sometimes induce syncope or dyspnoea; in one reported instance massive bilateral tumours led to suffocation.[11] Clinical manifestations are varied and include hoarseness, debilitating pain, deviation and even hemiatrophy of the tongue (Fig. 2), dysphagia, Horner's syndrome and, rarely, the carotid sinus syndrome.[19,20,24] An unconventional clinical feature may be the development of transient ischaemic attacks or, conceivably, stroke caused by pressure on the internal carotid artery, particularly if it is atheromatous.[27] Tumour spread around the internal carotid artery extending intracranially eventually leads to fatality.[11,28] Cardiovascular manifestations such as episodic flushing, dizziness, palpitations, ventricular tachycardia and hypertension, may rarely occur either when the tumour is secretory or when a phaeochromocytoma co-exists with it.[17,29,30]

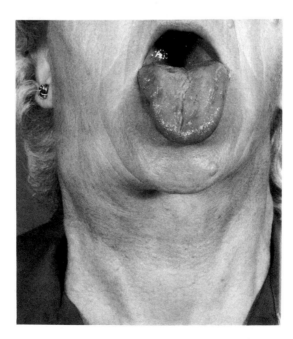

Fig. 2. A right-sided carotid body tumour associated with some hemiatrophy and deviation of the tongue due to involvement of the hypoglossal nerve.

Given its location, a CBT is often mistaken for more commonly observed conditions such as cervical lymphadenopathy, whether that be inflammatory, lymphomatous or neoplastic, carotid artery aneurysms, branchial cysts or a number of other unusual conditions.[31] Even when the surgeon has been vigilant and considered the possible presence of a CBT, the clinical signs may not be sufficiently diagnostic. The diagnosis should be established prior to any attempted exploration.

CONFIRM THE DIAGNOSIS OF CBT

Traditionally, contrast angiography has been used to establish a definitive diagnosis (Fig. 3).[11,22] Newer methods complement and may eventually replace angiography entirely. Radionuclide scanning using [99]mTechnitium is an inexpensive minimally invasive technique which demonstrates the vascularity of clinically unsuspected CBTs,[13,32] and is particularly applicable in locating recurrent tumours or in the periodic screening of the family of a patient with bilateral carotid body tumours. Imaging using a duplex colour Doppler is most effective as a screening method but is limited by its inability to define the detailed vasculature. Aided by contrast

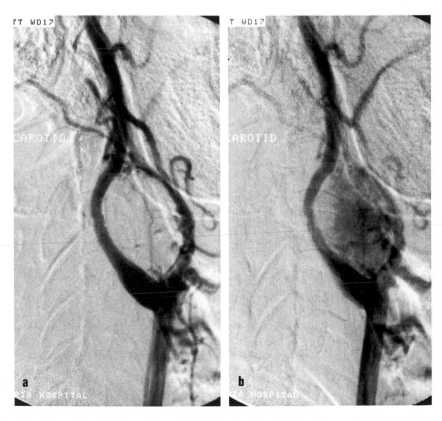

Fig. 3. Angiography. (a) Showing a CBT classically splaying the carotid bifurcation. (b) A later phase showing a 'blush' and a cloud of tumour vessels mainly derived from the external carotid artery and 'crotch'.

enhancement of the carotid arteries,[33] computed tomographic (CT) scans will clarify the dimensions and configuration of a tumour and are of especial value in defining the boundaries of an advanced tumour and in identifying invasion into the arterial system; this information is of immense value in planning surgical treatment. The main additional attribute of magnetic resonance imaging is that it will also demonstrate changes in blood flow caused by the tumour mass.[34]

Angiography carries a small but well known incidence of transient ischaemia and stroke, a conceivable complication in cases where cerebral flow may have already been compromised by extrinsic tumour pressure on the internal carotid artery.[13] This observation is particularly valid in the older patient with co-existing atheromatous disease of the internal carotid artery. Biplane films are desirable in planning operative approach and excluding ulceration or stenosis which may be a potential source of embolism while extirpating the tumour.[35] The pathognomonic radiological features of CBTs, exhaustively detailed in the literature are the 'lyre-like' or goblet-shaped splaying of the carotid bifurcation by a highly vascular tumour within a cloud of fine tortuous vessels indicating the key sources of blood supply to the tumour (Fig. 3). Angiography will also exclude a contralateral tumour and in some instances delineate a lymph node metastasis.[11] It might be argued that an early tumour which does not distort the carotid bifurcation and lacks a significant tumour circulation is liable to be missed.[36] A completely avascular tumour is unusual[4] but if some of the classical appearances are absent it is possible that another form of chemodectoma such as a glomus jugulare or glomus intravagale tumour may be present.[31]

Fine needle aspiration, widely used in cytological diagnosis of other tumours, carries the dangers of injury to cranial nerves and major arteries which might also be atheromatous, while being only partially successful and in rare instances leading to fatality.[37]

CONSIDER TREATMENT OPTIONS

The radio-resistance of CBTs and the complications of irradiation such as tissue necrosis, destruction of the mandible, carotid artery stenosis and laryngeal stricture contraindicate this therapeutic approach.[11,20,38] The subsequent effects of radiotherapy, namely fibrosis and obliteration of tissue planes, compound the inherent difficulties which attend operative removal, thereby rendering surgery doubly hazardous.[36] Reports of tumour aggression in response to radiation therapy[39] suggest that this treatment may be justified when used palliatively, in particular to relieve pain caused by bony metastases and deposits elsewhere.[40]

After the first review of the experience of surgery for 23 carotid body tumours early this century[41] numerous reports followed in which tumours were excised without a definitive preoperative diagnosis and wherein frequent ligation of the carotid artery inevitably led to a depressing mortality of 30% and a stroke rate of 30–50%.[23,38,42–44] Two observations heralded an improvement in the surgical management of CBTs: first, recognition that the carotid body closely involves the adventitia of the carotid arteries and, second, that a relatively avascular subadventitial plane of dissection or 'white line', permits complete tumour excision while preserving the integrity of the carotid arteries.[45] The adoption of this strict anatomical technique of removal, aided by advances in anaesthesia, blood transfusion and vascular surgical techniques led to safer operative results and a pre-eminent position for surgery in management. Despite such progress, the sobering fact remains that the incidence of cranial nerve palsies remains high and approximately half of these are permanent.[26,46,47] These complications most commonly follow the excision of the larger and more invasive Group II and Group III[20] tumours which ideally ought to be recognized and treated much earlier.

The rationale for surgery in CBTs is based on their relentless growth and pressure effects, local invasiveness and potential malignancy, and the inability of the tumour either to regress spontaneously or to respond to radiotherapy or any other therapeutic option.

ADHERE TO SURGICAL PRINCIPLES AND OBJECTIVES

When the diagnosis has been established the patient should be informed of the nature of the tumour and the implications of surgical removal, particularly if the mass is large and has been present for some time. In discussing treatment with the patient the merits of surgery should be clearly stated and the potential likelihood of complications such as cranial nerve palsy and stroke identified. It has been suggested that preoperative embolization will reduce the size and vascularity of the tumour thereby minimizing hazards of surgery.[48,49] Difficulties include the super-selective catherization of tiny 'feeder' vessels, incomplete embolization and the potential dangers of inadvertent 'spill' causing necrosis of unforeseen distal tissue sites in the head and face,[36] and the necessity to excise the devitalized tumours within a couple of days, the tissue specimen being usually unsuitable for histopathological or other analysis.

The aim of surgery would be to excise a tumour in its entirety while preserving the carotid system and adjacent nerves and keeping blood losses to a minimum. Occasionally, as in some Group III tumours, excision cannot be undertaken without injuring the common or internal carotid artery. In these instances the solution must be to sacrifice the vessel segment along with the tumour and then to reconstruct the artery by means of a graft. As a rule, all CBTs must be removed except in the face of compelling contraindications such as advanced malignant change, prohibitive concurrent cardiac and respiratory risks and senility.

Clear and well established principles of technique must be applied if safe and precise excision is to be achieved. The salient points are wide exposure, location of cranial nerves, control of the carotid arterial system, dissection in the prescribed plane, preparedness to proceed to intraluminal shunting and, if required, grafting to replace a sacrificed segment of artery. The relative technical ease with which a smaller tumour can be removed without damaging important neighbouring structures dispels any arguments against early surgical intervention.

When the differential diagnosis of a mass in the carotid area fails to include CBT, exploration or biopsy may be undertaken oblivious to that possibility, often precipitating a potentially dangerous situation. In one series, definitive surgery to remove a CBT was preceded by such intervention in as many as a third of the cases reported.[40] Having inadvertently exposed a tumour suspected to be a CBT, the general surgeon should wisely refrain from proceeding to biopsy and instead seek the assistance of a vascular surgeon accustomed to dealing with this condition. To proceed further without previous operative experience or the necessary surgical instruments is to court disaster. At one time planned open biopsy was actually recommended as a method of confirming the diagnosis of CBT.[42] It is worth remembering that the flow through a CBT approximates 2 litre/100 g/min,[50] a rate exceeding that of the brain. The deliberate incision of such a tumour, particularly by a surgeon untutored in this condition, is an alarming experience. Confronted by life-threatening haemorrhage, the surgeon may resort to hurried carotid clamping and ligation which in a bloody field invites the twin dangers of injury to cranial nerves and of arresting carotid flow which may be followed by stroke. As the practice of blind exploration becomes obsolescent the incidence of diagnostic surprise should recede.

ENSURE CAREFUL PREPARATION FOR OPERATION

Nasotracheal intubation allows the mouth to close, providing that little extra space behind the angle of the mandible so that one does not have to resort either to anterior subluxation of the mandible or to lateral mandibulotomy, measures which improve access when the tumour is exceptionally large. Care should also be taken during intubation to avoid compression of the carotid bifurcation. If a catecholamine-secreting tumour is present, then haemodynamic fluctuations may be provoked. In patients with atheroma of the carotid artery, plaque or thrombus could conceivably be dislodged by robust handling beneath the angle of the mandible. In the rare instance when plasma catecholamine levels are known to be elevated, α- and β-receptor blockade using phenoxybenzamine and propranolol respectively in the week prior to operation will prevent cardiovascular collapse; postoperatively in the intensive care unit fluid expansion of the extracellular space can be monitored to avert irreversible hypotension.[51,52] An arterial pressure line and continuous ECG monitoring are essential in the surveillance of all patients.

The patient is placed in the standard jack-knife position with a soft sandbag between the scapulae, the head laterally rotated and hyperextended as for a routine carotid endarterectomy. The ipsilateral upper long saphenous vein should be accessible in case a donor graft is required. Notwithstanding the presumed technical proficiency of the surgeon, adequate blood should be cross-matched.

MAINTAIN PRECISION OF OPERATIVE TECHNIQUE

An oblique cervical incision anterior to the sternomastoid, which can be extended up to the ear and around it, provides an adequate approach. Better access at the upper end is facilitated by division of the digastric muscle and stylohyoid tendon. After dividing the common facial vein the CBT becomes apparent. A small early tumour is usually confined within the cleft of the carotid bifurcation, whereas a larger tumour may entirely obscure the carotid system. A plethora of fine tortuous vessels, some of which course proximally down the common carotid artery, illustrate the

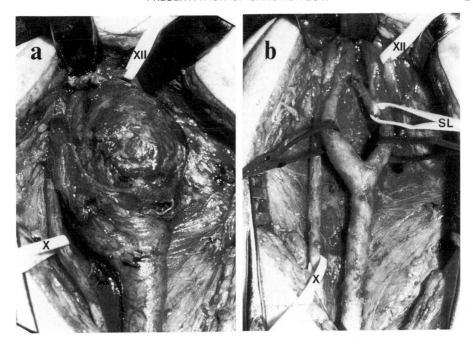

Fig. 4. Moderately early CBT. (a) Tumour–carotid relationships, the vagus (X) and hypoglossal (XII) nerves within silastic slings. (b) Tumour excision leaves the carotid system, vagus (X), its superior laryngeal branch (SL) and hypoglossal (XII) nerves intact. Reproduced from Ref. 36, with permission.

bleeding potential of the tumour (Fig. 4a). In advanced tumours, which may have a characteristic 'collar-stud' configuration, the deeper component which lies parapharyngeally is often deceptively large. Hypoglossal and vagus nerves are carefully freed if possible and encircled (Figs 4a, 5a).

In small tumours the common carotid artery and its two main branches are easily controlled. In larger tumours the branches of the external carotid artery are ligated so as to reduce tumour blood supply while at the same time allowing the tumour to be mobilized.

Sharp dissection in the subadventitial plane of cleavage or 'white line'[45] is a precept which must be adhered to if complete ablation of the tumour is to be achieved, while at the same time preserving the integrity of the arteries. Dissection commenced at the common carotid artery is advanced upwards, under magnification, maintaining haemostasis at each step. The denuded artery is continuously irrigated and any spasm and consequently any impairment of carotid flow, induced by intimate handling can be abolished by bathing the area in warm papaverine solution.[53] Dissection is continued up the external carotid artery, alert to the presence of the superior laryngeal nerve. The tumour margins are freed from the peripheral tissue if necessary by ligating branches of the external carotid artery. At the bifurcation the dissection should proceed up the internal carotid artery. Soon the carotid bifurcation shows signs of 'lifting off' the tumour mass and should be

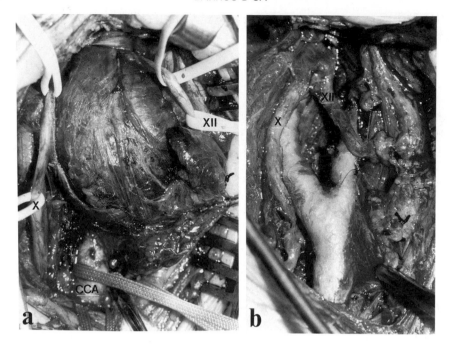

Fig. 5. Large CBT. (a) Completely surrounding the carotid system; the common carotid artery (CCA) is just visible, the vagus (X) and hypoglossal (XII) nerves are encircled by silastic slings. (b) Tumour excision leaves the carotid system, vagus (X) and hypoglossal (XII) nerves intact. Reproduced from Ref. 36, with permission.

freed further. At this stage, a large feeding vessel arising directly from the 'crotch' of the bifurcation becomes apparent and has to be controlled by a fine prolene stitch.

It is important to take stock of the surrounding anatomy, particularly as the tumour tissue tapers upwards along the internal carotid artery, converging with the IXth, Xth, XIth and XIIth cranial nerves, medial to which lie the upper sympathetic trunk and superior cervical ganglion. The tumour should be regarded as virtually inoperable if it invades the styloid or mastoid process. Patience and precision are vital in the final stages of excision to ensure that the artery and nerves are not damaged (Figs 4b, 5b).

It is possible that flow through the internal carotid artery, which may already be compromised by the tumour mass, could be further impaired during operative manipulation. Prolonged retraction of the internal carotid by encircling silastic slings will impair or arrest carotid flow. Rotation of the tumour–arterial mass for access to the pharyngeal component of the tumour may cause the internal carotid artery to twist on its vertical axis with similar results. Any risk of thrombosis may be countered with a small intravenous bolus of heparin.

In order to avert the likelihood of ischaemia, an intraluminal shunt may be employed as a planned manoeuvre,[54] in turn facilitating an unhurried and careful technique which is essential in protecting the cranial nerves.[36,53] In an emergency, a tear in the carotid artery during dissection can be extended longitudinally away from the undissected tumour and an inlying shunt quickly inserted to maintain cerebral flow. If entry into the carotid artery seems imminent or if a prolonged arterial occlusion is anticipated, an outlying shunt may be placed in such a manner as to connect the proximal common to the distal internal carotid artery, isolating the intervening tumour-bearing arterial segment (Fig. 6a). A similar situation is likely to occur when the 'white line' is obliterated by a benign or invasive malignant tumour, in which circumstance the tumour–vessel mass is removed 'en bloc' while a shunt maintains flow (Fig. 6b).

If angiography had shown that the internal carotid artery was coincidentally atheromatous, complete resection of the affected segment along with the tumour is desirable. Immediately on detaching the tumour–vessel mass a shunt carrying a saphenous vein graft, harvested in readiness for this manoeuvre, is inserted to bridge the gap; the interposed vein graft is anastomosed distally and the shunt is extracted before completing the proximal anastomosis (Fig. 6c).

In a minority of advanced cases the hazards of excision are increased by tumour invasion of the artery, cranial nerves, internal jugular vein and lymph nodes. Even good preoperative CT scans may fail to differentiate between tumour invasion of the vagus nerve or of the jugular vein on the one hand and a co-existing tumour either of the ganglion nodosum or the glomus jugulare on the other. A segment of the external carotid artery can be removed en bloc with the tumour without much concern (Fig. 6d) but similar excision involving the internal carotid artery requires shunting and vein graft replacement. Adjacent infiltrated lymph nodes should be excised along with the tumour, if necessary by taking a segment of the internal jugular vein as well.

In dealing with the recurrent CBT, re-visiting the site of previous surgery can be a challenging prospect, not only due to fibrosis and obliteration of tissue planes but also because the arteries previously denuded of adventitia, are likely to be injured more easily during dissection.[36] These are persuasive arguments in favour of the complete ablation of the tumour at the time of initial operation. Clearly caution is advisable even in applying accepted vascular surgical skills in dealing with recurrent tumours and once again the techniques of shunting and vein graft replacement must be held in reserve.

REMAIN ALERT TO POSTOPERATIVE PROBLEMS AND COMPLICATIONS

The quality of carotid flow after tumour excision depends on good oxygenation. An important postoperative consideration is attention to the airway, either if vocal cord paralysis was present before operation or if it had resulted from inadvertent vagal damage or necessary vagal excision in removing a large invasive tumour. Endotracheal reintubation or temporary tracheostomy are only rarely required. Good haemostasis before closure and effective drainage will prevent haematoma and laryngeal oedema. If a contralateral CBT had been removed a short time previously, uncompensated baroreceptor dysfunction may manifest itself in the form of pulse rate and blood pressure fluctuations which potentially compromise carotid flow. Frequent neurological examination will alert the surgeon to the development of cerebrovascular ischaemia which may in turn call into question the likelihood of

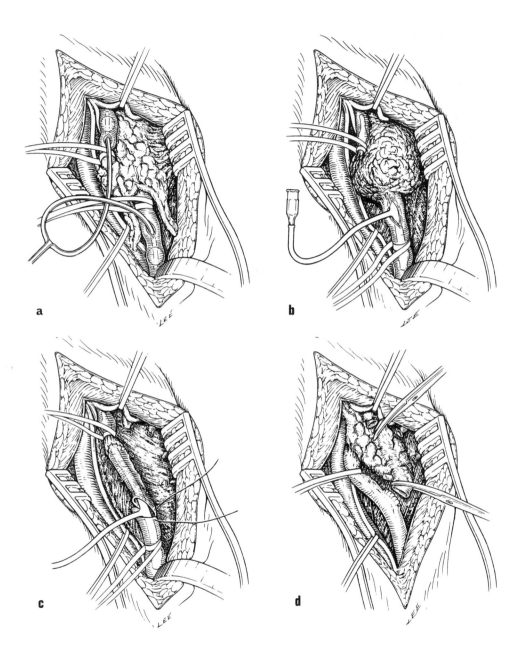

Fig. 6. (a) Outlying Pruitt shunt maintains cerebral flow via inadvertent tear in carotid trunk. (b) CBT inseparably adherent to carotid artery, to be removed en bloc while an inlying Brener shunt maintains cerebral flow. (c) Vein graft over distal Brener shunt anastomosed to internal carotid artery; shunt is removed before completion of proximal anastomosis. (d) Resection of external carotid artery en bloc with tumour. Reproduced from Ref. 53, with permission.

thrombotic occlusion or the vein graft or the carotid artery itself. Any doubts of this nature must be resolved by immediate angiography and, where indicated, by appropriate and expeditious surgical intervention.

The documented incidence of both morbidity and mortality in the face of commendable surgical skills reflects the increasing technical challenge as the intimacy of the tumour–vessel relationship increases from a Group I to Group III tumour. The occurrence of stroke, cranial nerve damage and recurrence from inadequate excision, are the three main sources of concern, particularly in operations on Group III tumours.

The unacceptably high postoperative mortality of 30% and a hemiplegic stroke rate of 50% which used to occur in the aftermath of en bloc removal or carotid ligation should be regarded as historical. In one large series modern surgical techniques have seen a reduction in the perioperative mortality to 6% and the stroke rate to 2.7%.[46] In a personal series of 30 cases which was uncomplicated either by mortality or stroke, one case of transient cerebral ischaemia was precipitated by graft thrombosis immediately postoperatively and the problem was quickly resolved by graft revision (unpublished data). These rewarding results are a testimony to disciplined and precise operative technique, improved management, the employment of intraluminal shunts to ensure cerebral perfusion when required and reconstruction of the internal carotid artery when it had to be sacrificed. There should be no room, however, for complacency on the part of the vascular surgeon who must remain vigilant to such occurrences as arterial spasm, thrombosis and even shunt failure.

Permanent nerve injury is often the product of surgical inexperience, limited exposure, scanty knowledge of anatomy and failure to identify and protect a nerve, particularly in the final stages of excision. Of course, a nerve may have to be sacrificed deliberately if it has been invaded by a tumour or in the process of block dissection.

Complete tumour excision is possible in most cases with a 6% local recurrence rate interestingly observed only in familial tumours.[55] As postoperative survival has been shown to be equal to that of age- and sex-matched controls, long-term indefinite follow-up is therefore important in order to detect late recurrence or metastases. In good hands, the probability of leaving behind a residue of tumour is small but the inexperienced surgeon will find his technique severely tested. Fears of haemorrhage, cranial nerve damage and cerebral ischaemia may create sufficient anxiety to discourage complete excision. In contrast, a vascular surgeon who regularly operates on the carotid artery and has a personal interest in CBTs will attract a modest number of referrals from which experience he will gain the necessary confidence. It is therefore in his interest to be thorough at the initial operation with the objective of averting a return to the scene where re-operation is attended by distinct pitfalls.

REFERENCES

1. Glenner GG, Grimley PM: Tumors of the extra-adrenal paraganglion system (including chemoreceptors). Atlas of Tumour Pathology, series 2, fascicle 9. Washington: Armed Forces Institute of Pathology, 1974
2. Smith P, Jago R, Heath D: Anatomical variation and quantitative histology of the normal and enlarged carotid body. J Pathol 137: 287–304, 1982

3. Eyzaguirre C, Zapata P: Perspectives in carotid body research. J Appl Physiol 57: 931–957, 1984

4. Saldana MJ, Salem LE, Traveean R: High altitude hypoxia and chemodectomas. Hum Pathol 4: 251–263, 1973

5. Pacheco-Ojeda L, Durango E, Rodriguez C, Vivar N: Carotid body tumors at high altitudes: Quito, Ecuador 1987. World J Surg 12: 856–860, 1988

6. Chedid A, Jao W: Hereditary tumors of the carotid bodies and chronic obstructive pulmonary disease. Cancer 33: 1635–1641, 1974

7. Lack EE: Carotid body hypertrophy in patients with cystic fibrosis and cyanotic congenital heart disease. Hum Pathol 8: 39–47, 1976

8. Edwards C, Heath D, Harris P: The carotid body in emphysema and left ventricular hypertrophy. J Pathol 104: 1–13, 1971

9. Hirsch JH, Killen FC, Troupin RH: Bilateral carotid body tumors and cyanotic heart disease. Am J Radiol 134: 1073–1075, 1980.

10. Wilson H: Carotid body tumours: familial bilateral. Ann Surg 171: 847–848, 1970

11. Dent TL, Thompson NW, Fry WJ: Carotid body tumours. Surgery 80: 365–372, 1976

12. Parry DM, Li FP, Strong LC et al.: Carotid body tumors in humans: genetics and epidemiology. J Natl Cancer Inst 68: 573–578, 1982

13. Hamilton JRL, Barros D'Sa AAB: Radionuclide angiography and surgery for familial bilateral chemodectomas. Br J Vasc Surg 1: 97–105, 1987

14. Larraza-Hernandez O, Albores Saavedra J, Benavides G et al.: Multiple endocrine neoplasia. Pituitary adenoma, multicentric papillary thyroid carcinoma, bilateral carotid body paraganglionoma, parathyroid hyperplasia, gastric leiomyoma, and systemic amyloidosis. Am J Clin Pathol 78: 527–532, 1982

15. Pritchett JW: Familial concurrence of carotid body tumor and pheochromocytoma. Cancer 49: 2578–2579, 1982

16. Sundaram M, Cope V: Paraganglioma in the neck. Br J Surg 73: 182–185, 1973

17. Glenner GG, Grout JR, Roberts WC: A non-adrenaline secreting carotid body-like tumour. Lancet ii: 439, 1961

18. Strauss M, Nicholas GG, Abt AB, Harrison TS, Seaton JF: Malignant catecholamine-secreting carotid body paraganglioma. Otolaryngol Head Neck Surg 91: 315–321, 1983

19. Davidge-Pitts KJ, Pantanowitz D: Carotid body tumors. In Surgery Annual, Nyhus LM (Ed.), Norwalk, Conn: Appleton-Century-Crofts, Vol. 16: pp. 203–227, 1984

20. Shamblin WR, Remine WH, Sheps SG, Harrison EG: Carotid body tumor (chemodectoma): clinicopathologic analysis of ninety cases. Am J Surg 122: 732–739, 1971

21. Pryse-Davis J, Dawson IM, Westbury G: Some morphologic, histochemical and chemical observations on chemodectomas and the normal carotid body, including a study on the chromaffin reaction and possible ganglion cell elements. Cancer 17: 185–202, 1964

22. Van Asperen De Boer FRS, Terpstra JL, Vink M: Diagnosis, treatment and operation complications of carotid body tumours. Br J Surg 68: 433–438, 1981

23. Lees GD, Levine HL, Beven EG, Tucker HM: Tumors of carotid body: experience with 41 operative cases. Am J Surg 142: 362–365, 1981

24. Lack EE, Cubilla AL, Woodruff JM, Farr HW: Paragangliomas of the head and neck region. Cancer 39: 397–409, 1977

25. Gaylis H, Davidge-Pitts K, Pantanowitz D: Carotid body tumours. A review of 52 cases. South Afr Med J 72: 493–496, 1987

26. Krupski WC, Effeney DJ, Ehrenfeld WK, Stoney RJ: Cervical chemodectoma: Technical considerations and management options. Am J Surg 144: 215–220, 1982

27. Sanchez AC, de Seijas EV, Matesanz JM, Trapero VL: Carotid body tumour: Unusual cause of transient ischaemic attacks. Stroke 19: 102–103, 1988

28. Javid H, Dye WS, Hunter JA, Najafi H, Julian OC: Surgical management of carotid body tumour. Arch Surg 95: 771–779, 1967

29. Bederal P, Bratten M, Cappelen C, Mylius EA, Walaas O: Noradrenaline–adrenaline producing nonchromaffin paraganglioma. Acta Med Scand 172: 249–257, 1962

30. Sato T, Saito H, Yoshinaga K, Shibota Y, Sasano N: concurrence of carotid body tumor and pheochromocytoma. Cancer 34: 1787–1795, 1974

31. Barros D'Sa AAB: Management of carotid body tumours. Curr Pract Surg 4(1): 36–48, 1992
32. Serafini AN, Weinstein MB: Radionuclide investigation of a carotid body tumor. J Nucl Med 13: 640–643, 1972
33. Ferris RA, Kirschner LP, Mero JH, Fields RL, Fulcher TM: Computed tomography of a carotid body tumor. J Comput Assist Tomogr 3: 834–835, 1979
34. Olsen WL, Dillon WP, Kelly WM, Norman D, Brant-Zawadski M, Newton TH: MRI imaging of paragangliomas. Am J Roentgen 148: 201–204, 1987
35. Gehweiler JA, Bender WR: Carotid arteriography in the diagnosis and management of tumors of the carotid body. Am J Roentgen 104: 893–898, 1968
36. Barros D'Sa AAB: Carotid body tumours—the premise of the vascular surgeon. In Vascular Surgery: Current Questions, Barros D'Sa AAB, Bell PRF, Darke SG, Harris PL (Eds). London: Butterworth Heinemann, pp. 31–49, 1991
37. Engzell U, Franzen S, Zajicek J: Aspiration biopsy of tumors of the neck. II. Cytologic findings in 13 cases of carotid body tumour. Acta Cytologica 15: 25–30, 1971
38. Lahey FH, Warren KW: A long-term appraisal of carotid body tumors with remarks on their removal. Surg Gynecol Obstet 92: 481–491, 1951
39. Mitchell DC, Clyne CAC: Chemodectomas of the neck: the response to radiotherapy. Br J Surg 72: 903–905, 1985
40. Browse NL: Carotid body tumours. Br Med J 284: 1507–1508, 1982
41. Keen WW, Funke J: Tumors of the carotid gland. JAMA 47: 468–479, 1906
42. Monro RS: The natural history of carotid body tumours and their diagnosis and treatment. Br J Surg 37: 445–453, 1950
43. Farr HW: Carotid body tumors: A thirty-year experience at Memorial Hospital. Am J Surg 114: 614–619, 1967
44. Pette JR, Woolner LB, Judd ES: Carotid body tumors (chemodectomas). Ann Surg 137: 465–477, 1953
45. Gordon-Taylor G. On carotid tumours. Br J Surg 28: 163–172, 1940
46. Hallet JW, Nora JD, Hollier LH, Cherry KJ, Pairolero PC. Trends in neurovascular complications of surgical management for carotid body and cervical paragangliomas: A fifty-year experience with 153 tumors. J Vasc Surg 7: 284–289, 1988
47. McPherson GAD, Halliday AW, Mansfield AO: Carotid body tumours and other cervical paragangliomas: Diagnosis and management. Br J Surg 76: 33–36, 1989
48. Borges LF, Heros RC, DeBrun G: Carotid body tumors managed with preoperative embolization: a report of two cases. J Neurosurg 59: 867–870, 1983
49. Schick PM, Hieschima GB, White RA et al.: Arterial catheter embolization followed by surgery for large chemodectoma. Surgery 87: 459–464, 1980
50. Ganong WF: Medical Physiology 8th edn, Los Altos, California: Lange Medical Publications, p. 504, 1977
51. Newland MC, Hurlbert BJ: Chemodectoma diagnosed by hypertension and tachycardia during anesthesia. Anesth Analg 59: 388–390, 1980
52. Glasscock ME, Jackson CG, Nissen AJ, Smith PG: Diagnosis and management of catecholamine-secreting glomus tumors. Laryngoscope 94: 1008–1015, 1984
53. Barros D'Sa AAB. Chemodectoma. In Surgical Management of Vascular Disease, Bell PRF, Jamieson CW, Ruckley CW (Eds). London: Baillière Tindall, pp. 721–737, 1991
54. Som ML, Silver CE, Seidenberg B: Excision of carotid body tumors using an internal vascular shunt. Surg Gynecol Obstet 122: 41–44, 1966
55. Nora JD, Hallet JW, O'Brien PC, Naessens JM, Cherry KJ, Pairolero PC: Surgical resection of carotid body tumours: Long-term survival, recurrence and metastasis. Mayo Clin Proc 63: 348–352, 1988

INTRAOPERATIVE MONITORING

Colour Coded Duplex Scanning During Carotid Endarterectomy

Hans O. Myhre, Ola D. Saether, Sven R. Mathisen and Bjørn A. J. Angelsen

INTRODUCTION

Following carotid surgery the endarterectomized surface must be clean and free of intimal flaps. Furthermore, there must be no residual stenoses at the end-points following closure of the arteriotomy. Even minor irregularities can become the source of either restenosis, reocclusion or embolism, with dramatic consequences.[1,2]

The incidence of postoperative neurological events is in the order of 2–6% even in recently published multicentre studies.[3,4] Taking into consideration the large number of carotid endarterectomies performed, it is critical to minimize the incidence of postoperative neurological events, especially those causing stroke with long-term disability. Although, some of these events may be caused by ischaemia during arterial cross-clamping, others are caused by technical complications such as intimal flaps, thrombosis and residual stenosis after the reconstruction.

Blaisdell found with completion arteriography that 25% of the performed carotid endarterectomies had unsuspected technical defects.[5] Similar results have been confirmed by others using intraoperative Doppler spectral analysis[6,7] and duplex scanning.[8-11] The clinical significance of some of these defects are difficult to define.[12] Nevertheless, it is likely that a method for intraoperative control during carotid endarterectomy is warranted.[10] Flow- and pressure measurements can give an indication of the haemodynamic significance of an obstruction, but will not detect minor irregularities. Angioscopy has been used by some surgeons, and provides an easy means of direct visual correction without having to reopen the arteriotomy.[13,14] However, the method has not found wide acceptance so far. Duplex scanning has been found valuable, especially during carotid surgery.[8,10] The practical use of this technique for intraoperative control during carotid endarterectomy is described.

TECHNIQUE

We have used a colour coded duplex scanner, Vingmed CFM 750 (Vingmed, Norway) for our investigations consecutively in 60 carotid endarterectomies. A specially designed 7.5 MHz annular array probe with a stand-off dome was used. For tissue imaging, the sector opening angle is 45 degrees, and the sector angle chosen for flow imaging is 25 degrees to obtain an adequate frame rate.[15] The dome has a front that is angled relative to the sector's centre axis, and by choosing the colour sector, adequate Doppler angle between the flow beams and the velocity direction is obtained (Fig. 1). The stand-off dome provides excellent nearfield imaging of vessel structures close to the probe. The shape of the dome is specially adapted for long

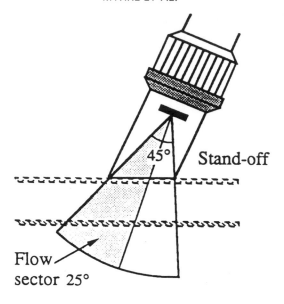

Fig. 1. A schematic illustration of the ultrasound probe specially designed for intraoperative use.

axis contact imaging of the vessel. Short axis images are easily obtained by rotating the probe 90 degrees around the probe axis.

The probe and the connecting cable was covered by a sterile plastic bag, which was distally filled with sterile acoustic coupling gel (Aquasonic 100, Parker laboratories Inc, USA). Sterile saline solution was applied in the operative field to the level of the vessel, and imaging was done with the probe in contact with the vessel wall.

The scan head was first placed along the longitudinal axis of the carotid artery and parallel scans were obtained around most of the vessel circumference. Finally, transverse scanning from the beginning of the endarterectomy in the common carotid artery to the end-point in the internal carotid artery were included. Also areas where vascular clamps or elastic tapes had been placed, were investigated. However, only the proximal part of the external carotid artery was included in this study.

In our own experience general anaesthesia was used and a shunt was applied on a selective basis, depending upon intraoperative pressure measurements, symptomatology and the extent of the arterial disease. Vein-patch graft angioplasty was performed in most cases. No attempt was made to compare the results of colour coded duplex scanning with other methods in this investigation.

RESULTS

In one patient an intimal flap was seen in the lumen giving rise to turbulent flow (Fig. 2). A revision confirmed a defect of 2×7 mm, and a repeat scan showed normal arterial lumen afterwards. Otherwise, a patent vessel with normal flow profile

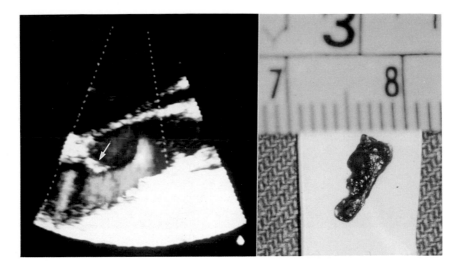

Fig. 2. An intimal defect is protruding into the arterial lumen (←). At reintervention an intimal flap (right) of 2 × 7 mm was identified and removed. Control investigation showed no irregularities in the arterial lumen.

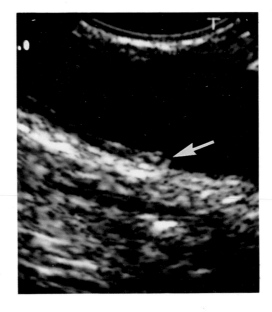

Fig. 3. A step in the intima can be demonstrated where the endarterectomy is starting in the common carotid artery (→).

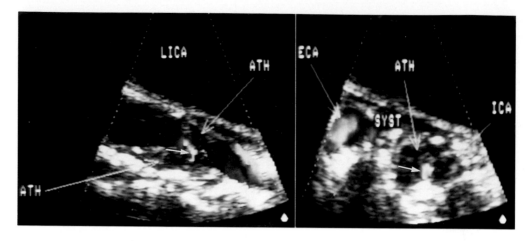

Fig. 4. Intraoperative prereconstruction scanning with severe carotid artery stenosis. Both longitudinal and transverse images are presented. A small lumen is seen in the central part of the plaque (→).

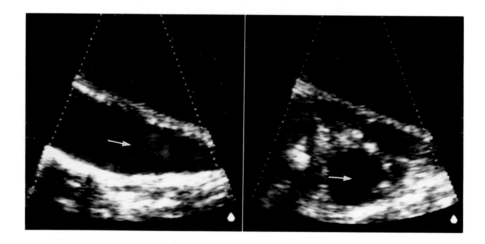

Fig. 5. Following endarterectomy colour coded duplex scanning revealed an open lumen without defects and non-turbulent flow. Both longitudinal and transverse images are presented.

and smooth endarterectomy surface was found by the duplex scanning. Also, the distal part of the endarterectomy and the patch graft angioplasty was visualized and found to be without stenoses. In most cases a definite step could be observed where the endarterectomy started in the common carotid artery (Fig. 3). However, no turbulence was observed at this site.

In this particular series one patient had a transient ischaemic attack (TIA) the first postoperative day. This occurred during a period with hypertension and a systolic blood pressure greater than 200. The patient had no neurologic sequelae. Otherwise, no postoperative complications such as haemorrhage or wound infection were observed.

In one case there was doubt about whether the internal carotid artery was open or had occluded at the time of surgery. Intraoperative prereconstruction investigation revealed that the artery was still open with a small central lumen and the operation was therefore continued as planned (Fig. 4). Postreconstruction scan revealed a satisfactory result (Fig. 5).

The investigation took approximately 5–10 minutes. The duplex image was interpreted by the surgeon and hard copies of the images could easily be obtained.

DISCUSSION

The applicability of colour coded duplex scanning for intraoperative investigation following carotid endarterectomy was confirmed by our study. Today such scanners are used intraoperatively by different surgical disciplines and are thus often available in the operating theatre. Most vascular surgeons are today accustomed with obtaining and interpreting ultrasound images and Doppler spectra. The investigation is expedient and does not extend the operating time significantly. Multiple images are obtained in various planes and the examination can be repeated following correction of technical defects. This method does not expose the patient nor the personnel to unnecessary X-ray irradiation. Additionally, the patient is spared from unnecessary exposure to contrast media and potential complications from puncture of the carotid artery.[16] Furthermore, the method provides haemodynamic data pertaining to the blood flow, which may give supplemental information of importance when the decision to reintervene is to be taken. The real-time feature gives information about the motion of intimal flaps, which is of importance for a precise definition of the defects observed. Since the same pre- and postoperative investigative method is also used intraoperatively, additional costs are limited to probes for intraoperative use.

It has been suggested that fewer unnecessary reexplorations need to be performed when the decision is based on intraoperative ultrasound compared with arteriography.[17] On the other hand, the method seems to be extremely sensitive, detecting changes too small to be of clinical significance. Thus, B-mode scanning is able to detect 67% of defects 1 mm and less and will detect all defects of 2 mm or more.[18,19] Some of these minor defects do not require corrections. However, the decision to reintervene must be based both on the size and location of the defect. Thus, a small defect in the internal carotid artery should probably always be corrected, whereas similar defects in the external carotid artery are perhaps not of the same importance. Also blood stasis can be visualized since static unclothed blood is echogenic when using images at frequencies above 5 MHz.[8]

It is often difficult to decide when to reintervene after having detected a defect following carotid endarterectomy. Following the policy of correcting defects of 1–2 mm or more in the internal carotid artery while leaving minor defects in the common and external carotid artery, no differences in the frequency of early and late neurological events and restenoses have been detected thus far.[12] A revision rate of 7–9% has been described by other authors.[8,17,20] The decision to intervene is based on experience and upon the size and location of the defect, together with the likelihood of improving patency after an eventual corrective procedure.

Ultrasound imaging is ideal for visualization of the endarterectomized site. However, the distal arterial tree can not be visualized, and for this purpose arteriography is a better method. Complications such as stroke have been reported following arteriography which has been abandoned by some surgeons for this reason.[16] However, digital imaging assistance for operating rooms and improved technique has also made this technique safer.[21] The time required to perform intraoperative arteriography is not necessarily longer than the time it takes to perform a duplex examination. However, only a single anteroposterior projection is usually obtained and no haemodynamic data are provided.[11] Oblique sections of the carotid arteries visualized by duplex scanning may be difficult to interpret and it is difficult to reach a very high bifurcation or the site of the distal end of the shunt if it has been located far from the arteriotomy.

There is a need for better probes designed for intraoperative use. It would be advantageous if these probes could be sterilized since it is cumbersome to have the probe in a plastic bag. Furthermore, the probe used in the present investigation is relatively large, although this is a minor disadvantage.

When using the percutaneous technique, depth penetration is obtained at the expense of high resolution obtained with high frequencies. This problem is eliminated during intraoperative use of ultrasound since the probe can be placed directly at the vessel wall. Thus, probes of 10 MHz or even higher frequencies can be used giving an excellent resolution.

The published reports are usually too small to show any statistical differences between the various methods since the percentage of neurological events in the immediate postoperative period is low. It is perhaps difficult to do a randomized series where one control method is compared with no intraoperative investigation at all. However, a long term follow-up comparison between intraoperative duplex scanning and arteriography seems warranted.[22,23] In this particular series only one defect was observed and corrected. Our overall postoperative incidence of TIA and stroke in 247 carotid endarterectomies is 3.2%. This only reflects that our experience is limited and that large series are necessary to show the benefit of intraoperative colour coded duplex scanning control. However, it is reassuring to know that the technical result of the reconstruction is satisfactory after closure of the arteriotomy. Another explanation for the low rate of pathological findings and revisions could be that only the first part of the external carotid artery was included in the investigation. More attention should be focused on this artery which is often endarterectomized in a 'blind manner'. If secondary thrombotic occlusion occurs, thrombotic material could extend into the lumen of the internal carotid artery giving rise to emboli with TIA and stroke.[20] Defects detected in this artery should therefore probably be corrected to a greater extent. Our operative technique is probably similar to most other centres. The procedure includes a long arteriotomy to visualize both end-points of the endarterectomy. The endarterectomized surface is carefully rinsed with haparin-saline solution removing all intimal flaps.

It is interesting to note that no turbulence was seen following endarterectomy of the internal carotid artery. This is probably advantageous with regard to the formation of secondary thrombosis or intimal hyperplasia.[1,2] It is a question of whether the flow pattern is fully normalized immediately after completion of an endarterectomy, or a turbulent flow pattern is observed later in the postoperative period since such a flow pattern is seen in normal patent carotid arteries.

CONCLUSION

Several investigators have demonstrated that colour coded duplex scanning is convenient for intraoperative use following carotid endarterectomy. In this setting the whole endarterectomized segment of the artery can be investigated. Multiple images can be obtained in various planes, and the investigation only takes 5–10 minutes. The method is inexpensive if the duplex equipment is available and only a specially built probe for intraoperative use is necessary. Standardization is advantageous since colour coded duplex scanning is used both for pre- and postoperative investigation. The staff is therefore familiar with the investigative procedure and interpretation of the results.

The technique is superior to arteriography in detecting intimal flaps and thrombosis, whereas the methods are equal for the detection of strictures.[22] The size and the location of the defect must be considered along with the likelihood of improving patency and reducing neurological complications by intraoperative corrective measures. About 1–2 mm flaps of the internal carotid artery should be corrected whereas such minor defects in the common or external carotid can probably be ignored. Hitherto, no differences have been observed regarding the immediate incidence of neurological events or late restenosis following this policy. Intraoperative use of colour coded duplex scanning and arteriography probably complement each other,[7,22,23] but it seems likely that with improved technology, colour coded duplex scanning has a definite place for intraoperative control of carotid endarterectomy.

REFERENCES

1. Bandyk DF, Kaebnick HW, Adams MB, Towne JB: Turbulence occurring after carotid bifurcation endarterectomy: A harbinger of residual and recurrent carotid stenosis. J Vasc Surg 7: 261–274, 1988
2. Smith RL, Blick EF, Coalson J, Stein PD: Thrombus production by turbulence. J Appl Physiol 32: 261–264, 1972
3. European carotid surgery trialists' collaborative group. MRC European carotid surgery trial: interim results for symptomatic patients with severe (70–99%) or with mild (0–29%) carotid stenosis. Lancet 337: 1235–1243, 1991

4. North American symptomatic carotid endarterectomy trial collaborators. Beneficial effect of carotid endarterectomy in symptomatic patients with high-grade carotid stenosis. N Engl J Med 325: 445–453, 1991
5. Blaisdell FW, Lim R Jr, Hall AD: Technical result of carotid endarterectomy: Arteriographic assessment. Am J Surg 114: 239–246, 1967
6. Barnes RW, Garrett WV: Intraoperative assessment of arterial reconstruction by Doppler ultrasound. Surg Gynecol Obstet 146: 896–900, 1978
7. Zierler RE, Bandyk DF, Thiele BL: Intraoperative assessment of carotid endarterectomy. J Vasc Surg 1: 73–83, 1984
8. Sigel B, Coelho JCU, Flanigan DP *et al.*: Detection of vascular defects during operation by imaging ultrasound. Ann Surg 196: 473–480, 1982
9. Flanigan DP, Doublas DJ, Machi J *et al.*: Intraoperative ultrasonic imaging of the carotid artery during carotid endarterectomy. Surgery 100: 893–898, 1986
10. Schwartz RA, Peterson GJ, Noland KA, Hower JF, Naunheim KS: Intraoperative duplex scanning after carotid artery reconstruction: A valuable tool. J Vasc Surg 7: 620–624, 1988
11. Okuhn SP, Stoney RJ: Intraoperative use of ultrasound in arterial surgery. *In* Surgical Clinics of North America, Pearce WH, Yao JST (Eds). Philadelphia: WB Saunders p. 70, 1990
12. Sawchuk AP, Flanigan DP, Machi J, Schuler JJ, Sigel B: The fate of unrepaired minor technical defects detected by intraoperative ultrasonography during carotid endarterectomy. J Vasc Surg 9: 671–676, 1989
13. Raithel D, Kasprzak P: Angioscopy after carotid endarterectomy. Ann Chir Gynaecol 81: 192–195, 1992
14. Olcott IV C. Clinical applications of video angioscopy. J Vasc Surg 5: 664–666, 1987
15. Angelsen BAJ, Kristoffersen K, Torp HG, Linker DT, Skjaerpe T: Color flow mapping with an annular array. *In* Textbook of Color Doppler Echocardiography, Nanda NC (Ed.). Philadelphia, London: Lea & Febiger, 1989
16. Anderson CA, Collins GJ Jr, Rich NM: Routine operative arteriography during carotid endarterectomy: A reassessment. Surgery 83: 67–71, 1978
17. Sigel B, Flanigan DP, Schuler JJ *et al.*: Imaging ultrasound in the intraoperative diagnosis of vascular defects. J Ultrasound Med 2: 337–343, 1983
18. Coelho JCU, Sigel B, Flanigan DP *et al.*: Detection of arterial defects by real-time ultrasound scanning during vascular surgery: An experimental study. J Surg Res 30: 535–543, 1981
19. Flanigan DP: Intraoperative use of the B-mode scan. *In* Arterial Surgery: New Diagnostic and Operative Techniques, Bergan JJ, Yao JST (Eds), Orlando: Grune & Stratton, 1988
20. Lane RJ, Ackroyd N, Appleberg M, Graham J: The application of operative ultrasound immediately following carotid endarterectomy. World J Surg 11: 593–597, 1987
21. Roon AJ, Hoogerwerf D: Intraoperative arteriography and carotid surgery. J Vasc Surg 16: 239–243, 1992
22. Coelho JCU, Sigel B, Flanigan DP *et al.*: An experimental evaluation of arteriography and imaging ultrasound in detecting arterial defects at operation. J Surg Res 32: 130–137, 1982
23. O'Donnel TF Jr, Erdoes L, Mackey WC *et al.*: Correlation of B-mode ultrasound imaging and arteriography with pathologic findings at carotid endarterectomy. Arch Surg 120: 443–449, 1985

Completion Angiography Following Carotid Endarterectomy

John A. Mannick, Anthony D. Whittemore and Magruder C. Donaldson

Completion angiography following peripheral arterial reconstruction has become standard practice in many centres. However, there are few published reports of carotid endarterectomies evaluated with completion angiograms and many experienced surgeons reject this procedure as being unnecessary, potentially misleading and possibly dangerous. Influenced by reports by Blaisdell and associates[1,2] and Courbier et al.,[3] we began in July of 1983 a trial of routine completion angiography following carotid endarterectomy and found that useful information was frequently obtained by this technique. It therefore has become standard practice on our vascular service since that time and has been used in all endarterectomies except for those performed simultaneously with coronary artery bypass surgery, where the technical difficulties in obtaining completion angiograms have prevented their routine use in this subset of patients.

We have recently reviewed our experience with 453 consecutive carotid endarterectomies studied with completion angiograms from July of 1983 until July of 1991. Carotid endarterectomy was routinely performed under general anaesthetic with selective shunting based on electroencephalographic (EEG) monitoring. The endarterectomies were performed in 386 patients, 285 (64%) were males and 186 (37%) were females. Their ages ranged from 40 to 89 years with a mean age of 67. Risk factors included diabetes in 79 patients (18%), smoking in 221 (49%), hypertension in 266 (59%), known coronary artery disease in 209 (46%), prior stroke in 107 (23.7%) and obstructive pulmonary disease in 55 (12%). The indications for carotid endarterectomy were transient ischaemic attack (TIA) in 66%, recent stroke in 6% and asymptomatic pre-occulsive stensosis in 28%.

Completion angiograms were performed by placing a cassette under the patient's neck and skull, a procedure which was simplified by the routine use of a cassette holding operating table. A portable X-ray machine was then used to take a single angiographic exposure. Approximately 10 ml of contrast medium were injected by hand through an angiographic tubing attached to a small 20 gauge intravenous cannula inserted directly into the common carotid artery proximal to the site of endarterectomy.

Patch angioplasty of autogenous vein, Dacron or polytetrafluoroethylene (PTFE) was used selectively and was performed in 24 (5.3%) patients prior to completion angiography to correct kinks or to compensate for very small arteries. Patch angioplasty was performed in 25 (5.5%) additional patients as part of the treatment of defects noted on completion angiography. A total of 8.4% of male patients and 11.7% of female patients (not statistically significantly different) received patch angioplasties. Defects on completion angiograms which warranted surgical correction were demonstrated in 57 operations, a surprising 13%. A kink and an adventitial band were repaired in two cases without reopening the arterotomy whereas in three cases no pathology was encountered after re-exploration of the artery. In 15 cases re-exploration was limited to the external carotid artery. It was our policy to repair pre-occlusive stenoses or acute occlusions of the external carotid in order to prevent possible embolization of fresh clot from the external carotid into the internal carotid system.

In 39 cases flaps, stenoses or platelet aggregates in the area of the endarterectomy were corrected by reopening part or all of the original arterotomy. After correction of defects noted on the initial angiogram, it was our policy to perform a second angiogram in order to show that a satisfactory technical result had ultimately been obtained. The patient was not allowed to leave the operating room until a technically satisfactory endarterectomy was confirmed by angiography (Fig. 1).

The operative morbidity for the 453 patients' endarterectomies included seven strokes (1.6%), both major and minor, and two transient ischaemic attacks. Death within 30 days of surgery occurred in three patients (0.7%). Two died of myocardial infarction and one died of a severe pulmonary disease. There were no detectable complications of the completion angiograms.

In 1987, routine postoperative duplex surveillance was instituted for all patients who had undergone carotid endarterectomy. After a mean follow-up of 15.4 months, restenosis of greater than 50% occurred in 18 (8.4%) of 214 evaluable arteries. Seven (3.3%) arteries developed high grade or symptomatic restenosis requiring reoperation.

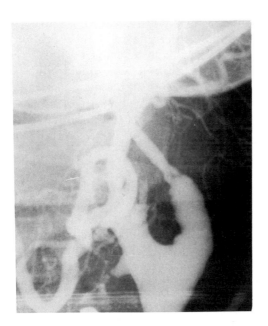 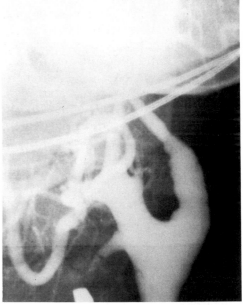

Fig. 1A (left).   Completion angiogram following carotid endarterectomy in a 69-year-old White male. Patch graft angioplasty was elected because of the relatively small size of the internal carotid artery. The angiogram shows a filling defect at the distal end of the endarterectomy.

Fig. 1B (right).   Second angiogram following opening of the patch graft and removal of a small intimal tag with attached platelet thrombus. The filling defect is no longer present.

As opposed to several recently reported series, the difference in restenosis rates between males (8.2%) and females (8.9%) was not significantly different (χ^2). There was also no significant difference in restenosis between patched (4.0%) and non-patched (9.5%) arteries though there was a trend in favour of the patched arteries. We have interpreted these results as suggesting that completion angiography permits selective patch angioplasty with a rate of restenosis comparable to that achieved in reported series of carotid endarterectomies in which angioplasty was routine.[4]

This experience of routine completion angiography following carotid endarterectomy over an 8-year period suggests that this technique is both safe and useful. It clearly detects a significant number of lesions which appear to require surgical correction. While we realize that there are reported series of carotid endarterectomies in which no completion angiograms or other imaging of the endarterectomy site was performed with comparable rates of postoperative stroke and mortality, it seems likely that patients benefit from correction of residual stenoses and technical defects at the time of the initial surgery. At the very least it seems likely that this will prevent some early recurrent stenoses which may very well represent residual stenoses uncorrected at the time of initial endarterectomy.

For 5 of the 8 years of the present study we have evaluated the area of endarterectomy intraoperatively with the hand-held Doppler at the completion of the procedure. Unfortunately, this technique has not revealed a number of significant defects seen on simultaneously performed completion angiograms. Therefore, we do not consider simple insonation of the endarterectomy site to be adequate for evaluation of the technical success of the endarterectomy.

We would agree with Zierler and associates[5] and Schwartz and coworkers[6] that the use of intraoperative duplex examination of carotid endarterectomy sites would also be an appropriate means of evaluating the technical adequacy of the procedure. Our recent experience with this technique has shown it to be very accurate but more time-consuming than completion angiography. In any case, our experience over the past 8 years with completion angiography suggests to us that some form of imaging of the carotid endarterectomy site should be performed routinely before the patient leaves the operating room.

REFERENCES

1. Blaisdell FW, Lim R, Hall A: Technical result of carotid endarterectomy. Arteriographic assessment. Am J Surg 114: 239–246, 1967
2. Blaisdell FW: Routine operative arteriography following carotid endarterectomy. Surgery 83: 114–115, 1978
3. Courbier R, Jausseran J-M, Reggi M et al.: Routine intraoperative angiography: its impact on operative morbidity and carotid restenosis. J Vasc Surg 3: 343–350, 1986
4. Hertzer NR, Beven EG: O'Hara PJ, Krajewski LP: A prospective study of vein patch angioplasty during carotid endarterectomy. Ann Surg 628–635, 1987
5. Zierler RE, Bandyk DF, Thiele BL: Intraoperative assessment of carotid endarterectomy. J Vasc Surg 1: 73–81, 1984
6. Schwartz RA, Peterson GJ, Noland KA, Hower JF, Naunhcim, KS: Intraoperative duplex scanning after carotid artery reconstruction: a valuable tool. J Vasc Surg 7: 620–624, 1988

Perioperative Transcranial Doppler Monitoring

C. V. Ruckley and A. R. Naylor

The interim results of the European Carotid Surgery Trial (ECST)[1] and the North American Surgeons Carotid Endarterectomy Trial (NASCET),[2] by highlighting the fine balance between operative risk and long-term benefit, have renewed interest in the operation of carotid endarterectomy and re-focused attention on the need to minimize operative mortality and morbidity.

How may the operation be made safe? First and foremost by meticulous and painstaking operative technique.[3] It is interesting, in this context, that one of the significant surgical risk factors identified in the ECST was fast surgery.[1] Another way in which the safety of the operation may be enhanced is by careful measurement and monitoring throughout. Such measurement and monitoring has several roles. These may be broadly divided into five categories:

1. Patient selection and preoperative identification of risk.
2. Assessment of the need for a shunt and monitoring shunt function.
3. Monitoring perioperative cerebral blood flow.
4. Detection of intraoperative events.
5. Quality control.

Unlike most other techniques employed to measure or monitor cerebral haemodynamics, transcranial Doppler (TCD) can contribute useful information in all of these categories and is therefore without doubt the most versatile and practical of available methods. We have employed TCD for perioperative carotid monitoring since 1988 and our experience is based on a consecutive series of more than 100 carotid endarterectomy operations performed by one surgeon.

PRINCIPLES OF TRANSCRANIAL DOPPLER ULTRASOUND

Before the introduction of TCD by Aaslid and his co-workers in 1982,[4] conventional Doppler ultrasound equipment was unable to penetrate the intact cranium and provide quality imaging data. However, the development of a low frequency (2.5 MHz) pulsed wave ultrasound beam together with the exploitation of areas where the skull is relatively thin (the cranial windows) permitted insonation of the arteries comprising the Circle of Willis and its principal branches. It is important to remember however that TCD measures blood flow velocity and not volume flow and this must be taken into account when evaluating data.

The most commonly used cranial window (especially for intraoperative monitoring) is through the relatively thin temporal bone. This permits insonation of most of the Circle of Willis, and in particular, the middle cerebral artery (MCA). Similarly, the transorbital window enables insonation of the carotid siphon, while the suboccipital window permits insonation of the distal vertebral arteries and basilar artery.[5] Transcranial Doppler has the capacity for range gating. This enables the 'focussing point' of the ultrasound beam to be adjusted over some distance in order to evaluate different components of the basal cerebral arteries. In addition, TCD discriminates between flow towards the Doppler probe (represented by a positive waveform deflection) and flow away from the probe (a negative waveform deflection).

The quality of the signal depends on the thickness of the cranium and in a proportion of patients (10% overall but up to 30% of elderly female subjects) a signal adequate for perioperative monitoring cannot be obtained.

It is customary to record both the systolic (peak) and mean velocities and all TCD machines include some type of pulsatility index measurement. It is, however, important simultaneously to monitor, and as far as possible maintain stable, systemic blood pressure and end-tidal CO_2 since both can substantially influence cerebral blood flow in the anaesthetized patient.

PREOPERATIVE EVALUATION

The selection of patients for carotid endarterectomy radically influences outcome; one of the dilemmas being that the patient who has most to gain from a successful operation is also the one who represents the highest operative risk. Since one of the documented risk factors is reduced cerebral vascular reserve (CVR),[6] its preoperative detection carries potential advantages in terms of risk assessment and the potential need for an intraoperative shunt. Transcranial Doppler can also provide a simple means of assessing CVR, based on the response of MCA blood flow velocity to a vasodilatory stimulus such as CO_2 or acetazolamide.[7]

A baseline preoperative study can easily be undertaken with a hand-held probe and a map produced of the anterior cerebral artery (ACA), MCA and posterior cerebral artery (PCA). This can sometimes be time consuming and complex, particularly in the presence of flow reversal in the ipsilateral ACA although the more recent development of a transcranial colour duplex probe may make this examination considerably easier.[8] Collateral flow may be evaluated during ipsilateral and contralateral common carotid artery (CCA) compression, provided this is done low in the neck and only after duplex or angiography has excluded significant CCA disease.

Figure 1 illustrates an example of the types of flow compensation mediated by the Circle of Willis. This patient presented with a left carotid territory stroke and had a 95% stenosis of the left internal carotid artery (ICA) and no significant disease in the right ICA. In the asymptomatic right hemisphere, there is the normal pattern of flow in the MCA and PCA, together with the normally reversed flow in the right ACA (as flow is away from the probe). Note however that velocity flow in the symptomatic left MCA is significantly less than on the right. Note also the enhanced flow in the left PCA and the abnormal flow reversal in the left ACA (now towards the probe and indicating that the contralateral ICA is partially supplying the hemisphere), both being evidence of recruitment of collateral flow. The fact that the contralateral ICA is the principal source of collateral flow to the symptomatic MCA can be demonstrated by brief contralateral CCA compression which causes flow velocity in the ipsilateral ACA to fall significantly (Fig. 2).

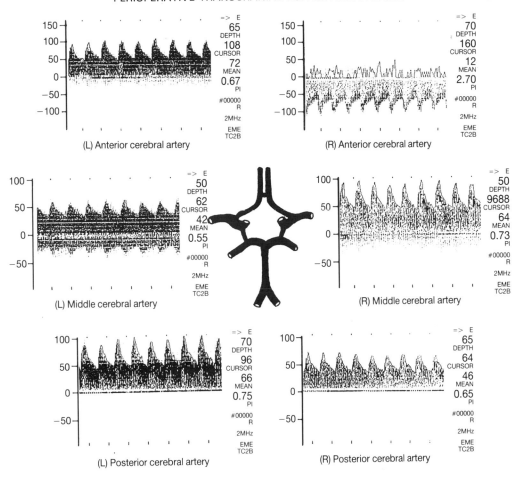

Fig. 1. Preoperative TCD study of the basal cerebral arteries in a patient presenting with a left carotid territory stroke and a left ICA stenosis of 95%. There is TCD evidence of recruitment of the collateral circulation to maintain left MCA flow as demonstrated by enhanced left PCA velocities and flow reversal in the ipsilateral ACA.

INTRAOPERATIVE MONITORING

Optimal intraoperative monitoring (almost invariably of the ipsilateral MCA) requires the use of a fixed head probe system which is protected from disturbance by a metal or plastic frame. Transcranial Doppler then enables continuous monitoring of each of the different phases of the procedure (Fig. 3).

Shunt deployment

The surgeon who prefers to use a shunt selectively can make effective use of TCD. Application of the ICA clamp usually causes a variable fall in MCA velocity, the

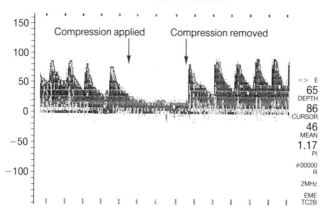

Fig. 2. In the presence of a subcritical ICA stenosis, MCA flow may be maintained by reversed flow in the ispilateral ACA, i.e. the inflow actually originates from the contralateral ICA. This phenomenon is demonstrated in this figure. The TCD is imaging the ispilateral ACA which has a positive waveform deflection (i.e. the opposite to normal and suggesting that flow is coming over from the opposite hemisphere). By compressing the contralateral common carotid artery the ACA flow signal falls significantly, confirming that the former is responsible for the vascularization of the symptomatic hemisphere.

degree being a reflection of the potential contribution from the collateral circulation. On some occasions, where there is immediate and effective reversal of flow in the ipsilateral ACA (Fig. 4), the subsequent drop in MCA velocity may be negligible, in which case a shunt is superfluous, as flow to the operated hemisphere is being maintained via inflow from the contralateral ICA. In association with others,[9] we have observed an overall correlation between MCA velocity, stump pressure and a subjective assessment of ICA backflow (Figs 5 and 6). In our hands,[10] a systolic stump pressure of 50 mmHg after clamping corresponds with a systolic MCA velocity of 40 cm/s and a mean MCA velocity of 30 cm/s and we have occasionally used this as a criterion for late shunt deployment should MCA velocity fall further during the endarterectomy phase of the operation. Such a policy does result in a higher rate of shunt usage (about 50%) than is strictly necessary, but avoids the need for, and costs of, additional monitoring such as electroencephalography (EEG) or somatosensory evoked potentials (SSEPs) which involve further equipment and a need for technical support. The linear relationship between MCA velocity and stump pressure has not, however, been a uniform finding in other series and may reflect the differential effects of loss of cerebral autoregulation and the use of various anaesthetic regimens.

Operative technique

The continuous monitoring of MCA velocities influences operative technique. It is surprising to the surgeon, when the method is first employed, to discover the extent to which manipulation of the carotid bifurcation affects MCA flow,[10] a warning as to how easy it may be to dislodge thrombotic debris into the cerebral circulation.

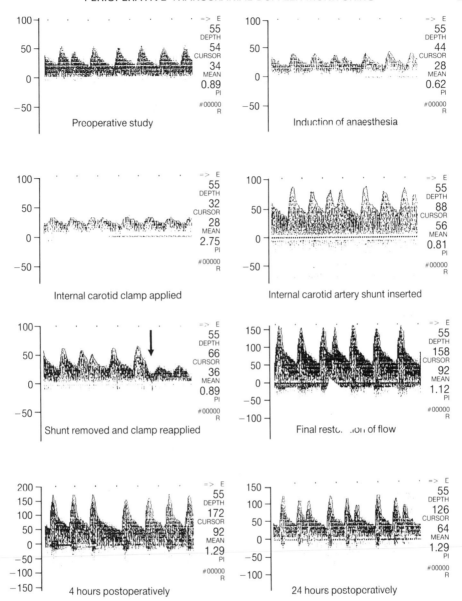

Fig. 3. Middle cerebral artery flow velocity profiles during carotid endarterectomy. Sequence of TCD waveforms from varying phases of the procedure. Note the effect of carotid clamping, the restoration of increased flow with shunting, the initial surge in MCA velocity following clamp release which then increases still further within 4 hours of operation.

Monitoring shunt function

Insertion of a shunt restores blood flow velocity to pre-clamp levels, and occasionally even higher (Fig. 3). One of the most valuable roles of TCD is to monitor velocity while the shunt is *in situ*. On several occasions we have been alerted to failure of flow in a shunt which to all external appearances was functioning satisfactorily. The

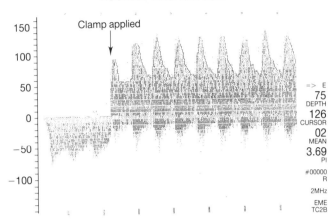

Fig. 4. This sequence shows the effect of carotid clamping on the ipsilateral anterior cerebral artery during carotid endarterectomy. Note the immediate reversal of flow when the clamp is applied. In such a situation, a shunt is often not necessary.

commonest cause of impaired shunt function is kinking, either in the midpoint or at the point of entry into the ICA. We have also experienced on two occasions, complete occlusion of a shunt when the balloon cuff was inflated, once in the ICA and once in the CCA. On neither occasion was it apparent, on external examination or by backbleeding through the side arm, that the shunt was not working and on each occasion, release of fluid from the balloon restored flow. Moreover, on a further occasion, thrombus formed unnoticed in the side arm of the shunt and gave rise to a number of emboli which were detected by TCD.

Cerebral perfusion

Measurement of MCA velocity, using TCD, gives only indirect information on cerebral blood flow. It has, however, become conventional, provided end-tidal CO_2

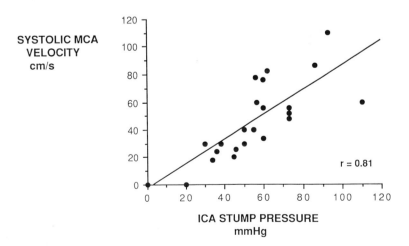

Fig. 5. Relationship between systolic MCA velocity and ICA systolic stump pressure.

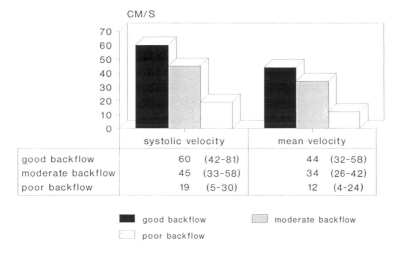

CM/S

	systolic velocity		mean velocity	
good backflow	60	(42–81)	44	(32–58)
moderate backflow	45	(33–58)	34	(26–42)
poor backflow	19	(5–30)	12	(4–24)

■ good backflow   ▨ moderate backflow
☐ poor backflow

data refer to the median and its 95% confidence interval

Fig. 6. Relationship between MCA velocity and a subjective assessment of ICA backflow after carotid clamping. Good backflow was defined as brisk, pulsatile flow, moderate as brisk but non-pulsatile, while the remainder were classified as poor.

and blood pressure remain stable, to assume that changes in velocity represent an index of change in blood flow. It does not, however, provide objective assessment of functional cerebral activity, for which EEG, SSEP or some other index of cerebral oxygenation is required. However, in the presence of near normal systemic arterial blood pressure and end-tidal CO_2 and MCA velocities in excess of 40 cm/s we have encountered no neurological events of haemodynamic origin.

Events

In addition to disturbances of flow due to dissection or deformity of the arteries or shunt malfunction, referred to earlier, the TCD can alert to embolic events. Emboli are most frequently detected at the time of shunt insertion and after final restoration of flow (Fig. 7) and produce a characteristic high-pitched staccato sound and a high energy signal superimposed on the waveform. The majority of these emboli are probably small air bubbles, but particulate debris may also be detected at times when no air can have entered the circulation.[10,11]

Although the clinical significance of all TCD embolic events remains unknown, there is increasing evidence that some are associated with neurological morbidity,[10] i.e. their presence and occurrence alerts the surgeon to potential imperfections in technique and can to a considerable extent be obviated.

Quality control

Insistence on the value of methods of quality control at the end of the operative procedure is a relatively new aspect of carotid surgery in the UK and several methods have been advocated. A good quality MCA signal after completion of the

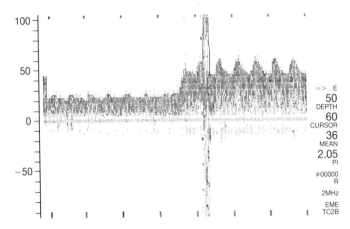

Fig. 7. Transcranial Doppler evidence of a single air/microparticulate embolus following clamp release and final restoration of flow.

endarterectomy and clamp release is a strong indicator of a functionally satisfactory operation and together with angioscopy and Doppler should ensure a more consistently good technical result. The potential value of TCD as a means of quality control has been highlighted by Laman *et al.* where TCD alerted the investigators to an intimal flap in the early postoperative period.[12] In addition, our use of TCD has warned us of the potential of the external carotid artery as a source of embolism.[10] It had previously been our practice liberally to flush the carotid vessels with heparinized saline upon completion of the endarterectomy. Irrigation of an unclamped external carotid artery often causes a large sequence of emboli to be detected in the ipsilateral MCA, due to reversed flow in the ophthalmic artery (Fig. 8). It is now clear that external carotid artery irrigation is a potentially dangerous manoeuvre which can readily propel clot or debris into the MCA territory. This

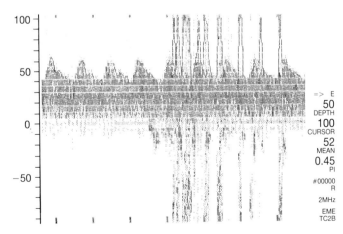

Fig. 8. Sequence of emboli in the MCA during irrigation of the external carotid artery (ICA still clamped). Emboli in this situation reach the cerebral circulation via reversed flow in the ophthalmic artery.

observation also highlights the importance of the external carotid collateral circulation in the presence of an occluded ICA.

POSTOPERATIVE MONITORING

It may often be difficult to decide on the best course of management for a patient who develops a cerebral ischaemic event postoperatively. Should the patient be returned immediately to the operating theatre?; should heparin be given?

The presence of an unchanged and unimpaired TCD signal from the ipsilateral MCA tends to exclude an acute carotid thrombosis (which can occur intraoperatively) and thus avoids an unnecessary, immediate return to the operating room. We would now screen with TCD (to exclude thrombosis) and then evaluate the endarterectomized segment with duplex or angiography. If no technical error is apparent, we would then proceed to a CT scan to exclude a cerebral haemorrhage.

A number of patients complain of non-specific neurological symptoms such as headache, dizziness and confusion following carotid endarterectomy. This may be due to the cerebral hyperperfusion syndrome which is particularly apt to occur in patients with hypertension and a very tight ICA stenosis. Serial TCD studies suggest that up to 30% of patients have an increase in MCA velocity in the first 72 hours after surgery, though only 1–2% of patients overall have significant symptoms.[13,14] The developing syndrome is usually apparent within 4 hours of surgery (Fig. 3) and may then return to normal limits within 12–36 hours or progress even further over the ensuing 48–72 hours. It is thought that the hyperperfusion syndrome is a consequence of a delayed resetting of cerebral autoregulation which has become defective preoperatively because of the chronic state of cerebral vasodilatation required to maintain normal cerebral blood flow above a critical ICA stenosis. Because TCD is non-invasive, it is an ideal means of studying this phenomenon.

SUMMARY

Transcranial Doppler monitoring is a simple, reliable non-invasive technique for carotid monitoring. It is versatile in that it fulfils most of the functions subserved by perioperative monitoring and it also enhances the safety of the procedure. By alerting to disturbances of MCA flow from a variety of causes and to embolic events, it can lead to improvements in operative technique. Furthermore, if neurological events occur in the perioperative period it is easier to identify their cause and to decide on appropriate treatment if TCD monitoring has been in operation.

REFERENCES

1. European Carotid Surgery Triallists Collaborative Group: MRC European Carotid Surgery Trial: Interim results for symptomatic patients with severe (70–99%) or with mild (0–29%) carotid stenosis. Lancet 337: 1235–1243, 1991
2. North American Symptomatic Carotid Endarterectomy Trial Collaborators: Beneficial effects of carotid endarterectomy in symptomatic patients with high-grade stenosis. N Engl J Med 325: 445–453, 1991

3. Naylor AR, Bell PRF, Ruckley CV: Monitoring and cerebral protection during carotid endarterectomy. Br J Surg 79: 735–741, 1992
4. Aaslid R, Markwalder T-M, Nornes H: Non-invasive transcranial ultrasound recording of flow velocity in basal cerebral arteries. J Neurosurg 57: 769–774, 1982
5. Naylor AR: Transcranial Doppler ultrasound. *In* Current Neurosurgery. Teasdale GM, Miller JD (Eds). Edinburgh: Churchill-Livingstone, pp. 77–100, 1992
6. Naylor AR, Merrick MV, Ruckley CV: Risk factors for intra-operative neurological deficits during carotid endarterectomy. Eur J Vasc Surg 5: 33–39, 1991
7. Bishop CCR, Powell S, Rutt D *et al.*: Transcranial Doppler measurement of middle cerebral artery velocity: A validation study. Stroke 17: 913–915, 1986
8. Naylor AR, Warlow CP: Transient ischaemic attacks. Current practice in surgery (in press)
9. Padayachee TS, Gosling RG, Bishop CC, Burnand K, Browse NL: Monitoring middle cerebral artery velocity during carotid endarterectomy. Br J Surg 73: 98–100, 1986
10. Naylor AR, Wildsmith JAW, McClure J, Jenkins AMcL, Ruckley CV: Transcranial Doppler monitoring during carotid endarterectomy. Br J Surg 78: 1264–1268, 1991
11. Spencer MP, Thomas GI, Nicholls SC, Sauvage LR: Detection of middle cerebral artery emboli during carotid endarterectomy using transcranial Doppler ultrasonography. Stroke 21: 415–423, 1990
12. Laman DM, Voorwinde A, Davies G, Van Duijn H: Intra-operative internal carotid artery re-stenosis detected by transcranial Doppler monitoring. Br J Surg 78: 1315–1316, 1989
13. Piepgras DG, Morgan MK, Sundt TM *et al.*: Intracerebral haemorrhage after carotid endarterectomy. J Neurosurg 68: 532–536, 1988
14. Powers AD, Smith RR: Hyperperfusion syndrome after carotid endarterectomy: A transcranial Doppler evaluation. Neurosurg 26: 56–60, 1990

Somatosensory Evoked Potential Monitoring During Carotid Surgery

Thomas F. Panetta, Alan D. Legatt and Frank J. Veith

The benefits of carotid endarterectomy have been proven in prospective, randomized trials.[1,2] However, controversy still exists over the technical aspects involved in performing carotid endarterectomy and in monitoring these patients. General versus regional anaesthesia, routine versus selective shunting, and the best method for determining the need for a shunt are but a few of the issues involved. The need for a shunt during surgery is based on whether or not cerebral ischaemia occurs during carotid artery clamping. Cerebral ischaemia has been estimated to occur in 4–33% of patients undergoing operation;[3] however, only one-fifth of all perioperative strokes can be attributed to ischaemic injury.[4-6] Even though the majority of perioperative strokes may be secondary to embolic or thrombotic events, the surgeon is still obligated to try to prevent intraoperative cerebral ischaemia which can lead to strokes, blood pressure fluctuations and hyperperfusion syndromes including cerebral haemorrhage. The increased risk of perioperative stroke in patients with contralateral internal carotid artery occlusion or a history of previous stroke mandates that a reliable method be found for evaluating and preventing cerebral ischaemia.

The use of somatosensory evoked potential (SEP) monitoring during carotid surgery is founded on the relationship between cerebral blood flow, brain metabolism, and the electrical responses of the nervous system to sensory stimulation.[7,8] Following stimulation of the median nerve at the wrist, the nerve impulses which contribute to the SEPs travel through the peripheral nerve and brachial plexus until they reach the spinal cord (Fig. 1). They are then conducted rostrally through the spinal cord dorsal columns (fasciculus cuneatus) to the medulla, where they synapse in the nucleus cuneatus. Second-order somatosensory axons originating in this nucleus cross to the contralateral side and ascend in the medial lemniscus to the nucleus ventralis posterolateralis of the thalamus, which in turn sends out extensive projections to the somatosensory cortex. The N20 (N = negative direction, average latency = 20 mseconds (ms)) component of the medial nerve SEP is generated in the primary somatosensory cortex, and may also receive a contribution from the thalamocortical projection fibres.[9-11] Since the somatosensory cortex and the thalamocortical projection fibres are supplied by the cortical branches of the middle cerebral artery, interruption of blood flow caused by clamping the internal carotid artery specifically affects neuronal pathways monitored by median nerve SEPs.

The amplitude of the N20 component (Fig. 2) of median nerve SEPs is an index of the vascular integrity as well as the adequacy or inadequacy of collateral circulation to the primary somatosensory cortex and the thalamocortical projection fibres. Cortical SEPs are progressively attenuated as regional cerebral blood flow falls below 18 ml/100 g/min and disappear at about 15 ml/100 g/min or below[7] (Fig. 3). Massive increases in extracellular potassium concentration, which signify membrane ion

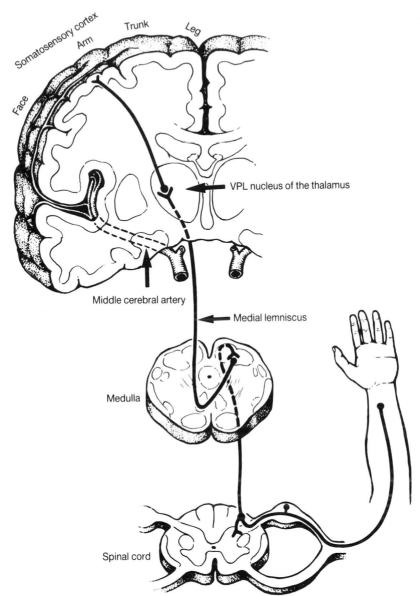

Fig. 1. Association of the neural cell pathway monitored by median nerve SEPs and the blood supplied to the brain by the internal carotid and middle cerebral arteries. (Modified from Kandel ER: Central representation of touch. *In* Principles of Neural Science, 2nd edn, Kandel ER, Schwartz JH (Eds). New York: Elsevier Science Publishing Co Inc., p. 317, 1985.)

pump failure and probable irreversible cell damage, occur at flows below 10 ml/100 g/min,[7,8] although blood flows below 15 ml/100 g/min may cause permanent neuronal damage if they are sustained for longer than 30 minutes.[12]

The differences in regional cerebral blood flow thresholds for electrical and ion pump failures provide a 'window' in which monitoring of cerebral electrical

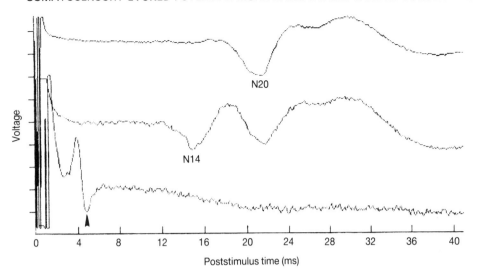

Fig. 2. Typical intraoperative SEPs to median nerve stimulation. The stimulus was delivered at the beginning of the waveforms (arrow). Negativity is shown as a downward deflection in this and subsequent figures. The cortical and cervicomedullary components are labelled according to their polarity (N) and mean peak latency in normal individuals. A triphasic compound action potential is recorded over the peripheral nerve.

activity may detect cerebral ischaemia resulting from carotid artery clamping before irreversible neurologic damage has occurred. Thus, routine use of SEP monitoring in patients undergoing carotid surgery is a valid technique for determining the need for intraoperative shunting.[13,14] The technical aspects, results of a clinical series, and comparison with other monitoring techniques are presented.

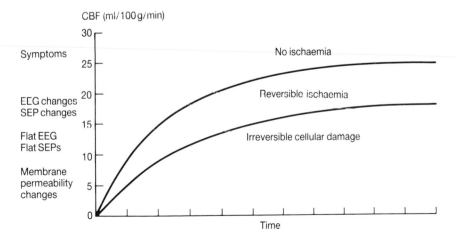

Fig. 3. The relationship between duration of ischaemia, severity of ischaemia, symptoms, thresholds for monitoring techniques and membrane permeability changes.

TECHNICAL ASPECTS OF SEP RECORDING AND INTERPRETATION

Somatosensory evoked potentials are elicited by electrical stimulation of the median nerves at the wrist. Two surface electrodes are placed about 3–4 cm apart over each median nerve just proximal to the wrist crease. Typical stimulus parameters are a duration of 200 microseconds, a rate of 6.1 pulses/s, and an intensity of 20–30 mA/pulse delivered by a constant-current stimulator. Stimuli are delivered unilaterally, but both cerebral hemispheres are alternately monitored during each operation. The SEPs generated in the brain contralateral to the carotid artery that will be clamped provide a control for monitoring systemic factors such as fluctuating levels of anaesthesia and blood pressure changes which may alter SEPs.

N20, the primary cortical SEP, is recorded over the parietal scalp,[15,16] while N14, a component generated at the level of the cervicomedullary junction[10,17] is recorded at the inion (the external occipital protuberance). It is very difficult to repair or replace electrodes that malfunction when the patient is draped and the operation is underway. Therefore, backup recording electrodes should always be placed, and careful attention should be given to the manner in which both the stimulating and the recording electrodes are attached.

Peripheral nerve SEPs are recorded as a backup in order to identify any technical problems that might occur with the stimulator or the stimulating electrodes. In diagnostic studies, these SEPs are usually recorded at the supraclavicular Erb's points overlying the brachial plexus. However, these sites are too close to the operative sterile field. Therefore, peripheral nerve SEPs should be recorded from a mid-line antecubital electrode referred to a nearby electrode on the lateral aspect of the elbow. If both the cortical and the peripheral nerve SEPs are lost simultaneously, the problem can be localized to the stimulator, the stimulating electrodes, or the distal peripheral nerve. In contrast, loss of the cortical SEP with persistence of the peripheral nerve and cervicomedullary SEP components reflects cortical dysfunction.

Cerebral ischaemia can, therefore, be documented by demonstrating ipsilateral cortex findings in the absence of changes in the contralateral hemisphere or the peripheral nerve SEPs. Bilateral decreases in cortical SEP amplitudes can usually be attributed to anaesthesia or changes in blood pressure, except in those patients with contralateral carotid artery occlusion.

In general, cortical SEPs are too small to be seen in the raw data, and signal averaging must be employed to examine the SEP waveforms. The electrophysiologic data are amplified and digitized by a multi-channel evoked potential averager. The improvement in signal-to-noise ratio is proportional to the square root of the number of data epochs included in the average. Thus, the number of averages required for each patient is a function of the size of the SEP as well as the magnitude of the background noise. Typically, each average consists of several hundred sweeps, which may take one or two minutes to acquire. The resultant SEP is the average of the brain's responses over this time interval. Cerebral ischaemia following carotid artery test clamping persists as long as the artery is clamped and unshunted.

Cerebral ischaemia initially causes an amplitude attenuation of the cortical SEPs. A latency delay may also be seen, but this usually occurs later. Because SEP amplitudes are, in general, more variable than latencies and affected more by alterations in the anaesthetic regimen, they therefore have a correspondingly higher threshold for identifying a significant SEP change. A 50% amplitude attenuation or a 10% latency delay of the N20 is indicative of significant hemispheric dysfunction and possible cerebral ischaemia. These changes are relative to a baseline which is established at a steady-state anaesthetic regimen after the induction of general anaesthesia and just prior to clamping the internal carotid artery. SEPs will change considerably during induction of anaesthesia, and an awake SEP is not a valid baseline for the interpretation of intraoperative SEPs in an anaesthetized patient.

An example of a significant SEP change that would mandate shunting is shown in Fig. 4. The cortical SEP attenuated repeatedly whenever flow through the distal internal carotid artery was interrupted, but recovered when flow was restored either with a shunt or with unclamping after completion of the endarterectomy. Minor cortical SEP changes—typically a 20% drop in amplitude—are commonly seen with carotid artery clamping and do not indicate a need for shunting.

SEPs are affected by most general anaesthetics and the N20 component is affected to a much greater degree than the N14 and peripheral nerve SEPs.[17] Thus, anaesthetic effects may mimic SEP changes caused by cerebral ischaemia. Anaesthetic changes are bilateral, and concurrent monitoring of the SEPs generated in the

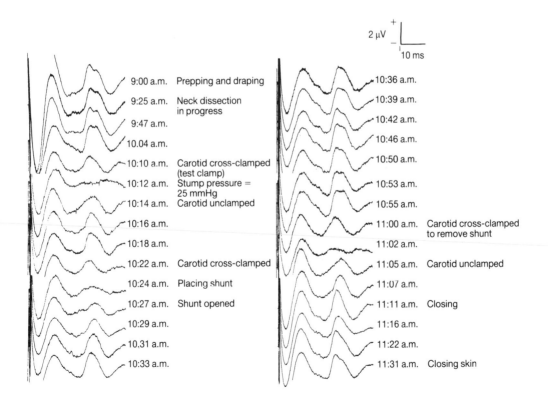

Fig. 4. Cortical SEPs to right median nerve stimulation recorded during a left carotid endarterectomy in a 66-year-old woman. Note the marked SEP attenuations when the distal internal carotid artery blood flow was interrupted at 10:10 a.m., 10:22 a.m. and 11:00 a.m., and the improvement when the shunt was opened.

hemisphere contralateral to the carotid artery being endarterectomized can help differentiate between anaesthetic-related changes and ischaemic SEP changes (it should be noted, however, that if the contralateral carotid artery is occluded, bilateral cerebral ischaemia may conceivably develop following carotid artery clamping). Those performing the SEP monitoring must be aware of the anaesthetic regimen and should maintain a dialogue with the personnel administering the anaesthesia. High concentrations of inhalational agents should be avoided as they can suppress the cortical SEPs. Equally important is the avoidance of large changes in the anaesthetic regimen close to the time of carotid artery clamping, since they could confound the interpretation of any SEP changes at that point (Fig. 5).

Neuromuscular blockade will not alter the SEPs and, if any muscle activity is blocked, it may improve the quality of the recordings. Much of the EEG activity picked up by the scalp electrodes is filtered out by a bandpass of 30 Hz–30 000 Hz, and much of the remaining noise originates in muscle activity.

RESULTS OF THE MONTEFIORE SERIES

In 50 carotid endarterectomy procedures monitored by SEPs, major changes in SEPs (>50% decrease in amplitude) occurred in five cases (10%). All five patients were shunted with no adverse neurological sequelae. Two of the five patients had contralateral carotid artery occlusions with stump pressures of 17 and 30 mmHg; the stump pressures in the three patients in whom the contralateral carotid arteries were patent (although stenotic) were 25, 36, and 40 mmHg. Eleven patients were shunted for other reasons, e.g., because of contralateral carotid artery occlusion, even if the SEPs were unchanged when the carotid artery was clamped. No shunts were used in the remaining 34 patients who had no major SEP changes at carotid artery clamping, despite stump pressures as low as 18 mmHg; none of these 34 patients had an intraoperative stroke.

During four operations, the SEPs were stable through the initial carotid artery clamping, but showed significant attenuation in association with decreases in the systemic blood pressure which was present at other times (Fig. 6). The latter were frequently related to alterations of the anaesthetic regimen, but the SEP changes were considerably larger than those caused by similar anaesthetic doses in the absence of hypotension at other points during the operation. In each case, the SEP changes did not occur at blood pressure levels which by themselves would be alarming; in three patients the SEP changes occurred reproducibly when the systolic pressure decreased to 100–110 mmHg.[18] Nonetheless, the SEP alterations suggested that the mild, relative hypotension was causing significant cerebral ischaemia and the patients' blood pressures were pharmacologically increased in response to the SEP changes. In all four cases, the SEPs returned to baseline concurrent with the improvement in the blood pressure, and none of the patients had new postoperative neurological deficits.

COMPARISON WITH OTHER TECHNIQUES

Other techniques that have been used to assess the adequacy of cerebral circulation during carotid endarterectomy including measurement of internal carotid artery stump

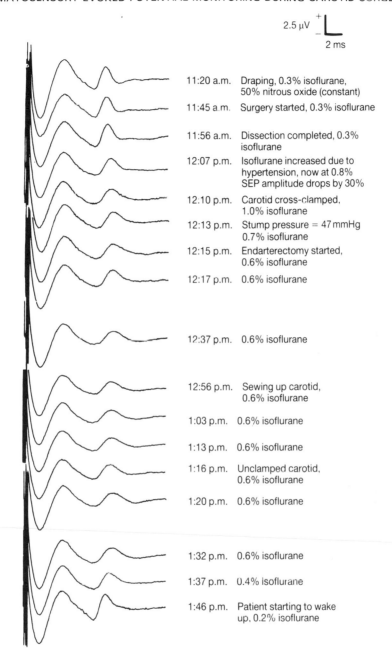

2.5 µV $^+_-$ L

2 ms

11:20 a.m.   Draping, 0.3% isoflurane,
             50% nitrous oxide (constant)

11:45 a.m.   Surgery started, 0.3% isoflurane

11:56 a.m.   Dissection completed, 0.3%
             isoflurane

12:07 p.m.   Isoflurane increased due to
             hypertension, now at 0.8%
             SEP amplitude drops by 30%

12:10 p.m.   Carotid cross-clamped,
             1.0% isoflurane

12:13 p.m.   Stump pressure = 47 mmHg
             0.7% isoflurane

12:15 p.m.   Endarterectomy started,
             0.6% isoflurane

12:17 p.m.   0.6% isoflurane

12:37 p.m.   0.6% isoflurane

12:56 p.m.   Sewing up carotid,
             0.6% isoflurane

1:03 p.m.   0.6% isoflurane

1:13 p.m.   0.6% isoflurane

1:16 p.m.   Unclamped carotid,
             0.6% isoflurane

1:20 p.m.   0.6% isoflurane

1:32 p.m.   0.6% isoflurane

1:37 p.m.   0.4% isoflurane

1:46 p.m.   Patient starting to wake
             up, 0.2% isoflurane

Fig. 5. Cortical SEPs to right median nerve stimulation recorded during a left carotid endarterectomy in a 60-year-old woman. Three minutes prior to clamping of the carotid artery, at 12:07 p.m. the isoflurane concentration was increased because of hypertension; the expired isoflurane concentration increased from 0.3% to 0.8% and then to 1.0%. There was an immediate 30% decrease in the amplitude of the SEP N20 component, with no further change when the carotid artery was clamped. If the time interval had been shorter and the anaesthetic effects greater, the SEP changes could have been interpreted as indicating significant ischaemia due to clamping of the carotid artery. The stump pressure was 47 mmHg, no shunt was used, and the patient had no postoperative neurologic deficits.

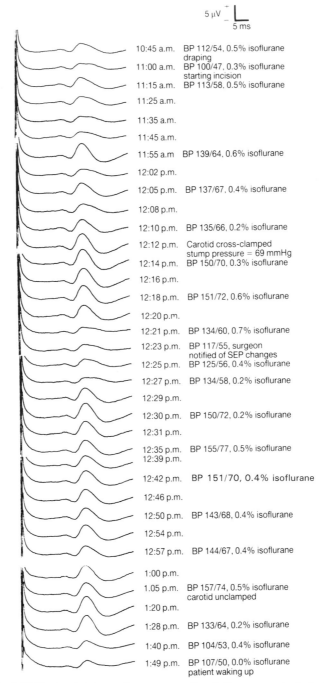

5 µV
5 ms

10:45 a.m.   BP 112/54, 0.5% isoflurane
              draping
11:00 a.m.   BP 100/47, 0.3% isoflurane
              starting incision
11:15 a.m.   BP 113/58, 0.5% isoflurane

11:25 a.m.

11:35 a.m.

11:45 a.m.

11:55 a.m   BP 139/64, 0.6% isoflurane

12:02 p.m.

12:05 p.m.   BP 137/67, 0.4% isoflurane

12:08 p.m.

12:10 p.m.   BP 135/66, 0.2% isoflurane

12:12 p.m.   Carotid cross-clamped
              stump pressure = 69 mmHg
12:14 p.m.   BP 150/70, 0.3% isoflurane

12:16 p.m.

12:18 p.m.   BP 151/72, 0.6% isoflurane

12:20 p.m.

12:21 p.m.   BP 134/60, 0.7% isoflurane

12:23 p.m.   BP 117/55, surgeon
              notified of SEP changes
12:25 p.m.   BP 125/56, 0.4% isoflurane

12:27 p.m.   BP 134/58, 0.2% isoflurane

12:29 p.m.

12:30 p.m.   BP 150/72, 0.2% isoflurane

12:31 p.m.

12:35 p.m.   BP 155/77, 0.5% isoflurane
12:39 p.m.

12:42 p.m.   BP 151/70, 0.4% isoflurane

12:46 p.m.

12:50 p.m.   BP 143/68, 0.4% isoflurane

12:54 p.m.

12:57 p.m.   BP 144/67, 0.4% isoflurane

1:00 p.m.

1.05 p.m.   BP 157/74, 0.5% isoflurane
              carotid unclamped
1:20 p.m.

1:28 p.m.   BP 133/64, 0.2% isoflurane

1:40 p.m.   BP 104/53, 0.4% isoflurane

1:49 p.m.   BP 107/50, 0.0% isoflurane
              patient waking up

Fig. 6. Cortical SEPs to right median nerve stimulation recorded during a left carotid endarterectomy in a 62-year-old woman. The SEPs were not attenuated by carotid artery clamping, but were affected by systemic blood pressure. Compare the SEP at 1:40 p.m., when the blood pressure was 104/53 with that at 12:18 p.m. when the blood pressure was 151/72. The former was attenuated compared with the latter, even though a higher concentration of isoflurane was being administered at 12:18 p.m.

pressure, monitoring of clinical status under regional (local) anaesthesia, recording of EEG, both unprocessed and converted to frequency spectra, and measurement of cerebral blood flow using Xenon-133.[19-23] Although the stump pressure is the simplest to obtain, it correlates poorly with both blood flow measurements and electrophysiologic indices of the adequacy of cerebral perfusion[21,23,24] as well as with the appearance of neurologic deficits during carotid endarterectomies performed under regional anaesthesia.[25]

Some centres use a conventional paper-recorded EEG to monitor carotid surgery. A 50% or greater increase in the theta or delta activity, or a decrease in alpha or beta activity indicates cerebral dysfunction. Since the frequency distribution of the EEG is often affected, machines which calculate and display EEG power spectra, and sometimes the spectral edge or other derived parameters, are also frequently employed.[26] These measures may reveal changes not obvious on inspection of the raw EEG[27] data. Other measures used include total EEG power and a single frequency variable based on a baseline crossing the algorithm.[28] Although the EEG has proven to be a valuable tool for intraoperative carotid monitoring, it has been suggested that the false positive rate for detecting ischaemia is higher than that for SEPs.[29]

In a group of 42 consecutive patients undergoing carotid endarterectomy in whom both SEP monitoring and measurement of distal carotid artery stump pressures were employed,[30] there was a general correlation between the two measures (Fig. 7). However, there was also considerable overlap in stump pressure values between patients in whom SEP changes at carotid artery clamping were indicative of significant cerebral ischaemia and those patients without major SEP changes. Patients in whom the SEPs indicated cerebral ischaemia had stump pressure values ranging from 17 to 40 mmHg. Of the 37 patients without major SEP changes, 16 had stump pressures below 40 mmHg. Ten of these patients with patent contralateral internal carotid arteries were not shunted and there were no perioperative strokes, demonstrating that shunting was unnecessary. Thus, there was no single stump pressure threshold value which correctly differentiated between patients who displayed SEP evidence of cerebral ischaemia at carotid artery clamping and those in whom shunting was clearly unnecessary.

Somatosensory evoked potential monitoring and transcranial Doppler monitoring for measurement of middle cerebral artery flow velocities can be performed simultaneously. The transcranial Doppler–middle cerebral artery flow velocity measurement is very sensitive to the small changes in middle cerebral artery blood flow. Since it is difficult to maintain precise positioning of the transcranial Doppler transducer throughout the operation, the transcranial Doppler–middle cerebral artery flow velocity signal can occasionally be lost or attenuated arti-factually. In such circumstances, SEP monitoring may demonstrate the adequacy of cerebral perfusion despite the changes in the transcranial Doppler–middle cerebral artery flow velocities (Fig. 8). Since averaging of an SEP may take over a minute while transcranial Doppler–middle cerebral artery flow velocity changes are rapid but subject to false positive changes, the two techniques are comp-lementary and may be used together for monitoring during carotid artery surgery.

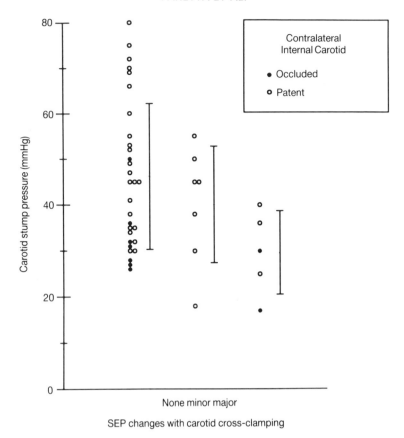

SEP changes with carotid cross-clamping

Fig. 7. Relationship between distal internal carotid artery stump pressures and intraoperative SEP findings in 42 successive operations in which both were measured. For each SEP category, the vertical bar denotes the mean stump pressure ± 1 SD. Shunts were used in the patients with contralateral carotid artery occlusion (filled circles) and in patients with major SEP changes at carotid artery clamping. None of the other patients included in this figure were shunted, even if the stump pressure measurement was as low as 18 mmHg, and none of them suffered a perioperative stroke.

REPERFUSION CEREBRAL INJURY

Clamping the internal carotid artery, for even short durations, can result in ischaemia and reperfusion mediated neurochemical events that can cause reversible or irreversible brain injury depending on the duration and severity of the ischaemic insult. Initial neurochemical events include the activation of phospholipases A_2 and C which leads to the release of second messengers, including free polyunsaturated fatty acids, diacylglycerols and platelet activating factor.[31] Reperfusion of ischaemic cerebral tissue liberates vasoactive cyclooxygenase and lipoxygenase reaction products and oxygen-derived free radicals. The role of these biochemical events in the clinical setting has yet to be determined, but recent evidence suggests some

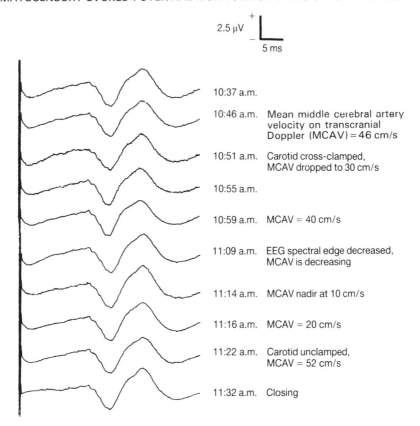

2.5 μV

+

−

5 ms

10:37 a.m.

10:46 a.m.   Mean middle cerebral artery
velocity on transcranial
Doppler (MCAV) = 46 cm/s

10:51 a.m.   Carotid cross-clamped,
MCAV dropped to 30 cm/s

10:55 a.m.

10:59 a.m.   MCAV = 40 cm/s

11:09 a.m.   EEG spectral edge decreased,
MCAV is decreasing

11:14 a.m.   MCAV nadir at 10 cm/s

11:16 a.m.   MCAV = 20 cm/s

11:22 a.m.   Carotid unclamped,
MCAV = 52 cm/s

11:32 a.m.   Closing

Fig. 8. Cortical SEPs recorded during a right carotid endarterectomy in a 70-year-old woman. Middle cerebral artery blood velocities were being measured by transcranial Doppler. SEPs were stable during the initial clamping of the carotid artery, but the transcranial Doppler–middle cerebral artery flow velocity signal was transiently lost, and the patient was shunted. The transcranial Doppler–middle cerebral artery flow velocity signal was also transiently attenuated when the carotid artery was clamped for removal of the shunt, and at one point early in the operation before the initial clamping; the SEPs were stable throughout. The patient was neurologically unchanged postoperatively.

relevance.[32] In addition, the association of non-stroke complications with preexisting high-grade carotid artery stenoses implicates reperfusion cerebral injury as a contributing factor. These complications include blood pressure fluctuations, cerebral hyperperfusion, haemorrhage, headaches, seizures, oedema, fatigue, somnolence, psychiatric disturbances, inappropriate antidiuretic hormone syndrome and changes in cerebral vasoreactivity.

Reperfusion cerebral injury, which is defined as a deterioration of SEPs at the onset or shortly after carotid artery unclamping, was identified in 27% of patients.[33] An additional 12% of patients developed overt hypotension after carotid artery unclamping. Both phenomena were short-lived and unrelated to each other. Deterioration of cortical SEPs ipsilateral to the operated side occurred in 21 of 77 patients. These patients had no change in SEPs recorded from the contralateral cortex, thus ruling out anaesthetic or blood pressure related events. These changes were reversible, occurred immediately after carotid artery unclamping and resolved within 10 minutes in the majority of cases. Reperfusion cerebral injury was more common in patients with previous strokes (37%) and less common in diabetics (16%). In contrast, reperfusion hypotension was more common in patients with contralateral carotid artery occlusions (29%). There were no perioperative strokes in either group of patients.

Reperfusion injury appears to be a subclinical finding on SEP monitoring, since it occurs in the absence of neurological symptoms. The aetiology of reperfusion cerebral injury may be related to microemboli or the effects of vasoactive metabolites on cerebral vasculature. Using a combination of SEP and transcranial Doppler monitoring in patients undergoing carotid surgery may help to elucidate the aetiology and clinical significance of these phenomena.

ACKNOWLEDGEMENTS

This chapter was supported in part by the James Hilton Manning and Emma Austin Manning Foundation, the Anna S. Brown Trust and The New York Institute for Vascular Studies.

REFERENCES

1. North American Symptomatic Carotid Endarterectomy Trial Collaborators: Beneficial effect of carotid endarterectomy in symptomatic patients with high-grade carotid stenosis. New Engl J Med 325: 445–507, 1991
2. Towne JB, Weiss DG, Hobson RW, II: First phase report of cooperative Veterans Administration asymptomatic carotid stenosis study—Operative morbidity and mortality. J Vasc Surg 11: 252–259, 1990
3. Rosenberg N: Monitoring and use of a shunt during carotid surgery. *In* CRC Handbook of Carotid Artery Surgery: Facts and Figures. Boca Raton, Florida: CRC Press, pp. 151–170, 1989
4. Krul JMJ, van Gijn J, Ackerstaff RGA *et al.*: Site and pathogenesis of infarcts associated with carotid endarterectomy. Stroke 20: 324–328, 1989
5. Naylor AR, Bell PRF, Ruckley CV: Monitoring and cerebral protection during carotid endarterectomy. Br J Surg 79: 735–741, 1992
6. Horsch S, De Vleeschauwer P, Ktenidis K: Intraoperative assessment of cerebral ischemia during carotid surgery. J Cardiovas Surg 31: 599–602, 1990
7. Branston NM, Symon L: Cortical EP, blood flow and potassium changes in experimental ischemia. *In* Evoked Potentials, Barber C (Ed.). Baltimore: University Park Press, pp. 527–530, 1980
8. Astrup J, Symon L, Branston NM, Lassen NA: Cortical evoked potential and extracellular K^+ and H^+ at critical levels of brain ischemia. Stroke 8: 51–57, 1977
9. Allison T, Goff WR, Williamson PD *et al.*: On the neural origin of early components of the human somatosensory evoked potential. *In* Clinical Uses of Cerebral, Brainstem and Spinal Somatosensory Evoked Potentials, Desmedt JE (Ed.). Progress in Clinical Neurophysiology, Vol. 7. Basel: Karger, pp. 51–68, 1980
10. Emerson RG, Pedley TA: Generator sources of median somatosensory evoked potentials. J Clin Neurophysiol 1: 203–218, 1984
11. Lueders H, Lesser RP, Hahn J *et al.*: Cortical somatosensory evoked potentials in response to hand stimulation. J Neurosurg 58: 885–894, 1983

12. Nuwer MR: Evoked Potential Monitoring in the Operating Room. New York: Raven Press, 1986
13. Markand ON, Dilley RS, Moorthy SS, Warren C, Jr: Monitoring of somatosensory evoked responses during carotid endarterectomy. Arch Neurol 41: 375–378, 1984
14. Schweiger H, Kamp H-D, Dinkel M: Somatosensory-evoked potentials during carotid artery surgery: Experience in 400 operations. Surgery 109: 602–609, 1991
15. American Electroencephalographic Society: Guidelines for clinical evoked potential studies. J Clin Neurophysiol 1: 3–53, 1984
16. Legatt AD: Intraoperative neurophysiologic monitoring. *In* Clinical Anesthesia in Neurosurgery, 2nd edn, Frost EAM (Ed). Stoneham, Mass: Butterworth, pp. 63–127, 1991
17. Yamada T: The anatomic and physiologic bases of median nerve somatosensory evoked potentials. Neurol Clin 6: 705–733, 1988
18. Legatt AD, Veith FJ, Schroeder CE *et al.*: Usefulness of somatosensory evoked potentials during carotid endarterectomy. J Cardiovasc Surg 30: 21, 1989 (abstract)
19. Sundt TM, Jr, Sharbrough FW, Piepgras DG *et al.*: Correlation of cerebral blood flow and electroencephalographic changes during carotid endarterectomy. With results of surgery and hemodynamics of cerebral ischemia. Mayo Clin Proc 56: 533–543, 1981
20. Rampil IJ, Holzer JA, Quest DO, *et al.*: Prognostic value of computerised EEG analysis during carotid endarterectomy. Anesth Analg 62: 186–192, 1983
21. Blume WT, Sharbrough FW: EEG monitoring during carotid endarterectomy and open heart surgery. *In* Electroencephalography: Basic Principles, Clinical Applications and Related Fields, 2nd edn, Niedermeyer E, Lopes da Silva F (Eds). Baltimore: Urban & Schwartzenberg, pp. 645–656, 1987
22. Wilkinson HA, Wright RL, Sweet WH: Correlation of reduction in pressure and angiographic cross-filling with tolerance of carotid occlusion. J Neurosurg 22: 241–245, 1965
23. Sundt TM, Houser OW, Sharbrough FW *et al.*: Carotid endarterectomy: Results, complications and monitoring techniques. *In* Advances in Neurology, Thompson RH, Green JR (Eds). New York: Raven Press, pp. 97–119, 1977
24. Beebe HG, Pearson JM, Coatsworth JJ: Comparison of carotid artery stump pressure and EEG monitoring in carotid endarterectomy. Am Surg 44: 655–660, 1978
25. Kwaan JHM, Peterson GJ, Connolly JE: Stump pressure: An unreliable guide for shunting during carotid endarterectomy. Ann Surg 115: 1083–1085, 1980
26. Ahn SS, Jordan SE, Nuwer MR, Marcus DR, Moore WS: Computed electroencephalographic topographic brain mapping. A new and accurate monitor of cerebral circulation and function for patients having carotid endarterectomy. J Vasc Surg 8: 247–254, 1988
27. Chiappa KH, Burke SR, Young RR: Results of electroencephalographic monitoring of 367 carotid endarterectomies. Use of a dedicated minicomputer. Stroke 10: 381–388, 1979
28. Ashburn MA, Mitchell LB, Dean DF *et al.*: The power spectrum analyser as an indicator of cerebral ischaemia during carotid endarterectomy. Anaesth Intens Care 13: 387–391, 1985
29. Lam AM, Manninen PH, Ferguson GG, Nantau W: Monitoring electrophysiologic function during carotid endarterectomy. A comparison of somatosensory evoked potentials and conventional electroencephalogram. Anesthesiology 75: 15–21, 1991
30. Legatt AD, Veith FJ, Schroeder CE, *et al.*: Somatosensory evoked potential monitoring during surgery for carotid stenosis. Electroenceph Clin Neurophysiol 76: 21P–22P, 1990 (abstract)
31. Panetta T, Marcheselli VL, Braquet P, Spinnewyn B, Bazan NG: Effects of a platelet activating factor antagonist (BN 52021) on free fatty acids, diacylglycerols, polyphosphoinositides, and blood flow in the gerbil brain: Inhibition of ischemia-reperfusion induced cerebral injury. Biochem Biophys Res Comm, 149: 580–587, 1987
32. Panetta TF: Cerebral ischemia-reperfusion injury during carotid endarterectomy: Significance and consequences. *In* Current Surgical Therapy, 4th edn, Cameron JL (Ed.). Mosby Year Book, St Louis, Missouri, pp. 702–709, 1992
33. Panetta TF, Legatt AD, Veith FJ, Gupta SK, Wengerter KR: Reperfusion hypotension during carotid endarterectomy: Frequency and correlation with somatosensory evoked potentials. J Cardiovasc Surg 32: 63, 1991 (abstract)

Shunting and Neuromonitoring: A Prospective Randomized Study

Wilhelm Sandmann, Frank Willeke, Ralf Kolvenbach, Reiner Benecke and Erhard Godehardt

Carotid endarterectomy (CEA) is frequently performed to prevent ischaemic stroke, although ironically, the most serious complication after CEA is stroke. The main causes for stroke are thromboembolism before and after clamping, perfusion ischaemia and technical failure. The risk of thromboembolism and technical defects can be reduced by a meticulous surgical performance, but a minimal risk of spontaneous thromboembolism still remains until the internal carotid artery (ICA) is clamped. The significance of perfusion ischaemia and the consequence of shunting has been a subject of extensive discussion[1-4] and will undoubtedly continue.

Interestingly the stroke rates reported by non-shunters, selective and routine-shunters are all very low, but with the involvement of neurologists the surgical stroke rates became substantially different.[5,6] Non-shunters usually point out that shunting complicates the surgical procedure and may cause thromboembolism or dissection, while shunters claim that, without shunting, many more patients would have developed a perioperative stroke, especially when brain function was monitored by EEG for selective shunting.[7]

At our institution we started the use of a shunt in 1971 and abandoned it in 1978. There were more neurological complications in shunted patients. However, the two groups could not be compared, because the annual case load in the first series was low and most of the complications could be easily explained by technical failures. In order to avoid the influence of the learning curve and to investigate the significance of clamping ischaemia, shunting was prospectively randomized in 503 cases.

MATERIAL AND METHOD

From March 1986 to December 1989 the use of the intraluminal JAVID-shunt was prospectively randomized in a continuous series of 503 carotid endarterectomies (male 350, female 153) in 472 patients (Table 1). Unilateral procedures were performed in 441 and bilateral, staged procedures in 31 patients. Patients with bilateral simultaneous procedures and those undergoing reconstruction of the supraaortic branches and

Table 1. Material of the study

Study period	3/1986–12/1989
Patients	472
Mean age	64 years
Cases	503
Male/female	350/153

Table 2.   Randomized shunt study: Status of the contralateral ICA and neurological outcome

	Unchanged	TIA	Stroke no. (%)	Total
Normal	193	2	5 (2.5)	200
Normal postop.	28	—	1 (3.4)	29
Ulcer	3	—	—	3
<50%	68	1	—	69
50–80%	72	3	2 (2.6)	77
80–99%	27	—	1 (3.6)	28
Occluded	63	—	8 (11.3)	71
Occluded postop.	1	—	1 (50)	2
Aneurysm	1	—	—	1
Unknown	21	—	2 (8.7)	23
Total	477	6	20	503

Normal/occlusion $p<0.01$

Table 3.   Randomized shunt study

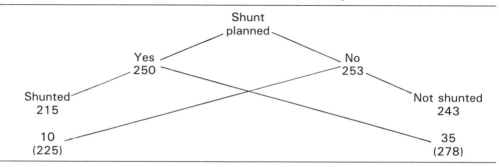

Table 4.   Randomized shunt study: Shunt planned but not shunted

	Postoperative			
Preoperative	Unchanged	TIA	Stroke	Total
Asymptomatic	7	—	—	7
TIA	19	—	—	19
Post stroke	8	—	1	9
Total	34	—	1 (2.9%)	35

Table 5.   Randomized shunt study: Planned placebo but shunted

	Postoperative			
Preoperative	Unchanged	TIA	Stroke	Total
Asymptomatic	3	—	1	4
TIA	4	—	—	4
Post stroke	1	—	1	2
Total	8	—	2 (20%)	10

the carotid bifurcation at the same time and patients with reconstruction of the ICA at the base of the skull were not entered into the study.

Doppler sonography and computed tomographic (CT) scan were performed in every case both before and after surgery. Duplex studies and transcranial Doppler sonography were used in selected cases. Arteriographic studies were performed in 90% of the patients. The ICA to be reconstructed was stenosed at least 70% or more, while the contralateral ICA was patent in 200 (39.8%), patent after prevous CEA in 29 (6%), stenosed <50% in 72 (14.3%), 50–80% in 77 (15.3%), 80–99% in 28 (5.6%), occluded in 71 (14.1%), occluded after previous surgery in two (0.4%) cases and aneurysmal in one (0.2%) case (Table 2). In 23 (4.6%) of the cases useful information about the contralateral ICA was not available. The patients were examined by an independent neurologist before surgery (asymptomatic 73, transient ischaemic attack (TIA) 243, poststroke 187). In patients with major strokes CEA was delayed 6 weeks to 3 months according to multiple CT scans.

Selected patients with small, fixed deficits underwent CEA within 14 days of stroke. Patients with severe bilateral disease, subtotal unilateral occlusion and those presenting with crescendo TIAs were heparinized and waited in hospital for surgery. Surgery was performed under general anaesthetic and electroencephalogy (EEG) and/or somatosensory-evoked potentials (SEP) monitoring was used. Of 250 cases randomized to shunting, 35 (14%) could not be shunted for technical reasons, while of 253 cases planned without shunting, 10 (4%) received a shunt during endarterectomy because neuromonitoring showed significant changes 2–40 minutes after clamping (Tables 3, 4, 5).

After CEA the arteriotomy was closed by direct suture in 20 and by a saphenous vein patch in 483 cases (Table 6). After the clamps had been released the quality of the blood flow through the internal carotid artery was evaluated by means of Doppler spectral analysis to detect possible technical defects.[8]

In 143 (28.4%) cases the blood flow was significantly disturbed or turbulent and the ICA was reopened to achieve laminar flow by further reconstruction. In 243 (47.9%) cases kinking, which was present primarily or occurred after CEA, was corrected either by plication in 14 (2.8%) or by resection of the internal carotid artery in 221 (43.9%) cases before the artery was closed with a vein patch. In seven (1.4%) cases CEA failed (Table 6). Reconstruction was achieved in five (1%) cases using a vein interposition graft and in two (0.4%) the ICA had to be ligated.

Postoperative neurological examination, Doppler sonography and CT scans were performed in all patients after each procedure. All patients who developed TIA or stroke had CT scans taken within 24 hours of onset of symptoms and repeat CT scans thereafter.

Table 6. Randomized shunt study: Reconstruction techniques

	Shunt no. (%)	Placebo no. (%)	Total no. (%)
CEA, direct closure	8 (40)	12 (60)	20 (4)
CEA, patch	143 (59)	98 (41)	241 (48)
CEA, plication, patch	5 (36)	9 (64)	14 (3)
CEA, resection, patch	93 (42)	128 (58)	221 (44)
Vein interposition graft	0	5 (100)	5 (1)
Ligation	1 (50)	1 (50)	2 (0.4)
Total	250	253	503 (100)

SANDMANN *ET AL.*

Table 7. Randomized shunt study: Operative and postoperative mortality

	Survival	Death	Total
Planned with shunt	248	2 (0.8%)	250
shunted	213	2 (0.9%)	215
not shunted	35	—	35
Planned without shunt	246	7 (2.8%)	253
not shunted	237	6 (2.5%)	243
shunted	10	1 (10%)	10
Total	494	9 (1.8%)	503

Table 8. Randomized shunt study: Neurological outcome — planned *vs* definitive treatment

Procedure	Unchanged	Stroke no. (%)	Total
Planned with shunt	240	10 (4)	250
shunted	206	9 (4.2)	215
not shunted	34	1 (2.9)	35
Planned without shunt	243	10 (4)	253
not shunted	235	8 (3.3)	243
shunted	8	2 (20)	10

Table 9. Randomized shunt study — ischaemic strokes: Neurological outcome compared with neuromonitoring

EEG/SEP	Total	Periop. stroke no. (%)	Postop. stroke no. (%)	Without stroke
Normal/minor changes	484	6 (1.2)	3 (0.6)	475
Significant changes	19	8 (42)	1 (5)	10
Total	503	14 (2.8)	4 (0.8)	485

$p < 0.000000002$

Table 10. Randomized shunt study — total series: Preoperative *vs* postoperative status

Stage preoperative	Postoperative			
	Unchanged	TIA	Stroke no (%)	Total no. (%)
I Asymptomatic	71	0	2 (2.7)	73 (15)
II TIA	237	4	2 (0.8)	243 (48)
IV Post stroke	169	2	16 (8.6)	187 (37)
Total	477	6	20 (4)	503 (100)

I + II/IV $p < 0.001$

Table 11. Randomized shunt study — planned with shunt: Preoperative vs postoperative status

Stage preoperative	Postoperative			
	Unchanged	TIA	Stroke no (%)	Total no. (%)
I Asymptomatic	34	0	0	34 (14)
II TIA	119	2	2 (1.6)	123 (49)
IV Post stroke	84	1	8 (8.6)	93 (37)
Total	237	3	10 (4)	250 (100)

I + II/IV $p < 0.01$

RESULTS

The overall mortality rate was 1.8% (Table 7). Five patients died from coronary artery disease, three from intracranial haemorrhage and one from ischaemic stroke. The difference between patients randomized with and without shunt was not statistically significant.

The overall stroke rate (including three patients* with intracranial haemorrhage and four patients with strokes from the non-operated hemisphere) was 4% (ischaemic 3.4%, haemorrhagic 0.6%) (Table 8). There was no statistical difference between the groups with and without shunting. Nineteen cases showed severe EEG/SEP changes during anaesthesia and 11 during clamping. In one of the first 70 patients the EEG and SEP changed significantly to a zero line 40 minutes after clamping. The same patient had undergone CEA with a shunt on the contralateral side without neurological complications. The randomization protocol did not allow shunting of the patient during the second operation. The patient awoke with an ipsilateral stroke. The neurological deficit improved markedly within the next 6 weeks.

Since that event the following ten patients, who developed severe changes by means of neuromonitoring during the period of clamping were subsequently heparinized and shunted.

In eight patients the EEG/SEP changes disappeared after the shunt had been inserted and the postoperative course was uneventful. In two patients who developed stroke, the EEG/SEP changes remained despite the shunt. In eight patients EEG/SEP changes developed before (2) or after (6) but not during shunting. Five patients developed perioperative stroke and in all of them technical failures could be identified (Table 9). Three patients awoke without stroke and the reason for the changes in neuromonitoring could not be identified.

In 484 procedures EEG/SEP remained normal or showed only minor changes. Six patients awoke with a stroke, with three in the ispilateral hemisphere. Technical failures could be identified in three patients. The ischaemic stroke rate in patients with severe changes in neuromonitoring was 42% and in patients without changes 1.2% (6/484) ($p < 2 \times 10^{-9}$).

---

*Two patients showed primary haemorrhage, one patient developed haemorrhage after ischaemic stroke.

If assumed that all patients receiving a shunt because of significant EEG/SEP changes during clamping would have developed a stroke without shunting, the non-shunted patients would have ended up with a stroke rate of 7.1%. Patients with postoperative strokes did not show changes in neuromonitoring during clamping.

Four groups of patients showed statistical significance of stroke rates, which were not influenced by shunting:

1. In 73 patients with occlusion of the ICA there was a 12.8% stroke rate compared with 2.0% in 301 patients with a patent or insignificantly stenosed contralateral ICA ($p<0.01$) (Table 2).
2. Of 187 cases with a preoperative stroke, 16 (8.6%) developed a recurrent or new stroke compared with four (1.3%) of 316 asymptomatic/TIA cases ($p<0.001$). The same findings resulted if positive and negative preoperative CT scans were compared (Tables 10, 11, 12, 13).
3. In 360 cases with primary optimal reconstruction according to Doppler spectral analysis, stroke developed in 2.2%, while 143 cases with attempted correction of technical inadequacy had strokes in 8.5% ($p<0.05$) (two patients with ligation of the ICA did not develop stroke) (Tables 14, 15).
4. In 167 procedures performed by the most experienced surgeon, there was a stroke rate of 1.8% (shunt 2.3%, without 1.3%), while 336 reconstructions were carried out by the associates and surgeons in training with a stroke rate of 5.1% (shunted 4.9%, non-shunted 5.2%) ($p<0.1$) (Tables 16, 17).

Table 12. Randomized shunt study — planned without shunt: Preoperative *vs* postoperative status

Stage preoperative	Postoperative			
	Unchanged	TIA	Stroke no (%)	Total no. (%)
I Asymptomatic	37	0	2 (5)	39 (15.4)
II TIA	118	2	0	120 (47.4)
IV Poststroke	85	1	8 (8.5)	94 (37.2)
Total	240	3	10 (4)	253 (100)

I + II/IV $p<0.01$

Table 13. Randomized shunt study: Preoperative CT scan compared with neurological outcome

CT scan	Neurological outcome			
	Unchanged	TIA	Stroke	Total
Normal	187	2	2 (1.1)	191
Vasopathy	37	0	2 (5.1)	39
Small infarct	86	2	8 (8.3)	96
Large infarct	19	0	1 (5)	20
Multiple infarcts	48	2	1 (2)	51
Contralateral infarct	36	0	4 (10)	40
No CT scan	64	0	2 (3.6)	66
Total	477	6	20 (4)	503

CT scan normal/pathologic $p<0.005$

Table 14. Randomized shunt study — shunt planned: Doppler spectral analysis and neurological outcome

No. of clamping procedures	Unchanged	TIA	Stroke no. (%)	Total
= 1	165	2	4 (2.8)	171
> 1	72	1	6 (7.6)	79
Total	237	3	10 (4)	250

= 1/< 1 p < 0.1

Table 15. Randomized shunt study — no shunt planned: Doppler spectral analysis and neurological outcome

No. of clamping procedures	Unchanged	TIA	Stroke no. (%)	Total
= 1	182	3	4 (2.1)	189
> 1	58	0	6 (9.4)	64
Total	240	3	10 (4)	253

= 1/> 1 p < 0.025

Table 16. Randomized shunt study: Most experienced surgeon and neurological outcome

Randomization	Unchanged	TIA	Stroke no. (%)	Total
Shunt group	85	1	2 (2.3)	88
Placebo group	77	1	1 (1.3)	79
Total	162	2	3 (1.8)	167

Most experienced/less experienced p < 0.1

Table 17. Randomized shunt study: Less experienced surgeon and neurological outcome

Randomization	Unchanged	TIA	Stroke no. (%)	Total
Shunt group	152	2	8 (4.9)	162
Placebo group	163	2	9 (5.2)	174
Total	315	4	17 (5.1)	336

Most experienced/less experienced p < 0.1

Table 18. Randomized shunt study — total series: Reconstruction time and neurological outcome

Clamping/shunting	Unchanged	TIA	Stroke	Total
< 45 min	101	—	2 (1.9%)	103
> 45 min	376	6	18 (4.5%)	400
Total	477	6	20 (4%)	503

Unchanged/stroke p < 0.1

Table 19. Randomized shunt study — placebo planned: Reconstruction time and neurological outcome

Clamping	Unchanged	TIA	Stroke	Total
<45 min	55	—	—	55
>45 min	185	3	10 (5.4%)	198
Total	240	3	10	253

<45/>45 p<0.1

Table 20. Randomized shunt study — shunt planned: Reconstruction time and neurological outcome

Clamping/shunting	Unchanged	TIA	Stroke	Total
<45 min	152	—	2 (1.3%)	155
>45 min	85	3	8 (8.4%)	95
Total	237	3	10	250

<45/>45 p<0.05

DISCUSSION

In the literature the occurrence rates of stroke after CEA vary substantially between 0% and 21%.[5,9] Prospective studies and those in which neurologists were involved usually reported higher stroke rates than retrospective and pure surgical works.[10,11] Surgeons tend to relate stroke to the operated side and usually focus on ischaemic strokes only, while neurologists include haemorrhagic strokes and also those located in the contralateral hemisphere.

The terms 'major' and 'minor' may be useful to describe the significance of this complication on the patient's life, but even a minor stroke remains a stroke. Also a prolonged, reversible ischaemic neurological deficit (PRIND), a reversible ischaemic neurological deficit (RIND), and a TIA may be strokes, if the patient is examined carefully by a neurologist and routine CT scans are performed pre- and postoperatively.

The same problem exists for the judgement of new strokes superimposed upon chronic strokes. In order to discuss on the same terms it is necessary to have neurologists involved in pre- and postoperative patient examination. In the present study we tried to overcome these shortcomings, but there were other problems.

The design of the study had to be changed early in its course, because it was felt to be unethical to leave a patient without shunt in the presence of a zero line in EEG/SEP monitoring. Therefore, the conclusion drawn from the statistics are less valid if compared with a pure scientific design. However, this study proved that carotid clamping may cause perfusion ischaemia and subsequent stroke.

There are many reasons why the stroke rates in the groups planned with and without shunting were not significantly different. One reason may be that eight out of ten patients with severe EEG/SEP changes during clamping responded to secondary shunting (Table 9). Otherwise, the group of non-shunted cases could have ended up with a stroke rate of 7.1% and this would have shown at least a trend in favour of shunting. However, the main reason seems to be the rate of technical problems which occurred slightly more often in the shunt group. Probably the JAVID-shunt makes optimal reconstruction more difficult, because straightening of the artery by carotid resection or plication after desobliteration was more often used in the non-shunted group of patients. Most interestingly, in patients with positive preoperative CT scans and/or preoperative stroke and/or occlusion of the contralateral internal carotid artery, significantly higher rates of stroke were found. Many of the patients with preoperative strokes were operated upon by vascular surgeons in training with less favourable results in terms of clamping time, quality of locally restored flow and neurological outcome (Tables 18, 19, 20). Therefore, the higher stroke rates are more likely related to the performance of the CEA but are also dependent on the clinical stage of extracranial arterial disease. These findings are similar to those in the literature, but the influence of the surgeon in relation to the stroke rate has not yet been calculated.

CONCLUSION

From our study we conclude that EEG and/or SEP are useful methods to monitor brain perfusion during carotid endarterectomy.

The chance of developing a stroke in the presence of a normal EEG/SEP pattern is about 1%, regardless of the use of a shunt.

The perioperative stroke rate in the presence of critical EEG/SEP changes was 42%, but could increase up to 84% without secondary shunting.

The difference in outcome of patients with preoperative strokes and/or positive CT scans compared with asymptomatic and TIA patients and/or negative scans is not only disease related; many patients were operated upon by vascular surgeons in training with less favourable results regarding clamping time and quality of reconstruction. For an experienced surgeon the occurrence rate of clamping ischaemia is expected to be 0.5%, vs 5% for a less experienced surgeon. In patients with previous stroke and/or positive CT scan, clamping ischaemia occurs more often. Therefore, since the study finished, we have been using the intraluminal shunt prophylactically in patients who have had a stroke before the operation, in patients with contralateral carotid artery occlusion and in patients with a positive CT scan. We probably should use the shunt routinely if the operation is performed by a vascular surgeon in training. However, this study demonstrated that clamping ischaemia is only one among many problems which can cause a perioperative stroke.

REFERENCES

1. Ferguson CG: Response (letter). Stroke 14: 116–117, 1983
2. Sundt TM: The ischemic tolerance of neural tissue and the need for monitoring and selective shunting during carotid endarterectomy. Stroke 14: 93–98, 1983
3. Halsey JH: Risks and benefits of shunting in carotid endarterectomy. Stroke 23 (11): 1583–1587, 1992
4. Baker WH, Littooy FN, Hayes AC, Dorner DB, Stubbs D: Carotid endarterectomy without shunt: The control series. J Vasc Surg 1 (1): 50–56, 1984
5. Easton JD, Sherman DG: Stroke and mortality rate in carotid endarterectomy: 228 consecutive operations. Stroke 8: 565–568, 1977

6. Dyken ML, Pokras R: The performance of endarterectomy for disease of the extracranial arteries of the head. Stroke 15 (6): 948–950, 1984

7. Callow AD, O'Donnell TF Jr: EEG Monitoring in cerebrovascular surgery. *In* Cerebrovascular Insufficiency, Bergan JJ, Yao JST (Eds). New York: Grune & Stratton, pp. 327–341, 1983

8. Sandmann W, Kniemeyer H, Peronneau P: Carotid bifurcation doppler spectrum analysis at surgery. *In* Diagnostic Techniques and Assessment: Procedures in Vascular Surgery, Greenhalgh RM (Ed.). New York: Grune & Stratton, pp. 123–127, 1985

9. Thompson JE, Talkington CM, Garrett WV: Asymptomatic carotid bruit: Course and surgical management. *In* Cerebrovascular Insufficiency, Bergan JJ, Yao JST (Eds). New York: Grune & Stratton. pp. 227–237, 1983

10. Javid H: Intraluminal shunting during carotid endarterectomy. *In* Cerebrovascular Insufficiency, Bergan JJ, Yao JST (Eds). New York: Grune & Stratton, pp. 309–325, 1983

11. Brott T, Thalinger K: The practice of carotid endarterectomy in a large metropolitan area. Stroke 15 (6): 950–955, 1984

NATURAL HISTORY AND OBSERVATIONAL STUDIES

The Natural History of Asymptomatic Carotid Artery Disease

J. W. Norris

Early success in medical prophylaxis of stroke with first, aspirin[1] and later, even more powerful antiplatelet drugs such as ticlopidine,[2] was followed by even more powerful stroke prevention with carotid endarterectomy in symptomatic patients.[3,4] The situation in asymptomatic disease is more controversial, and recent published results of a randomized trial of surgical *vs* conservative treatment for asyptomatic carotid stenosis indicates little beneficial effect of carotid endarterectomy on the outcome of either stroke or death.[5]

In the light of these problems, accurate information of the natural evolution and outcome of asymptomatic carotid disease becomes even more critical. Although early prospective community studies of asymptomatic carotid stenosis gave little room for optimism for carotid surgery[6,7] development of accurate non-invasive neurovascular imaging suggested that asymptomatic high risk subgroups exist which might justify surgical hazards.[8]

In view of the proliferation of drug trials in stroke prevention in the last decade, it is surprising that no such attempt has yet been made to prevent stroke in asymptomatic carotid disease. In our study in Toronto, in patients followed clinically for up to 8 years with asymptomatic carotid disease, over one-third were already prescribed long-term aspirin by their own physicians.[9] This indiscriminate aspirin therapy, now widespread throughout the Western world, is probably affecting outcome, not only for stroke, but also for myocardial ischaemic and peripheral vascular disease, since all types of vascular disease are benefited by long-term aspirin therapy.[10] The counter-argument against this unscientific strategy is that such widespread aspirin use may inadvertently increase the chance of stroke by removing the most powerful and significant warning of stroke, transient ischaemic attacks (TIAs).[11]

The decline of stroke, and all other types of vascular disease in recent decades, must also be considered in evaluating outcome in these patients. Effective antihypertensive drugs with few side-effects, developed in recent years, are probably the major factor in producing a 5% annual fall each year in North America for the last 15–20 years[12] (Fig. 1).

However, there are many other incalculable factors in the changing pattern of stroke. The seminal role of hypertension has been questioned, and it has been convincingly argued that control of hypertension accounts only for 15–25% of the observed decline.[13] Other factors include the escalating practice of carotid endarterectomy, which reached epidemic proportions until recent years,[14] and the dramatic decrease in smoking in the community.[12]

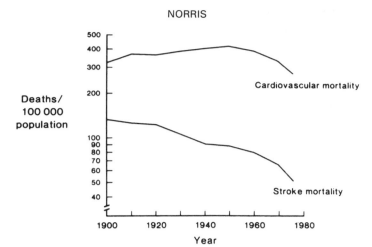

Fig. 1. Annual rates per 100 000 population in the USA for all cardiovascular and stroke mortalities, age adjusted to 1940 US population, for 1900–1976. From Ref. 52, with permission.

STROKE AND DEATH RATE IN ASYMPTOMATIC CAROTID STENOSIS

Early reports of community surveys revealed a surprisingly low incidence of stroke of 1–2% annually and a surprisingly high incidence of myocardial infarction, with vascular death (usually cardiac) far out-stripping death from stroke, usually two- to fourfold.[6,7] Even more relevant, was the assumption that stroke, when it occurred, was random in distribution (compared to the side of carotid stenosis) and was as likely to be haemorrhagic as ischaemic.[7] However, non-invasive vascular imaging and the advent of computed tomographic (CT) of the brain, fortunately soon proved both these obervations to be false.[8,15]

Prospective surveys, using careful clinical and carotid Doppler monitoring over years, indicated that certain subgroups, especially patients with severe (>75%) carotid stenosis, had annual stroke risk rates of 5%.[15–17] This figure is similar to the stroke outcome of TIAs where none doubts that carotid surgery is justified. A similar hierarchy of stroke risk with increasing carotid stenosis was seen in the North American Symptomatic Carotid Endartectomy Trial (NASCET), at least for tenth percentiles over 70%[3] (Fig. 2, Tables 1, 2)

However, the parallel risk of myocardial infarction and vascular death (Table 1) implies that the very patients in which surgical hazards are justified, also have the highest chance of dying, either perioperatively or soon after;[9] but most patients, when faced with this option, would rather face the surgical hazard of death at surgery compared with the quality of life of survival with a severe hemiplegia, and all that it implies.

IPSILATERALITY OF STROKE WITH CAROTID STENOSIS

Prior to the widespread use of non-invasive vascular imaging techniques, such as carotid Doppler and magnetic resonance angiography (MRA), neck bruits were

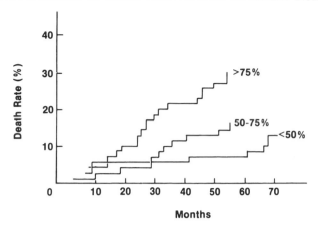

Fig. 2. Cumulative event rates of vascular deaths in patients with mild (< 50%), moderate (50–75%), and severe (> 75%) carotid stenosis. From Ref. 51, with permission.

thought to be simply markers of diffuse atherosclerosis, with a major impact on myocardial infarction and death.[15] We now know, however, that carotid bruits are poor localizers of underlying carotid disease, and may occur in otherwise normal arteries, arteries with minor stenoses contralateral to severely stenosed or occluded carotids, or simply be conducted from the heart.[18] In over 1000 patients with asymptomatic neck bruits who underwent duplex and phonoangiographic evaluation, carotid stenosis could not be readily predicted, and in any case had no relationship to the severity of the lesion.[19]

Other studies do not agree with this, and angiographic and carotid duplex surveys indicate that the type and location of neck bruits have some degree of predictive value for underlying carotid stenosis.[20,21] In our study in Toronto we found that neck bruits close to the angle of the jaw carried a two-thirds chance of an underlying, Doppler-detectable, carotid stenosis, with a one-third chance of a silent carotid stenosis on the other side[21] (Fig. 3).

In both asymptomatic and symptomatic patients, we found that approximately 75% of strokes (nearly all ischaemic) occur ipsilateral to the most stenosed carotid artery. For instance, in 102 patients with cerebral ischaemic events, 35 had no carotid lesions. In the remaining 67, 17 had either contralateral carotid stenosis or were vertebrobasilar, leaving 50 with ipsilateral carotid stenosis, i.e. 50 of 67 patients with events had ipsilateral carotid stenosis.[9] This has major implications for the success of carotid surgery, since an overall risk of 3.3% per year is reduced to 2.5% per year

Table 1. Annual percentage rate of vascular events over period of follow-up

Degree of stenosis	TIA	Stroke	Cardiac	Vascular death
< 50% (mild)	1.0	1.3	2.7	1.8
50–75% (moderate)	3.0	1.3	6.6	3.3
> 75% (severe)	7.2	3.3	8.3	6.5

TIA: transient ischaemic attack.
From Ref. 51, with permission.

Table 2.   Ipsilateral stroke rate at 18 months in patients with TIA or minor stroke treated with conservative treatment versus carotid endarterectomy (NASCET)

% stenosis	Medical group (%) (n = 295)	Surgical group (%) (n = 300)
90–99	33	6
80–89	28	8
70–79	19	7
Overall	25	7

when the ipsilaterality risk factor is included.[9] Unfortunately, this raises the stakes for surgical success even further, and even then is restricted to patients with stenoses >75%. For asymptomatic patients with carotid stenosis below this critical level, the stroke risk is reduced to around 1% per year, and once ipsilaterality is factored in, there surely can be no way surgical procedures can improve on the natural course of the lesion.

FREQUENCY OF WARNING TIAs

Initial impressions of the natural outcome of asymptomatic carotid stenosis suggested that in most cases, TIAs preceded the onset of cerebral infarction. Therefore, once the patients with significant carotid stenosis were identified by some form of screening, they only needed to be educated in TIA recognition and early physician notification.[8,22] Unfortunately, later data from most prospective series did not bear out this impression.[9,15]

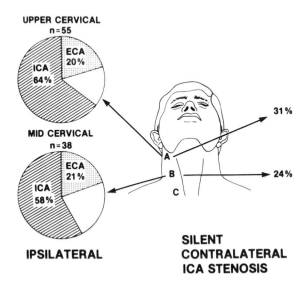

Fig. 3.   Doppler findings in 93 patients with unilateral carotid bruits. Where carotid and subclavian bruits were heard on the same side of the neck, the carotid bruit was regarded as the most relevant. ICA = internal carotid artery stenosis of at least 35%. ECA = external carotid artery stenosis. From Ref. 21, with permission.

TIAs precede ischaemic strokes in over 50% of cases, when patients are carefully questioned, even retrospectively.[23] However, the quality and quantity differ in prospective reviews, and in the Toronto series of asymptomatic carotid lesions, we found that amaurosis fugax (transient monocular blindness) was the commonest manifestation. This is never reported in retrospective surveys, indicating how easily both patients and physicians dismiss these transient symptoms. This probably explains the relative frequency of small infarctions in asymptomatic patients and those with TIAs.[24]

'SILENT' INFARCTS IN ASYMPTOMATIC CAROTID STENOSIS

The advent of CT scanning indicated that patients with carotid stenosis, but otherwise without symptoms, not infrequently had multiple small infarctions throughout the brain stem and hemispheres. Frequencies vary from 10 to 70%, depending upon the study population, since patients with even fleeting TIAs or amaurosis fugax have more asymptomatic lesions than truly asymptomatic patients[25,26] (Table 3).

In our study, 19% of patients with asymptomatic carotid stenosis had small, lacunar-sized infarcts, which occurred in 30% of patients with TIAs without carotid disease and 48% of those with TIAs and carotid stenosis.[26] None of these infarctions was the wedge-shaped lesion seen in thromboembolic stroke, but it is becoming increasingly evident that the distinction between hypertensive, small vessel 'lacunes' and small thromboembolic infarcts is less clear.[27] Again, in our study, the frequency of these tiny lesions related strongly to the degree of carotid stenosis, being found in 10% of those with stenosis <50%, 17% in those with stenosis 50–75%, and 30% in those with severe stenosis, >75%.

Whether these infarcts remain 'silent' depends on a number of factors. They are small, and so not likely to produce a significant clinical deficit, unless placed in an eloquent area of the brain. Their distribution to 'silent' areas, such as the frontal lobes, is unlikely to be accompanied by symptoms. TIAs occurring during sleep will never be reported, and finally, transient symptoms are easily dismissed or forgotten, particularly in the elderly.

Table 3. Frequency of central and peripheral infarction in symptomatic and asymptomatic patients

| Group | n | Mean age | Men : Women | Computed tomographic scan results | | |
				Peripheral infarcts	Central infarcts	Positive CT (%)
ACS	115	69	66 : 49	12	10	19
TIA −	63	66	33 : 30	11	8	30
TIA +	203	66	135 : 68	60	36	47*

ACS patients with asymptomatic carotid stenosis.
TIA − transient ischaemic attack patients without carotid stenosis.
TIA + TIA patients with carotid stenosis.
*p<0.0001.
From Ref. 26, with permission.

PATHOLOGY OF THE CAROTID PLAQUE

Although the relationship of the carotid plaque to cerebral ischaemia was first suggested by Chiari nearly 90 years ago,[28] it was only in 1951 that Miller Fisher's astute observations opened the way to a therapeutic approach.[29] In 1954, Eastcott and others published the first carotid surgical procedure to ablate the offending carotid plaque.[30]

However, even today, many questions remain concerning the type of plaque producing symptoms. Severity of stenosis remains the single, certain entity related to outcome, but what about ulceration, with and without stenosis? Can symptomatic plaques (or better, presymptomatic plaques) be distinguished from asymptomatic plaques? And if so, can this be performed by non-invasive techniques?

In a study of largely uncontrolled, retrospective observations of surgically removed plaques, Imparato et al. speculated that the major factor producing symptoms was plaque haemorrhage.[31] This idea has been developed by other observers, such as Lusby et al.[32] It has major implications. For instance, haemorrhagic areas (or, at least, echolucent equivalents) can be readily identified on B-mode ultrasound real-time imaging.[33] Also, drugs such as anti-platelet and anti-coagulant agents used to prevent stroke in patients with TIAs might, in fact, hasten haemorrhagic disruption of the plaque and paradoxically produce stroke.

Subsequent, more carefully controlled studies have, however, failed to confirm this observation. Although it is likely that haemorrhage into the plaque produces 'instability' and a tendency to rupture and liberate debris upstream[34] (Fig. 4), the relationship of this to symptoms is, at best, tenuous. Prospective studies indicate

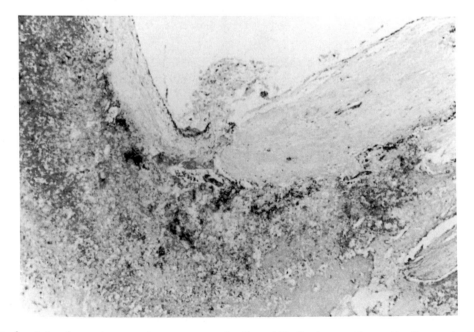

Fig. 4. Intraplaque haemorrhage communicating with the lumen through a fissure in the fibrous cap. From Ref. 36, with permission.

that plaque haemorrhage is closely related to severity of stenosis, irrespective of symptoms.[35,36] More recently, a prospective study relating symptoms to plaque pathology by comparing plaques from symptomatic (NASCET) and asymptomatic (ACAS) multicentre studies, have so far shown no difference.[37]

The question of plaque ulceration remains similarly controversial. When carotid surgery in a recently symptomatic patient reveals webs of fresh clot in a ragged carotid ulcer, it seems difficult to deny a direct relationship. However, angiography has been repeatedly shown to be a poor method of visualizing these ulcers, as has B-mode ultrasound imaging.[33,38] So prospective evaluation by non-invasive or invasive imaging is difficult. It is probable that severe ulceration relates to subsequent cerebral ischaemic events, as proposed in detail by Moore and co-workers,[39] but we still await the definitive study.

CHANGING PATTERNS IN STROKE

Marked changes in lifestyles, at least in the Western world, over the last few decades are having enormous impact on disease patterns, especially in vascular disease. This, coupled with widespread treatment of hypertension and indiscriminate prescription of a variety of antiplatelet drugs, are also affecting the site and pattern of atherosclerosis.[12]

The profiles of risk factors for ischaemic cardiac, cerebral and peripheral vascular disease are surprisingly different. For instance, lipoprotein changes, consisting of raised serum low-density lipoprotein (LDL) levels and low high-density (HDL) fractions, are unequivocal risk factors of coronary and leg ischaemia[40-42] (Fig. 5), but play little or even no role in cerebrovascular disease.[27] Therefore, it is probable that the dietary changes indulged in by Western societies may have little effect on carotid plaque pathology or outcome.

Nevertheless, not only is stroke mortality declining, but the severity of stroke is also declining (at least in women), a well documented effect over the last three decades.[27] This may represent a decrease in diffuse cerebral atherosclerosis, since size of infarction is directly related to the health of the adjoining collateral blood supply.

One of the most dramatic changes in the environment over recent years has been a decrease in smoking, a potent risk factor for all forms of vascular disease, and more recently demonstrated for cerebrovascular disease also.[27,43] The target area for arterial disease may also be changing, and there is evidence that cigarette smoking is a more powerful risk factor for intracranial arterial stenosis than blood lipids.[44]

The plethora of drugs, taken by design or default, present in today's world may also be changing the pattern of arterial disease, especially in the elderly. Drugs which change cardiac output and arterial laminar flow also affect the pattern of atherosclerosis, especially at flow dividers such as the carotid bifurcation[45] and antiplatelet drugs may interfere with plaque growth by changing platelet adhesiveness.[46] We know that the haemodynamic idiosyncrasy of the carotid sinus is a major factor in determining it as a prime site for atherosclerosis. Flow separation in the carotid bulb produces a rapid laminar flow on the inner wall, leaving a slower flow in the opposite direction on the outer wall. This low shear effect is a major factor in producing the

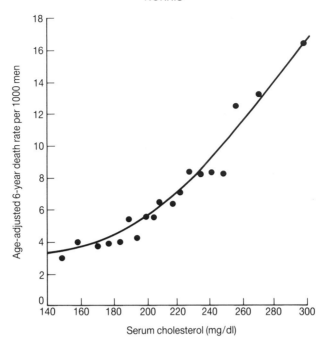

Fig. 5. Data from the MRFIT Study showing the relationship between serum cholesterol levels and age-adjusted 6-year death rate from CHD. The risk increases steadily, and particularly above 200 mg/dl. The magnitude of the increased risk is large — fourfold in the top 10% compared with the bottom 10%. From Ref. 53, with permission.

pattern and site of atherosclerosis lesions in the carotid bulb, and explains why this area is a rich and early source of embolism to the brain[47] (Fig. 6).

Epidemiological studies in Greenland Eskimos suggest that marine oils (a high content of their rich fish diet) contain n-3 omega fatty acids, which are hypolipidaemic, and anti-atherogenic.[48] Just how this affects plaque growth is uncertain, but it is likely that small soft early plaques are in a state of flux, and so may be influenced by systemic factors, unlike the fibrous, calcified state of established, larger plaques.[49]

Finally the question of gender and vascular risk is intriguing. Although virtually all epidemiological studies indicate that men have more vascular disease than women, carotid bruits are almost equally distributed. However, in women (who have a slight excess in incidence of neck bruits in the general population) severity of carotid stenosis is much less. This curious discrepancy remains unanswered, including comparison of arterial calibre, haematocrit and different body habitus.[50]

CONCLUSION

The natural evolution and outcome data of asymptomatic carotid stenosis indicate more that carotid plaques represent markers of diffuse atherosclerosis than a serious

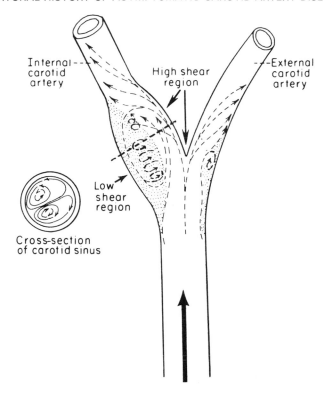

Fig. 6. Schematic representation of flow patterns in the carotid bifurcation. The inner wall of the carotid sinus is a region of higher shear stress, while the outer wall is a low shear region corresponding to the site of predilection for atherosclerotic plaques. From Ref. 54, with permission.

risk of stroke. They may, therefore, represent a target group for screening for other vascular lesions, such as coronary artery disease.

The pathology of these plaques may be changing, judging by secondary effects such as the decline in incidence, mortality and severity of stroke. It is clear that the stroke risk for these lesions, especially those below 75% stenosis, is low. Even with current randomized surgical studies underway and some early publications, the role of surgical prophylaxis still remains uncertain.

REFERENCES

1. Easton JD: Antiplatelet therapy in the prevention of stroke. Drugs 42: 39–50, 1991
2. Haynes RB, Sandler RS, Larson EB, Pater JL, Yatsu FM: A critical appraisal of ticlopidine, a new antiplatelet agent. Arch Intern Med 152: 1276–1380, 1992
3. NASCET Collaborators: Beneficial effect of carotid endarterectomy in symptomatic patients with high-grade carotid stenosis. N Engl J Med 325: 445–453, 1991
4. European Carotid Surgery Trialists' Collaborative Group: MRC European Carotid Surgery Trial: Interim results for symptomatic patients with severe (70–99%) or with mild (0–29%) carotid stenosis. Lancet 337: 1235–1243, 1991

5. Hobson RW, Weiss DG *et al.*: Efficacy of carotid endarterectomy for asymptomatic carotid stenosis. New Engl J Med 1993 (in press)
6. Heyman A, Wilkinson WE, Heyden S *et al.*: Risk of stroke in asymptomatic persons with cervical arterial bruits. A population study in Evans County, Georgia. N Engl J Med 302: 838–841, 1980
7. Wolf PA, Kannel WB, Sorlie P, McNamara P: Asymptomatic carotid bruit and risk of stroke. The Framingham Study. JAMA 245: 1442–1445, 1981
8. Chambers BR, Norris JW: Outcome in patients with asymptomatic neck bruits. N Engl J Med 315: 860–865, 1986
9. Chambers BR, Norris JW: The case against surgery for asymptomatic carotid stenosis. Stroke 15: 964–967, 1984
10. Antiplatelet Trialists' Collaboration: Secondary prevention of vascular disease by prolonged antiplatelet treatment. Br Med J 296: 320–331, 1988
11. Asymptomatic Carotid Atherosclerosis Study Group: Study design for randomized prospective trial of carotid endarterectomy for asymptomatic atherosclerosis. Stroke 20: 844–849, 1989
12. Whisnant JP: The decline of stroke. Stroke 15: 160–168, 1984
13. Bonita R, Beaglehole R: Increased treatment of hypertension does not explain the decline in stroke mortality in the United States, 1970–1980. Hypertension 13 (Suppl I): 1–69, 1989
14. Report of the American Academy of Neurology, Therapeutics and Technology Assessment Subcommittee: Interim assessment: carotid endarterectomy. Neurology 40: 682–683, 1990
15. Hennerici M, Hulsbomer H-B, Hefter H, Lammerts D, Rautenberg W: Natural history of asymptomatic extracranial arterial disease. Brain 110: 777–791, 1987
16. Roederer GO, Langlois YE, Jager KA *et al.*: The Natural history of carotid arterial disease in asymptomatic patients with cervical bruits. Stroke 15: 605–613, 1984
17. Bogousslavsky J, Despland PA, Regli F: Asymptomatic tight stenosis of the internal carotid artery: long-term prognosis. Neurology 36: 861–863, 1986
18. Norris JW. Head and neck bruits in stroke prevention. *In* Prevention of Stroke, New York: Springer-Verlag, pp. 103–112, 1991
19. Howard VJ, Howard G, Harpold GJ *et al.*: Correlation of carotid bruits and carotid atherosclerosis detected by B-Mode real-time ultrasonography. Stroke 20: 1331–1335, 1989
20. Ingall TJ, Homer D, Whisnant JP, Baker HL, O'Fallan WM: Predictive value of carotid bruit for carotid atherosclerosis. Arch Neurol 46: 418–422, 1989
21. Chambers BR, Norris JW: Clinical significance of asymptomatic neck bruits. Neurology 35: 742–745, 1985
22. Levin SM, Sondheimer FK, Levin JM: The contralateral disease but asymptomatic carotid artery: to operate or not? An update. Am J Surg 140: 203–205, 1980
23. Mohr JP, Gautier JC, Pessin MS: Internal carotid artery disease. *In* Stroke, Barnett HJM, Stein BM, Mohr JP, Yatsu FM (Eds). New York: Churchill Livingstone, pp. 285–335, 1986
24. Herderschee D, Hijdra A, Algra A *et al.*: for the Dutch TIA Trial Study Group: Silent stroke in patients with transient ischemic attack or minor ischemic stroke. Stroke 23: 1220–1224, 1992
25. Grigg MJ, Papadakis K, Nicolaides AN *et al.*: The significance of cerebral infarction and atrophy in patients with amaurosis fugax and transient ischemic attacks in relation to internal carotid artery stenosis: a preliminary report. J Vasc Surg 7: 215–222, 1988
26. Norris JW, Zhu CZ: Silent stroke and carotid stenosis. Stroke 23: 483–485, 1992
27. Wolf PA, D'Agostino RB, O'Neal MA *et al.*: Secular trends in stroke incidence and mortality: The Framingham Study. Stroke 23: 1551–1555, 1992
28. Chiari H: Uber das verhalten des tielungswinkels der carotis commonis bei der endarteritis chronica deformans. Verh Dtsch Ges Pathol 9: 326–330, 1905
29. Fisher CM, Adams RD: Observations on brain embolism with special reference to the mechanism of haemorrhagic infarction. J Exp Neurol 10: 92, 1951
30. Eastcott HHG, Pickering GW, Rob CG: Reconstruction of internal carotid artery in a patient with intermittent attacks of hemiplegia. Lancet ii: 994–996, 1954

31. Imparato AM, Riles TS, Gorstein F: The carotid bifurcation plaque: Pathologic findings associated with cerebral ischemia. Stroke 10: 238–241, 1979
32. Lusby R: Consensus statement on the management of patients with asymptomatic carotid lesions. 1993 (in press)
33. Widder B, Paulat K, Hackspacher J et al.: Morphological characterization of carotid artery stenoses by ultrasound duplex scanning. Ultrasound Med Biol 16: 349–354, 1990
34. Bornstein NM, Norris JW: The unstable carotid plaque. Stroke 20: 1104–1106, 1989
35. Lennihan L, Kupsky WJ, Mohr JP et al.: Lack of association between carotid plaque hematoma and ischemic cerebral symptoms. Stroke 18: 879–881, 1987
36. Bornstein NM, Krajewski A, Lewis AJ, Norris JW: Clinical significance of carotid plaque hemorrhage. Arch Neurol 47: 958–959, 1990
37. Fisher M, Martin A, Cosgrove M, Pirisi A, Norris J: Carotid artery plaques in the NASCET and ACAS projects. Neurology 42 (Suppl 3): 204, 1992
38. Estol C, Classen D, Hirsch W, Wechsler L, Moossy J: Correlative angiographic and pathologic findings in the diagnosis of ulcerated plaques in the carotid artery. Arch Neurol 48: 692–694, 1991
39. Moore WS, Boren C, Malone JM et al.: Natural history of nonstenotic, asymptomatic ulcerative lesions of the carotid artery. Arch Surg 113: 1352–1359, 1978
40. Senti M, Pedro-Botet J, Nogues X, Rubiew-Prat J, Vidal-Barraquer F: Lipoprotein profile in men with peripheral vascular disease: Role of intermediate density lipoproteins and apoprotein E phenotypes. Circulation 85: 30–36, 1992
41. Austin MA, King MC, Vranizan KM, Krauss RM: Atherogenic lipoprotein phenotype: A proposed genetic marker for coronary heart disease risk. Circulation 82: 495–506, 1990
42. Adult treatment panel, the national cholesterol education program, National Heart, Lung and Blood Institute. Cholesterol, current concepts for clinicians. Updated version. US Department of Health and Human Services, Public Health Service. Bethesda: National Institutes of Health, 1988
43. Donnan GA, McNeil JJ, Adena MA et al.: Smoking as a risk factor for cerebral ischemia. Lancet ii: 643–645, 1989
44. Ingall TJ, Homer D, Baker HL et al.: Predictors of intracranial carotid artery atherosclerosis. Arch Neurol 48: 687–691, 1991
45. Spence JD: Effects of antihypertensive agents on blood velocity: implications for atherogenesis. Can Med Assoc J 127: 721–724, 1982
46. Dhawan V, Ganguly NK, Majumdar S, Chakravarti RN: Effect of indomethacin on serum lipids, lipoproteins, prostaglandins and the extent and severity of atherosclerosis in Rhesus monkeys. Can J Cardiol 8: 306–312, 1992
47. Grottum P, Svindland A, Walloe L: Localization of early atherosclerotic lesions in the right carotid bifurcation in humans. Acta Path Microbiol Immunol Scand Sect A 91: 65–70, 1983
48. Harris WS: Fish oils and plasma lipid and lipoprotein metabolism in humans: a critical review. J Lipid Res 30: 785–807, 1989
49. Loscalzo J: Regression of coronary atherosclerosis (letter). New Engl J Med 323: 1337, 1990
50. Norris JW: Changing perspectives in asymptomatic carotid stenosis. In Stroke, Barnett HJM (Ed.), London: Churchill Livingstone, 1992
51. Norris JW, Zhu CZ, Bornstein NM, Chambers BR: Vascular risks of asymtomatic carotid stenosis. Stroke 22: 1485–1490, 1991
52. Whisnant JP: The role of the neurologist in the decline of stroke. Ann Neurol 14: 1–7, 1983
53. Jenkins DJA, Hegele RA: Diet in the treatment of hyperlipidemia. Ann RCPSC 24: 283–289, 1991
54. Lie JT: Pathology of occlusive disease of the extracranial arteries. In Occlusive Cerebrovascular Disease: Diagnosis and Surgical Management, Sundt TM (Ed.). Philadelphia/London: WB Saunders, p. 26, 1987

Single Centre Observation of Asymptomatic Carotid Artery Disease

Peter J. Franks, Mary R. Ellis and Roger M. Greenhalgh

INTRODUCTION

The results of two recently published trials have highlighted the benefit of carotid endarterectomy in symptomatic patients with high grade stenoses of the carotid arteries.[1,2] However, the benefits of surgery in asymptomatic disease are unknown. Improvements in diagnostic techniques have led to screening programmes for asymptomatic arterial disease with continuous wave Doppler used to determine the prevalence and progression of asymptomatic carotid disease. These results may then be related to the development of symptoms, stroke and mortality to determine the relative importance of carotid stenoses on these end-points.

PREVALENCE

Prevalence studies of asymptomatic disease have rarely been performed on random samples of the population. Because of the nature of the disease, studies have been performed primarily in surgical or neurological units. In 1987 Josse et al.[3] reported a study of 528 patients referred to a neurology clinic with reasons other than peripheral or cardiac disease with no evidence of cerebral symptoms. They found that carotid artery stenosis >50% went from zero prevalence in patients aged 45–54 up to 6.1% in men and 6.9% in women at age 75–84. In a study of 2009 asymptomatic carotid patients with other forms of arterial disease or risk factors (375 peripheral, 264 coronary and 1370 with atherosclerotic risk factors) prevalence of >50% carotid artery stenosis was 32.8%, 6.8% and 5.9% respectively.[4] Klop et al.[5] screened 374 patients with peripheral arterial disease and found a prevalence of 50–75% stenosis in 10.6%, 76–99 in 8% and complete occlusion in 8%, giving an overall prevalence of 26.6%. Faggioli et al.[6] recorded prevalence in 539 patients undergoing coronary artery bypass and found >75% stenosis in 8.7%. The best estimate of population prevalence was described by Colgan et al.[7] who examined 348 volunteers attending hospital sponsored health fairs. Overall they found a prevalence of >50% carotid stenosis in 13 (4%) and only three patients with >80% stenosis. However, it must be acknowledged that this was not a random sample of the population and the results may have been biased by subject self-selection.

INCIDENCE

To date there have been no direct investigations of incidence of asymptomatic carotid disease though other studies have alluded to this problem. Moll et al.[8] determined stenosis in 262 men and 107 women. In all, 17% of the 302 patients who were normal at first visit developed a haemodynamically significant unilateral stenosis and 3% a bilateral stenosis within 2 years, increasing to 55% and 8% respectively within 5 years.

SYMPTOM DEVELOPMENT IN ASYMPTOMATIC CAROTID DISEASE

Epidemiological studies of asymptomatic carotid disease are rare and have relied on carotid bruit as an indicator of carotid disease.[9,10] The Framingham study found an increased stroke risk in patients with carotid bruit, but this occurred more often in a territory other than that predicted by the site of bruit.[9] Similarly, the Evans county study found a higher risk of stroke in men with bruit but not in women.[10] Cervical bruits were found to be a risk factor for death from ischaemic heart disease demonstrating its role as an indicator of generalized atherosclerosis.[11]

Since the widespread application of continuous wave Doppler in vascular units the degree of stenosis has been estimated non-invasively. Several studies have since shown that bruit is not a good indicator of stenosis, though there is little evidence on the relative importance of these factors in the prediction of subsequent cerebrovascular morbidity or mortality.[12-14]

The lack of evidence on the relative importance of stenosis and bruit on stroke and symptom development prompted a study which would screen patients at risk of carotid stenosis and observe the development of stroke, cerebrovascular symptoms and mortality in patients with differing grades of stenosis.

CHARING CROSS ASYMPTOMATIC CAROTID STUDY

Over a period of 5 years all patients attending the Vascular Surgical Service at Charing Cross Hospital for symptoms ascribed to peripheral arterial disease or aortic aneurysm with no history of stroke, transient ischaemic attack (TIA) or amaurosis fugax were screened. The degree of internal and common carotid stenosis was recorded using continuous wave Doppler. Significant stenosis was described as a stenosis of at least 50% in either common or internal carotid arteries, whilst severe stenosis was described as >80% diameter reduction in either common or internal carotid arteries.

Of the 1198 screened 1034 (86.3%) were without stenosis, 130 (10.9%) were found to have a unilateral stenosis >50% and 34 (2.8%) bilateral stenoses. The prevalence of stenosis was age-specific being 6.9% in men under 60 years increasing to 20.8% in the over 80s with similar rises in women (Fig. 1). Prevalence of >80% stenosis was 2.8% (34/1198) with one patient suffering from bilateral stenosis. The prevalence was similar between the sexes at 2.9% (95%CI 2.3–3.5%) for men and 2.4% (95%CI 1.6–3.2%) for women.

Patients with no detectable stenosis (0–49%) continued to be seen at annual follow-up clinics where carotid scans were performed. Over the period of follow-up 37 of the 1034 patients developed a unilateral stenosis of greater than 50%. Total annual incidence was 3.9% (95%CI 2.2–5.6%) per year in the men and 4.9% (95%CI 2.0–7.8%) in the women with no obvious difference for age.

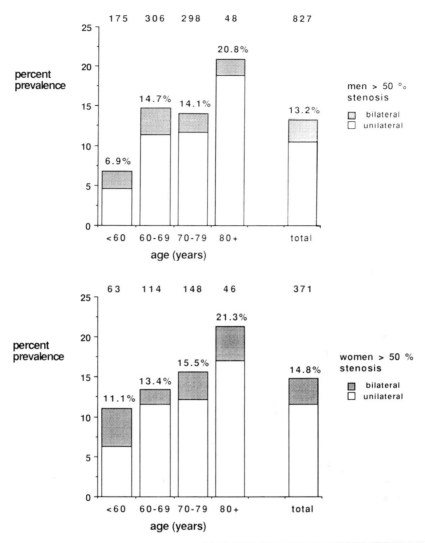

Fig. 1. Prevalence of asymptomatic carotid disease in patients with peripheral arterial disease or aortic aneurysm. Numbers refer to the number of patients in each age band; (a: upper) men, (b: lower) women.

Careful note was taken whenever a cerebrovascular symptom developed in any of the patients with or without significant asymptomatic carotid disease. These were categorized into (i) stroke, (ii) TIA or amaurosis fugax. Deaths were obtained from flagging patients through the Office of Populations, Censuses & Surveys from where death certificates were obtained. Patients who did not attend for follow-up were contacted wherever possible to determine their reason for non-attendance.

There were 27 patients who developed a stroke over the period of follow-up and 33 other neurological events (TIA or amaurosis fugax). In all there were 155 deaths of which 11 were due to strokes.

Life tables were plotted for patients with unilateral and bilateral disease. For statistical analysis the patients with unilateral and bilateral disease were combined and compared with patients with stenoses <50%. The results were expressed as a risk of patients with unilateral or bilateral stenoses >50% relative to those with no significant stenosis (relative risk). Patients with at least one >50% stenosis had a significantly higher risk of symptom development (TIA or stroke) with a relative risk of 2.98 (95%CI 1.68–5.29, $p<0.001$) compared with patients with 0–49% stenosis (Fig. 2a). When corrected for age and sex this difference remained (RR 2.95, 95%CI 1.65–5.30, $p<0.001$). For patients with at least one >80% stenosis the relative risk was higher at 4.47 (95%CI 1.58–12.65, $p<0.001$) which was also maintained after correction for age and sex (RR=4.27, 95%CI 1.49–12.29, $p<0.001$) (Fig. 2b).

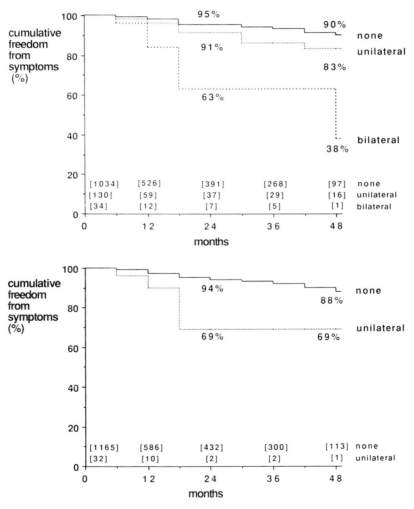

Fig. 2. Life table analysis for the development of cerebrovascular symptoms. (a: upper) Patients with at least one >50% stenosis had an increased risk of symptom development (RR = 2.98, 95%CI 1.68–5.29, $p<0.001$). (b: lower) Patients with at least one >80% stenosis also had an increased risk (RR = 4.47, 95%CI 1.58–12.65, $p<0.001$).

The relative risk of stroke alone was high in patients with at least one >50% stenosis at 1.78 but did not achieve statistical significance (95%CI 0.66–4.80, $p=0.275$), Fig. 3a. No strokes occurred in the 33 patients with a stenosis >80% and a relative risk could not be calculated (Fig. 3b).

Mortality was significantly higher in patients with at least one >50% stenosis (RR=1.69, 95%CI 1.13–2.53, $p=0.013$). A significantly higher mortality was also demonstrated in patients with a stenosis >80% (RR=3.05, 95%CI 1.32–7.04, $p=0.023$).

Bruit was also significantly associated with the development of stroke or TIA (RR=2.16, 95%CI 1.23–3.81, $p=0.010$) and mortality (RR=1.78, 95%CI 1.24–2.54, $p=0.002$), but also failed to achieve significance for stroke alone (RR=1.46, 95%CI

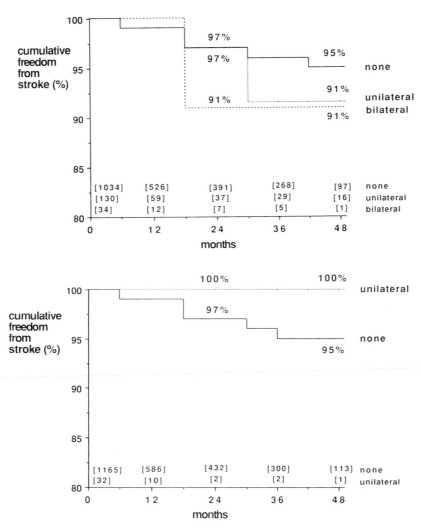

Fig. 3. Stroke risk analysed by life table. (a: upper) The risk was higher in patients with at least one > 50% stenosis (RR = 1.78) but did not achieve statistical significance (95%CI 0.66–4.80, $p = 0.275$). (b: lower) No strokes occurred in the 33 patients with >80% stenosis so the relative risk could not be computed.

0.58–3.68, $p = 0.431$). The only independent risk factors for stroke or TIA development was >50% stenosis. When corrected for this, neither >80% stenosis or bruit were significantly associated with symptom development.

DISCUSSION

The results from this study have found a high proportion of patients with peripheral arterial disease and aortic aneurysms with significant carotid stenosis. Nevertheless, the prevalence of 13.7% overall is considerably lower than previously reported, but may be the result of observing different patient populations.[4,5]

The results of this study have major implications for the investigation of asymptomatic carotid disease in patients with peripheral vascular disease. They show that carotid stenosis is common in these patients and that the incidence of stenosis development is similar for all age groups. The data demonstrate that patients with carotid disease have an increased risk of developing a cerebrovascular symptom of either stroke or TIA. The risk of death from cardiovascular disease was high, though principally from non-stroke deaths. This has been found consistently in previously reported studies.[8,15,16]

Prospective randomized trials conducted jointly by vascular surgeons and neurologists will determine the potential benefit of surgery against conservative methods of treatment. The Veterans Administration have initiated a trial to compare carotid endarterectomy with no surgery, all patients receiving 1300 mg aspirin daily.[17] Of the 211 patients who received surgery, 30-day mortality was 1.9% with a postoperative stroke rate of 2.4% and TIA of 0.9%. The results comparing this group and the 233 randomized to no surgery have yet to be published. The Asymptomatic Atherosclerosis Study Group has initiated a larger trial with randomization of 750 patients into both arms of the trial with all receiving 325 mg aspirin per day.[18] The results of these trials are eagerly awaited to determine the optimum treatment of patients with asymptomatic disease.

REFERENCES

1. NASCET Collaborators: North American Symptomatic Carotid Endarterectomy Trial—first results. N Engl J Med 325: 445–453, 1991
2. European Carotid Surgery Trialists Collaborative Group: MRC European carotid surgery trial: interim results for symptomatic patients with severe (70–99%) or with mild (0–29%) carotid stenoses. Lancet 337: 1235–1243, 1991
3. Josse MO, Touboul PJ, Mas JL, Laplane D, Bousser MG: Prevalence of asymptomatic internal carotid artery stenosis. Neuroepidemiology 6: 150–152, 1987
4. Hennerici M, Aulich A, Sandmann W, Freund H-J: Incidence of asymptomatic extracranial arterial disease. Stroke 12: 750–758, 1981
5. Klop RBJ, Eikelboom BC, Taks ACJM: Screening of the internal carotid arteries in patients with peripheral vascular disease by colour-flow Duplex scanning. Eur J Vasc Surg 5: 41–45, 1991
6. Faggioli GL, Curl GR, Ricotta JJ: The role of carotid screening before coronary artery bypass. J Vasc Surg 12: 724–731, 1990
7. Colgan MP, Strode GR, Sommer JD, Gibbs JL, Sumner DS: Prevalence of asymptomatic carotid disease: results of duplex scanning in 348 unselected volunteers. J Vasc Surg 8: 674–678, 1988

8. Moll F, Eikelboom BC, Vermeulen FEE, van Lier HJJ, Schulte BPM: Risk factors in asymptomatic patients with carotid bruit. Eur J Vasc Surg 1: 33–39, 1987
9. Wolf PA, Kannel WB, Sorlie P, McNamara P: Asymptomatic carotid bruit and risk of stroke. The Framingham study. JAMA 245: 1442–1445, 1981
10. Heyman A, Wilkinson WE, Heyden S et al.: Risk of stroke in asymptomatic persons with cervical arterial bruits. N Engl J Med 302: 838–841, 1980
11. Ellis MR, Greenhalgh RM: Management of asymptomatic carotid bruit. J Vasc Surg 5: 869–873, 1987
12. Barnes RW, Marszalek PB, Rittgeers SZ: Asymptomatic carotid disease in preoperative patients. Stroke 11: 136A, 1980
13. Hennerici M, Rautenberg W, Mohr S: Stroke risk from symptomless extracranial arterial lesions. Lancet ii: 1180–1183, 1982
14. Zhu CZ, Norris JW: Role of carotid stenosis in ischemic stroke. Stroke 21: 1131–1134, 1990
15. Bogousslavsky J, Despland P-A, Regli F: Asymptomatic tight stenosis of the internal carotid artery: long-term prognosis. Neurology 36: 861–863, 1986
16. Knudsen L, Sillesen H, Schroeder T, Hansen HJB: Eight to ten years follow-up after carotid endarterectomy: Clinical evaluation and Doppler examination of patients operated on between 1978–1980. Eur J Vasc Surg 4: 259–264, 1990
17. Towne JB, Weiss DG, Hobson RW: First phase report of cooperative Veterans Administration asymptomatic carotid stenosis study—operative morbidity and mortality. J Vasc Surg 11: 252–259, 1990
18. Asymptomatic Carotid Atherosclerosis Study Group: Study design for randomized prospective trial of carotid endarterectomy for asymptomatic atherosclerosis. Stroke 20: 844–849, 1989

Antiplatelet or Anticoagulant Therapy After Carotid Endarterectomy: Results of a Trial and an Analysis Supported by Postdata Matching

Georg Kretschmer, Georg Bischof, Thomas Pratschner, Martin Kail, Martina Mittlböck, Edwin Turkof, Stefan Puig and Peter Polterauer

INTRODUCTION

Carotid endarterectomy combined with postoperative pharmacotherapy *vs* medical therapy alone reduces the risk of stroke or death among symptomatic patients with high grade stenosis (see pp. 369–382, this volume).[1,2]

The beneficial effect of 'surgical pharmacotherapy' has been addressed recently. Acetylsalicylic acid (ASA) and anticoagulants (AC) seem to be the drugs most obvious to discuss.[3,4] The Oxford Trial Metaanalysis produced evidence for the value of ASA in reducing vascular events in general.[5]

Since carotid artery disease frequently heralds the presence of lesions in the coronary vascular bed,[6] it seems most likely that postsurgical pharmacotherapy using either drug after carotid endarterectomy might prolong postoperative survival, probably by reducing coronary events.

In this article we report the results of a clinical trial and an analysis using postdata matching,[7] with both studies devoted to the question of postoperative pharmacotherapy after carotid thrombendarterectomy (TEA). Patient survival was used as the final end-point of evaluation.

PATIENTS AND METHODS

Eligible for analysis were 402 patients with lesions of the carotid bifurcation, in whom elective surgery was considered to be indicated. Of these, 115 were asymptomatic, whereas 287 had experienced one or more transient ischaemic attacks. Preoperative clinical status was assessed according to clinical neurologic investigation.

The operative procedure was a typical TEA of the carotid bifurcation under general anaesthesia without intraluminal shunting. The arteriotomy was closed with direct suture.[8] Ultrasound examinations were used to monitor patency of the endarterectomized vessel during the early postoperative period.[9]

Perioperative management included a daily dosage of up to 1.5 g of ASA ($n=216$), or oral anticoagulants ($n=37$) or no antithrombotic medication at all ($n=149$).

Regular postoperative control examinations were carried out on an out-patient basis with intervals of 3 months initially and of 6 months in the long term or whenever otherwise required. Particular attention was directed to confirming reliable consumption of the medication. A thrombotest between 5 and 12% was considered safe and within therapeutic limits. In general, medical therapy was continued for more than 1 year or until patient's death. It was the surgeon's decision to prescribe AC, ASA, or nothing at all.

The prospective trial was initiated in 1982. By November 1985, a total of 66 patients had undergone TEA and were assigned either to the therapy group ($n=32$) starting 1.0 g ASA 2 days prior to surgery or the control group ($n=34$), which remained without medication.

Survival was chosen as the primary end-point of evaluation. The survival status of trial participants was finally assessed by the end of 1988, and of the patients eligible for the matched analysis by the end of 1991.

Standard laboratory tests were used to assess hypercholesterolaemia and hyperlipidaemia.

STATISTICAL METHODS

The information concerning causes of disease and details of therapeutic procedures were obtained using the documentation system of the Austrian Vascular Surgical Society (180 variables per surgical intervention, more than 8000 operations stored since 1965). For the purpose of the present investigation the system was modified to allow discrimination between patients of the analysis from those participating in the prospective trial.

Statistical procedures were carried out with the IBM 4381 main frame computer of the Medical Faculty at the University of Vienna.

For data storage and retrieval, SAS-Software,[10] (which also facilitated scheduling and organization of follow-up appointments and out-patient examinations) was used. BMDP-1L software allowed survival analysis.[11] Within the prospective trial, patients were assigned to either group by means of adaptive randomization.[12] Prognostic factors that were accounted for included patient sex, age, history of diabetes mellitus, hypertension, smoking habits and preoperative clinical staging.

Survival curves were estimated according to the Kaplan–Meier method;[13] possible statistical differences were calculated with the tests of Breslow[14] and Mantel[15] in bi-tailed mode. The graphical design of Kaplan–Meier curves followed the recommendations established by the Ad Hoc Committee on reporting standards of the Society for Vascular Surgery and the North American Chapter of the International Society for Cardiovascular Surgery.[16]

The most recent information regarding the survival was conveyed through the Austrian Central Statistical Office (Österr. Statistisches Zentralamt, Vienna, Austria) and transferred to the Computer at least once a year by electromagnetic tape. (See appendix for the current legislation in Austria, regarding reporting of residency and causes of death, as well as obtaining permission for postmortem examination.) Analysis of the data revealed different risk factors for peripheral arterial occlusive diseases which were unevenly distributed among patient groups. Therefore a logistic regression analysis was used to explore these factors, which independently influenced the outcome in a relevant way.[17] These particular factors were then employed for case-control postdata matching. To each case on the basis of similarity with respect to the above mentioned variables, one or more controls were selected. One should expect to screen four to five times as many controls to match the case series. Depending on the size of the available clinical series, we have used a constant case-control ratio of 1 : 2; in other words, each case had two 'selected' i.e. matched controls.[7]

The data was analysed employing the intention to treat principle.[18]

RESULTS

Clinical trial: (n = 66; follow-up: 5 years)

The various risk factors were evenly distributed among 66 patients recruited for the trial, as shown in Table 1 (treatment group: TG $n=32$, control group: untreated $n=34$). During the follow-up period of 5 years 20 patients died, six in the treatment group and 14 in the control group. In both groups the median survival was more than 60 months. The probability of survival differed significantly among groups ($p<0.033$ Mantel; $p<0.024$ Breslow; Fig. 1).

Although surgery was performed using antiaggregate therapy in one group, there was no difference in the frequency of local haematoma (ASA: 3/32 patients; controls: 3/34 patients). Cerebral deaths were similarly distributed (one in each group), whereas the incidence of cardiac deaths was different (none in the treatment group and 9 in the control group).

Table 1. Prospective trial: balancing of risk factors in the untreated group *vs* the ASA (1000 mg/day) group

Variable	Description	ASA n = 32	Untreated n = 34
Age	⩽55	5	4
	55–65	12	14
	>65	15	16
Diabetic state	Non-diabetic	20	20
	Diabetes I	9	14
	Diabetes II	3	0
Cardiac pathology	None	13	15
	Arrhythmia	3	3
	Ischaemia/infarction	2	2
	Other	9	9
Hyperlipidaemia	Yes	17	18
	No	15	16
Sex	Male	24	23
	Female	8	11
Hypertension	<160/90 mmHg	20	21
	>160/90 mmHg	12	13
Smoking habits	Non-smoker	16	16
	<10 cig./day	3	4
	>10 cig./day	13	14
Clinical stage	I	12	13
	II	20	21

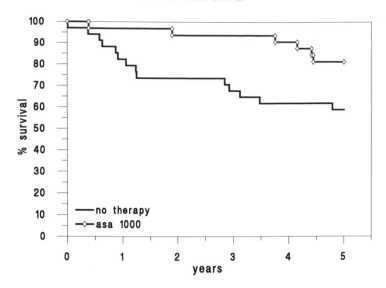

Fig. 1.   The prospective trial. Probability of patient survival; Kaplan–Meier estimates; At
5 years, there remain 26 *vs* 20 patients at risk, the SEM being 0.06 *vs* 0.08.[16]

Matched pair analysis: (*n* = 402; follow-up: 10 years)

Data of 402 patients were available for evaluation. During follow-up 20 patients died
in the AC-group, 78 in the ASA-group and 87 in the untreated group. The median
survival was 8.48±0.54 (SEM) years, 6.52±0.38 years and 5.94±1.13 years
respectively. The difference in the probability of survival was significant (*p* < 0.082

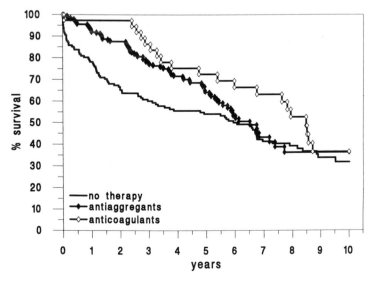

Fig. 2.   Analysis of the clinical series. Probability of patient survival; Kaplan–Meier estimates.

Table 2. Uneven distribution of risk factors between groups before matching

Variable	Description	AC n=37	ASA n=216	Untreated n=149
Age	≤55	6	20	16
	55–65	10	47	50
	>65	20	90	69
Diabetic state	Non-diabetic	24	143	82
	Diabetes I	11	53	48
	Diabetes II	2	17	19
Cardiac pathology	Nil	13	89	65
	Arrhythmia	5	10	10
	Ischaemia/infarction	13	82	58
	Other	6	34	16
Hyperlipidaemia	Yes	25	112	105
	No	12	104	44
Sex	Male	29	150	103
	Female	8	66	46
Hypertension	<160/90 mmHg	25	122	93
	>160/90 mmHg	12	94	56
Smoking habits	Non-smoker	10	58	44
	<10 cig./day	6	21	16
	>10 cig./day	19	110	82
Clinical stage	I	15	42	58
	II	22	174	91

Mantel; $p<0.003$ Breslow) (Fig. 2). since the risk factors were distributed as summarized in Table 2, the results were considered of limited value.

Employing a logistic regression analysis, the factors of age, ischaemic cardiac disease and diabetic metabolic state adversely influenced survival as shown in Table 3. Using the afore mentioned three factors, the technique of data matching was applied to adjust the recognized risk factors as demonstrated in Table 4.

For analysis 185 patients were eligible (AC: $n=37$; ASA: $n=74$, untreated: $n=74$). During follow-up 88 patients died: 20 in the AC group, 24 in the ASA group, but 44 in the non-medicated group. The median survival was 8.48 ± 0.54 (SEM) years (AC-group); the 75% quantile was 3.69 ± 0.47 years in the ASA-group and the median survival was 6.07 ± 1.54 years in the untreated group respectively. The probability of survival was $p<0.076$ Mantel, and $p<0.011$ Breslow, but no difference was observed between the two medical treatment options ($p<0.85$ Mantel; $p<0.61$ Breslow; Fig. 3).

The leading cause of death was ischaemic myocardiopathy (68% AC; 40% ASA, 39% untreated group, but the incidence of cerebral deaths was equal among groups (11% AC; 10% ASA; 9% untreated group).

Table 3. Stepwise logistic regression analysis for significant prognostic factors

Variable	p	Risk ratio
Age	0.0001	1.73
Cardiac pathology (ischaemia)	0.0001	2.26
Diabetes I	0.0026	1.44
Diabetes II	0.0001	2.53
Cardiac pathology (arrhythmia)	0.342	1.35
Other cardiac pathology	1.123	1.46

Table 4.   Data matching (1 : 2 : 2; i.e. each AC patient was matched with two ASA patients
and two patients without therapy)
The following risk factors were well distributed

Variable	Description	AC n = 37	ASA n = 74	Untreated n = 74
Age	≤ 55	6	12	12
	55–65	11	22	22
	> 65	20	40	40
Diabetic state	Non-diabetic	24	49	52
	Diabetes I	11	21	18
	Diabetes II	2	4	4
Cardiac pathology	None	13	31	31
	Arrhythmia	5	8	8
	Ischaemia/infarction	13	27	26
	Other	6	8	9
Hyperlipidaemia	Yes	25	35	57
	No	12	39	17
Sex	Male	29	55	48
	Female	8	19	26
Hypertension	< 160/90 mmHg	25	42	47
	> 160/90 mmHg	12	32	27
Smoking habits	Non-smoker	10	15	17
	< 10 cig./day	6	6	10
	> 10 cig./day	19	40	44
Clinical stage	I	15	14	30
	II	22	60	44

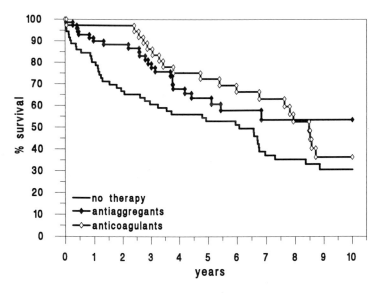

Fig. 3.   Analysis of the clinical series using postdata matching.
Probability of patient survival; Kaplan–Meier estimates. At 9 years
there are six patients at risk, the SEM exceeds 10% (AC); at 8.5
years there are six patients at risk, the SEM exceeds 10% (ASA);
at 10 years there are six patients at risk, the SEM exceeds 10%
respectively (no therapy).[16]

DISCUSSION

The object of these investigations was to evaluate the impact of postoperative 'surgical' pharmacotherapy in patients with occlusive arterial disease. The results of both studies seemed to be in accordance and in favour of postoperative medical therapy using either antiplatelet or anticoagulant drugs.

The study dealt with a limited series of patients from one single centre, but was uniformly assessed, managed and followed up. Patient survival was used as the end-point of evaluation, a criterion which is beyond any doubt. Current legislation in Austria made complete follow-up covering 5 and 10 years possible. In the clinical trial the recruited sample of patients was small, but by the end of 5 years the number of patients at risk was of sufficient size and the standard error remained below 10%; the results appeared acceptable.[16] The analysis of the clinical series seemed to duplicate the result of the trial, but referred to a larger number of patients which were followed up for up to 10 years. The statistical tools which have been employed in the analysis of the clinical series, namely the multivariate logistic regression analysis, are accepted methods. In addition we have already used case control postmatching to adjust the risk factors in two series of patients in order to obtain comparable groups.[19]

It is established that carotid lesions are associated with coronary artery disease and that cardiac events determine the fate of patients following carotid TEA.[6,20] In this series myocardial ischaemic events proved to be the decisive factors. Therefore it is tempting to argue for postoperative medication in order to reduce the incidence of cardiac events and to prolong the life of these vascular patients.

The Kaplan–Meier estimates constantly decline over the years, pointing at the fact that the risk of dying from underlying ischaemic cardiac disease remains fairly constant. Long-term treatment and surveillance might be indicated.

In cerebrovascular arterial disease, the value of ASA and AC has been investigated in two metaanalyses, but these did not produce convincing evidence in favour of any medication.[27,28] It has been demonstrated that ASA is of value in reducing vascular events in general[5,21] and probably cerebral ischaemic attacks.[22]

A variety of studies have shown the beneficial effect of AC in preventing myocardial infarction and reinfarction, thereby prolonging patient survival.[23-25] In addition, cancellation of AC-therapy, once initiated, may cause adverse events.

Both drugs, ASA and AC, theoretically have the potential danger of inducing cerebral haemorrhage. In our two studies the incidence of cerebral deaths was equal between groups treated and untreated. It remained around 10% during long-term observation up to 10 years. Thus the risk might be overestimated.[4]

Of course long-term AC therapy needs a system to control the level of anticoagulation as frequently as necessary in any individual patient, but compliance is easy to check. Although ASA is simple to prescribe, the exact adherence of patients to regular drug intake might be difficult to assess.[26] In our analysis, survival of ASA patients declined between 5 and 10 years, although the reason is not known. Progression of underlying disease, advanced age or reduced compliance beyond 5 years of continuous medical therapy might be responsible.

According to our investigations both drugs are similar in their effectiveness. Switching from one drug to the other seems justified in case of drug intolerance, but not depending upon the kind of surgery, which has been performed.

APPENDIX

In Austria under the Act on Reporting of Residency, residents are obliged to report their place of residence (and all changes thereof) to the local authorities or to the police. In addition, if a person dies in hospital, then the director of the clinic or the physician, who performed the coroner's inquest, has to report to the local authorities the cause of death to enable the local authorities to pass that information on to the Austrian Central Statistical Office. This leads to an estimated postmortem examination frequency of 70–75%, thereby rendering accurate information about patient survival and possible cause of death.

ACKNOWLEDGEMENT

We wish to thank the Austrian Central Statistical Office, Vienna, Austria for making available to us the survival status of the patients.

REFERENCES

1. North American Symptomatic Carotid Endarterectomy Trial (NASCET) Steering Committee: North American Symptomatic Carotid Endarterectomy Trial. Methods, patient characteristics and progress. Stroke 22: 711–720, 1991
2. European Carotid Surgery Trialists' Collaborative Group: MRC European Carotid Surgery Trial: interim results for symptomatic patients with severe (70–99%) or with mild (0–29%) carotid stenosis. Lancet 337: 1235–1243, 1991
3. Dormandy J: Surgical pharmacotherapy: Eur J Vasc Surg 3: 379–380, 1989
4. Van Urk H, Kretschmer G: What is the role of oral anticoagulants and platelet inhibition in peripheral vascular surgery? Eur J Vasc Surg 4: 553–555, 1990
5. Peto R, Gray R, Collins R *et al.*: Randomised trial of prophylactic daily aspirin in British male doctors. Br Med J 296: 313–316, 1988
6. Berkhoff A, Levine RL: Management of the vascular patient with multisystem atherosclerosis. Progr Cardiovasc Dis 29: 347–368, 1987
7. Schlesselmann JJ: Case control studies, design, conduct, analysis. *In* Monographs in Epidemiology and Biostatistics. Oxford: Oxford University Press, pp. 105–123, 1982
8. Polterauer P, Huk I, Hölzenbein Th *et al.*: Carotisendarteriektomie: Indikation, Technik, Ergebnisse. J Vasc Dis Suppl. 26: 159–162, 1988
9. Ehringer H, Bockelmann L, Konecny U *et al.*: Verschlußkrankheit der extracraniellen A. carotis: Spontanverlauf und frühe Phase nach Thrombendarteriektomie im bildgebenden Ultraschall. J Vasc Dis Suppl. 20: 71–76, 1987
10. SAS/STAT Users Guide Version 6, Cary, NC, SAS-Institute, 1990
11. Dixon WJ, Brown MD, Engelman L *et al.*: BMDP Statistical Software Manual. Berkeley California: University of California Press, 1990
12. Pocock SJ, Simon R: Sequential treatment assignment with balancing for prognostic factors in the controlled clinical trial. Biometrics 31: 103–115, 1975
13. Kaplan EL, Meier P: Non-parametric estimation from incomplete observations. J Am Stat Assoc 53: 457–481, 1958
14. Breslow NA: Generalized Kruskal-Walis test for comparing k-samples subject to unequal patterns of censorship. Biometrika 57: 163–165, 1965
15. Mantel N: Evaluation of survival data and two new rank order statistics arising in its consideration. Cancer Chemother Rep 50: 163–165, 1965

16. Ad Hoc Committee on Reporting Standards/Society for Vascular Surgery/North American Chapter International Society for Cardiovascular Surgery: Suggested standards for reports dealing with lower extremity ischemia. J Vasc Surg 4: 80–94, 1988
17. Cox DD: Regression models and life tables. J R Stat Soc 34B: 187–196, 1972
18. Pocock SJ: Clinical Trials. New York: John Wiley, pp. 176–184, 1984
19. Kretschmer G, Niederle B, Schemper M, Polterauer P: Extraanatomic femoro–femoral crossover bypass (FF) vs. unilateral orthotopic ilio–femoral bypass (IF): an attempt to compare results based on data matching. Eur J Vasc Surg 5: 75–82, 1991
20. O'Donnel TF, Callow AD, Willet G et al.: The impact of coronary artery disease on carotid endarterectomy. Ann Surg 198: 705–712, 1983
21. UK-TIA Study Group: United Kingdom transient ischaemic attack aspirin trial: interim results. Br Med J 296: 316–320, 1988
22. Klimt CHR, Knatterud GL, Stamler J, Meier P: Persantin–aspirin–reinfarction study, part II. Secondary coronary prevention with persantin and aspirin. J Am Coll Cardiol 7: 251–269, 1986
23. De Smit P, Van Urk H: The Dutch oral anticoagulation trial. Acta Chir Austr 24: 5–7, 1992
24. Smith P, Arnesen H, Holde I: The effect of Warfarin on mortality and reinfarction after myocardial infarction. N Engl J Med 323: 147–152, 1990
25. Kretschmer G, Wenzl E, Schemper M: Influence of postoperative anticoagulant treatment on patient survival after femoro popliteal vein bypass surgery. Lancet i: 797–799, 1988
26. Franks PJ, Sian M, Kenchington GF, Alexander CE, Powel JT: Femoro–popliteal bypass trial participants. Aspirin usage and its influence on femoro–popliteal vein graft patency. Eur J Vasc Surg 5: 75–82, 1991
27. Sze PC, Reitman D, Pincus MM, Sacks HS, Chalmers TC: Antiplatelet agents in the secondary prevention of stroke: meta-analysis of the randomized control trials. Stroke 19: 436–442, 1988
28. Jonas S: Anticoagulant treatment in cerebrovascular disease: review and metaanalysis. Stroke 19: 1043–1048, 1988

CLINICAL TRIALS

Can Reported Carotid Surgical Results be Misleading?

W. Bruce Campbell

INTRODUCTION

Few operations in the history of modern surgery have produced such controversy and debate about their role and benefit as carotid endarterectomy. Only very recently have really good data about the proper place of carotid surgery been published[1,2] but there are still areas of uncertainty.

The doubts about carotid endarterectomy over so many years seem incredible, considering the volume of literature on the results of the operation. However, surgical series show great variation and may mislead the reader because, by and large, they probably fail to reflect the overall results of the majority of surgeons who do not publish their results.[3-6] Surgeons are understandably reluctant to report poor or mediocre results and editors generally prefer to publish 'respectable' ones. There are ample data (presented below) to suggest that the low morbidities which dominate the literature, and which authoritative voices demand, are better than the average.[3]

The situation has been clouded still further by lack of good information on the natural history of non-operated carotid disease, and because comparative studies of surgery against conservative management have failed in the past to deliver a sufficiently clear message.[4,7]

This chapter identifies some of the factors which may contribute to the variations in published results of carotid surgery, and which may mislead the reader unless they are recognized.

THE ERA REPORTED

In general, the outcome of arterial surgery has improved with each decade, and so the era from which a series was drawn is likely to influence the results. The Joint Study of Extracranial Arterial Occlusion[7] provides an example. The authors noted a difference in mortality between the first and second halves of the study, and the overall perioperative stroke rate (9.5%) and mortality (3.5%) of these patients — operated on during the 1960s — was higher than the two recent multicentre studies.[1,2] Brott and Thalinger[8] and Cafferata and Gainey[9] both documented decreasing perioperative stroke and mortality rates during the early 1980s, and a review of other surgical series published during the 1970s and early 1980s also indicated a gradual trend to decreasing morbidity and mortality.[10]

Improvements in investigative techniques over the years have also had an influence on morbidity, patient selection, and the recognition of problems and complications. The introduction of duplex scanning has abolished the hazards of arteriography for many patients and has led to more patients being investigated for carotid stenosis with a view to operation. It has also allowed recognition of different types of plaque[11] which confer differing levels of risk if left untreated. Finally, duplex surveillance has allowed the recognition of recurrent stenoses which remained largely undetected when follow-up was by clinical means alone.[12]

Digital subtraction arteriography has also reduced the risks of arteriography, compared with older intraarterial studies which had a stroke and mortality rate additional to that of operation.[13]

Finally the introduction of computed tomographic (CT) scanning has allowed recognition of areas of cerebral infarction, haemorrhage, and other intracerebral lesions preoperatively, and also asymptomatic postoperative emboli.[14] These generally remained undetected in earlier years and may alter surgical decisions and results,[15] although their relevance is still a matter for debate.

REFERRAL PATTERNS

The experience of the UK-TIA (transient ischaemic attack) study group reported in 1982 provides a good example of differing practices among referring physicians.[16] Requests for angiography by neurologists in this trial varied from 3 to 100%, and among 515 patients judged to be good clinical candidates for surgery, the angiography rates varied from 5 to 85%.

Responses to a questionnaire by vascular surgeons in the UK in 1985–6 also showed marked differences in the frequency of referrals from different specialists.[17] For instance, 66% of surgeons received referrals from neurologists 'often' or 'sometimes' while 34% 'rarely' or 'never' did so. Corresponding figures for referrals from ophthalmologists were 42% and 48%. These striking differences mean that different surgeons were probably receiving very different proportions of patients in their localities who had suffered neurological or ocular ischaemia due to carotid disease. This might well have had a significant influence on their surgical statistics.

CASE SELECTION

The morbidity of endarterectomy is related to the presence and severity of neurological problems[18,19] and to the medical condition of the patient.[1] Series with large numbers of asymptomatic stenoses and medically fit patients would therefore be expected to have lower morbidities than those with symptoms and unfit patients. Different philosophies in case selection probably go a long way to explaining the fact that some poorer results have been reported from the UK (where operations for asymptomatic stenoses are very uncommon)[17] than from the USA over the years. Questionable case selection in a number of American hospitals has already been referred to above.[20] An even larger study of 1302 patients suggested that endarterectomy had been undertaken for equivocal indications in 32% and inappropriately in a further 32%, many of whom had stenoses less than 50% and some even without ischaemic symptoms in the carotid territory.[5] These figures suggest substantial bias of results by case selection in many hospitals. On a national level, the operation has probably been overutilized in the USA and underutilized in the UK.[17]

We know that the degree and type of stenosis have an important effect on the outcome of carotid surgery but in many series these details have not been reported. The age ranges vary[21] and so, presumably, does the medical condition of those operated upon in different hospitals.[5,6] This suggests either a referral bias or perhaps case selection on the part of some surgeons to exclude higher risk patients. The European Carotid Surgery Trial (ECST) study[1] allowed clinicians to randomize those patients about whom they were 'substantially uncertain' and noted considerable differences in the types of patients and carotid lesions entered into the study. This approach was statistically valid and meant that a great diversity of patients was included, but it emphasized the wide differences in selection policy for carotid surgery in different hospitals across Europe.

One of the challenges in case selection is that some of the patients at highest risk of stroke may also be those with the highest risk of complications and death from surgery.

MEASUREMENT OF CAROTID STENOSES

The exact method by which the degree of carotid stenosis was calculated varies between different studies. In others it is not specified at all, and this suggests two possibilities which may bias results. First, measurements may have been inaccurate in some cases. Second, knowledge of patient outcome might bias measurements in marginal cases in retrospective series.

SURGEON EXPERIENCE

There have been suggestions within the UK that surgeons performing less than ten carotid endarterectomies per year may have higher complication rates than those undertaking more, and one study from the USA showed a tendency to more complications among surgeons performing less than three procedures per year compared with those doing more than twelve.[22] However, most studies which have compared the results of surgeons doing small numbers of endarterectomies with those doing more have failed to show any significant differences in complication rates.[9,21,23–25] Many of these studies included large numbers of low risk patients with asymptomatic stenoses, and the possibility remains that less experienced surgeons chose to deal with higher proportions of these cases.

Cafferata and Gainey reported a severe bias of results due to a single neurosurgeon. It is interesting and relevant that in some countries a gulf exists both in communication and in publication of results between vascular surgeons and neurosurgeons undertaking carotid endarterectomy.

TYPE OF HOSPITAL

Glimpses of the results from different hospitals[3–6,9,26 28] leave the observer in serious doubt whether the overall outcome of carotid endarterectomy is as good as the minimum standard demanded by leading voices in the field.[5] Many of the factors presented here probably contribute to poor results, and it is particularly difficult to separate hospital and surgeon variables.

Rubin et al.[29] found that mortality was higher in hospitals where fewer carotid endarterectomies were undertaken. By contrast, a review by Hsia et al.[6] documented higher mortalities in large, urban and teaching hospitals. They suggested that these institutions might be operating on higher risk patients than smaller hospitals. Some reports failed to show any difference in morbidity between hospitals, but these have investigated smaller numbers of selected institutions.[21,27]

OPERATIVE TECHNIQUES

Many surgical series do not specify details of technique which may have an influence on results. Great differences exist in policies on shunting, the use of patches, and ways of dealing with the carotid sinus nerve,[17] while some departments use unconventional techniques such as 'closed' endarterectomy.[30]

Differences in perioperative medical therapy are often not specified at all. The use of aspirin throughout the perioperative period is common (but not invariable) and the use of intraoperative heparin is not universal. These may not influence serious morbidity, but aspirin certainly increases operative oozing, and heparin increases the incidence of postoperative bleeding unless reversed by protamine sulphate.[31]

DEFINITIONS

In publications on carotid surgery, the variation in definitions and in the exclusion of neurological events makes comparison between series very difficult. Many authors have excluded from their analyses strokes which were 'temporary',[32] 'transient',[33] 'prolonged temporary',[34] 'cleared before discharge'[35] or were 'not permanent'.[36] These cannot properly be compared with studies which have included all neurological events in their results. Series which fail to make clear whether or not transient neurological events have been excluded cause even more of a problem.

Who diagnoses and defines postoperative neurological events is also important. Surgeons themselves may underdetect and record fewer minor strokes, while neurologists are likely to be impartial and probably more assiduous at diagnosing postoperative deficits.

TIME PERIOD SELECTED AND SIMPLE EXCLUSIONS

In any retrospective review, starting or finishing the series just before or after a 'bad patch' can have an important effect on results. For example, if a series of 100 patients is contrived to end just before the occurrence of two strokes, the stroke rate is 'improved' by 2%. If the resulting stroke rate of such a series is only 2%, then this manoeuvre has halved the stroke rate.

Another way of lowering morbidity rates is simply to exclude inconvenient patients. Excuses may include unusual circumstances surrounding the operation, non-standard technique, its performance by a trainee or visitor, or simple failure to document the postoperative problem. Although vigorously denied by senior authors, this is a phenomenon recognized by most trainees who have been involved in retrospective reviews but its incidence is impossible to discover.

PRESENTATION OF RESULTS

Two main problems in presentation can make results misleading. First, many series do not separate out patients with clear ipsilateral carotid TIAs from a mass of other patients undergoing endarterectomy. Second, it is often not made clear whether data on postoperative stroke rate include those patients who died as a result of stroke.

Another aspect of presentation has been a tendency over the years for authors to compare surgical results with natural history studies showing the least favourable outcomes from untreated carotid disease.[10]

DURATION AND MANNER OF FOLLOW-UP

Surgical series have generally concentrated on the immediate postoperative period (usually the first 30 days) and on simple clinical outcome. For many purposes this is adequate but it has not contributed to our knowledge of the longer term results of endarterectomy. We now know that the incidence of restenosis and occlusion may only be determined by postoperative imaging,[12] and may be related to technical aspects of the surgery.[37]

In controlled studies it is essential that patients lost to follow-up are fully documented, but this has not always been done.[7]

LOCAL COMPLICATIONS

Most of the discussion on the morbidity of carotid endarterectomy centres on stroke and death. Less serious complications such as bleeding and nerve injury are often neglected in surgical series but when reported their incidence varies quite markedly.[2,21,24,31,38] This may point to meticulous technique in series with low incidences, but variations like this always suggest the possibility that 'minor' complications have not been documented thoroughly, often because local definitions vary on what constitutes, for example, a 'postoperative bleed'.

CONCLUSION

The North American Symptomatic Carotid Endarterectomy Trial (NASCET)[2] and The European Carotid Surgery Trial (ECST)[1] series have set new standards in study design for the investigation of carotid endarterectomy. Most of the points raised in this critique were considered and dealt with in order to eliminate the possibility of misleading results.[39,40] These studies, and others now in progress[41] are clarifying many aspects of management. They should reduce the likelihood of inappropriate patient selection and set an example in the presentation of results.

REFERENCES

1. European Carotid Surgery Trialists' Collaborative Group: MRC European Carotid Surgery Trial; interim results for symptomatic patients with severe (70–99%) or with mild (0–29%) carotid stenosis. Lancet 337: 1235–1243, 1991
2. North American Symptomatic Carotid Endarterectomy Trial Collaborators: Beneficial effect of carotid endarterectomy in symptomatic patients with high-grade carotid stenosis. N Engl J Med 325: 445–453, 1991
3. Dyken ML, Pokras R: The performance of endarterectomy for disease of the extracranial arteries of the head. Stroke 15: 948–950, 1984
4. Shaw DA, Venables GS, Cartlidge NEF, Bates D, Dickinson PH: Carotid endarterectomy in patients with transient cerebral ischaemia. J Neurol Sci 64: 45–53, 1984
5. Winslow CM, Solomon DH, Chassin MR et al.: The appropriateness of carotid endarterectomy. N Engl J Med 318: 721–727, 1988
6. Hsia DC, Krushat WM, Moscoe LM: Epidemiology of carotid endarterectomies among Medicare beneficiaries. J Vasc Surg 16: 201–208, 1992
7. Fields WS, Maslenikov V, Meyers JS et al.: Joint study of extracranial arterial occlusion. JAMA 211: 1993–2003, 1970
8. Brott T, Thalinger K: The practice of carotid endarterectomy in a large metropolitan area. Stroke 15: 950–955, 1984
9. Cafferata HT, Gainey MD: Carotid endarterectomy in the community hospital. A continuing controversy. J Cardiovasc Surg 27: 557–560, 1986
10. Warlow C: Carotid endarterectomy: does it work? Stroke 15: 1068–1076, 1984
11. Feeley TM, Leen EJ, Colgan MP et al.: Histologic characteristics of carotid artery plaque. J Vasc Surg 13: 719–724, 1991
12. Knudsen L, Sillesen H, Schroeder T, Buchardt Hansen HJ: Eight to ten years follow-up after carotid endarterectomy: clinical evaluation and doppler examination of patients operated on between 1978–1980. Eur J Vasc Surg 4: 259–264, 1990
13. Faught E, Trader SD, Hanna GR: Cerebral complications of angiography for transient ischemia and stroke: prediction of risk. Neurology 29: 4–15, 1979.
14. Berguer R, Sieggrreen MY, Lazo A, Hodakowski GT: The silent brain infarct in carotid surgery. J Vasc Surg 8: 442–447, 1986
15. Graber JN, Vollman RW, Johnson WC et al.: Stroke after carotid endarterectomy: Risk as predicted by pre-operative computerised tomography. Am J Surg 147: 492–497, 1984
16. UK-TIA Study Group: Variation in the use of angiography and carotid endarterectomy by neurologists in the UK-TIA aspirin trial. Br Med J 286: 514–517, 1983
17. Murie JA, Morris PJ: Carotid endarterectomy in Great Britain and Ireland. Br J Surg 73: 867–870, 1986
18. Fode NC, Sundt TM, Robertson JT, Peerless SJ, Shields CB: Multicenter retrospective review of results and complications of carotid endarterectomy in 1981. Stroke 17: 370–376, 1986
19. Moore DJ, Modi JR, Finch WT, Sumner DS: Influence of the contralateral carotid artery on neurologic complications following carotid endarterectomy. J Vasc Surg 1: 409–414, 1984.
20. Merrick NJ, Brook RH, Fink A, Solomon DH: Use of carotid endarterectomy in five California Veterans Administration Medical Centers. JAMA 256: 2531–2535, 1986
21. Krupski WC, Effeney DJ, Goldstone J et al.; Carotid endarterectomy in a metropolitan community: Comparison of results from three institutions. Surgery 98: 492–499, 1985.
22. Richardson JD, Main KA: Carotid endarterectomy in the elderly population: a statewide experience. J Vasc Surg 9: 65–73, 1989.

23. Slavish LG, Nicholas GG, Gee W: Review of a community hospital experience with carotid endarterectomy. Stroke 15: 956–959, 1984
24. Kempczinski RF, Brott TG, Labutta RJ: The influence of surgical specialty and caseload on the results of carotid endarterectomy. J Vasc Surg 3: 911–916, 1986
25. Kirshner DL, O'Brien MS, Ricotta JJ: Risk factors in a community experience with carotid endarterectomy. J Vasc Surg 10: 178–186, 1989
26. Easton JD, Sherman DG: Stroke and mortality rate in carotid endarterectomy: 228 consecutive operations. Stroke 8: 565–568, 1977
27. Bouchier-Hayes D, de Costa A, Macgowan WAL: The morbidity of carotid endarterectomy. Br J Surg 66: 433–437, 1979
28. Eriksson S-E, Link H, Alm A, Radberg C, Kostulas V: Results from 88 consecutive prophylactic carotid endarterectomies in cerebral infarction and transitory ischaemic attacks. Acta Neurol Scand 63: 209–219, 1981
29. Rubin JR, Pitluk HC, King TA et al.: Carotid endarterectomy in a metropolitan community: the early results after 8535 operations. J Vasc Surg 7: 256–260, 1988
30. Diaz FG, Ausman JI, Malik GM: Pitfalls during carotid endarterectomy. Acta Neurochir (Wien) 91: 87–94, 1988
31. Treiman RL, Cosman DV, Foran RF et al.: The influence of neutralizing heparin after carotid endarterectomy on postoperative stroke and wound hematoma. J Vasc Surg 12: 440–446, 1990
32. Whitney DG, Kahn EM, Estes JW, Jones CE: Carotid artery surgery without a temporary indwelling shunt. 1917 consecutive procedures. Arch Surg 115: 1393–1398, 1980
33. Haynes CD, Dempsey RL: Carotid endarterectomy. Review of 276 cases in a community hospital. Ann Surg 189: 758–761, 1979
34. Park YH: Five years experience with carotid endarterectomy in a small community hospital. Vasc Surg 13: 191–201, 1979
35. Stanford JR, Lubow M, Vasko JS: Prevention of stroke by carotid endarterectomy. Surgery 83: 259–263, 1978
36. Carmichael JD: Carotid surgery in the community hospital. 467 consecutive operations. Arch Surg 115: 937–939, 1980
37. Barnes RW, Nix ML, Nichols BT, Wingo JP: Recurrent versus residual carotid stenosis. Incidence detected by doppler ultrasound. Ann Surg 203: 652–660, 1986
38. Bergqvist D, Ljungstrom K-G: Hemorrhagic complications resulting in reoperation after peripheral vascular surgery: A fourteen-year experience. J Vasc Surg 6: 134–138, 1987
39. Barnett HJM: Symptomatic carotid endarterectomy trials. Stroke 21 (Suppl iii): iii-2-5, 1990
40. North American Symptomatic Carotid Endarterectomy Trial Steering Committee: North American Symptomatic Carotid Endarterectomy Trial. Methods, patient characteristics, and progress. Stroke 22: 711–720, 1991
41. Moore WS, Mohr JP, Najafi H et al.: Carotid endarterectomy: Practice guidelines. J Vasc Surg 15: 469–479, 1992

Carotid Endarterectomy for Asymptomatic Carotid Stenosis: Results of the Veterans Administration Cooperative Clinical Trial

Robert W. Hobson II and the VA Cooperative Asymptomatic Carotid Artery Stenosis Study Group*

INTRODUCTION

Justification for carotid endarterectomy in patients with asymptomatic carotid stenosis has constituted a controversial and poorly defined aspect of the surgical management of extracranial carotid occlusive disease. Data from recently published clinical trials on the efficacy of carotid endarterectomy in symptomatic carotid occlusive disease have defined the indications for operation in the symptomatic patient with high-grade stenosis.[1-3] Other major studies, funded by the Veterans Administration (VA)[4] as well as the National Institutes of Health (NIH),[5] will influence decisions regarding carotid endarterectomy in the asymptomatic patient. Results of the VA trial[6] were published recently, while release of data from the NIH trial is anticipated within the next year. The purpose of this chapter is to summarize the results of the VA trial on asymptomatic carotid stenosis and to compare these data with other clinical observations.

METHODS

This prospective randomized clinical trial was conducted at 11 Department of Veterans Affairs Medical Centres (see Appendix) to define the influence of carotid endarterectomy on the combined incidence of neurological outcome events, including transient ischaemic attack, transient monocular blindness, and stroke in patients with asymptomatic carotid stenosis.

Data on 444 adult male patients with asymptomatic carotid stenosis, shown arteriographically to reduce the diameter of the arterial lumen by 50% or more (in the presence of positive Gee-OPG[7] or duplex scan,[8] a 75% area stenosis) were studied. Patients were randomized to optimal medical management including aspirin therapy and carotid endarterectomy ($n=211$) vs optimal medical management alone ($n=233$).

All patients were followed independently by a vascular surgeon and neurologist at each participating centre during a mean follow-up of 47.9 months. The mean age of the clinical population was 64.5 years and clinical characteristics of randomized patients at entry are summarized in Table 1.

In 32% of the trial's patients there was a history of ischaemic events due to contralateral stenoses and 80% of these events were reported as transient ischaemic

---

*See Appendix at end of this chapter for details.

Table 1. Patient characteristics at entry*

	Surgical	Medical
No. of patients	211	233
Mean age (SD)	64.1 (6.8)	64.7 (6.7)
Race (%)		
Caucasian	88	86
Afro American	6	8
Hispanic	1	3
Native American	2	3
Asian American	2	0
Previous contralateral symptoms (%)	32	33
Daily smoker (%)	52	49
Previous smoker (%)	43	42
History of (%)		
Diabetes	30	27
Myocardial infarct	28	25
Angina pectoris	30	25
Congestive heart failure	5	7
Hypertension	63	64
Arrhythmia	17	14
Peripheral vascular disease	61	59

*No significant differences between treatment groups. From Ref. 6, with permission.

attacks. Two-thirds of the sample involved patients with bilaterally asymptomatic cerebral hemispheres. Medical exclusionary criteria included previous cerebral infarction, previous endarterectomy with restenosis, previous extracranial to intracranial bypass, high surgical risk due to associated medical illness, chronic anticoagulant therapy, aspirin intolerance or chronic higher dose aspirin therapy, life expectancy less than 5 years, surgically inaccessible lesions, non-compliance or refusal to participate in the protocol.

All patients underwent arteriographic confirmation of significant stenosis. The threshold lesion for randomization was a stenosis of 50% or more (comparing the least transverse diameter at the point of maximal stenosis with the measured diameter of the postbulbar internal carotid artery once its diameter had become uniform, which in the presence of positive non-invasive studies[7,8] was considered to be an area reduction of 75%). Patients randomized to carotid endarterectomy underwent operation within 10 days of randomization.

PATIENT FOLLOW-UP

The study initiated enrolment of patients on 1 April 1983 and patient acquisition was completed in October 1987, while clinical follow-up ended on 31 March 1991. Mean follow-up, as measured from time of entry to first neurological event, death or lost to follow-up, was 47.9 months.

All patients received initial dosages of aspirin (650 mg, twice daily), which were modified to a lower dose regimen (325 mg, daily) for patients with aspirin intolerance[9,10] during the subsequent clinical follow-up. Patients who experienced clinically defined neurological outcome events were evaluated independently by the vascular surgeon and neurologist at each centre and their conclusions submitted for blinded review and adjudication to the Endpoints Committee.

SURGICAL MORBIDITY AND MORTALITY

Morbidity and mortality data for carotid endarterectomy have been published previously.[11] The 30-day operative mortality was 1.9% (4/211), three deaths as a result of myocardial infarction and one with myocardial infarction followed by stroke. Five postoperative strokes (non-fatal) occurred for an incidence of 2.4% (5/211). Three non-fatal strokes (0.4%, 3/714) occurred as a result of arteriography; one was associated with significant hemiparesis (0.15%) and two were associated with minimal neurological deficits. The 30-day postrandomization permanent stroke and death rate was 4.7% for the surgical group, assigning all complications of arteriography for this trial to the surgical group. In contrast, during the first 30 days after assignment of patients to the medical group, one death due to suicide (0.4%), and two neurological events (0.9%) occurred: one permanent stroke and one transient ischaemic event.

NEUROLOGICAL OUTCOME EVENTS

The results of all neurological events, contralateral and ipsilateral, are summarized in Table 2. Eighty-four events were observed, 27 (12.9%) in the surgical group and 57 (24.5%) in the medical group, which represented an absolute risk reduction of 11.6% ($p<0.002$; relative risk 0.51; 95% confidence interval: 0.32, 0.81). Results for ipsilateral events only are presented in Table 3. There were 65 ipsilateral events, 17 (8.0%) in the surgical group and 48 (20.6%) in the medical group. The absolute risk reduction was 12.6% ($p<0.001$; relative risk 0.38; 95% confidence interval: 0.22, 0.67). Analysis of the ipsilateral neurological events in the medical group for stenoses of 50–75% and 76–99% demonstrated an incidence of 24 events (19.2%; 12 strokes, seven transient ischaemic attacks, five episodes of transient monocular blindness) for stenoses of 50–75% and 24 events (22.4%; 10 strokes, eight transient ischaemic attacks, six episodes of transient monocular blindness) for stenoses of 76–99%, which did not represent a significant difference.

Table 2. Combined neurologic endpoints of transient ischaemic attack, transient monocular blindness, and stroke (non-fatal and fatal) for ipsilateral and contralateral events

	Surgical		Medical	
	No.	%	No.	%
No. of patients	211		233	
Transient ischaemic attack	9	4.3	17	7.3
Transient monocular blindness	1	0.5	12	5.2
Stroke	17	8.1	28	12.0
Total*	27	12.9	57	24.5

*$p<0.002$; relative risk, 0.51; 95% confidence interval: 0.32, 0.81. From Ref. 6, with permission.

Table 3. Combined neurologic endpoints of transient ischaemic attack, transient monocular blindness, and stroke (non-fatal and fatal) for ipsilateral events only

| | Surgical | | Medical | |
	No.	%	No.	%
No. of patients	211		233	
Transient ischaemic attack	6	2.8	15	6.4
Transient monocular blindness	1	0.5	11	4.7
Stroke*	10	4.7	22	9.4
Total**	17	8.0	48	20.6

*$p = 0.056$.
**$p < 0.001$; relative risk, 0.38; 95% confidence interval: 0.22, 0.67.
From Ref. 6, with permission.

The temporal distribution of neurological outcome events over the duration of follow-up was determined by construction of Kaplan-Meier survival curves, where survival was defined as time until first neurological event. Data for ipsilateral events are summarized in Fig. 1. The numbers (*n*) of patients remaining event free and on study at the beginning of each 12-month interval are provided under the graph. Treatment group comparisons by the log-rank test demonstrated significant differences in favour of the surgical group ($p < 0.001$).

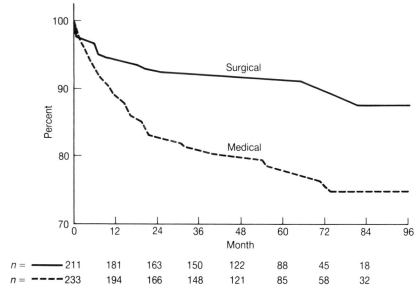

Fig. 1. Event free rates for first ipsilateral stroke and transient ischaemic attack including transient monocular blindness. These are Kaplan-Meier curves of an analysis of time until first event for surgical and medical groups. The numbers (*n*) of patients remaining event free and on study at the beginning of each 12-month period are provided under the graph. Treatment group comparisons by the log-rank test demonstrated significant differences in favour of the surgical group ($p < 0.001$). The relative risk (surgical *vs* medical) was 0.38 (95% confidence interval: 0.22, 0.67). From Ref. 6, with permission.

STROKE AND DEATH ANALYSIS

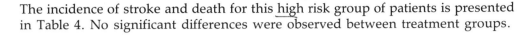

The incidence of stroke and death for this high risk group of patients is presented in Table 4. No significant differences were observed between treatment groups.

DISCUSSION

The results of this clinical trial indicate that carotid endarterectomy when combined with optimal medical management reduces the incidence of ipsilateral neurological outcome events in high-risk male patients with arteriographically confirmed asymptomatic carotid stenosis. In addition, the incidence of ipsilateral stroke alone (Table 3) was significantly ($p=0.056$) reduced in the surgically managed group. However, when the four perioperative deaths (1.9%) were added to this analysis, the 30-day perioperative stroke and death rates between groups were not significantly different. Emphasizing the importance of maintaining low perioperative complication rates among operative patients, our current clinical evaluation of these patients also includes a rigorous evaluation of the coronary circulation using stress-thallium scans as indicated.[12] Carotid endarterectomy is indicated in patients with high-grade asymptomatic stenosis who have received clearance for the risks of coronary artery disease and are expected to live 5 or more years. Although this trial was unable to confirm the influence of carotid endarterectomy on the combined incidence of stroke and death, a modest effect could not be excluded because of this trial's sample size. However, data from the ACAS trial[5] with an anticipated sample size of 1500 patients may be able to address this important question.

This trial included transient ischaemic attacks (TIA) with stroke alone in the analysis of neurological outcomes. The investigators determined that this was justified because of the importance of TIA as an indicator or predictor of stroke. Furthermore, differences between transient ischaemic attack and stroke with or without minimal disability may constitute an unnecessarily rigid distinction in view of their similarity in clinical definition,[13] the subsequent risk of stroke after transient events,[1-3] and the acknowledged 30–40% incidence of abnormal computed tomography and magnetic resonance scans in patients with transient ischaemic attack alone.[14,15] The

Table 4. Stroke, stroke death, and all other deaths*

| | Surgical | | Medical | |
	No.	%	No.	%
No. of patients	211		233	
Non-fatal stroke	17	8.0	25	10.7
Stroke death	1	0.5	4	1.7
MI/cardiac/sudden**	44	20.9	47	20.2
Other medical	19	9.0	17	7.3
Unknown	6	2.8	10	4.3
Total*	87	41.2	103	44.2

*No significant difference (relative risk, 0.92; 95% confidence interval: 0.69, 1.22).
**Includes four perioperative deaths; MI = myocardial infarction.
From Ref. 6, with permission.

NASCET[1] and ECST[2] trial results confirmed that transient ischaemic attack in the presence of high-grade stenosis is an important factor for predicting stroke. Patients with transient ischaemic attack or non-disabling stroke, ipsilateral to a 70% or greater carotid stenosis, were reported to have a 26% incidence of stroke, on lifetable analysis, during the first 2 years of follow-up. An analysis of relevant data (Fig. 1) from our trial demonstrated that 26 of the 32 ipsilateral strokes occurred during the first 2 years of the clinical trial. Furthermore, as observed in our studies of the medical treatment group, one-half of the neurological outcome events were strokes, which were not preceded by transient ischaemic attack.

Surgical complications included an operative mortality of 1.9%, a permanent stroke rate of 2.4% and associated strokes due to arteriography of 0.4%. Although the combined perioperative stroke and death rate of 4.7% was higher than the 3.0% cited by Callow and colleagues,[16] multiple individual institutional reports have demonstrated performance well within the 3% combined stroke and death rate.[17-21] As a more rigorous clinical review of patients' coronary risk factors is exercised, many institutions will achieve extremely low or 0% mortality. These institutional reports further emphasize the potential value of carotid endarterectomy in selected patients with high-grade asymptomatic carotid stenosis.

One approach to the performance of carotid endarterectomy for asymptomatic stenosis has been the identification of a high-risk subset of patients who might benefit from operative intervention. Degree of stenosis has emerged as an important risk factor. Chambers and Norris[22] prospectively followed 500 asymptomatic patients with carotid bruits and observed ischaemic cerebral vascular events in 18% (5.5% strokes) of patients with more than 75% reduction in cross-sectional area in the first year and 22% for the first 2 years. In patients with stenoses of less than 75%, the rates were less than 3% and 6% for the first 1 and 2 years, respectively. Although the threshold lesion in this trial was a 50% diameter reducing stenosis on arteriography, the added requirement of a positive non-invasive study in most patients resulted in a comparably significant stenosis approximating a 75% area reduction. This probably accounts for the comparability of ipsilateral neurological event rates between the Toronto data[22] and this clinical trial.[5] Exclusion of patients with high-grade stenosis or rapid progression in the severity of stenosis from a recently reported clinical trial,[23] allocating them to surgical management, may have neutralized potentially significant differences between the surgical and medical groups.

In summary, we conclude that carotid endarterectomy, when combined with optimal medical management including antiplatelet therapy, can reduce the incidence of ipsilateral neurological outcome events in high-risk male patients with arteriographically confirmed asymptomatic carotid stenosis. However, caution must be observed and all patients are not considered operative candidates. The primary cause of death in these patients remains coronary atherosclerosis and this must be carefully evaluated prior to considering operation in the asymptomatic patient. Each surgeon also has the responsibility of defining by local clinical audit the institutional complication rate for carotid endarterectomy. Without thorough clinical evaluation and knowledge of the morbidity and mortality of carotid endarterectomy, operative intervention can not be recommended routinely. Although carotid endarterectomy did not appear to have a significant effect on the combined incidence of stroke and death in this study, a firm conclusion on this important aspect of treatment must await publication of data from clinical trials involving larger numbers of patients.

REFERENCES

1. NASCET Collaborators: Beneficial effect of carotid endarterectomy in symptomatic patients with high-grade carotid stenosis. N Engl J Med 325: 445–453, 1991
2. European Carotid Surgery Trialists' (ECST) Collaborative Group: MRC European Carotid Surgery interim results for symptomatic patients with severe (70–99%) or mild (0–29%) carotid stenosis. Lancet 337: 1235–1243, 1991
3. Mayberg MR, Wilson SE, Yatsu F et al.: Carotid endarterectomy and prevention of cerebral ischemia in symptomatic carotid stenosis. JAMA 266: 3289–3294, 1991
4. Veterans Administration Cooperative Study Group: Role of carotid endarterectomy in asymptomatic carotid stenosis. Stroke 17: 534–548, 1986
5. The Asymptomatic Carotid Atherosclerosis Study Group: Study design for randomized prospective trial of carotid endarterectomy for asymptomatic atherosclerosis. Stroke 20: 844–849, 1989
6. Hobson RW, Weiss DG, Fields WS et al.: Efficacy of carotid endarterectomy for asymptomatic carotid stenosis. N Engl J Med 328: 221–227, 1993
7. Gee W, Mehigan JT, Wylie EJ: Measurement of collateral cerebral hemispheric blood pressure by ocular pneumoplethysmography. Am J Surg 130: 121–127, 1975
8. Blackshear WM Jr, Phillips DJ, Thiele BL et al.: Detection of carotid occlusive disease by ultrasonic imaging and pulsed Doppler spectrum analysis. Surgery 86: 698–706, 1979
9. Krupski WC, Weiss DG, Rapp JH, Corson JD, Hobson RW, and the VA Cooperative Asymptomatic Carotid Artery Stenosis Study Group: Adverse effects of aspirin in the treatment of asymptomatic carotid artery stenosis: Complications related to high and low dose protocols. J Vasc Surg 16: 588–600, 1992
10. Hobson RW, Krupski WC, Weiss DG and the VA Cooperative Asymptomatic Carotid Artery Stenosis Study Group: Influence of aspirin in the management of asymptomatic carotid stenosis. J Vasc Surg 17: 257–265, 1992
11. Towne JB, Weiss DG, Hobson RW II: First phase report of Veterans Administration asymptomatic carotid stenosis study — operative morbidity and mortality. J Vasc Surg 11: 252–259, 1990
12. Eagle KA, Coley CM, Newell JB et al.: Continuing clinical and thallium data optimizes preoperative assessment of cardiac risk before major vascular surgery. Ann Intern Med 110: 859–866, 1989
13. Toole JF. The Willis Lecture: Transient ischemic attacks, scientific method, and new realities. Stroke 22: 99–104, 1991
14. Perrone P, Candelise L, Scott G, DeGrandi C, Scialfa G: CT evaluation in patients with transient ischemic attack: Correlation between clinical and angiographic findings. Eur Neurol 18: 217–221, 1979
15. Awad I, Modic M, Little JR, Furlan AJ, Weistein M: Focal parenchymal lesions in transient ischemic attacks: Correlation of computed tomography and magnetic resonance imaging. Stroke 17: 399–403, 1985
16. Callow AD, Caplan LR, Correll JW et al.: Carotid endarterectomy: What is its current status? Am J Med 85: 835–838, 1988
17. Thompson JE, Patman RD, Talkington CM. Asymptomatic carotid bruits — long-term outcome of patients having endarterectomy compared to unoperated controls. Ann Surg 188: 308–316, 1978
18. Wylie EJ. Is an asymptomatic carotid stenosis a surgical lesion? In Arteriopathies Cerebrales Extra-craniennes Asymptomatiques, Courbier R, Jausseran JM, Reggi M (Eds). pp. 231–240, Lyon, France: Médicale Observal, 1980

19. Moore DJ, Miles RD, Gooley NA, Sumner DS. Noninvasive assessment of stroke risk in asymptomatic and nonhemispheric patients with suspected carotid disease. Five-year follow-up of 294 unoperated and 81 operated patients. Ann Surg 202: 491–504, 1985
20. Treiman RL, Cosman DV, Foran RF, Levin PM, Cohen JL: The risk of carotid endarterectomy for the asymptomatic patient: An argument for prophylactic operation. Ann Vasc Surg 4: 29–33, 1990
21. Anderson R, Hobson RW, Padberg FT *et al.*: Carotid endarterectomy for asymptomatic carotid stenosis: A ten year experience with 120 procedures in a fellowship program. Ann Vasc Surg 5: 111–115, 1991
22. Chambers BR, Norris JW: Outcome in patients with asymptomatic neck bruits. N Engl J Med 315: 860–865, 1986
23. CASANOVA Study Group: Carotid surgery versus medical therapy in asymptomatic carotid stenosis. Stroke 22: 1229–1235, 1991

APPENDIX: STUDY ORGANIZATION

Planning Committee

Robert W. Hobson II, MD, Study Chairman
William S. Fields, MD
Andrew Gage, MD
Jerry Goldstone, MD
Clair Haakenson, RPh, MS
Wesley S. Moore, MD
Jonathan B. Towne, MD
David G. Weiss, PhD
Creighton B. Wright, MD

Executive Committee

Robert W. Hobson II, MD, Study Chairman
Cindy Colling, RPh, MS, Study Pharmacist
William S. Fields, MD, Consultant in Neurology
Jerry Goldstone, MD, Consultant in Vascular Surgery
Wesley S. Moore, MD, Consultant in Vascular Surgery
Jonathan B. Towne, MD, Consultant in Vascular Surgery
David G. Weiss, PhD, Assistant Chief, CSPCC Perry Point
Creighton B. Wright, MD, Consultant in Vascular Surgery

Study Administrative Coordinator

Sandy Rossos, MS, Adele George, RN

Data Monitoring Board

Allan D. Callow, MD, PhD, Chairman
Roger E. Flora, PhD
James C. Grotta, MD
Anthony Imparato, MD

Central Neuroradiologist

In Sook Song, MD

Endpoint Committee

Louis R. Caplan, MD
William S. Fields, MD
Jerry Goldstone, MD
Wesley S. Moore, MD
Creighton Wright, MD

VA Cooperative Studies Programme Coordinating Centre

C. James Klett, PhD, Joseph F. Collins, ScD, David G. Weiss, PhD, Peggy Jackson, Dorothy Morson, Bertha D. Carter, Barbara McMullen, Robert Kuhn, PhD, Barbara Miller, MS, Mike Lee, MS, Diana Preston, Debra Davis, Linda Linzy, Cathy Lucas

VA Cooperative Studies Programme

Daniel Deykin, MD, Janet Gold, Ping Huang, PhD

Participating Centres

Atlanta, GA VAMC

Robert B. Smith, MD, John Ammons, MD, Rita Giannetti, RN

Boston, MA VAMC

Rudolph W. Vollman, MD, Willard Johnson, MD, Russell Butler, MD, Carlos Kase, MD, Janis Hamilton, RN, Nancy Walker, RN

Buffalo, NY VAMC

Andrew A. Gage, MD, C. Steven Powell, MD, Emilio Soria, MD, Walter A. Olszewski, MD, Ireneo Gutierrez, MD, Delores E. Young, RN, Karen Burch, RN

East Orange, NJ VAMC

Thomas G. Lynch, MD, Frank Padberg, MD, Said Shanawani, MD, Dolores A. Johnson, RN, Carolyn Rogers, RN

Iowa City, IA VAMC

Loren F. Hiratzka, MD, John Corson, MD, William T. Talman, MD, Cheryl Martin, RN, Vickie B. Griffith, RN, John Yutzy, RN, Brenda Lutes, RN

Little Rock, AR VAMC

Bernard W. Thompson, MD, Diane Morgan, RN, Colette McDonald, RN

Los Angeles, CA (Sepulveda) VAMC

J. Dennis Baker, MD, E. Jeffrey Metter, MD, Nadine Rabey, AS, DeEtte Dix, PA

Milwaukee, WI (Wood) VAMC

Jonathan B. Towne, MD, Dennis Bandyk, MD, Varun K. Saxena, MD, John Navine, RN, Kathy Catarozoli, RN, Debra Lanza, RN, Pat Parson, RN

San Francisco, CA VAMC

William C. Krupski, MD, Joseph Rapp, MD, Frank Sharp, MD, Sande Perez, RN

Tucson, AZ VAMC

Jerry Goldstone, MD, Victor Bernhard, MD, Enrique Labadie, MD, Martha Nash, RN, Barbara Phelps, RN, Jennifer Vance, RN, Gary Anderson, VS

West Los Angeles (Wadsworth) VAMC

R. Eugene Zierler, MD, Bruce Stabile, MD, Samuel E. Wilson, MD, Stanley Cohen, MD, Lynne Emma, RN, Cathy Hubbert, RN

Cooperative Studies Programme Clinical Research Pharmacy Coordinating Centre

Clair Haakenson, RPh, MS, Dennis Toussaint, RPh, MS, Larry Young, RPh, MS, Cindy Colling, RPh, MS

Asymptomatic Carotid Atherosclerosis Study

James F. Toole

Between 1970 and 1989, mortality for stroke in the USA declined steadily at the rate of about 5% per annum. Disappointingly, morbidity did not decline at a similar rate so that each year about 450 000 new symptomatic infarctions occur, increasing the prevalence of disabled survivors. Because of this pool of disabled survivors, the cost of stroke to the nation is estimated to exceed 15 billion dollars per year and is increasing. Cerebral infarction accounts for about 85% of strokes; of these 50% are thought to be the result of carotid bifurcation atherosclerosis. This has excited intense interest in carotid endarterectomy as a means for reduction of stroke risk. The customary practice has been to await the onset of transient ischaemic attacks (TIAs), which cause patients to seek medical attention as the means to identify those at excess risk. However, with the advent of non-invasive systems—mainly ultrasound—for evaluation of the carotid bifurcation many physicians now suspect that endarterectomy should be performed before TIAs have occurred in order to prevent TIAs and unheralded stroke. The reasons for this are several:

1. nearly half the cerebral infarctions (CIs) due to carotid lesions occur without preceding TIAs;
2. 10–15% of these infarctions are silent;
3. TIAs are not necessarily 'benign' and many who have apparently complete recovery demonstrate residual infarctions on brain imaging;
4. operative complications are higher in patients with symptomatic stenosis.

Most of our knowledge of the natural history of asymptomatic stenosis is derived from longitudinal studies of unoperated stenotic arteries contralateral to endarterectomies for symptomatic disease. Of patients having endarterectomy for symptomatic carotid artery atherosclerosis, 30–40% have greater than 50% stenosis of the asymptomatic, contralateral carotid artery.[1-4] In the distribution of the previously asymptomatic carotid artery, TIAs occurred in 3–18% and CIs in up to 3% of patients available for follow-up during 1–20 years.[5-9] In Podore's retrospective study, there was an annual stroke rate of 0.9% and an overall 4.5% incidence of CIs on the asymptomatic side. The combined annual cerebral infarction and TIA rate was 4% on the asymptomatic side.[10] In other studies, annual rates of combined TIA and stroke in the distribution of the asymptomatic carotid are 1.5–7.4%. Mortality rates are consistently in the 4–6% per year range, usually resulting from coronary artery disease.[9,11-14] In a prospective study using Doppler to identify carotid stenosis, Barnes et al. found that CI occurred on the side of stenosis in 1.6% and TIA in 7.9%.[15]

Declining operative morbidity and mortality from endarterectomy performed by experienced surgeons has encouraged many physicians to recommend surgical intervention for asymptomatic patients,[8,11,16] because their surgical risk is distinctly less than that for the TIA group. In contrast, others have pointed out the excessive risk for coronary death (5–10% per year) of these patients so restrict longevity that endarterectomy for stroke prevention is not justified.[17]

Furthermore, the natural history of carotid occlusion is not a benign one. In one prospective study of 47 patients with carotid occlusion causing mild or no neurologic phenomena, at the time of occlusion, 11 patients (23.5%) subsequently suffered cerebral infarction of which seven were ipsilateral to the carotid occlusion for a stroke rate distal to the occluded internal carotid artery of likelihood of ipsilateral cerebral infarction in individuals with high-grade stenosis or occlusion followed for 3 years.[18]

Lastly, antiplatelet therapy has not been shown to be effective in a properly designed prospective in asymptomatic patients with carotid stenosis as it has in symptomatic patients. Consequently, the Asymptomatic Carotid Artery Study (ACAS) was initiated.[11]

The Asymptomatic Carotid Artery Study is a prospective, multicentre, randomized clinical trial designed to determine whether the addition of carotid endarterectomy to aspirin plus risk factor modification reduces the incidence of TIA, retinal and cerebral infarction in patients with asymptomatic carotid stenosis. In the USA and Canada, 38 clinical centres are participating in this study funded by the US Public Health Service NINDS.

Patients who have unilateral or bilateral surgically accessible stenosis of the common or internal carotid artery of at least 60% diameter stenosis, patients who have never had TIA/stroke symptoms ipsilateral to the stenosis and, with respect to the contralateral artery, not had a stroke or TIA within the last 45 days, may be eligible. All patients receive counselling and interventions for risk factor reduction which includes hypertension, obesity, tobacco abuse, and other recognized risk factors for strokes. All the patients receive one tablet of aspirin (325 mg) daily; one-half are randomly assigned to undergo a carotid endarterectomy.

PRIMARY OBJECTIVES

1. To determine whether the addition of carotid endarterectomy to aspirin 325 mg + best medical management will reduce the incidence of TIA and CI in asymptomatic patients with haemodynamically significant carotid stenosis.

2. To determine whether endarterectomy for asymptomatic patients provides an increment of safety and prophylaxis which exceeds that of surgery deferred until the patient becomes symptomatic.

3. To determine the incidence to TIA and CI not only in the hemisphere of the randomized artery but also in the control hemisphere and vertebrobasilar arterial distribution.

SECONDARY OBJECTIVES

1. To determine the surgical success in lesion removal and the incidence of recurrent carotid stenosis following carotid endarterectomy.

2. To determine the rate of progression (or regression) of carotid atherosclerosis in the medically treated group and in the control carotid arterial system.

3. To determine incidence of coronary artery events (angina pectoris, non-fatal and fatal myocardial infarction) during follow-up.

The original study utilized a three-step aspirin dose regimen starting with a dose of 1200 mg daily. The final aspirin protocol is for all patients to receive low dose aspirin, 325 mg daily. Enteric-coated aspirin may be prescribed at physician discretion.

Cranial computed tomography (CCT) is performed on *all* randomized patients at entry into the study. Patients having a verified end-point will also receive a clinically indicated CCT. Each patient, at completion of his/her 5-year follow-up, will receive an exit CCT.

The ACAS has included a detailed method for accounting for or following non-randomized eligible patients. The minimum eligibility/baseline data and reason for non-randomization are documented on all patients of an ACAS physician who are probably eligible but who for any reason are not randomized. If consent is given, these patients are followed on a schedule corresponding to the telephone follow-up schedule of randomized patients.

Patients can be randomized if Doppler shift in the stenotic artery exceeds the previously established 95% confidence interval for that artery.[16] All patients randomized to surgery receive an artereiogram in addition. Repeat Doppler studies are required at verified end-point or at exit.

All patients are scheduled to be seen for a 1-month follow-up visit, designed to coincide with the 30-day postoperative visit for surgical patients (42-days post-randomization for the medical group.) Follow-up continues until death of the patient or for a minimum of five years. For the first 2 years of the study, beginning 3 months after randomization, follow-up includes clinic visits every 6 months for comprehensive evaluation including a physical and neurological examination, Doppler, event detection questionnaire, and drug counts. Questionnaire by telephone for event detection and adherence data are undertaken at 3-month intervals after each clinic visit. For the last 3 years, follow-up is similar, except that the Doppler exam is done annually; CCT is performed at study entry and exit, or after a verified end-point.

Quality assurance is a major component in the study and includes training and certification of personnel, monitoring morbidity and mortality rates by surgeon[12] and institution, central evaluation of samples of angiograms, Doppler,[16] OPG-Gee, CCT, and external blinded verification of all suspected end-points.

More than 1315 patients have been enrolled in this study as of 31 October 1992; the goal is 1500. With the accrual rate currently at approximately 40 patients per month, recruitment is projected to be completed by February 1993.

The baseline characteristics of the first 1315 patients indicate that there is a male to female ratio of 2 : 1; approximately 85% of the patients are 60 and older and half are between the ages of 60 and 69. About one-fourth have had a previous hemispheric event contralateral to the study artery and one-fifth have had a previous contralateral endarterectomy. Sixty-nine percent of the patients were found to have a bruit associated with the study artery. Recognized risk factors for stroke such as hypertension, obesity, etc. are balanced between the two treatment groups.

The primary analysis will be the comparison of the probability of cerebrovascular events in the surgically and medically treated groups after 5-year follow-up; a primary end-point is a verified TIA or cerebral infarction occurring in the distribution of the randomized artery, or any TIA, stroke, or death in the perioperative period. Major secondary analyses will be stroke in the distribution of the randomized artery, TIA/stroke in any distribution, all-cause mortality, comparisons of other morbidity such as myocardial infarction, analysis according to treatment actually received (instead of treatment assigned), and analysis for certain high risk groups. Comparison will also be made for different lengths of follow-up periods. Besides primary and secondary hypotheses being evaluated, ancillary findings in such areas as CCT, pathology, Doppler/angiogram correlation, progression of stenosis, TIA and stroke, etc. will provide valuable information for the management of patients.

EXCLUSIONS

1. Patients with asymptomatic bilateral stenoses greater than 60% are eligible. If two arteries are eligible for randomization, the artery selected for randomization is the artery with the greater degree of stenosis as determined by angiography, if available. If an angiogram is not available, the artery selected is the artery with the higher peak systolic frequency on the Doppler examination. If both arteries have exactly the same degree of stenosis, the left artery is randomized. (The number of eligible arteries was added as a randomization stratum.)

2. The eligible age range is 40–79 years.

3. Only distal stenosis with minimal residual lumen (MRL) less than the MRL of the operable stenosis is reason for exclusion.

4. Cerebral aneurysm, arteriovenous malformation, or other abnormal angiographic findings exclude the patient only if the ACAS physician feels the condition increases the risk of morbidity or mortality, or is a contraindication to endarterectomy.

5. Patients are excluded for any other medical problem or medical therapy, such as anticoagulant therapy, contraindicating aspirin.

ACKNOWLEDGEMENTS

This paper was supported by USPHS National Institute of Neurological Disorders & Stroke Grant No NS22611.

REFERENCES

1. The CASANOVA Study Group: Carotid surgery versus medical therapy in asymptomatic carotid stenosis. Stroke 22: 1229–1235, 1991
2. Warlow C: Carotid endarterectomy: does it work? Stroke 15: 1068–1076, 1984

3. European Carotid Surgery Trialists' Collaborative Group: MRC European Carotid Surgery Trial: Interim results for symptomatic patients with severe (70–99%) or with mild (0–29%) carotid stenosis. Lancet 337: 1235–1243, 1991

4. Barnett JHM: North American Symptomatic Carotid Endarterectomy Trial (NASCET): Rationale and progress. *In* Current Critical Problems in Vascular Surgery, Veith FJ (Ed.). St Louis, Missouri: Quality Medical Publishing, pp. 573–576, 1989

5. North American Symptomatic Carotid Endarterectomy Trial (NASCET) Investigators: Clinical alert: Benefit of carotid endarterectomy for patients with high-grade stenosis of the internal carotid artery. National Institute of Neurological Disorders and Stroke, Stroke and Trauma Division. Stroke 22: 816–817, 1991

6. North American Symptomatic Carotid Endarterectomy Trial Collaborators: Beneficial effect of carotid endarterectomy in symptomatic patients with high-grade carotid stenosis. N Engl J Med 325: 445–453, 1991

7. Mayberg MR, Wilson SE, Yatsu F *et al.* for the Veterans Administration Cooperative Studies Program 309 Trialist Group: Carotid endarterectomy and prevention of cerebral ischemia in symptomatic carotid stenosis. JAMA 266: 3289–3294, 1991

8. Mayo Asymptomatic Carotid Endarterectomy Study Group: Effectiveness of carotid endarterectomy for asymptomatic carotid stenosis. Design of a clinical trial. Mayo Clin Proc 64: 887–904, 1989

9. Marler JR, Carotid endarterectomy clinical trials (editorial). Mayo Clin Proc 64: 1026–1028, 1989

10. Podore PC, DeWeese JA, May AG *et al.*: Asymptomatic contralateral carotid artery stenosis: a five year follow-up study following carotid endarterectomy. Surgery 88: 748–752, 1980

11. The Asymptomatic Carotid Atherosclerosis Study Group: Study Design for randomized prospective trial of carotid endarterectomy for asymptomatic atherosclerosis. Stroke 20: 844–849, 1989

12. Moore WS, Vescera CL, Robertson JT *et al.*: Selection process for participating surgeons in the Asymptomatic Carotid Atherosclerosis Study (ACAS). Stroke 22: 1353–1357, 1991

13. Hobson RW, Towne J: Carotid endarterectomy for asymptomatic carotid stenosis (editorial). Stroke 20: 575–576, 1980

14. Hobson RW, Weiss D, Fields W *et al.* and the VA Cooperative Study Group: Efficacy of carotid endarterectomy for asymptomatic carotid stenosis. N Engl J Med 328: 221–227, 1993

15. Barnes RW, Liebman PR, Marszalek PB *et al.*: The natural history of asymptomatic carotid disease in patients undergoing cardiovascular surgery. Surgery 90: 1075–1083, 1981

16. Howard G, Chambless LE, Baker WH *et al.*: A multicenter validation study of Doppler ultrasound versus angiogram. J Stroke Cerebrovasc Dis 1: 166–173, 1991

17. Norris JW, Zhu CZ: Silent stroke and carotid stenosis. Stroke 23: 483–485, 1992

18. Roederer GO, Langlois JE, Jager KA *et al.*: The natural history of carotid arterial disease in asymptomatic patients with cervical bruits. Stroke 15: 605–613, 1984

The Management of Asymptomatic Carotid Disease

G. Geroulakos, T. N. Sonecha and A. N. Nicolaides

INTRODUCTION

It is important to recognize that patients with asymptomatic carotid disease do not constitute a homogeneous group: the truly asymptomatic individuals, the patients with vertebrobasilar symptoms only, the patients without cerebrovascular symptoms but with symptoms indicating atherosclerotic disease elsewhere (e.g. claudication or angina) and the patients who have had a carotid endarterectomy in the past for focal hemispheric symptoms and are now asymptomatic with a stenosis on the unoperated side may have a different natural history in terms of transient ischaemic attacks (TIAs), stroke, death and operative risk. It is therefore necessary for reports dealing with asymptomatic carotid disease to clearly specify the types and selection of patients studied. In the past many authors have not made such distinctions.

It should also be recognized that cervical bruit or carotid bifurcation bruit (mid-cervical bruit) is not the same as internal carotid stenosis and may also be different in terms of natural history. Clinical assessment of a cervical or bifurcation bruit by auscultation cannot reliably indicate localization and severity of carotid bifurcation disease.

This report will deal with two types of asymptomatic carotid disease: (a) that which exists in individuals or patients who never had any focal hemispheric or vertebrobasilar symptoms and (b) that which is found in patients who in the past have had a carotid endarterectomy for focal hemispheric symptoms and are now asymptomatic with carotid stenosis on the unoperated side.

SIGNIFICANCE AND RISK

Clinical decisions for a particular group of patients depend upon the balance of risks as a result of the natural history or possible complication of a particular therapy, against the benefits of such therapy. Therefore, it follows that the natural history and potential risk/benefit of different therapeutic measures should be defined as accurately as possible.

'ASYMPTOMATIC' BRUIT

The finding of a cervical bruit by auscultation does not always indicate carotid bifurcation disease. Many such bruits may arise from the heart (e.g. aortic valve) or great vessels at the base of the neck (e.g. subclavian). Thus, only some of the cervical bruits are the result of carotid bifurcation disease. A bruit heard maximally in the mid-cervical region indicates a high likelihood of carotid bifurcation disease, but it does not necessarily indicate internal carotid stenosis, because it may arise from the external carotid artery. Furthermore, the absence of cervical or mid-cervical bruit does not exclude severe stenosis or occlusions. It is well established that stenosis of either external or internal carotid artery greater than 85% is often not associated with a bruit because of the diminished flow.

The presence of a cervical bruit indicates that internal carotid stenosis greater than 50% in diameter will be found in approximately 50% of such patients and stenosis greater than 75% will be found in 23%.[1] The presence of a bifurcation bruit indicates that internal carotid stenosis greater than 75% will be found in 75–90% of patients, the rest of the bruits arising from the external carotid.[2-4]

Two prospective epidemiological studies of the residents over 45 years old in Evans County, Georgia[5] and Framingham, Massachusetts[6] have found a carotid (mid-cervical) bruit prevalence of 4.4% and 4.8% respectively (Table 1). This prevalence rose to 7% in people over the age of 65. Although there was a fourfold increase in the incidence of stroke and a twofold increase in the incidence of death from cardiovascular disease in the population with bruit, the actual incidence of stroke was low: 2.3% and 3% per year. In addition, only 30% of strokes were due to infarction ipsilateral to the bruit. These population studies indicate that bruit *per se* is not a good indicator of infarction in the territory of the affected carotid artery.

Studies of the natural history based on the presence of a bruit suggest that a bifurcation bruit as opposed to cervical bruit doubles the risk of developing symptoms.[7] Nevertheless the risk of hemispheric TIAs (1.6–7% per year) and stroke (0.7–4.6% per year) is low. The ratio of TIAs/stroke was on average 1.3/1 indicating that approximately 65% of patients who developed cerebrovascular symptoms presented with a TIA and had a carotid endarterectomy in most centres. Those who developed a stroke did so in most instances without any 'warning' TIAs. In the studies the incidence of death from myocardial infarction (1.9–6.8% per year) was 1–4.5 times higher than stroke.

Furthermore, as stated in some studies, TIAs and stroke were not always related to the cerebral territory appropriate to the carotid bruit.[7,8] Thus, studies on the natural history of patients with asymptomatic carotid bruit demonstrate that bruit is not a good indicator of patients at high risk of stroke, but rather of patients with an increased incidence of generalized atherosclerotic disease and death from myocardial infarction.

INTERNAL CAROTID STENOSIS

Although patients with asymptomatic carotid stenosis have overall a very low risk of stroke, there is general agreement that a subgroup of patients with a high grade stenosis has a significantly increased incidence of cerebrovascular events. Roederer *et al.*, using duplex scan followed up 167 asymptomatic patients with carotid stenosis for a mean of 3 years. During follow-up, ten patients became symptomatic (six with TIAs, and four with strokes). While no spontaneous strokes occurred in patients with a stenosis less than 80%, the incidence was 12.5% in patients with an 80–99% stenosis.[9] Comparable results were more recently reported by Norris *et al.* in a prospective study of 696 patients with asymptomatic carotid stenosis who were

Table 1. Prospective epidemiological studies of cervical bruits and stroke/death risk

Study	Cervical bruit	Number (age > 44)	Prevalence of bruit (%)	Mean follow-up (%)	Incidence of stroke	Relative risk of stroke in the presence of bruit	Relative risk of death in the presence of bruit Cardiovascular deaths	
							Men	Women
Heyman et al., 1980[5]	Present	72	2.3	4.4	6	4:1	3.4:1	1.9:1
	Absent	1548	0.57					
Wolf et al., 1981[6]	Present	171	3.0	4.8	4	3:1	1.7:1	1.9:1
	Absent	3538	1.0					

followed up for a mean period of 4 months.[10] The annual stroke rate was 1.3% in patients with carotid stenosis ⩽75% and 3.3% in those with stenosis >75%. Ipsilateral stroke rate was 2.5% in patients with >75% stenosis. In another natural history study, a cohort of 188 randomly selected asymptomatic patients with carotid artery disease was followed up for a mean of 4 years.[11] The incidence of TIAs and stroke in 129 patients who had <80% stenosis was 1.5% and 4.6% respectively. In the 59 patients with >80% stenosis, 7% suffered a TIA and an additional 7% a stroke.

These studies clearly indicate that carotid surgery can be of no value in patients with stenosis ⩽75%. Even in those with carotid stenosis >75%, the yearly stroke rate remained low. It is apparent that we cannot rely exclusively on the degree of stenosis to identify a high risk group.

PLAQUE CHARACTERIZATION

High resolution B-mode ultrasound has the major advantage over arteriography in that it can be used to characterize atherosclerotic plaques. In 1983 Reilly proposed the ultrasonic classification of carotid plaques as homogeneous or heterogeneous.[12] The distinction was based on the echogenicity of non-carotid calcified tissue. Pathological studies performed on plaques with homogeneous ultrasound pattern which were removed from carotid endarterectomy patients demonstrated a predominantly fibrotic collagenous composition with no evidence of haemorrhage. By contrast, there was a strong correlation between heterogeneous plaques, intraplaque haemorrhage and a high lipid and cholesterol content.

An expansion of the above classification was presented in 1988 by Gray-Weale *et al.*[13] Four plaque types were defined: Type 1: dominantly echolucent, Type 2: substantially echolucent with small areas of echogenicity, Type 3: dominantly echogenic with small areas of echolucency, and Type 4: uniformly echogenic plaques. From the same group, Steffen *et al.* demonstrated that in symptomatic carotids, irrespective of the degree of stenosis, Types 1 and 2 were predominant, whereas in the asymptomatic patients, the most common lesions were Types 3 and 4.[14] Geroulakos *et al.* studied symptomatic and asymptomatic patients with plaques producing >70% stenosis and found that the finding of Steffen *et al.* holds for this subgroup with severe stenosis.[15] Interestingly, there was a more prominent shift to the echolucent types of plaques in the symptomatic high grade stenosis group than what was previously reported for symptomatic patients irrespective of the degree of stenosis. These results support the hypothesis that echolucent plaques are unstable and tend to embolize.

There are very few reports on the natural history of carotid stenosis in relation to plaque morphology. Johnson *et al.*, focussing on the contribution of plaque characterization to the development of symptoms, studied prospectively with real-time B-mode ultrasound 297 carotid arteries in asymptomatic patients for 3 years.[16] At the end of follow-up, only three patients of the original 42 with echolucent plaques and more than 75% stenosis remained asymptomatic. Twenty-six of the original 42 patients with the same degree of stenosis and echodense plaques developed symptoms.

In another study on the ultrasonic features of carotid plaque and the risk of subsequent neurologic deficit,[17] Sterpetti showed that the severity of stenosis and the presence of heterogeneous plaque were statistically correlated with the occurrence of new deficits. It is noteworthy that multivariate analysis confirmed that the ultrasonic pattern and degree of stenosis were independent variables.

The ability of B-mode real-time ultrasound to identify individuals at a high risk seems to be well established. Future studies which fail to examine the important aspect of plaque morphology should be considered obsolete and would give incomplete information on the natural history of asymptomatic carotid stenosis.

CEREBRAL COLLATERAL CIRCULATION

The progress of asymptomatic carotid stenosis to total occlusion is not always followed by cerebrovascular events. Obviously, the severity of carotid stenosis *per se* is less relevant for the final brain perfusion than the configuration of the Circle of Willis.

Meager *et al.* studied 50 patients with TIAs who underwent computed tomographic (CT) scanning and cerebral angiography.[18] In 15 patients infarcts showed on CT scan. Only 14% of these silent infarcts occurred in patients with normal collateral reserve capacity while 71% occurred in patients with impaired reserve capacity. The identification of a high risk group should also include the detection of an inadequate cerebrovascular reserve as a result of an incomplete Circle of Willis.

Recent reports have suggested that the assessment of the intracranial circulation by transcranial Doppler is a feasible non-invasive and reproducible technique that allows selection and quantification of the patients with true cerebrovascular insufficiency.[19] This may prove to have great importance in predicting clinical outcome.

THE CONTRALATERAL NON-OPERATED CAROTID ARTERY STENOSIS

Studies on the natural history and optimal management at the unoperated asymptomatic carotid artery contralateral to endarterectomy are few.

Roederer *et al.* followed 134 patients after unilateral carotid endarterectomy for a period extending to 48 months.[9] Four patients of eight with >80% stenosis developed TIAs (7%). No patient had a stroke in this population.

Langsfield *et al.* studied the natural history of the contralateral artery in 289 patients who underwent carotid endarterectomy with a mean follow-up of 22 months and the carotid arteries of 130 patients who had no surgical treatment and had been symptom-free.[20] In the contralateral asymptomatic group, 31 patients (10.7%) developed symptoms with ten patients (3.5%) having stroke. Fourteen of 130 (10.8%) patients in the primary asymptomatic group developed symptoms with only two strokes occurring (1.4%).

Steffen *et al.* reported on the carotid plaque ultrasound appearance.[14] Three groups were studied: (a) asymptomatic vessels in asymptomatic patients ($n = 184$), (b) symptomatic vessels in symptomatic patients ($n = 134$), and (c) asymptomatic contralateral vessels in symptomatic patients ($n = 134$). In symptomatic arteries echolucent plaques were predominant while in the asymptomatic arteries echogenic plaques were prominent.

Evaluation of the asymptomatic contralateral vessel in the symptomatic patients showed a pattern of plaque type distribution between the other two groups. These data demonstrate that although there may be some difference between asymptomatic carotid stenosis in patients who had contralateral carotid endarterectomy and carotid stenosis in truly asymptomatic individuals, the overall incidence of strokes is so low that there is no obvious advantage to prophylactic surgery. These patients however should be educated in the importance of minor warning signs of threatening stroke.

CARDIAC ASSESSMENT OF PATIENTS WITH EXTRACRANIAL CEREBROVASCULAR DISEASE

Coronary artery disease and extracranial cerebrovascular disease not uncommonly coexist. As many as 50% of patients with cerebrovascular disease will have symptomatic coronary artery disease[21-23] and thus the natural history of these two disease states is clearly intertwined.[24,25]

The risk of myocardial infarction after carotid endarterectomy has long been recognized. Indeed, myocardial infarction is the most common cause of both early and late mortality after carotid endarterectomy. Even in patients with asymptomatic carotid stenosis, the mortality from myocardial infarction is four times higher than from stroke.[6]

With the increasing realization that a substantial number of patients presenting with carotid bifurcation disease may have coexistent coronary artery disease, clearly more attention needs to be directed towards the detection of the latter. Unfortunately, it is expensive and not practical to undertake routine coronary angiography in order to achieve this. A non-invasive and relatively inexpensive screening test that could identify patients likely to have multivessel coronary disease or left main stem disease would enable the clinician to consider coronary angiography in selected cases.

The ECG-chest wall mapping (CWM) stress test is a non-invasive method that has been claimed to be predictive not only of the presence of coronary artery disease but also of its severity in terms of the number of coronary artery territories involved. The technique of chest wall mapping is based on the work of Fox and coworkers[26-27] which was subsequently modified and validated in our department. Briefly, CWM of ST-segment changes during and after exercise, and of Q waves at rest was performed using 16 electrocardiographic electrodes and bicylce ergometry in 150 patients presenting with chest pain suggestive of angina. All patients underwent coronary angiography.[28] By using multiple criteria (ST-segment depression, Q waves at rest and appearance of inverted U waves) the diagnostic accuracy was improved. The principle of this test is based on the observation that ECG changes obtained with an electrode at a point on the chest wall reflect changes in the myocardium immediately beneath that point. The position of the leads was such that they would monitor changes in the distribution of all three major coronary arteries, thus providing spatial information. The electrodes were positioned in four vertical rows. Rows A and B were along lines going through the right and left sternoclavicular joints respectively, C along the anterior axillary line and D on the back, 6 cm medial to the posterial axillary line. Electrode C3 was on the anterior axillary line at the fifth intercostal space corresponding to the conventional V5 position: this determined the horizontal levels of A3, B3 and D3. The distance between B3 and C3 was used to determine the distance between the horizontal rows.

The presence or absence of significant ($\geqslant$50% stenosis) coronary artery disease was detected with a sensitivity of 90% and a specificity of 88%. The identification of lesions in individual coronary arteries was also possible: there was a sensitivity of 98% and a specificity of 85% for lesions of the right coronary artery; and a sensitivity of 86% and a specificity of 80% for lesions of the circumflex artery. The absence of significant coronary artery disease and the presence of single, double or triple vessel disease was correctly predicted in 70% of patients. Errors occurred in 25% of patients because the disease was missed or falsely diagnosed in one coronary artery territory. Errors in more than one vessel occurred in only 5% of patients. Left main stem coronary disease present in 11 patients was in every case demonstrated as ECG changes in LAD/Diagonal and circumflex regions.[28]

In a pilot study involving 100 consecutive claudicants who underwent an ECG–CWM stress test, we found that approximately one-third of patients had a positive effort test, and in one-third of the latter, the test revealed the presence of multivessel disease.[29] They were selected for coronary angiography and left ventriculography which confirmed the presence of multivessel disease.

Subsequently, a study validating the ECG–CWM stress test in arteriopaths was performed.[30] When coronary angiography was performed in a series of 70 patients with two- or three-vessel coronary territory disease indicated by the ECG–CWM stress test, it was found that multivessel coronary disease was correctly predicted in 90%. The results should be interpreted with caution because coronary angiography was not performed in all patients irrespective of the outcome of the ECG–CWM stress test. However, a prospective follow-up of 144 arteriopaths demonstrated that ECG–CWM stress test indicating two- or three-vessel coronary disease can predict an increased cumulative cardiac event rate (47% at 7 years) in comparison with those with a negative test or one-vessel coronary territory disease (13% at 7 years).[31] Thus, identification of a subset of arteriopaths with an increased risk of myocardial infarction is possible using the non-invasive technique of ECG–CWM stress test which can fill the gap between clinical evaluation and coronary angiography.

On the basis of future studies, this may become a new method for the selection of patients for angiography. The patients who cannot attain the requisite level of haemodynamic stress necessary to obtain a meaningful result during the ECG–CWM stress test (30% of claudicants when bicyle ergometry is used) should be considered for dipyridamole 201-T1 scintigraphy, preferably using a quantitative approach.[32] The risk of an ischaemic cardiac event in patients with a redistribution defect has been shown to be higher in the perioperative period, particularly in the presence of clinical markers such as unstable angina, recent myocardial infarction, congestive heart failure (indicating poor left ventricular (LV) function) or diabetes mellitus.[33,34] On the other hand fixed defects on dipyridamole 201-T1 scan have been shown to correlate with long-term survival.[35]

Patients with an ECG–CWM stress test result indicative of multivessel coronary artery disease or dipyridamole 201-T1 scintigraphy suggestive of multisegment redistribution defects should be considered for coronary angiography with a view to prior myocardial revascularization before carotid endarterectomy is contemplated. This rather oversimplified approach is outlined only in order to provide a broad guideline but the management clearly has to be individualized for each patient according to the presenting clinical situation (e.g., this strategy would not be appropriate for patients with symptoms requiring urgent carotid operation in the presence of a threatening lesion).

The initial non-invasive cardiac assessment as depicted would obviate the need for coronary angiography in the majority of patients. Using this approach approximately only 15% of patients will require coronary angiography, i.e. those in whom the non-invasive tests suggest two- or three-vessel coronary disease. This is more cost-effective than coronary angiography being performed in patients with a positive conventional ECG stress test. Ambulatory ST-segment Holter monitoring and dipyridamole echocardiography would provide alternative means of non-invasive cardiac assessment leading to identification of patients at a higher risk of an ischaemic cardiac event, and indeed may complement the preoperative cardiac evaluation in selected cases.

MEDICAL TREATMENT OF CAROTID BIFURCATION DISEASE

A number of new studies have brought better understanding of the impact of aggressive risk factor intervention on the reduction of strokes and cerebral ischaemic attacks. A meta-analysis of 14 randomized trials of anti-hypertensive drugs involving 37 000 individuals for a mean treatment duration of five years showed that a reduction of the diastolic blood pressure by a mean of 5–6 mmHg is associated with about 35–40% less stroke and 20–25% less coronary artery disease. Non-vascular mortality appears unchanged.[36]

The place of antiplatelet therapy is well established in symptomatic carotid bifurcation disease. A review of 25 randomized trials showed a significant reduction of non-fatal stroke ($p < 0.001$) and non-fatal myocardial infarction ($p < 0.001$) in patients on antiplatelet treatment. Aspirin is now accepted as the standard antiplatelet treatment. Adding dipyridamole is of little or no value.[37,38] The appropriate dose of aspirin as secondary prophylaxis after cerebrovascular ischaemic events is not known and doses ranging from 75 mg to 1500 mg have been used in various trials.[39] However, it was emphasized that the balance of risk and benefit might be different for 'primary' prevention among people at a low risk if antiplatelet treatment produced even a small increase in the incidence of cerebral haemorrhage.[37] Asymptomatic carotid stenosis represents precisely a low risk group and there are no trials on the reduction of stroke by antiplatelet therapy. Despite this, many physicians recommend aspirin therapy because of the reduction (40%) in deaths from myocardial infarction.

The place of lipid lowering agents in patients with carotid artery disease has not yet been determined. Some preliminary evidence suggests that a marked reduction of total and low density lipoprotein cholesterol and serum fibrinogen results in significant plaque volume reduction.[40] However, in view of the reduction in coronary events and regression in coronary plaques, aggressive lipid lowering therapy is recommended.[41-44]

Cigarette smoking is correlated with extracranial carotid artery plaque thickness. This effect is independent of age, hypertension and diabetes. Smoking abatement should be an important element in the management of all arteriopaths.[45]

Optimal control of diabetes is also recommended. It has been suggested that any stroke that occurs in poorly controlled diabetics tends to be more extensive and disabling than when diabetes is under good control. It is considered that the over-abundance of glucose in the brain in the absence of oxygen, produces more toxic free radicals which decrease recovery from cerebral thrombosis.[46]

Alcohol has been recognized as a possible risk factor for stroke from as early as 1725.[47] Heavier drinking is related to higher prevalence of cardiomyopathy,[48] hypertension[49] and haemorrhagic stroke.[50] The possibility that lighter alcohol use (one to two drinks per day) protects against coronary artery disease[51] and occlusive stroke[52] has been raised in several population studies. Light drinkers should not be advised to abstain from alcohol for the purpose of lessening the risk of cardiovascular mortality.

SURGICAL TREATMENT AND CONCLUSIONS

In patients with asymptomatic internal carotid stenosis of less than 75% in diameter there is no value for surgical management. Although patients with a high grade stenosis have an increased rate of spontaneous stroke,[53] this risk is so low that even the slightest perioperative mortality and morbidity could easily tilt the balance of risk benefit against surgery.[54] Several multicentre randomized trials of carotid endarterectomy and best medical treatment *vs* best medical treatment alone in patients with asymptomatic carotid stenosis are now in progress. They are based on the hypothesis that in centres where the combined perioperative stroke and death rate is less than 3%, carotid endarterectomy will confer benefit. Until the results of such studies become available, operation on asymptomatic carotid stenosis cannot be recommended as a routine procedure. There is no doubt that a natural history study is urgently needed incorporating new concepts such as the combination of degree of stenosis, plaque morphology and collateral cerebral circulation in an attempt to identify a high risk group which may clearly benefit from surgery.

In the meantime, one should not forget the most important message: the diagnosis of asymptomatic carotid stenosis indicates that underlying cardiac disease is a greater threat than the threat of stroke. These patients should be screened at presentation for underlying ischaemic heart disease and should be referred to vascular physicians who are skilled in their management. The latter should include an aggressive risk-factor intervention since there is now convincing evidence that this has an effect on the reduction of strokes and the reduction of cardiac morbidity and mortality.

REFERENCES

1. Check WA: Ultrasound shows carotid stenosis in just half of cervical bruit cases. JAMA 252: 593–594, 1984
2. Thompson JE, Kartchner MM, Austin DJ et al.: Clinical considerations in the surgical management of strokes. Circulation 33 (Suppl. 1): 162–172, 1966
3. David TE, Humphries AW, Young JR et al.: A correlation of neck bruits and arteriosclerotic carotid arteries. Arch Surg 107: 729–731, 1973

4. Gautier JC, Rosa A, Lhermitte F: Auscultation carotidienne. Correlations chez 200 patients avec 332 angiographies. Rev Neurol 131: 175–184, 1975
5. Heyman A, Wilkinson WE, Heden S *et al.*: Risk of stroke in asymptomatic persons with cervical bruits; a population study in Evans County, Georgia. N Engl J Med 302: 838–841, 1980
6. Wolf PA, Kannel WB, Sorlie P, McNamara P: Asymptomatic carotid bruit and the risk of stroke—The Framingham Study. JAMA 245: 1442, 1981
7. Kartchner MM, McRay LP: Noninvasive detection and evaluation of stroke-prone patients. Angiology 28: 750–759, 1977
8. Chambers BR, Norris JW: Outcome in patients with asymptomatic neck bruits. N Engl J Med 315: 860–865, 1986
9. Roederer GO, Langlois YE, Jager KA *et al.*: The natural history of carotid arterial disease in asymptomatic patients with cervical bruits. Stroke 15: 605–613, 1984
10. Norris JW, Zhu CZ, Bornstein NM, Chambers BR: Vascular risks of asymptomatic carotid stenosis. Stroke 22: 1485–1490, 1991
11. Shanik GD, Moore JD *et al.*: Asymptomatic Carotid Stenosis: A benign lesion? Eur J Vasc Surg 6: 10–15, 1992
12. Reilly LM, Lusby RJ *et al.*: Carotid plaque histology using real-time ultrasonography. Am J Surg 146: 188–193, 1983
13. Gray-Weale AC, Graham JC, Burnett JR: Carotid artery atheroma: comparison of preoperative B-mode ultrasound appearance with carotid endarterectomy specimen pathology. J Cardiovasc Surg 29: 676–681, 1988
14. Steffen CM, Gray-Weale AC *et al.*: Carotid atheroma ultrasound appearance in symptomatic and asymptomatic vessels. Aust NZ J Surg 59: 529–534, 1989
15. Geroulakos G, Ramaswami G, Labropoulos N *et al.*: Ultrasonic differences between symptomatic and asymptomatic plaques. Br J Surg 79: 1235, 1992
16. Johnson JM, Kennelly MM *et al.*: Natural history of asymptomatic carotid plaque. Arch Surg 120: 1110–1012, 1985
17. Sterpetti AV, Schultz RD, Feldhaus RJ *et al.*: Ultrasonographic features of carotid plaque and the risk of subsequent neurological deficits. Surgery 104: 652–660, 1988
18. Meager E, Grace PA and Bouchier-Hayes D: Are CT infarcts a separate risk factor in patients with transient cerebral ischaemic episodes? Eur J Vasc Surg 5: 165–167, 1991
19. Ringelstein EB, Sievers C, Ecker S *et al.*: Noninvasive assessment of CO_2-induced cerebral vasomotor response in normal individuals and patients with internal carotid artery occlusion. Stroke 19: 963–969, 1988
20. Langsfeld M, Gray-Weale AC, Lusby RJ: The role of plaque morphology and diameter reduction in the development of new symptoms in asymptomatic carotid arteries. J Vasc Surg 9: 548–557, 1989
21. Tomatis LA, Fierens EE, Verbrugge GP: Evaluation of surgical risk in peripheral vascular disease by coronary arteriography: a series of 100 cases. Surgery 71: 429, 1972
22. Ennix CL, Lawrie GM, Morris GC *et al.*: Improved results of carotid endarterectomy in patients with asymptomatic coronary artery disease: an analysis of 1546 consecutive carotid operations. Stroke 10: 122, 1979
23. Jones EL: Combined carotid and coronary surgery—when is it necessary? J Cardiovasc Med 8: 676, 1983
24. Mehigan JG, Buch WS, Pipkin RD, Fogarty TJ: A planned approach to coexistent cerebrovascular disease in coronary artery bypass candidates. Arch Surg 112, 1403, 1977
25. Wolf PA, Kannel WB, Sorlie P, McNamara P: Asymptomatic carotid bruit and the risk of stroke—The Framingham Study. JAMA 245: 1442, 1981
26. Fox KM, Selwyn AP, Shillingford JP: Projection of electrocardiographic signs in precordial maps after exercise in patients with ischaemic heart disease. Br Heart J 42: 416, 1979
27. Fox K, Selwyn A, Oakley D *et al.*: Relation between the precordial projection of ST segment changes after exercise and coronary angiographic findings. Am J Cardiol 44: 1068, 1979
28. Salmasi AM, Nicolaides AN, Vecht RJ *et al.*: Electrocardiographic chest wall mapping in the diagnosis of coronary artery disease. Br Med J 2: 9, 1983
29. Sonecha TN, Nicolaides AN, Salmasi A-M *et al.*: Non-invasive detection of coronary artery disease in patients presenting with claudication. Int Angiol 9: 79, 1990

30. Sonecha TN: PhD Thesis, Ch. 6, University of London, 1992
31. Sonecha TN: PhD Thesis, Ch. 7, University of London, 1992
32. Lette J, Waters D, Lassonde J et al.: Multivariate clinical models and quantitative dipyridamole–thallium imaging to predict cardiac morbidity and death after vascular reconstruction. J Vasc Surg 14: 160, 1991
33. Eagle KA, Singer DE, Brewster DC et al.: Dipyridamole–thallium scanning in patients undergoing vascular surgery. Optimising the preoperative evaluation of cardiac risk. J Am Med Ass 257: 2185, 1987
34. Eagle KA, Coley CM, Newell JB et al.: Continuing clinical and thallium data optimises preoperative assessment of cardiac index before major vascular surgery. Ann Intern Med 110: 859, 1989
35. Cutler BS, Leppo JA: Dipyridamole thallium 201 scintigraphy to detect coronary artery disease before abdominal aortic surgery. J Vasc Surg 5: 91, 1987
36. Collins R, Peto R, MacMahon S et al.: Blood pressure, stroke and coronary heart disease. Part 2, Short term reductions in blood pressure: overview of randomised drug trials in their epidemiological context. Lancet 335: 827–838, 1990
37. Antiplatelet Triallists' Collaboration. Secondary prevention of vascular disease by prolonged antiplatelet treatment. Br Med J 296: 320–331, 1980
38. O'Brien JR: Effects of salicylates on human platelets. Lancet i: 779–783, 1968
39. The SALT Collaborative Group: Swedish Aspirin Low-dose Trial (SALT) of 75 mg aspirin as secondary prophylaxis after cerebrovascular ischaemic events. Lancet 338: 1345–1349, 1991
40. Hennerici M, Kleophas W and Gries FA: Regression of carotid plaques during low density lipoprotein cholesterol elimination. Stroke 22: 989–992, 1991
41. Neaton JD, Kuller LH, Wentworth D et al.: Total and cardiovascular mortality in relation to cigarette smoking, serum cholesterol concentration and diastolic blood pressure among black and white males followed up for five years (MRFIT). Am Heart J 108: 759, 1984
42. Lipid Research Clinics Program: The Lipid Research Clinics Coronary Primary Prevention Trial Results: I. Reduction in the incidence of coronary heart disease. JAMA 251: 351, 1984
43. Canner PL, Berge KG, Wenger NK et al.: Fifteen year mortality in coronary drug project patients: Long term benefit with niacin. J Am Coll Cardiol 8: 1245, 1986
44. Frick MH, Elo O, Haapa H et al.: Helsinki Heart Study: Primary prevention trial with gemfibrozil in middle-aged men with dyslipidaemia. N Engl J Med 317: 1237, 1987
45. Dempsey RJ, Moore RW: Amount of smoking independently predicts carotid artery atherosclerosis severity. Stroke 23: 693–696, 1992
46. Kushner M, Nencini P et al.: Relation of hyperglycaemia early in ischaemic brain infarction to cerebral anatomy, metabolism and clinical outcome. Ann Neurol 28: 129–135, 1990
47. Sedgwick J: A new treatise on liquors, wherein the use and abuse of wine, malt drinks, water, etc., are particularly considered in many diseases, institutions and ages with proper manner of using them hot or cold either as physic, diet or both. London: Rivington, 1725
48. Regan TJ: Alcoholic cardiomyopathy. Prog Cardiovasc Dis 27: 141–152, 1984
49. Klatsky AL: Blood pressure and alcohol intake. In Hypertension: Pathophysiology, Diagnosis and Management, Laragh JH, Brenner BM (Eds). pp. 277–294, New York: Raven Press, 1990
50. Donahue RP, Abbott RD, Reed DW et al.: Alcohol and haemorrhage stroke: the Honolulu Heart Program. JAMA 255: 2311–2314, 1986
51. Stampfer MJ, Colditz GA, Willett WC et al.: Prospective study of moderate alcohol consumption and the risk of coronary artery disease and stroke in women. N Engl J Med 319: 267–273, 1988
52. Klatsky AL, Armstrong MA, Friedman GD et al.: Alcohol use and subsequent cerebrovascular disease hospitalisations. Stroke 70: 741–746, 1989
53. Thompson JE, Don Patman R, Talkington CM: Longterm outcome of patients having endarterectomy compared with unoperated controls. Ann Surg 188: 308–316, 1978
54. Dorazio RA, Ezzet F, Nesbitt NZ: Longterm follow-up of asymptomatic carotid bruits. Am J Surg 140: 212–213, 1980

55. Busuttil RW, Baker JD, Davidson RD, Mechleder HI: Carotid artery stenosis—hemodynamic significance and clinical course. JAMA 245: 1438–1441, 1981
56. Cullen SJ, Correa MC, Calderon-Oritz M *et al.*: Clinical sequelae in patients with asymptomatic carotid bruits. Circulation 68: (II), 83–87, 1983
57. Colgan MP, Kingston W, Shanik DG: Asymptomatic carotid stenosis: is prophylactic endarterectomy justifiable? Br J Surg 72: 313–314, 1985

The European Carotid Surgery Trial (ECST)

P. M. Rothwell and C. P. Warlow

The European Carotid Surgery Trial (ECST) is an attempt to define the role of carotid endarterectomy in the management of patients with transient ischaemic attack (TIA) or minor ischaemic stroke in the carotid territory. It is a multicentre trial involving numerous collaborators working in 97 centres in 12 European countries. Randomization began in 1981 and, to date, it is the largest trial of any surgical procedure. Nearly 3000 patients have been randomized to either endarterectomy and medical treatment, or medical treatment alone. In 1991, preliminary results were published[1] showing that endarterectomy was beneficial in recently symptomatic patients with a 'severe' carotid stenosis (>70%), but was of no value in patients with 'mild' stenosis (<30%). Recruitment of patients with 'moderate' stenosis (30–70%) continues and, in a few years, the balance of risk and benefit from surgery in this group will also be known.

BACKGROUND

Stroke is the third commonest cause of death in 'developed' countries, and the commonest cause of serious long-term disability. Each year in the UK approximately 20 000 patients present to medical attention with a TIA;[2] of these around 5% will have a stroke each subsequent year.[3] In the early 1980s there was much doubt amongst neurologists and some vascular surgeons about the efficacy of carotid endarterectomy, which at that time was certainly not of proven value. Many surgical series of endarterectomy patients had been published,[3,4] with varying rates of surgical stroke (4–21%), but only two small controlled trials of surgery versus medical treatment alone had been reported.[5,6] Despite the fact that neither trial showed surgery to be clearly beneficial, carotid endarterectomy became the commonest vascular surgical procedure performed in the USA.[7] Although, the procedure was much less popular in the UK, there was still considerable disagreement amongst clinicians about which patients, if any, would benefit.[8]

HISTORY OF ECST

In the late 1970s the UK-TIA Aspirin Trial was launched by a group of British neurologists. Once the machinery for this trial was in place, the possibility of a randomized trial of carotid endarterectomy in a similar cohort of patients became apparent. In March 1980, a group of neurologists and vascular surgeons met in London to draw up a protocol for such a study. The following year funding was obtained from the Medical Research Council, and recruitment began in September 1981. It soon became clear that recruitment from the UK alone would be insufficient to provide any answers before the twenty-first century. Wider collaboration was therefore sought, with French centres joining in 1982 and Dutch centres in 1983. By 1987 there were 63 collaborating centres in 12 countries. In February 1991, 2518 patients having been randomized, the data monitoring committee revealed interim results showing that endarterectomy was of value in patients with severe stenosis, but not in those with mild stenosis. Follow-up of all patients and randomization of patients with moderate stenosis continues, and the trial is funded until 1997; so far a total of 2833 patients have been recruited.

OBJECTIVES

In general terms the trial is an attempt to define the risks and benefits of carotid endarterectomy in patients who have recently suffered a TIA or minor ischaemic stroke in the carotid territory. In specific terms it aims to answer the following questions in each of the three main categories of stenosis—mild, moderate and severe:
1. What is the risk of death or stroke in the 30 days following endarterectomy?
2. In patients who survive surgery for 30 days without a stroke, what is the long-term risk of disabling or fatal stroke?
3. What is the risk of stroke in patients not treated with surgery?

ELIGIBILITY

Eligibility is determined using the 'uncertainty principle' (Fig. 1). If the patient fulfils the eligibility criteria outlined below, and is willing to consider surgery, then only if the neurologist or surgeon are 'substantially uncertain' whether to recommend surgery can the patient be entered into the trial. This method of selection avoids any ethical difficulties and tends to maximize the heterogeneity, and hence the amount of information available from the trial, i.e. the trial will provide answers for a wide variety of patients, old and young, with mild and severe stenosis etc. Any patient irrespective of age, sex, or race, who, within the 6 months prior to randomization, has experienced any combination of TIA, amaurosis fugax, retinal infarction, minor ischaemic stroke or non-disabling major ischaemic stroke within the distribution of one or both internal carotid arteries (ICA), and who has a stenosing and/or ulcerating lesion of the symptomatic artery(s) at its origin in the neck, is eligible for the trial.

EXCLUSION CRITERIA

Patients are excluded on the following grounds: a) patient preference; b) poor general health; c) little if any carotid stenosis; d) ICA occlusion, or distal stenosis more severe than at the bifurcation; e) a lesion thought to be technically inoperable; f) other more likely sources of embolism (e.g. recent myocardial infarction, mitral stenosis, atrial fibrillation, etc) whose TIAs are thought not to be due to atherothromboembolism; g) vertebrobasilar events only; h) previous carotid endarterectomy of the symptomatic artery.

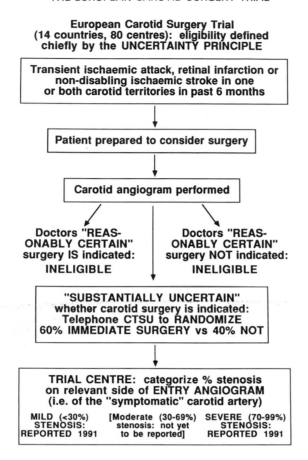

Fig. 1. Trial eligibility based on uncertainty principle. Reproduced by permission of *The Lancet*.

INVESTIGATIONS PRIOR TO RANDOMIZATION

Some of the data recorded on the randomization form are detailed in Table 1. It is also recommended that collaborators check the platelet count, erythrocyte sedimentation rate, urea, syphilis serology, chest X-ray, and echocardiogram if indicated, but no systematic record of these investigations is kept. Computed tomographic (CT) brain scans are recommended for all patients. Prior to January 1991, copies of all abnormal scans were sent to the Trial Office. Although the majority of patients now undergo duplex carotid ultrasound scanning as a screening test, results are not requested. All patients are required to undergo angiography. Selective angiograms are preferred, but as an absolute minimum, biplanar views of the origin of the symptomatic ICA, with as good a view as possible of the intracranial circulation on that side, are requested. Although not mandatory, views of the contralateral ICA are recommended. The exact method of angiography is not specified, however, because of the considerable variation in practice between departments of radiology. Copies of all angiograms are sent to the Trials Office. For the purpose of later subgroup analysis, the exact degree of stenosis is then measured.

Table 1. Baseline characteristics of randomized patients

	Severe stenosis (70–99%)	Mild stenosis (0–29%)
No. with data in computer	778	374
Mean age (years)	62.2	59.7
Male (%)	70	72
Prior transient cerebral ischaemic attack/amaurosis fugax (%)	78	59
Prior stroke, residual neurological signs or infarct on pre-randomization CT (%)	50	61
Prior retinal infarction (%)	5	8
Mean delay (days) from last ischaemic event to randomization	57	56
Prior myocardial infarction and/or angina (%)	27	13
Peripheral vascular disease (%)	19	13
Diabetic (%)	9	9
Mean systolic blood pressure (mmHg)	151	148
Mean diastolic blood pressure (mmHg)	86	87
Mean cholesterol (mmol/l)	6.5	6.3
Current cigarette smokers (%)	56	55
Mean obesity index (kg/m^2)	24.8	25.1

RANDOMIZATION AND TREATMENT

Patients are randomized by a telephone call to the Clinical Trials Service Unit at the University of Oxford to 'immediate surgery' (60%) or 'no immediate surgery' (40%). Clinicans are asked to ensure that patients in both groups receive the 'best medical treatment', which in practice usually includes aspirin, treatment of hypertension, and advice to stop smoking. All surgeons must be designated collaborators in the trial and must not delegate surgery to junior colleagues. Surgery should be performed as soon as possible after randomization, although it is recommended that operation is delayed for about 4 weeks after a stroke. Any strokes occurring after randomization but prior to surgery are included in the surgery group for subsequent analysis. No other elective surgical procedures, including contralateral endarterectomy, should be perfomed under the same anaesthetic. The surgeon is requested to give details of the operation including duration, type of anaesthesia, stump pressure if measured, ICA occlusion time, whether or not a shunt or patch were used, the degree of stenosis, whether the plaque was ulcerated or had adherent thrombus, anticoagulation during surgery, and postoperative blood pressure.

FOLLOW-UP AND OUTCOME MEASURES

The main outcome events are detailed in Table 2. Patients are seen by a collaborating physician, usually a neurologist, at 4 months and 1 year after randomization, and annually thereafter. Any patient not attending hospital is followed up through their family or other doctor. Information collected at each follow-up includes details of any new strokes since last review, any previous strokes with persisting symptoms, any

Table 2. Main outcome events in the European Carotid Surgery Trial

Type of outcome event	Definition
0. 'Unrelated' death	All non-stroke deaths except those occurring within 30 days of carotid surgery
1. Surgery-associated death or stroke (SADS)	Either death from any cause within 30 days of surgery, or stroke of any pathology or site within those 30 days
2. Haemorrhagic stroke	All strokes (except those associated with surgery) classified by CT scan, lumbar puncture or postmortem as definitely or probably primary intracerebral haemorrhage or spontaneous subarachnoid haemorrhage
3. Vertebrobasilar ischaemic stroke	All other strokes that were definitely in the vertebrobasilar arterial distribution
4. Contralateral ischaemic stroke	All other strokes that were definitely contralateral to the 'relevant' (i.e. symptomatic) carotid artery
5. Ipsilateral ischaemic stroke	All other strokes that were ipsilateral to the relevant carotid artery (plus any of uncertain territory)

myocardial infarcts, TIAs, angina or symptoms of peripheral vascular disease, medications, smoking status, and blood pressure. All patients are followed up until death.

TRIAL PERFORMANCE

A number of measures of trial performance are worthy of note. The number of patients being randomized each year has tended to increase as the trial has progressed, at least until the interim results were revealed, after which few mild and severe stenosis patients have been randomized (Fig. 2). Although some patients have been followed up for over 10 years, the mean period of follow-up is still less than 4 years. The time elapsing between randomization and surgery is important, because the risk of stroke following TIA falls appreciably with time.[9] Thus a short delay may reduce the benefit of surgery. The median delay following randomization was under 2 weeks, and 90% of patients received surgery within 5 weeks (Fig. 3). Only one patient randomized to surgery suffered a disabling stroke prior to surgery. Only six patients are definitely lost to follow-up. The 'uncertainty principle' criteria for eligibility has produced a wide range of patients both in terms of age and sex (Fig. 4), and severity of carotid stenosis (Fig. 5).

GENERALIZABILITY AND BIAS

During the first 10 years of ECST approximately 1000 patients from the UK were randomized. Thus less than 1% of patients presenting to medical attention with TIA

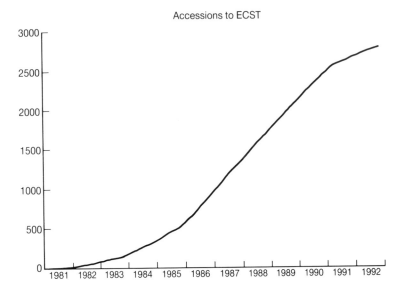

Fig. 2. The cumulative number of patients randomized in ECST.

in the UK were entered into the trial. Even this is likely to be an overestimate as many patients randomized had a minor ischaemic stroke rather than a TIA. This raises the important question: is the cohort of ECST patients representative of, and the results of the trial therefore generalizable to, the majority of TIA patients? The use of the 'uncertainty principle' tends to limit any bias regarding inclusion of

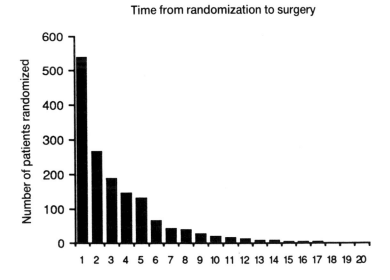

Fig. 3. The time elapsing between randomization of patients in ECST and performance of carotid endarterectomy.

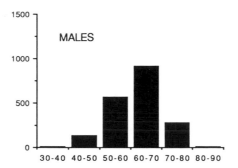

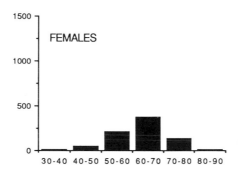

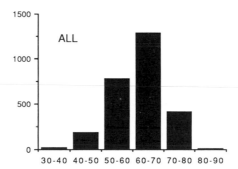

Fig. 4. The number of patients in ECST classified by degree of stenosis of the symptomatic ICA.

patients in the trial. It seems likely that patients seen by neurologists and vascular surgeons will differ from those seen by geriatricians, or those not referred to hospital at all, although the significant proportion of patients in the trial over 75 years of age argues against this. Clearly the international base of the trial increases generalizability. In any event, the generalizability of this, or any other, trial result is

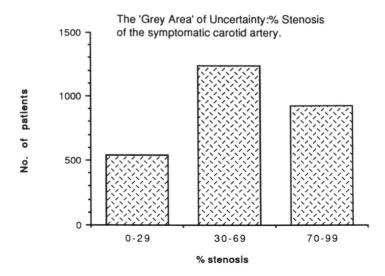

Fig. 5. The number of patients in ECST in each of the three main stenosis groups.

determined in practice by comparing the type of patient in the trial with the individual patient about whom a surgical decision has to be made.

It is not possible for a trial of a major surgical procedure to be blind! It is also difficult to blind the follow-up clincians, without giving all patients scars. Unblinded trials are of course susceptible to bias, but it is unlikely that measurements of hard end-points such as disabling stroke will be significantly affected. In ECST the outcome events of main concern (stroke lasting more than 7 days and all deaths) are reviewed by a clinical audit committee which is blinded to treatment allocation.

BASELINE CHARACTERISTICS OF RANDOMIZED PATIENTS

The baseline characteristics in the mild and severe stenosis patients analysed in January 1991 are shown in Table 1. The severe stenosis group contained a higher proportion of patients presenting with TIA or amaurosis fugax, and a lower proportion of patients with a previous stroke, residual neurological signs or an infarct on CT scan. Previous myocardial infarction or angina, and peripheral vascular disease were predictably more frequent in the severe stenosis group. There was no significant difference in any characteristics between the 'surgery' and 'no surgery' groups.

INTERIM RESULTS

The results outlined below are derived from the 2200 patients in whom data were complete in January 1991. These results are further restricted to the 1152 patients who had either a mild or severe stenosis on the pre-randomization angiogram.

Surgical mortality and morbidity

There were seven deaths within 30 days of operation compared with no deaths in 'no surgery' patients over an identical period. Death or disabling stroke occurred in 22 'surgery' patients (3.3%), and if all strokes producing symptoms for more than 7 days are included, the figure rises to 44 (7.5%) patients. There was a non-significant trend for stroke to be more frequent in the severe stenosis group.

Intercurrent mortality

Excluding the small number of deaths within 30 days of surgery and deaths from stroke, the number of deaths during follow-up due to any other cause were similar in the 'surgery' and 'no surgery' groups (8.3% vs 8.6%) and similar in the mild and severe stenosis groups (8.0% vs 9.8%).

Disabling or fatal strokes

During the mean follow-up period of 3 years, in patients with severe stenosis, there was an eightfold reduction in the number of ipsilateral ischaemic strokes in patients allocated to surgery compared with no surgery (5/455 vs 27/323, $2p < 0.0001$, Fig 6a). In patients with mild stenosis there was no difference in the number of ipsilateral ischaemic strokes between the 'surgery' and 'no surgery' groups (1/219 vs 0/155), although disabling or fatal strokes in general were more frequent in the 'surgery' group (11/219 vs 2/155, $p < 0.05$).

Strokes lasting more than 7 days

In patients with tight stenosis there was a sixfold reduction in strokes lasting more than 7 days in the surgery group (9/455 vs 44/323, $2p < 0.0001$, Fig. 6b). In patients with mild stenosis there was no statistically significant difference (6/219 vs 2/155), although the frequency of any stroke lasting more than 7 days was greater in the 'surgery' group (24/219 vs 9/155, $p < 0.05$).

Do baseline characteristics predict risk of ipsilateral ischaemic stroke and surgery-associated events? In 'no surgery' patients a logrank analysis of time to ipsilateral ischaemic stroke revealed three interrelated adverse prognostic factors, other than degree of carotid stenosis—a history of stroke, residual neurological signs, and infarction on the pre-randomization CT scan. The other baseline factors in Table 1 were not predictive. Among 'surgery' patients the factors predicting an adverse 30-day outcome were systolic blood pressure above 160 mmHg, and performance of surgery in under 1 hour.

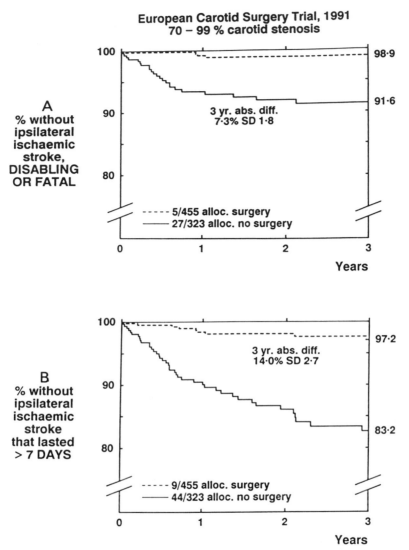

Fig. 6. Main analysis of strokes (A, disabling or fatal: odds redn. 84%; SD 17; log-rank 2p<0.0001), (B, lasting more than 7 days: odds redn. 84%; SD 13; log-rank 2p<0.0001) for patients with severe stenosis on the pre-randomization angiogram. Reproduced by permission of *The Lancet*.

DISCUSSION

The trial has achieved each of the objectives outlined earlier in the chapter with regard to patients with mild or severe stenosis. Carotid endarterectomy is associated with a small but significant risk of death or disabling stroke, at least when performed by European surgeons on European patients. Patients with a tight stenosis who undergo surgery without suffering a stroke, subsequently have only a very small risk of ipsilateral ischaemic stroke. In contrast severe stenosis patients give medical treatment alone have an appreciable, cumulative risk of ipsilateral ischaemic stroke. Conversely, in patients with a mild stenosis, whilst the mortality and morbidity from surgery are similar to tight stenosis patients, the risk of stroke with medical treatment alone is very low. Indeed, the excess of disabling or fatal strokes in the 'surgery' group reaches statistical significance. One could therefore argue that unless a surgeon is able to perform endarterecomy without any mortality or morbidity at all, then to operate on patients with mild stenosis is now unethical. Even assuming that complication-free surgery was possible, the procedure would hardly be a cost-effective way of preventing stroke.

The generalizability of the benefit of surgery in severe stenosis patients cannot be in doubt, the relative risk reduction for ipsilateral ischaemic stroke being so extreme. However, the risk–benefit equation for surgery contains a number of variables which deserve mention:

1. In order to apply the conclusions of ECST to their patients, clinicians must know the risk of death or disabling stroke following endarterectomy in their own institution.

2. The majority of surgeons require all patients to undergo cerebral angiography prior to endarterectomy. The neurological morbidity from this procedure in TIA patients is 4% and the disabling stroke rate is at least 1%.[10] Complications of angiography are not included in the ECST results as the procedure was performed prior to randomization, but must clearly be considered in clinical practice.

3. The recommendations of both ECST and the North American Symptomatic Carotid Endarterectomy Trial (NASCET)[11] rely on the measurement of the degree of stenosis of the origin of the symptomatic internal carotid artery. Clinicians therefore need to know what was measured, and how it was done, if they are to extrapolate the results of these trials to their own practice. Similarly, in any meta-analysis, methodological differences must be taken into account. The degree of stenosis was indeed calculated differently in each trial. In both cases the diameter of the lumen at the site of maximal stenosis was measured on the angiographic view showing the greatest degree of stenosis. However, the diameter which this was compared with to calculate the percentage diameter stenosis was different (Fig. 7). In ECST an estimate of the carotid bulb diameter at the site of the stenosis was used, whereas NASCET used the diameter of a 'disease-free' segment of proximal internal carotid artery. These methods will clearly give differing results because the diameter of the carotid bulb is greater than that of the ICA. A recent study measuring 700 ECST angiograms by both methods[12] showed that only 48% of patients classified as tight stenosis by ECST would have been included in the NASCET tight stenosis group. The 70% NASCET cut-off measures over 80% by the ECST method. Since risk of stroke increases with degree of stenosis this is likely to explain why the absolute benefit of surgery appears greater in NASCET tight stenosis patients.

4. It may be possible to identify further which patients are at high risk of surgical complications and which patients are at low risk of stroke on medical treatment alone, thereby selecting those patients with the most to gain and the least to lose from surgery. The surgical risk may be reduced by more rigorous treatment of preoperative hypertension which ECST has shown to be a risk factor for surgery associated stroke. The subgroup of 'no surgery' patients with a history of stroke, residual neurological signs, or infarction on CT scan, appear to be at increased risk of subsequent stroke. Thus, while endarterectomy benefits certain patients, further research is needed to

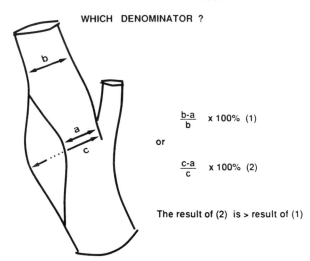

WHICH DENOMINATOR ?

$$\frac{b-a}{b} \times 100\% \quad (1)$$

or

$$\frac{c-a}{c} \times 100\% \quad (2)$$

The result of (2) is > result of (1)

Fig. 7. The NASCET (1) and ECST (2) methods of measuring the degree of ICA stenosis on an angiogram.

define predictive criteria other than simply the degree of ICA stenosis in order to best target the procedure and further improve its cost effectiveness.

5. A further important point concerns the difficulty in diagnosis of TIA. Transient neurological symptoms have a wide differential diagnosis, and there is considerable inter-observer variation in the diagnosis of TIA.[13] All patients randomized in ECST were seen by a neurologist and it is likely that many patients referred as possible candidates for endarterectomy were felt not to have suffered a carotid circulation TIA. Thus, the ECST results must be applied to patients reviewed by an experienced neurologist or a physician with an interest in stroke.

6. The ECST results can only be extrapolated to patients who have had a relatively recent TIA or minor ischaemic stroke. The median time from symptoms to surgery was 2 months, and 90% of patients received surgery within 5 months of the event on which randomization was based. Since the risk of stroke falls appreciably with time, it is possible that patients with less recent symptoms will benefit less from surgery.

The benefit of surgery seen in tight stenosis patients in ECST cannot be generalized to patients with asymptomatic tight stenosis. However, the results do provide justification for well conducted controlled trials in this area, with the proviso that since the risk of stroke appears to be lower in asymptomatic patients,[14] any such trials will probably have to be considerably larger than ECST in order to give any meaningful answers.

Extrapolating the results of surgery in ECST, severe stenosis patients, 1000 endaterectomies must be performed in symptomatic patients to prevent about 50 fatal or disabling and 50 non-disabling strokes over the subsequent 3 years. This benefit may increase with further follow-up, although Fig. 6a appears not to support this assumption. The cost effectiveness of endarterectomy in lower risk asymptomatic patients is therefore likely to be marginal.

Finally, it is to be hoped that following the results of ECST and NASCET, the frequency with which carotid endarterectomy is performed will fall considerably in certain institutions and increase in others. Over the past 30 years, for the want of a large controlled trial, many thousands of patients have been subjected to a dangerous surgical procedure with very little to gain, and many others have been denied the benefit of an effective surgical treatment. One can only hope that 'nihilistic' physicians and 'over-zealous' surgeons will now adapt their behaviour in the light of some long overdue evidence.

REFERENCES

1. European Carotid Surgery Trialists' Collaborative Group: MRC European Surgery Trial: Interim results for symptomatic patients with severe (70–99%) or mild (0–29%) carotid stenosis. Lancet 337: 1235–1243, 1991
2. Dennis M, Warlow CP: Strategy for stroke. Br Med J 303: 636–638, 1991
3. Hankey GJ, Warlow CP: Prognosis of symptomatic carotid artery occlusion: an overview. Cereb Dis 1: 245–256, 1991
4. Easton JD, Sherman DG: Stroke and mortality rate in carotid endarterectomy: 228 consecutive operations. Stroke 8: 565–568, 1977
5. Fields WS, Maslenikov V, Meyer JS et al.: Joint Study of Extracranial Arterial Occlusion. V. Progress report of prognosis following surgery or non-surgical treatment for transient cerebral ischaemic attacks and cervical carotid artery lesions. J Am Med Assoc 211: 1993–2003, 1970
6. Shaw DA, Venables GS, Cartlidge NEF, Bates D, Dickenson PH: Carotid endarterectomy in patients with transient cerebral ischaemia. J Neurol Sci 64: 45–53, 1984
7. Thompson JE, Garrett WV: Peripheral arterial surgery. N Engl J Med 302: 481–494, 1980
8. UK-TIA Study Group: Variation in the use of angiography and carotid endarterectomy by neurologists in the UK-TI Aspirin Trial. Br Med J 286: 514–517, 1983
9. Dennis MS, Bamford JD, Sandercock PAG, Warlow CP: Prognosis of transient ischaemic attack in the Oxford Community Stroke Project. Stroke 21: 848–853, 1990
10. Hankey GJ, Warlow CP, Sellar RJ. Cerebral angiographic risk in mild cerebrovascular disease. Stroke 21: 209–222, 1990
11. NASCET Collaborators: Beneficial effect of carotid endarterectomy in symptomatic patients with high-grade carotid stenosis. N Engl J Med 325: 445–453, 1991
12. Sharp B, Sellar RJ: Agreement and reliability of angiographic measurement in the assessment of atherosclerosis of the internal carotid artery. 1992. Unpublished data.
13. Kraaijeveld CL, Van Gjin J, Schouten HJA, Staal A: Interobserver agreement for the diagnosis of transient ischaemic attacks. Stroke 4: 723–725, 1984
14. Chambers BR, Norris JW: Outcome of patients with asymptomatic neck bruits. N Engl J Med 315: 860–865, 1986

The North American Symptomatic Carotid Endarterectomy Trial (NASCET)

H. J. M. Barnett

THE RATIONALE FOR NASCET

The launching of randomized trials to evaluate endarterectomy as an established strategy for stroke prevention was the natural outcome of several factors: stroke was declining; measures other than endarterectomy were responsible for much if not all of this decline; platelet-inhibiting drugs were becoming established as of definite benefit; there was an annual increase in the numbers of endarterectomies being performed; health-care providers were concerned that the appropriateness of the procedure had not been determined by rigorous modern scientific study. Two early randomized trials had been negative, but they had been done prior to the perfecting of the technique of endarterectomy and in the early stages of modern neuroanaesthesia and postoperative care.[1,2]

THE DESIGN AND CONDUCT OF NASCET

Patients with definite focal retinal and hemispheric events within 120 days of entry, and related to arteriosclerotic stenosis of 30% or greater were eligible for randomization. The two treatment categories consisted of those assigned to best medical and those who received the same to which was added endarterectomy. Patients with organ failure, potential cardioembolic sources of cerebral ischaemia, without good extra- and intracranial arteriographic views of the cerebral circulation and unable to give informed consent were not eligible.

A set of Stopping Rules were designed so that the early demonstration of benefit or harm, judged by ongoing confidential analyses would not jeopardize the safety of the study patients. Three years after the beginning of randomization, when 659 patients had been assigned to the medical ($n=331$) and the surgical ($n=328$) categories, the analyses determined that for those with severe ($\geqslant 70\%$) stenosis, the benefit was unequivocal and that the study should stop for this group of patients.[3] For those patients with <70% stenosis, there was no indication to do other than continue the trial.

THE RESULTS OF PATIENTS WITH SEVERE STENOSIS

The results of the analyses defining benefit may be summarized best by quoting the original manuscript: "Life table estimates of the cumulative risk of any ipsilateral stroke at 2 years were 26% in the 331 medical patients and 9% in the 328 surgical patients—an absolute risk reduction ($\pm$SE) of $17\pm3.5\%$ ($p<0.001$). For a major or fatal ipsilateral stroke, the corresponding estimates were 13.1% and 2.5%—an absolute risk reduction of $10.6\pm2.6\%$ ($p<0.001$). Carotid endarterectomy was still found to be beneficial when all strokes and deaths were included in the analysis ($p<0.001$)."[3] Analysing for any major stroke or death still yielded significant benefit and detected a p value <0.01. The benefit from surgery became apparent after a mere 3 months had elapsed as is evident in Fig. 1.

The strength of the results is further exemplified in the tabulation of absolute and relative risk reductions for the analyses of three outcome events (ipsilateral stroke, all stroke, all stroke and death) which counted minor non-disabling and transient strokes as well as three outcome event analyses comparing only serious strokes and death (Table 1).

Functional status of all patients was evaluated at each 3-monthly follow-up visit. The persistence of a better level of functioning on the North American Symptomatic Carotid Endarterectomy Trial (NASCET) scale for the surgical patients compared with the medical patients is clear from Fig. 2. Even when deaths from all causes during follow-up were added and the mean functional status was calculated for each treatment group after assigning the highest score on the scale for 'death', the mean functional status for surgical patients was statistically significantly better at 2 years than for the medical patients. (NASCET—unpublished data.)

Transient ischaemic attacks were recorded at each follow-up visit. The reduction after surgery compared with medical care of such events, is illustrated in the Kaplan-Meier survival curve in Fig. 3. This reduction is considered a clinical bonus for the surgical patients; by itself transient ischaemic attack (TIA) reduction was not regarded as a goal of the NASCET investigators. This is not said to diminish the importance of TIAs as heraldic symptoms for stroke. However, by comparison with stroke or death, NASCET's major outcome events, TIAs alone are of minor consequence. They may diminish the sense of well-being of the patients while they are occurring, but are not in themselves disabling. Preventing them, without reducing stroke and death,

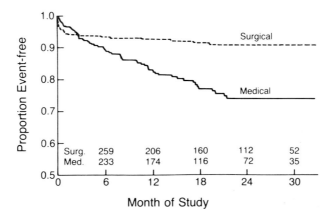

Fig. 1. Kaplan-Meier survival curves of the outcome event if ipsilateral stroke as a treatment failure after randomization to medical or surgical cohort. (Significant by Mantel-Haenszel χ^2 test, $p<0.001$.) Reproduced from Ref. 3, with permission.

Table 1. Risk reductions

	Absolute %	Relative %
Ipsilateral stroke	17	65
Any stroke	15	54
Any stroke or death	16.5	51
Major ipsilateral stroke	10.6	81
Major stroke	9.4	72
Major stroke or death	10.1	56

and at the risk of stroke and death, is not regarded as a worthy pursuit. Hence their reduction was not reported as one of our primary analyses.

Vascular risk factors which impact on arteriosclerotic disease regardless of its location, and some factors which peculiarly add to cerebral vascular risk, constitute a risk profile which has been developed for the NASCET patients. The preliminary analyses of the impact of this profile on outlook for patients with severe carotid stenosis and symptoms due to it, has been reported.[3] For patients who had less than five of the 13 specified risk factors, the likelihood of stroke in 2 years was 17%; with six of the risk factors the stroke rate at 2 years rose to 23%; with ⩾ seven factors the corresponding risk was 39%. The risk profile did not influence in a significant way the hazard of endarterectomy. These and other risks peculiar to carotid stenotic disease which will be described below are being catalogued for patients with moderate stenosis in the phase of NASCET which is ongoing. The possibility exists that in these lower-risk patients, the cut-off point for surgical benefit will require consideration not only of the degree of stenosis but also the impact of the risk profile as recorded in each individual patient.

CERTAIN SUBGROUP OBSERVATIONS

Contralateral disease

Bilateral selective carotid arteriography was a requirement for entry of patients into the trial. All angiograms were measured and recorded in the Central Office by the

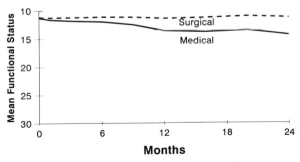

Fig. 2. Functional status over time averaged for medical and surgical patients, with severe stenosis, in NASCET. The functional status is the sum of the first ten domains — range = 10–70. Dead patients censored at death.

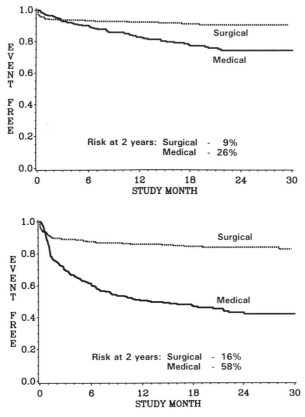

Fig. 3. The survival curves are plotted on a scale different to Fig. 1 and show the outcome of ipsilateral stroke 3(a: upper) in the medical (*n* = 331) and surgical (*n* = 328) groups and the outcome for ipsilateral stroke or TIA 3(b: lower). There is substantial evidence that endarterectomy reduces TIA occurrence, in addition to stroke and death.

Principal Neuroradiographer. In the patients randomized with ipsilateral severe stenosis, most (281 in the medical, and 280 in the surgical cohorts) had less than 70% stenosis in the opposite carotid artery. Thirty of the medical cohort and 25 of the surgical cohort had ⩾70% stenosis on the contralateral side; the figures for contralateral occlusion were 20 each in the medical and surgical groups. Figure 4 illustrates the fact that at 18 and 24 months there was substantial decrease in stroke-free survival for those treated medically with contralateral occlusion, but little impact if the contralateral lesion was short of occlusion (NASCET unpublished data). For the patients with contralateral occlusion, the 32-day stroke and death rate in the medical group was no different to that in the surgical group (10%). Surgery reduced the 2-year risk of stroke or death from 56.4% in the medical group to 20.4% in the surgical group. The numbers involved were too small to be accorded statistical significance but the conclusion appears to be valid that contralateral disease in this group of patients with ipsilateral symptomatic and severe stenosis, does not contraindicate surgery on the symptomatic side.

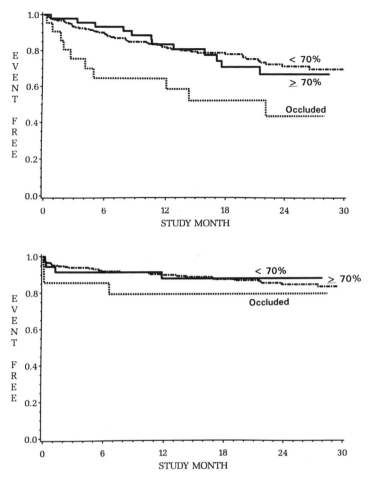

Fig. 4. The survival curves indicate that in patients entered into NASCET with severe ipsilateral stenosis, occlusion of the contralateral artery imposed a major hazard (56.4%) for the medical group (a: upper) over 30 months. While there was increased risk of surgery in the perioperative period (10%) the risk for the surgical patients (b: lower) was substantially improved in the long-term follow-up. Severe contralateral stenosis in this small group imposed no additional risk.

Retinal hemispheric ischaemia

It has been postulated that retinal symptoms with carotid disease are less threatening than are hemisphere symptoms. NASCET data confirm this hypothesis.[4] In the patients with severe disease, there were 59 who had experienced only retinal events and 70 whose history recorded only hemisphere events. Figure 5 graphically depicts the likelihood in these patients of stroke (fatal or non-fatal) occurring at 2 years; 44% of the hemisphere but only 17% of the retinal group had reached a stroke outcome.

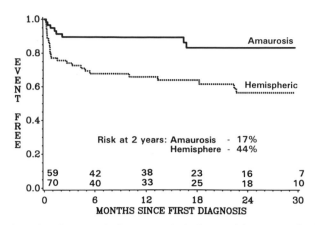

Fig. 5. Ipsilateral stroke. Amaurosis fugax carried a lower risk, as seen in the survival curves, than did hemisphere events of TIA presenting as the singular prerandomization symptoms in NASCET patients.

Ulceration in the involved carotid artery

The identification, with certainty, of an ulcerative lesion in the artery is not always easy to accomplish preoperatively. Review of 593 of the 659 angiograms in the patients with severe stenosis in NASCET lead to the recognition of ulceration with reasonable certainly in 34% of those assigned to the medical group and in 36% of those assigned to surgery.[5] At 2 years a non-fatal stroke or vascular death had occurred in 30% of the group with ulcer assigned to medical care alone and in 17% of those without ulcer. As expected, surgery eliminated the extra risk in the ulcerated group, rendering them no more likely to serious outcome events in postsurgical follow-up than the non-ulcerated group.

Silent brain infarction

The era of computed tomography (CT) has disclosed that 10–20% of reported series of patients who have had only TIA as evidence of carotid disease, nevertheless have evidence of a CT lesion compatible with infarction. Of the 352 NASCET patients who presented with TIA related to their high-grade stenosis, the incidence of asymptomatic brain infarction was 34.4%.[6] The outlook with medical therapy for these patients compared with those not found to have a CT lesion is depicted in Fig. 6 (NASCET— unpublished data).

Age as a risk for medical and surgical patients

The NASCET experience has enabled us to conclude that age is not a barrier to successful and beneficial carotid surgery. Dividing the patients with severe stenosis into those below 65 years and those aged 65–80 (the upper limit in the first phase of

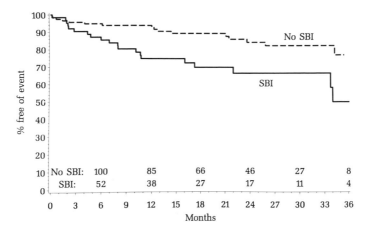

Fig. 6. The outlook for stroke in medical patients with silent brain infarction (SBI) was worse over time than for those who entered NASCET without this CT finding.

NASCET), yielded 143 patients with an average age of 56.3 years and 188 patients with an average age of 70.8 years. Figure 7 confirms that the older patients without surgery had a worse outlook than the younger patients. By contrast, surgery was equally beneficial in both age groups. Our conclusion is that there is no evidence to support an upper age limit for carotid endarterectomy provided the assessment of the overall condition of the patient determines that they do not have other complications such as organ failure or uncontrolled vascular risk factors, which will add to the hazard of anaesthesia and surgery (NASCET—unpublished data).

ONGOING QUESTIONS

The most important question still to be answered in respect to the benefit of carotid endarterectomy is the application of the procedure with less than 70% stenosis. The

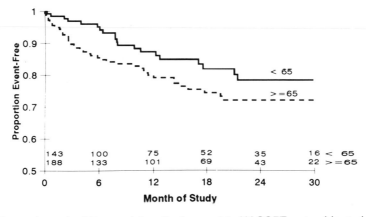

Fig. 7. Older patients ($\geq$65 years) (medical group) in NASCET not subjected to endarterectomy were more likely to experience ipsilateral stroke than younger (<65 years) patients.

percentage which has been found beneficial refers to the linear measurements of the most severe stenosis and utilizing the diameter beyond the bulb and beyond the diseased segment as the denominator in the calculation. In addition, the European trial has detected no benefit for patients with less than a 30% stenosis. NASCET has determined a declining benefit as the degree of stenosis declines from the 10th to the 8th deciles. The absolute difference of ipsilateral stroke at 2 years between the medical and surgical groups was 26.1% in those with 90–99% stenosis, was 17.9% with 80–89% and down to 12.5% in those with 70–79% stenoses. No data exist to confirm or deny benefit below 70%. Despite this there is evidence that the results of NASCET are being extrapolated to include patients who have less than 70% stenosis. The final results of the two major trials may prove that justification will be found for endarterectomy for patients at least with the more severe degrees of moderate stenosis or for some of them with moderate degree of stenosis and a high risk profile.

Even in NASCET centres fewer patients at the upper levels are being randomized since the declaration of benefit for those with severe disease than was the case in the early years of the study (Fig. 8). Partly this can be explained on the basis of the natural enthusiasm of physicians to utilize what they honestly believe to be definitive treatment for their patients. Partly it is due to the measurement of the degree of stenosis by more casual methods than demanded in NASCET. A sampling of 174 examples of arteriograms showing moderate and 76 examples showing severe stenosis, precisely measured by the NASCET Principal Neuroradiographer utilizing a jeweller's eye piece and calipers, was presented to three neurologists, three general radiologists and two non-study neuroradiologists. They were asked to estimate carefully the degree of stenosis. Overestimation was more common than underestimation by all three groups. The variance in each direction was between 5 and 15%.[7]

The persistence of a definite, albeit minimal (0.4–1%), risk of cerebral ischaemia caused by arteriography makes the search for a safe and reliable alternative imaging technique a compelling one. Duplex scanning allows the investigator to identify the characteristics and changes in the wall of the artery and in the lesion. Possibly

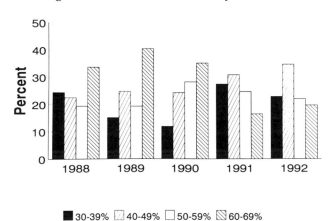

Fig. 8.   The randomization into NASCET of fewer patients in the higher moderate (60–69%) range of stenosis in 1991 and 1992 reflects an extrapolation of NASCET results to patients with levels of stenosis for which hard data do not yet exist.

echolucent plaques will be shown to be of more consequence than 'fibrous' plaques.[8] Unfortunately there are two serious shortcomings depriving duplex of a role as the ideal and safe imaging methods. First of all, the known benefit of endarterectomy relates not to duplex studies but to a linear measure by arteriography. Comparisons of duplex and arteriography in NASCET and in the Veterans Administration symptomatic trial have determined a 15–20% level of underestimating and over-estimating of the degree of stenosis. Similarly the observations published from the asymptomatic carotid artery study (ACAS) reflect at least a 10% discrepancy as does another large and recent meticulous comparison.[9,10] In addition extracranial ultrasound studies fail to recognize concomitant and possibly serious intracranial disease in the cavernous portion of the artery and they overlook coincidental intracranial aneurysms. Patients in this group are particularly prone to aneurysm and it was noted in 2.8% of the NASCET patients. In two of these the aneurysm was not given sufficient attention and lead to subarachnoid haemorrhage after the endarterectomy, in one with fatal consequences. The possibility of missing an aneurysm may be averted when refined magnetic resonance angiography is generally available. When this technology is perfected it may replace both ultrasound and conventional angiography.

REFERENCES

1. Fields WS, Maslenikov V, Meyer JS et al.: Joint study of extracranial arterial occlusion. V. Progress report of prognosis following surgery or nonsurgical treatment for transient cerebral ischemic attacks and cervical carotid artery lesions. JAMA 211: 1993–2003, 1970
2. Shaw DA, Venables GS, Cartilidge NEF, Bates D, Dickinson PH: Carotid endarterectomy in patients with transient cerebral ischemia. J Neurol Sci 64: 45–53, 1984
3. North American Symptomatic Carotid Endarterectomy Trial Collaborators: Beneficial effect of carotid endarterectomy in symptomatic patients with high-grade carotid stenosis. N Engl J Med 325: 445–453, 1991
4. Streifler JY, Benavente OR, Harbison JW, Eliasziw M, Hachinski VC, Barnett HJM: Prognostic implications of retinal versus hemispheric TIA in patients with high grade carotid stenosis: Observations from NASCET. (Abstract) Stroke 23: 159, 1992
5. Streifler JY, Fox AJ, Hachinski VC, Barnett HJM: The importance of plaque ulceration in symptomatic patients with high grade carotid stenosis: Observation from NASCET. (Abstract) Stroke 23: 160, 1992
6. Streifler JY, Fox AJ, Wong CJ, Hachinski VC, Barnett HJM: Importance of 'silent' brain infarctions in TIA patients with high-grade carotid stenosis: Results from NASCET. (Abstract) Neurology 42 (Suppl 3): 204, 1992
7. Pelz DM, Fox AJ, Eliasziw M, Barnett HJM: Review article—MOCOMP/PIAP Angiography measurement of carotid bifurcation stenosis. J Can Ass Radiologists 1993 (in press).
8. Langsfeld M, Gray-Weale AC, Lusby RJ. The role of plaque morphology and diameter reduction in the development of new symptoms in asymptomatic carotid arteries. J Vasc Surg 9: 548–557, 1989
9. Howard G, Chambless LE, Baker WH et al.: A multicenter validation study of doppler ultrasound versus angiography. J Stroke Cerebrovasc Dis 1: 166–173, 1991
10. Riles TS, Eidelman EM, Litt AW et al.: Comparison of magnetic resonance angiography, conventional angiography, and duplex scanning. Stroke 23: 341–346, 1992

Platelet Inhibitors After Carotid Endarterectomy

D. Bergqvist and B. Lindblad

Several factors may increase the risk of development of thrombosis in the reconstructed area after vascular surgical procedures. Generally the surgical trauma renders the patient prone to develop thrombosis, especially in the venous system. Locally, the reconstructed segment is thrombogenic, and this is true whether it is a bypass or an endarterectomized artery. The process is multifactorial and thereby it is not easy to optimize the study design to modify the local reaction.[1]

A factor always seen is the immediate activation of platelets, which adhere in a monolayer to the de-endothelialized area and which is a part of the repair process. However, in certain situations the process progresses with the formation of platelet aggregates and activation of the coagulation system, and a thrombus can develop which may continue to occlusion of the vessel or may embolize peripherally. The process of embolization is especially deleterious after carotid endarterectomy, the brain being the target organ, and the worst possible outcome would be a completed irreversible stroke or death.

Platelet adhesion and aggregation do occur after carotid endarterectomy and it should therefore be logical to presume that thrombosis and embolization can be prevented with antiplatelet drugs. However, the occurrence of transient neurological deficits and stroke after carotid surgery is multifactorial (embolization during dissection, ischaemic damage during cross-clamping, postendarterectomy thrombosis, postoperative hyperperfusion with haemorrhage, embolization from extracarotid source). It is not possible to control all of these by antiplatelet substances, or the expertise of the surgeon.

Although scientific support has been lacking, some authors still, on the basis of historical data, recommend postoperative use of antiplatelet drugs to prevent stroke.[2,3] Others have extrapolated from results of studies on stroke prevention with antiplatelet substances in non-surgical patients and advocated such a treatment also in the postoperative period. Since the arteriosclerotic plaque is removed the treatment of operated patients would seem to be quite different.

PATHOPHYSIOLOGICAL RATIONALE FOR PLATELET INHIBITION THERAPY

After carotid endarterectomy with exposed muscle tissue and collagen there is an activation of platelets, which accumulate on the endarterectomized segment.[4-7] In a dog model loss of platelet uptake was reached at re-endothelialization,[4] complete re-endothelialization not being seen until 3 months after surgery.[8] After 3 weeks the platelet activity seems to be reduced in humans.[4,5] By using [111]Indium-labelled platelets it has been shown that acetylsalicyclic acid (ASA) in combination with dipyridamole can reduce the uptake at least during the first couple of days postoperatively, findings indirectly supporting the role of platelets.[7,9] Interestingly enough the platelet uptake seems to be increased when a patch is used to close the carotid arteriotomy.[7] These observations in patients give support to findings in animal experiments where angiography and microscopy was used during a 3-month postendarterectomy course[10] and also studies on platelet uptake and its inhibition after percutaneous transluminal angioplasty.[11]

Using histopathological examination of the endarterectomy specimen, Pratschner *et al.*[12] described the existence of two types of plaques, one inert and the other with an active inflammatory cell population. They suggested that these two types correspond to one stable and one progressive form of arteriosclerotic disease process and further that the latter should perhaps be treated with antiplatelet drugs postoperatively.

When platelets aggregate and undergo release reaction, potent aggregatory and vasoconstrictive substances are released, but also substances which may be important for the reparative process in the long-term. Such a substance is the mitogen PDGF (platelet derived growth factor). By stimulation of smooth muscle cells, especially their migration, it is believed to play a role in the development of pseudointimal hyperplasia. Already within hours of injury smooth muscle cells in the media start to proliferate, and the proliferation continues for a number of days. Thereafter the smooth muscle cells migrate across the internal elastic lamina to the intima underneath the platelet layer.[13] An extracellular matrix is deposited, mainly consisting of elastin, collagen and proteoglycans. There is experimental evidence of a link between the immediate platelet activation and the late pseudointimal thickening.[14]

Although the knowledge is just starting to accumulate, the pseudointimal hyperplasia seems to play an important role in the development of restenosis. Platelet derived growth factor is just one possible factor in this process and there are potentially several others in the plasma and the vessel wall. This type of restenosis occurs and is probably important during the first one or two postoperative years. Restenoses occurring later in the postoperative course frequently are due to the progressive nature of the arteriosclerotic process. At reoperation, the early fibrotic restenosis forms a smooth whitish glistening, fairly firm narrowing process, rarely with fresh thrombus material attached to it.[15]

NATURAL HISTORY AFTER CAROTID ENDARTERECTOMY

From the literature it is obvious that there are great variations in outcome and it is important to point out the many potential differences between various studies: in design, in patient populations, in indications for surgery, in operative techniques and surgical skill, in follow-up routines and time, in adjuvant pharmacological therapy and not least in definitions of neurological symptomatology. The use of a standardized classification is of utmost importance to make it at all possible to undertake comparisons.[16,17] This is illustrated in Fig. 1 where data from Malmö, Sweden, are shown.

Neurological symptoms

As indicated above there are several reasons why neurological events may occur after carotid endarterectomy. As this is prophylactic surgery, it has been stated that

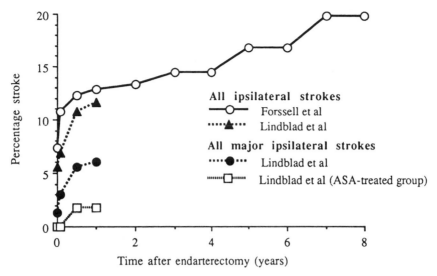

Fig. 1. Stroke frequencies in four populations of endarterectomized patients in Malmö, Sweden.

the immediate postoperative complication frequency (summarizing frequencies of neurological deficits and deaths) should not exceed 5–7%. It may be interesting to recall the data from the European Carotid Surgery Trial (ECST)[18] and the North American Symptomatic Carotid Endarterectomy Trial (NASCET).[19] In Table 1 these results are compared with frequencies from a population-based register from Sweden, Swedvasc[20] and a community-based random sample from the USA.[21] Table 1 also shows results from Malmö (patients operated on 1971–1982), the centre having performed the largest series of carotid endarterectomies in Sweden.[22]

Figure 1 shows that most cerebrovascular events occur during the first few postoperative months whereafter the rate is low, constant and around 1% per year on the operated side.[23] This is consistent with the findings from ECST[18] and

Table 1. Results after carotid endarterectomy

	ECST[18]		NASCET[19]		Swedvasc[20]	Forssell[22,23]	Brook[21]
	Med	Surgery	Med	Surgery	Surgery	Surgery	Surgery
No. of patients	323	455	331	328	383	414	1302
All stroke/mortality 30 days		7.5%	3%	7%	4.4%	7.7%	9.6%
All ipsilateral stroke 2 years			27.6%	9%		13%	
All stroke/mortality 2 years			32.3%	15.8%			
All stroke/mortality 3 years	21.9%	12.3%					

ECST European Carotid Surgery Trial; NASCET North American Symptomatic Carotid Endarterectomy Trial; Swedvasc Vascular registry in Sweden

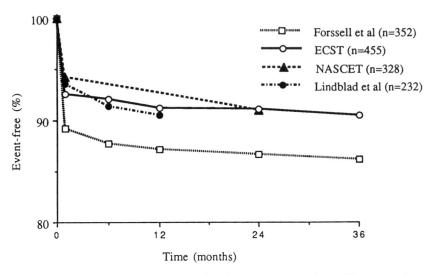

Fig. 2. Event-free rate after carotid endarterectomy in four different series. The Forssell study is from the period 1971 to 1982. The others are from the turn of the decade 1980–90.

NASCET[19] trials (Fig. 2). For comparison, a more recent series from Malmö (1985–1991) is also shown.[24]

The frequency chosen as well as the follow-up time obviously will have great influence on sample size calculations when designing interventional studies. When discussing antiplatelet therapy the most interesting period seems to be the first few postoperative months, during which most of the neurological complications occur.

The frequency of restenosis is a function of time, all other things being constant. It is therefore important to clearly define the time for follow up. The frequency of detected restenosis is also a function of diagnostic methodology and definitions used for pathological findings and because of these factors there has been some variation in literature reports.[25] In recent years, using various types of ultrasonographic techniques, the rate of at least 50% restenosis seems to be somewhere between 5 and 20%.[26-36] Several risk factors for recurrent stenosis have been reported such as female gender, continued smoking, lipid disorder, hypertension, multifocal arteriosclerosis, surgical technique with use of patch, individual surgeon.[27-29,31,36-39] The individual studies, however, vary in the number of risk factors given and the risk factor profile seems to be complex.

The immediate and important question is whether there is an increased risk of neurological symptoms in patients developing a restenosis. The answer to this question will have an impact on indications for surgical treatment for recurrent stenosis, which at least has been considered an indication by some authors.[29,40-43] Many authors have, however, not been able to show any relation between recurrent stenosis and development of neurological symptoms.[28,32,34,36] In contrast, Bernstein et al.[33] found that patients with restenosis had both a significantly greater life expectancy and a less likely risk for stroke and subsequent neurological events to occur. The data seem to show that prevention of restenosis does not necessarily indicate a prophylactic effect on symptomatic recurrence in the long-term. When treated with B-mode ultrasonography recurrent lesions are relatively homogenous with a smooth surface which could be one reason why they do not frequently contribute to symptoms.[27] When treated with light microscopy, most recurrent stenoses show no thrombosis and/or intraplaque haemorrhage and the surface is to a large extent covered with cells exhibiting immunoreactivity for antifactor VIII, indicating endothelial coverage.[44] These ultrasonographic and microscopic findings in combination with a seemingly inert plaque at surgery may explain why restenoses rarely are associated with symptoms.

Survival

Long-term survival after carotid endarterectomy is to a large extent dependent on whether or not the patients have simultaneous coronary artery disease, late mortality being dominated by myocardial infarction.[23,34,35,45] Moreover, patients with bilateral carotid artery disease have a decreased life expectancy compared with those with unilateral lesions, indicating that a more generalized arteriosclerosis is a negative factor concerning survival.[23] In patients with unilateral carotid artery disease and without coronary artery disease the expected survival after carotid endarterectomy is that of a normal age- and sex-matched population.[23,33]

ANTIPLATELET SUBSTANCES IN CARDIOCEREBROVASCULAR DISEASE

Discussing antiplatelet prophylaxis in patients undergoing carotid artery surgery cannot be isolated from a discussion on the overall beneficial effect, which has been reported in recent years. Platelet inhibitors used for secondary prevention have been shown to reduce non-fatal myocardial infarction, non-fatal stroke and cardiovascular death.[46–52] The role of antiplatelet therapy for the prevention of ischaemic stroke has recently been summarized by Easton.[53] Some authors are, however, less enthusiastic in concluding antiplatelet drugs to be of benefit in the prevention of cerebral infarction.[46,54]

Most studies have been performed using ASA, sometimes in combination with dipyridamole, the additive effect of which, however, seems questionable.[53] There also seems to be at least a similar secondary preventive effect using ticlopidine.[55–57]

Many patients undergoing carotid artery surgery do have a generalized arterio-sclerosis and therefore many of them have undergone other types of peripheral arterial surgery or coronary bypass surgery (in Malmö, Sweden, about 20%). The evidence is growing that antiplatelet therapy increases patency of various types of bypasses, and a number of studies have been performed with ASA in various doses.[1,58–62] In a meta-analysis on antiplatelet and anticoagulant therapy after coronary artery bypass surgery, Henderson et al.[60] concluded that early initiation of these drugs significantly reduced the incidence of graft occlusion. All except three of the platelet inhibitory studies (one sulphinpyrazone, two ticlopidine) have some form of ASA regimen. Whether or not antiplatelet therapy increases graft patency, it could have a beneficial influence on subsequent myocardial infarction, stroke and survival.[63] All this means that a substantial proportion of patients undergoing carotid endarterectomy already has been prescribed some form of antiplatelet regimen. This also means that from now on it could be difficult making prospective studies on antiplatelet prophylaxis because of the 'background noise' of such therapy within the population.

ANTIPLATELET AGENTS AFTER CAROTID ENDARTERECTOMY

There are three potential indications for platelet inhibitors after carotid endarterectomy, prevention of thromboembolic symptoms from the operated site, prevention of other cardiovascular symptoms and mortality and prevention of restenosis.

Prevention of thromboembolic symptoms from the operated side

From the studies with uptake of [111]Indium-labelled platelets on endarterectomy sites and its inhibition with ASA, there is at least a rationale to motivate studies on this type of prophylaxis. There are five randomized prospective trials, summarized in Table 2. All except the study by Kretschmer et al.[64] were double-blind using placebo.

In the study by Fields et al.[65] randomization was made postoperatively (day 5 was intended and 60–70% (?) were randomized within 1 week of surgery). The 125 patients were recruited from ten institutions. The primary end-points were mortality, cerebral infarction and retinal infarction and there was no difference between placebo and ASA groups over a 24-month period. If 'deaths from causes other than cerebral and retinal infarction' were eliminated there was a significant difference in favour of ASA. There were also fewer 'unfavourable' outcomes in the ASA group (death within 6 months, cerebral or retinal infarction during 6 months, number of transient ischaemic attacks (TIAs) during 6 months, greater or equal to the number of TIAs reported 3 months prerandomization). These subgroup analyses should be interpreted with great caution and the main conclusion is that there was no difference between ASA and control groups.

Table 2

	No. of patients		Follow-up time (months)	Daily dose of ASA (mg)	Start of prophylaxis	No. of events	
	Control	ASA				Control	ASA
Fields[65]	60	65	24	1300	+5 days	8	8
Boysen[66]	151	150	25	50–100	+1 week to 3 months	39	39
Kretschmer[64]	34	32	life-table, 60	1000	−2 days	11	4
Harker[67]	80	83	12	975[a]	−1 day	5	6
Lindblad[24]	115	117	6	75	−1 day	24	15

[a]Combination with 225 mg dipyridamole
+ means postoperatively, − preoperatively

In the study by Boysen et al.[66] a very low dose of ASA (50 mg) was used but in some patients the dose was increased on the basis of in vitro studies on platelet aggregation (up to 100 mg in a few patients). The mean treatment period was 21 months and the events recorded were TIA, amaurosis fugax, retinal infarction, stroke, myocardial infarction, vascular death and non-vascular death. Disabling stroke and death were called terminatory events. The relative risk reduction with ASA for the combined outcome TIA, stroke, myocardial infarction and vascular death was 11% (but the 95% confidence limits −38% to +48%!). Just as in the study by Fields et al.[65] the start of prophylaxis was late in the postoperative course (between 1 week and 3 months).

The study by Kretschmer et al.[64] was initiated because of the results from a retrospective analysis (252 patients) where it was shown that patients given up to 3500 mg ASA/day showed a significantly prolonged survival, mainly by decreasing the incidence of cardiac deaths. The primary endpoint in the prospective trial, where 1000 mg ASA was started 2 days prior to surgery, was also survival. The groups did again differ significantly in the probability of survival in favour of ASA ($p < 0.021$ Breslow, $p < 0.048$ Mantel). The study was open and the sample size small (total 66 patients). This study was combined with a histopathological examination of extirpated plaques and the beneficial effect of ASA was especially seen in the subgroup with signs of progressive arteriosclerosis.[12] This subgroup analysis is, however, based on a small sample and quantification of the microscopic findings is not easy.

The primary aim with the study by Harker et al.[67] was to evaluate the effect of aspirin plus dipyridamole for prevention of restenosis. There was, however, no prophylactic effect of the medication. They used ASA 325 mg and dipyridamole 75 mg three times daily, starting 12 hours preoperatively with continuation for 1 year. In addition to restenosis, outcome was registered as new clinical symptoms which had anatomic correlation to the operated artery. In the placebo group one patient suffered from fatal stroke, one developed a minor but permanent neurologic deficit and three had transient symptoms. In the treatment group one developed a minor permanent deficit and five transient symptoms. Thus there was no difference in neurological clinical symptoms.

In the study by Lindblad et al.[24] again the daily dose of ASA was low (75 mg), the end-points being cerebrovascular events (stroke with or without restitution within 1 week, TIA, amaurosis fugax) and death. There was a significant difference in favour of ASA concerning stroke without restitution within the 6-month period (Table 3). The overall difference in neurological end-points did not reach statistical significance although the relative risk reduction was 39%. Neurological deficits without restitution and cerebrovascular death were seen in five patients in the ASA group compared with 24 in the control group ($p < 0.01$). This is shown in life-table format in Fig. 3.

The conclusion from these studies would be that the beneficial effect of ASA on neurological outcome after carotid endarterectomy is small if any but that survival seems to be prolonged. However, the study designs and ASA doses differ considerably and still we do not know the optimal study conditions. The variations are indeed too great to think of making a meta-analysis or compilation. This would not be meaningful. Still Clagett as late as 1990[52] made a fairly firm statement in saying 'aspirin (325 mg/day) can be recommended in patients undergoing carotid

Table 3. Events in the study on low dose ASA (75 mg daily) by Lindblad *et al.*[24]

	Placebo (n = 117)	ASA (n = 115)	p
Stroke without restitution	11	2	0.01
Stroke with restitution	2	7	0.97
TIA/amaurosis fugax	5	4	0.75
Contralateral TIA	1	1	1.00
Contralateral stroke	5	1	0.12
Death	10	4	0.11
Cerebrovascular death	10	2	0.08

endarterectomy. Therapy should be started at the time of presentation, maintained throughout the perioperative period and continued indefinitely'. A much more ambivalent position was taken by Rutherford and Pearce,[68] who also stated the necessity of making properly designed studies to increase our knowledge. Admittedly the statement by Clagett came a few years later.

When discussing antiplatelet drugs the problem with possible bleeding complications must be considered. In none of the studies in Table 2 were there any differences between groups in perioperative haemorrhagic complications. None the less, there is a significant dose-related increase in bleeding time when using ASA.[69,70] Most of the potential effect of ASA is obtained already at doses of 50 mg daily and at 100 mg all thromboxane A_2 seems to be effectively blocked.[70] Although it has been difficult to relate the effect to dosage, there is evidence that fewer side-effects are seen with low doses.[71]

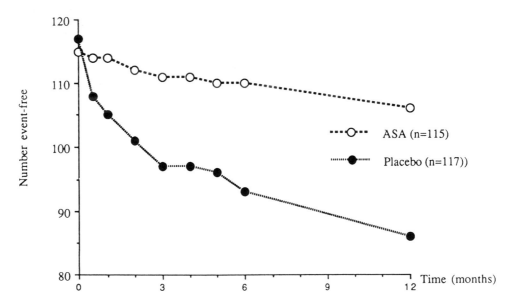

Fig. 3. Cerebrovascular death and any stroke without restitution within 7 days in patients having undergone carotid endarterectomy. Data from a randomized study comparing ASA and placebo[24] ($p < 0.01$).

Prevention of other cardiovascular symptoms and mortality

Extrapolating the knowledge from the studies dealing with the effect of antiplatelet drugs for secondary prevention as a whole there seems to be a beneficial effect, the relative risk reduction compared with no treatment being in the order of magnitude of 25–30%. For carotid artery surgery this view may be supported by data from the prospective study by Kretschmer et al.,[64] although we must be aware of the small size of that study (n=66). Until further evidence is presented the conclusion made by Clagett[52] could therefore still be valid and acceptable.

Prevention of restenosis

In the light of the discussion above on the lack of correlation between restenosis and neurological symptoms it may be of less interest to discuss preventive measures to reduce the frequency of restenosis. This is all the more so because we still know very little about the pathophysiological mechanisms causing a recurrent stenosis. As stated by Baker[25] there are several options to prevent restenosis, some being purely technical. Such an option is probably patching the arteriotomy, at least in some situations (i.e. small vessels in females). Regarding the potential link between early platelet activation and thrombosis and late restenosis, platelet inhibition may be of interest, but there will almost certainly be other substances worth evaluating such as growth factor inhibitors, agents with an effect on vasospasm or even heparin.

Data from retrospective studies have indicated that antiplatelet therapy does not reduce the frequency of recurrent carotid artery stenosis.[72,73] In our prospective randomized study on low dose ASA (75 mg daily) or placebo after carotid endarterectomy we did not find any difference between the groups on recurrent stenosis (Fig. 4) nor on progression of arteriosclerosis on the contralateral side (Fig. 5).[36] A similar lack of effect was also seen in a study where 975 mg ASA was combined with 225 mg of dipyridamol daily for 1 year.[67] The frequency of a >50% restenosis did not differ between the treatment and placebo group (16 and 14% respectively).

To conclude, at the present time there is no proven pharmacological method to prevent recurrent carotid artery stenosis.

DISCUSSION

There are several difficulties in drawing conclusions on the use of platelet inhibitors in connection with carotid artery surgery. This fact has to do with the difficulties in designing the correct studies on which to base conclusions. Some of these difficulties are summarized below.

Sample size

In a randomized study there must be biostatistical calculations on which sample sizes are necessary to answer a certain question. In the antiplatelet studies on

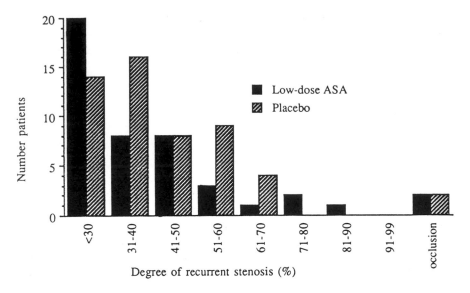

Fig. 4.   Frequency and degree of recurrent stenosis. Comparison between low-dose ASA and placebo after carotid endarterectomy (from Ref. 36).

postendarterectomy events this was made in three. If the studies are too small there is a risk for a type II statistical error. This problem was discussed in an Editorial[74] in *Stroke* when the Danish study[66] was published, but the points raised are valid to elucidate the problem in general. A lack of an effect may have this statistical reason

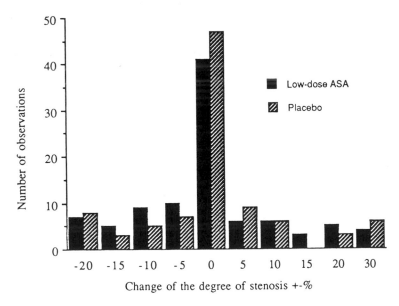

Fig. 5.   Development of arteriosclerosis in the contralateral non-operated carotid artery. The change of stenosis is correlated to the preoperative examination. Comparison between low-dose ASA and placebo (from Ref. 36).

besides being an effect of having chosen the wrong dosage of ASA (see below). A problem which has to do with biostatistics is the low frequency of end-points which requires rather large studies. Moreover, not all causes of postoperative neurological deficits can be influenced by platelet inhibitors.

End-point registration

End-points must be clearly defined and relevant.[75] As has already been discussed, recurrent stenosis is hardly a relevant end-point and the question is whether or not TIA/amaurosis fugax are. Most relevant from the patients' point of view would seem to be stroke with remaining symptoms, be it disabling or not, and certainly death. Trying to quantify the effect of stroke on the patients' life style is difficult but there are some disability scales, although several methodological problems still exist.[75] It is also important to decide on follow-up time during which end-points are of interest to register. In Table 2 this period varies between 6 and 60 months. Our choice of 6 months was motivated by the fact that most postoperative symptoms occurred within this time, whereafter the yearly risk was very low.[23,24]

Choice of substance, dose and administration routines

The vast majority of studies on platelet inhibitors in cardiocerebrovascular disease has been performed with ASA and only in a few have there been alternative substances. It would seem that every potential platelet function inhibitor is of interest but it is important to make the correctly designed studies from the very beginning.

Concerning ASA there is the problem of dosage, this again varying between the five studies in Table 2 (50–1300 mg daily). Low dose ASA is effective in inhibiting platelet aggregation and thromboxane generation[76–79] and is probably also effective at least in some clinical situations.[80] The Antiplatelet Trialists concluded on basis of a meta-analysis that the risk reduction was similar in studies using 900–1500 mg and those using 300–325 mg, but the lower dose was not investigated for cerebrovascular disease. A finding which may be of some importance was reported by Boysen et al.[66] They conducted analyses of platelet inhibition in an aggregation test and found that there was a satisfactory inhibition with 50 mg ASA daily in the majority or 76% of the patients. However, 13% needed 60 mg/day, 8% needed 70 mg and 3% needed 100 mg ASA daily. If this also reflects the in vivo situation is not known but it would indeed not be possible to require efficacy testing and dose adjustments in a large group of patients needing secondary prevention.

In a recent review Dyken[81] quoted data from the NASCET[19] trial, showing a lower frequency of ipsilateral stroke in patients receiving 1300 mg of ASA per day compared to those given 325 or 650 mg per day. The perioperative stroke rate was two to three times higher in patients receiving no or low dose ASA (<325 mg daily) compared with those receiving >650 mg daily.[82] The study, however, was not designed to answer the question of different doses postoperatively. Both from studies on coronary bypass surgery and peripheral graft surgery it can be concluded that platelet inhibitors are only effective if instituted before or in connection with the surgical procedure.[1,60] It is important to remember this when the studies in Table 2 are scrutinized.

Compliance with prescribed drugs

In the clinical situation, especially in long-term prophylaxis, there will always be patients that differ in their compliance, and compliance may moreover show variations with time in a single patient. Therefore, what really matters in this situation is efficacy on an intention to treat basis. When making scientific studies it would be of great importance to be able to know about compliance in a more reliable way than just asking the patients or calculating their remaining pills. When dealing with platelet inhibitors this can be checked analysing the effect on some platelet function tests in a blood sample. However, so doing there can only be random samples during a very limited period of the total study period. This was checked both by Fields et al.[65] and Boysen et al.[66] but in such case it is important to keep the information blinded from the trialists. An important study in this context is the one on the influence of ASA (300 mg×2) on femoropopliteal vein graft patency.[62] In a blood sample taken after 3 months salicylate analyses were undertaken. Interestingly 28% of the patients receiving placebo had salicylate concentrations higher than 50 ng/ml whereas 35% of patients receiving active treatment did not have any detectable salicylate in their serum. The 28% of patients taking ASA in spite of receiving placebo probably reflect an increasing problem in the future, that is self-medication with, or prescription of, ASA to a large number of cerebrocardiovascular patients, but also to fairly healthy individuals—'to be on the safe side'.

CONCLUSION

The number of studies on platelet inhibitory prophylaxis after carotid endarterectomy is very small and, in many respects there are great differences between the studies. There are several methodological obstacles to overcome in performing this type of study. Using ASA there seems to be a prolongation of survival after carotid endarterectomy and probably a small preventive effect on early postoperative neurological symptoms.

REFERENCES

1. Bergqvist D: Pharmacologic prevention of graft occlusion. Acta Chir Scand Suppl 529: 107–114, 1985
2. Edwards WH, Edwards WH Jr, Mulherin JL, Jenkins JM: The role of antiplatelet drugs in carotid reconstructive surgery. Ann Surg 201: 765–770, 1985
3. Edwards WH Jr, Jenkins JM, Edwards WH Sr, Mulherin JL: Prevention of stroke during carotid endarterectomy. Am Surg 54: 125–128, 1988
4. Lusby RJ, Ferrell LD, Englestad BL et al.: Vessel wall and Indium-111 labelled platelet response to carotid endarterectomy. Surgery 93: 424–432, 1983
5. Stratton JR, Zierler RE, Kazmers A: Platelet deposition at carotid endarterectomy sites in humans. Stroke 18: 722–727, 1987

6. Falk GL, Gray-Weale AC, Meyer H-J, Johnson S, Lusby RJ: Carotid endarterectomy. The timing of perioperative antiplatelet therapy by Indium 111 labelled platelets study in canines. J Cardiovasc Surg 29: 697–700, 1988

7. Meek AC, Chidlow A, Lane IF, Greenhalgh RM, McCollum CN: Platelet kinetics following carotid endarterectomy: the effect of aspirin and patch angioplasty. Eur J Vasc Surg 2: 99–104, 1988

8. Dirrenberger R, Sundt T: Carotid endarterectomy. Temporal profile of the healing process and effects of anticoagulation therapy. J Neurosurg 48: 201–219, 1978

9. Findlay JM, Lougheed WM, Gentili F et al.: Effect of perioperative platelet inhibition on postcarotid endarterectomy mural thrombus formation. J Neurosurg 63: 693–698, 1985

10. Deen HG, Sundt TM: The effect of combined aspirin and dipyridamole therapy on thrombus formation in an arterial thrombogenic lesion in the dog. Stroke 13: 179–183, 1982

11. Cunningham DA, Kumar B, Siegel BA, Gilula LA, Totty WG, Welch MJ: Aspirin inhibition of platelet deposition at angioplasty sites: demonstration by platelet scintigraphy. Radiology 151: 487–490, 1984

12. Pratschner Th, Kretschmer G, Prager M et al.: Antiplatelet therapy following carotid bifurcation endarterectomy. Evaluation of a controlled clinical trial. Prognostic significance of histologic plaque examination on behalf of survival. Eur J Vasc Surg 4: 285–289, 1990

13. Clowes A, Schwartz SM: Significance of quiescent smooth muscle migration in the injured rat carotid artery. Circ Res 56: 139–145, 1985

14. Fingerle J, Johnson R, Clowes A, Majesky M, Reidy M: Role of platelets in smooth muscle cell proliferation and migration after vascular injury in rat carotid artery. Proc Natl Acad Sci USA 86: 8412–8416, 1989

15. Gagne P, Riles T, Imparato A et al.: Redo endarterectomy for recurrent carotid artery stenosis. Eur J Vasc Surg 5: 135–140, 1991

16. Courbier R: Basis for an international classification of cerebral arterial diseases. J Vasc Surg 4: 179–183, 1986

17. Baker JD, Rutherford RB, Bernstein EF, Kempczinski RF, Zarins CK: Suggested standards for reports dealing with cerebrovascular disease. J Vasc Surg 8: 721–729, 1988

18. ECST. European Carotid Surgery Trialists Collaborative Group: MRC European Carotid Surgery Trial: interim results for symptomatic patients with severe (70–99%) or with mild (0–29%) carotid stenosis. Lancet 337: 1235–1243, 1991

19. NASCET. North American Symptomatic Carotid Endarterectomy Trial Collaborators: Beneficial effect of carotid endarterectomy in syptomatic patients with high-grade carotid stenosis. N Engl J Med 325: 445–453, 1991

20. Troëng T, Bergqvist D, Einarsson E, Elfström J, Norgren L: Kvalitetsmätning ger stöd för carotiskirurgi även i Sverige. Läkartidningen 88: 3266, 1991

21. Brook RH, Park RE, Chassin MR et al.: Carotid endarterectomy for elderly patients: predicting complications. Ann Intern Med 113: 747–753, 1990

22. Forssell C, Takolander R, Bergqvist D, Bergentz S-E, Olivecrona H: Risk factors in carotid artery surgery: an evaluation of 414 operations. Eur J Vasc Surg 2: 9–14, 1988

23. Forssell C, Takolander R, Bergqvist D, Bergentz S-E, Olivecrona H: Long-term results after carotid artery surgery. Eur J Vasc Surg 2: 93–98, 1988

24. Lindblad B, Persson NH, Takolander R, Bergqvist D: Does low dose acetylsalicylic acid prevent stroke after carotid surgery? A double-blind placebo controlled randomised trial. Manuscript, in prep.

25. Baker JD: Recurrent stenosis of the carotid artery: incidence, diagnosis, prognosis, and management. In Surgery for Cerebrovascular Disease, Moore WS (Ed.). Edinburgh: Churchill Livingstone, 1987

26. Thomas M, Otis SM, Rush M et al.: Recurrent carotid artery stenosis following endarterectomy. Ann Surg 200: 74–79, 1984

27. O'Donnell TF, Callow AD, Scott G et al.: Ultrasound characteristics of recurrent carotid disease: hypothesis explaining the low incidence of symptomatic recurrence. J Vasc Surg 2: 26–41, 1985

28. Nicholls SC, Phillips DJ, Bergelin RO et al.: Carotid endarterectomy. Relationship of outcome to early restenosis. J Vasc Surg 2: 375–381, 1985

29. Zbornikova V, Elfström J, Lassvik C et al.: Restenosis and occlusion after carotid surgery assessed by duplex scanning and digital subtraction angiography. Stroke 17: 1137–1142, 1986
30. Sanders EACM, Hoeneveld H, Eikelboom BC et al.: Residual lesions and early recurrent stenosis after carotid endarterectomy. A serial follow-up study with duplex scanning and intravenous digital subtraction angiography. J Vasc Surg 5: 731–737, 1987
31. Eikelboom BC, Ackerstaff GA, Hoeneveld H et al.: Benefits of carotid patching: a randomized study. J Vasc Surg 7: 240–247, 1988
32. Healy DA, Zierler RE, Nicholls SC et al.: Long-term follow-up and clinical outcome of carotid restenosis. J Vasc Surg 10: 662–669, 1989
33. Bernstein EF, Torem S, Dilley RB: Does carotid restenosis predict an increased risk of late symptoms, stroke, or death? Ann Surg 212: 629–636, 1990
34. Knudsen L, Sillesen H, Schroeder T, Buchardt Hansen HJ: Eight to ten years follow-up after carotid endarterectomy: clinical evaluation and doppler examination of patients operated on between 1978–1980. Eur J Vasc Surg 4: 259–264, 1990
35. Mattos M, Hodgson K, Londrey G et al.: Carotid endarterectomy: operative risks, recurrent stenosis, and long-term stroke rates in a modern series. J Cardiovasc Surg 33: 387–400, 1992
36. Hansen F, Lindblad B, Persson NH, Bergqvist D: Can recurrent stenosis after carotid endarterectomy be prevented by low-dose acetylsalicyclic acid? A double-blind, randomised and placebo controlled study. Eur J Vasc Surg (in press) 1993
37. Rapp JH, Qvarfordt P, Krupski WC, Ehrenfeld WK, Stoney RJ: Hypercholesterolemia and early restenosis after carotid endarterectomy. Surgery 101: 277–282, 1987
38. Hertzer N, Beven E, Ohara P, Krajewski P. A prospective study of vein patch angioplasty during carotid endarterectomy: three-year results from 801 patients and 917 operations. Ann Surg 206: 628–635, 1987
39. Mattos MA, Shamma AR, Rossi N et al.: Is duplex follow-up cost-effective in the first year after carotid endarterectomy? Am J Surg 156: 91–95, 1988
40. Clagett GP, Rich NM, McDonald PT et al.: Etiologic factors for recurrent carotid artery stenosis. Surgery 93: 313–318, 1983
41. Hunter GC, Palmaz JC, Hayashi HH et al.: The etiology of symptoms in patients with recurrent carotid stenosis. Arch Surg 122: 311–315, 1987
42. Piepgras D, Sundt T, Marsh W, Mussman LA, Fode NC: Recurrent carotid stenosis. Ann Surg 203: 205–213, 1987
43. Bartlett F, Rapp J, Goldstone J, Ehrenfeld W, Stoney R: Recurrent carotid stenosis; operative strategy and late results. J Vasc Surg 5: 452–456, 1988
44. Schwarcs TH, Yates GN, Ghobrial M, Baker WH: Pathologic characteristics of recurrent carotid artery stenosis. J Vasc Surg 5: 280–288, 1987
45. Hertzer NR, Arison R: Cumulative stroke and survival ten years after carotid endarterectomy. J Vasc Surg 2: 661–668, 1985
46. Sze PC, Reitman D, Pincus MM, Sacks HS, Chalmers TC: Antiplatelet agents in the secondary prevention of stroke: meta-analysis of the randomized control trials. Stroke 19: 436–442, 1988
47. Antiplatelet trialists' collaboration. Secondary prevention of vascular disease by prolonged antiplatelet treatment. Br Med J 296: 320–331, 1988
48. UK-TIA Study Group: United Kingdom transient ischaemic attack (UK-TIA) aspirin trial: interim results. Br Med J 296: 316–320, 1988
49. Hennekens CH, Buring JE, Sandercock P, Collins R, Peto R: Aspirin and other antiplatelet agents in the secondary and primary prevention of cardiovascular disease. Circulation 80: 749–756, 1989
50. Barnett HJM: Aspirin in stroke prevention. An overview. Stroke 21 (Suppl. IV): 40–43, 1990
51. Sivenius J, Riekkinen PJ, Smets P, Laakso M, Lowenthal A: The European Stroke Prevention Study (ESPS): Results by arterial distribution. Ann Neurol 29: 596–600, 1991
52. Clagett P: Antithrombotic drugs and vascular surgery. Perspect Vasc Surg 3: 79–102, 1990
53. Easton D: Antiplatelet therapy for the prevention of ischemic stroke. Cerebrovasc Dis 2 (Suppl 1): 6–13, 1992
54. Lekstrom JA, Bell WR: Aspirin in the prevention of thrombosis. Medicine 70: 161–178, 1991

55. Gent M, Easton JD, Hachinski VC et al. and the CATS Group: The Canadian American Ticlopidine Study (CATS) in thromboembolic stroke. Lancet i: 1215–1220, 1989

56. Hass WK, Easton JD, Adams HP et al. for the Ticlopidine Aspirin Stroke Study Group: A randomized trial comparing ticlopidine hydrochloride with aspirin for the prevention of stroke in high-risk patients. N Engl J Med 321: 501–507, 1989

57. Janzon L, Bergqvist D, Boberg J et al.: Prevention of myocardial infarction and stroke in patients with intermittent claudication; effects of ticlopidine. Results from STIMS, the Swedish Ticlopidine Multicentre Study. J Intern Med 227: 301–308, 1990

58. Lorenz RL, Weber M, Kotzur J et al.: Improved aortocoronary bypass patency by low-dose aspirin (100 mg daily). Lancet i: 1261–1264, 1984

59. Harter H, Burch J, Majerus P et al.: Prevention of thrombosis in patients on hemodialysis by low-dose aspirin. N Engl J Med 301: 577–579, 1979

60. Henderson WG, Goldman S, Copeland JG, Moritz TE, Harker LA: Antiplatelet or anticoagulant therapy after coronary artery bypass surgery. A meta-analysis of clinical trials. Ann Intern Med 111: 743–750, 1989

61. Pfisterer M, Jockers G, Regenass S et al.: Trial of low-dose aspirin plus dipyridamole versus anticoagulants for prevention of aortocoronary vein graft occlusion. Lancet ii: 1–6, 1989

62. Franks PJ, Sian M, Kenchington GF, Alexander CE, Powell JT, and the Femoro-popliteal Bypass Trial Participants: Aspirin usage and its influence on femoro-popliteal vein graft patency. Eur J Vasc Surg 6: 185–188, 1992

63. McCollum C, Alexander C, Kenchington G, Franks PJ, Greenhalgh R: Antiplatelet drugs in femoropopliteal vein bypasses: a multicenter trial. J Vasc Surg 13: 150–162, 1991

64. Kretschmer G, Pratschner T, Prager M et al.: Antiplatelet treatment prolongs survival after carotid bifurcation endarterectomy. Ann Surg 211: 317–322, 1990

65. Fields WS, Lemak NA, Frankowski RF, Hardy RJ: Controlled trial of aspirin in cerebral ischemia. Part II: surgical group. Stroke 9: 309–319, 1978

66. Boysen G, Soelberg Sørensen P, Juhler M et al.: Danish very-low-dose aspirin after carotid endarterectomy trial. Stroke 19: 1211–1215, 1988

67. Harker L, Bernstein E, Dilley R et al.: Failure of aspirin plus dipyridamole to prevent restenosis after carotid endarterectomy. Ann Intern Med 116: 731–736, 1992

68. Rutherford RB, Pearce WH: The use of antiplatelet drugs as an adjunct to the surgical management of extracranial arterial atheromatous disease. In Surgery for Cerebrovascular Disease, Moore WS (Ed.). Edinburgh: Churchill Livingstone, 1987

69. Boysen G, Hasager Boss A, Ødum N, Steen Olsen J: Prolongation of bleeding time and inhibition of platelet aggregation by low-dose acetylsalicylic acid in patients with cerebrovascular disease. Stroke 15: 241–243, 1984

70. Hasager Boss A, Boysen G, Steen Olsen J: Effect of incremental doses of aspirin on bleeding time, platelet aggregation and thromboxane production in patients with cerebrovascular disease. Eur J Clin Invest 15: 412–414, 1985

71. Hirsh J: Progress review: The relationship between dose of aspirin, side-effects and antithrombotic effectiveness. Stroke 16: 1–4, 1985

72. Crossman D, Callow AD, Stein A, Matsumoto G: Early restenosis after carotid endarterectomy. Arch Surg 113: 275–278, 1978

73. Clagett P, Rich N, McDonald PT et al.: Etiologic factors for recurrent carotid artery stenosis. Surgery 93: 313–318, 1983

74. Dyken M: Editorial: Transient ischemic attacks and aspirin, stroke and death; negative studies and type II error. Stroke 14: 2–4, 1983

75. van Gijn J: Measurement of outcome in stroke prevention trials. Cerebrovasc Dis 2 (Suppl 1): 6–13, 1992

76. Moncada G, Vane JR: Arachidonic acid metabolites and the interactions between platelets and blood-vessel walls. N Engl J Med 300: 1142–1147, 1979

77. Pedersen AK, Fitzgerald GA: Dose-related kinetics of aspirin. Presystemic acetylation of platelet cyclooxygenase. N Engl J Med 311: 1206–1211, 1984

78. Weksler BB, Tack-Goldman K, Subramanian VA, Gay WA Jr: Cumulative inhibitory effect of low-dose aspirin on vascular prostacyclin and platelet thromboxane production in patients with atherosclerosis. Circulation 71: 332–340, 1985

79. Bochner F, Lloyd J: Is there an optimal dose and formulation of aspirin to prevent arterial thrombo-embolism in man? Clin Sci 71: 625–631, 1986
80. The Dutch TIA Trial Study Group: A comparison of two doses of aspirin (30 mg vs 283 mg a day) in patients after a transient ischemic attack or minor ischemic stroke. N Engl J Med 325: 1261–1266, 1991
81. Dyken M: Meta-analysis in the assessment of therapy for stroke prevention. Cerebrovasc Dis 2 (suppl): 35–40, 1992
82. Clagett P: Soluble aspirin has a greater inhibitory effect on prostacyclin synthesis than enteric-coated slow-release aspirin. Commentary. Vasc Surg Outlook (7) 4: 5–6, 1992

Index

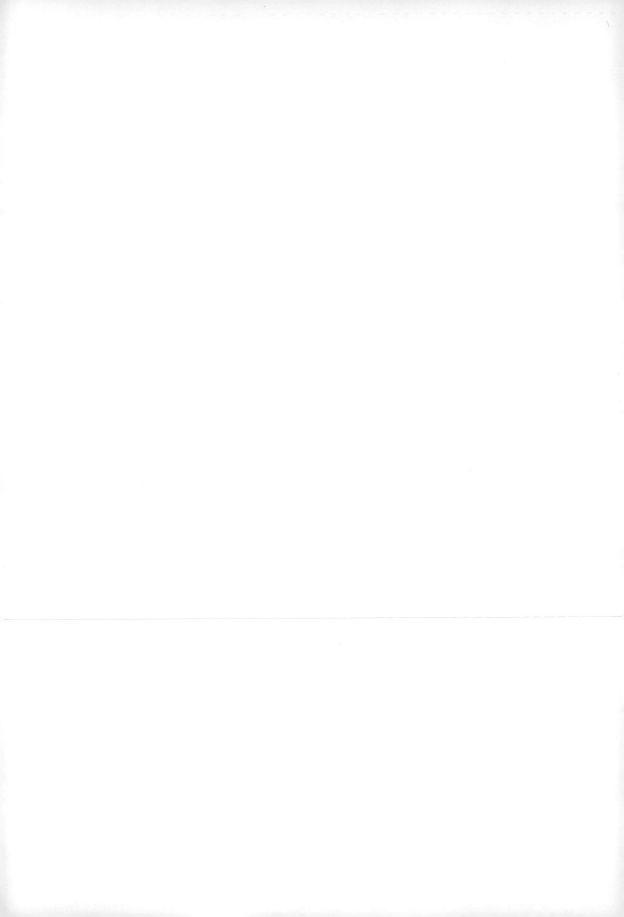